Political Science in Europe

Political Science in Europe

Achievements, Challenges, Prospects

Edited by
Thibaud Boncourt, Isabelle Engeli,
and Diego Garzia

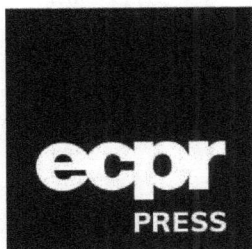

ecpr
PRESS

Published by the European Consortium for Political Research, Harbour House, 6–8 Hythe Quay, Colchester, CO2 8JF, United Kingdom

British Library Cataloguing in Publication Data
A catalogue record for this book is available from the British Library

ISBN: HB 978-1-78552-311-3
electronic 978-1-78552-312-0

Library of Congress Cataloging-in-Publication Data
Names: Boncourt, Thibaud, 1984– editor. | Engeli, Isabelle, 1977– editor. | Garzia, Diego, 1982– editor.
Title: Political science in Europe : achievements, challenges, prospects / edited by Thibaud Boncourt, Isabelle Engeli, and Diego Garzia.
Description: London, United Kingdom : ECPR Press | Includes bibliographical references and index. | Summary: "This collection reflects on the origins and development of European political science and provide a critical assessment of the achievements and challenges lying ahead"— Provided by publisher.

Identifiers: LCCN 2020009547 (print) | LCCN 2020009548 (ebook) |

ISBN 9781785523113 (cloth) | ISBN 9781785523120 (epub) | ISBN 9781538156919 (paper)
Subjects: LCSH: Political science—Europe. | Political science—Study and Teaching—Europe.
Classification: LCC JA84.E9 P564 2021 (print) | LCC JA84.E9 (ebook) | DDC 320.094—dc23
LC record available at https://lccn.loc.gov/2020009547
LC ebook record available at https://lccn.loc.gov/2020009548

ecpr.eu/shop

Contents

Acknowledgments

This fiftieth anniversary volume is the product of an amazing collective effort. We are extremely grateful to the Louise Soper, Madeleine Hatfield, Rebecca Gethen, and the Publication Committee at the ECPR for their admirable support, and to the Robert Schuman Centre for Advanced Studies at the European University Institute, Brigid Laffan, and Julia Hiltrop for their wonderful hosting of our authors' workshop in June 2019. Our warmest thanks go to Stefano Bartolini, Giliberto Capano, Rossella Ciccia, Mirjam Dageförde, Marta Fraile, Béla Greskovits, Ellen Immergut, Hanspeter Kriesi, Brigid Laffan, Yves Mény, Philippe Schmitter, Eniola Anuoluwapo Soyemi, and Luca Verzichelli for their insightful and constructive discussion of the draft chapters at the authors' workshop.

PREFACE

Chapter 1

Fifty Years of Political Science in Europe

An Introduction

Thibaud Boncourt, Isabelle Engeli, and Diego Garzia

The idea for a volume reflecting on the achievements of and challenges facing political science in Europe emerged in the course of discussions about the fiftieth anniversary of the European Consortium for Political Research (ECPR), to be celebrated in 2020. Decade anniversaries are symbolically important moments in the life of an association. ECPR's fortieth anniversary was celebrated with a pamphlet retracing the evolution of the consortium (Newton & Boncourt, 2010). The pamphlet highlighted the significant drive of the association to expand, diversify, and shape political science in Europe. Over the last ten years, the ECPR has strengthened its efforts in consolidating its institutional membership base and securing record attendance to the general conferences, joint sessions of workshops, and methods schools. More and more scholars from previously little represented regions—Eastern Europe, Southern Europe, and beyond—are joining ECPR activities. The ECPR journals and book series are publishing more than ever before. The ECPR has also significantly improved its commitment to gender equality in the profession by first publishing regular gender equality reports and then institutionalizing a gender equality plan and a code of conduct in 2018. In all these aspects, ECPR's fifty-year trajectory is a professional success story. It is safe to say that the Consortium has succeeded in shaping the political science landscape in Europe and supporting the development of a European political science community that has been taking a leading role at the international level.

For this fiftieth anniversary, the editors and the ECPR executive committee decided to move away from another history of the ECPR and, instead, reflect on the past, present, and prospects of political science in Europe. In lieu of focusing on the evolution of the ECPR as an association, we invited contributors to reflect on the evolution of and the prospect for our discipline within the broadly defined European perimeter.

Political science is now well established in Europe. Since the mid-twentieth century, the number of university departments, professional associations, and scientific journals dedicated to the discipline has steadily risen on the continent. Some of the discipline's venues are now solidly institutionalized. The International Political Science Association, for instance, is also celebrating an anniversary, its seventieth, in 2019. European journals like the *European Journal of Political Research*, the *Journal of European Public Policy*, *Party Politics*, *West European Politics*, and the *British Journal of Political Science* count among the most cited political science journals worldwide. The discipline also has a shared intellectual cannon, with a number of scholars widely recognized as key figures in the conceptual development of a blend of "European political science." The discipline has more professionals and produces strong cohorts of graduates and PhDs (e.g., Sapiro, Brun, & Fordant, 2019). Political science is also relatively successful in the disciplinary competition, as it manages to secure for itself a substantial share of the European funding available for the social sciences and humanities (Bach-Hoenig, 2017).

These achievements, however, also come with a number of challenges. Political science suffers from a general decline in the amount of public money available for research and from the rise of precariousness in academia. Along with other scientific disciplines like climate science, sociology, and gender studies, political science, and political scientists also come under fire from politicians and activists of different political persuasions, who criticize its alleged ideological biases and contest scholarly expertise altogether. The discipline is also being pressured to justify its market value by producing more and to prove its *impact* and *relevance* for society. Early career scholars are expected to publish at unseen quantity for the previous generations. The rise of open-access journals is a promising development toward a more inclusive publication environment, but it comes with the downside of a growing number of so-called "predatory" journals and conferences, which publish any work regardless of its quality—provided the author pays a substantial fee. At the same time, grant capture has become the symbol of academic success while funding success is still displaying some patterns of inequalities related to gender, the type of research, and the geographical location of universities across Europe. If these evolutions are driven by the specialization of knowledge production, they also follow a market bottom line. Failure to comply with the performance standards, or to do so in a way that fends off competition from neighboring disciplines, puts the very existence of political science under threat across local and national contexts. Such processes turn political science (as well as academia more generally) into an increasingly confusing and anomic universe, where it becomes harder for scholars to keep track of recent findings and to assess the quality of what is being produced.

In such a fluid and uncertain context, the purpose of this volume is to take stock of how the discipline has been built, what state it is in, what its achievements are, and what challenges it faces. It hopes to refine our understanding of the direction the discipline is going intellectually, and to feed professional debates about its structures and institutions.

1. BEYOND NUMBERS AND MEMORIES: A BROAD TAKE ON THE STATE OF EUROPEAN POLITICAL SCIENCE

Numerous fascinating publications have reflected on the historical state of political science in Europe. Building on this previous work, this volume offers a take on the common trends, opportunities and challenges across political science in Europe.

A number of these studies are shaped as retrospective accounts of personal experiences by senior members of the discipline. Such accounts often take the shape of stories that highlight the adventures and heroics of particular individuals—chiefly the so-called founding fathers of the discipline—and/or the paradigms and approaches they have contributed to develop, such as the "behavioral revolution" (e.g., Dahl, 1961). As the term "founding fathers" suggests, such histories are also primarily, not to say exclusively, written by and about senior male political scientists. The collective volume *Comparative European Politics: The Story of a Profession* (Daalder, 1997) is a prime example of this way of writing disciplinary history. By compiling individual autobiographies, the book offers a rich aggregate description of the development of a research area. More recently, Richard Rose's memoir *Learning about Politics in Time and Space* (Rose, 2014) builds upon the author's experiences to produce valuable considerations on the intellectual history and present state of the discipline.

Not all existing studies embrace disciplinary history in its entirety. Narratives often either put the emphasis on intellectual trends, in line with the history of political ideas, or focus on the social and institutional history and state of the profession. While it is increasingly rare for studies to turn a completely blind eye to either of these two sides of the coin, the fact remains that most focus on one of them, with the other less present. On the one hand, the contributions to the remarkable collective volume *Modern Political Science: Anglo-American Exchanges since 1880* (Adcock, Bevir, & Stimson, 2007) tend, for example, to prioritize "interpretation," with intellectual connections between U.S. and U.K. political science often clearer than the concrete circulations of scholars and books. On the other hand, volumes that focus on the "state of the discipline" often place a substantial emphasis on the discipline's numbers (in terms of professionals, students, books, journals, citations, etc.) with less focus on the conditions of knowledge production itself (see, for instance, Goodin & Klingemann, 1996).

Another substantial share of the existing literature studies political science in Europe through collections of country studies. While such collective efforts have different analytical focuses, they share the assumption that the accumulation of national cases creates the conditions for the analysis of more global processes. *Regime and Discipline: Democracy and the Development of Political Science* (Easton, Gunnell, & Graziano, 1991) uses country studies to tackle the more general question of how politics shaped the discipline. By contrast, volumes that aim to assess the "state of the discipline," such as the recent *Political Science in Europe at the Beginning of the 21st Century* (Krauz-Mozer, Borowiec, Kulakowska, & Scigaj, 2015), tend to privilege country descriptions that are rich in country-related information and peculiarities of national trajectories over the identification of common structures and questions to foster the emergence of a comparative narrative.

This volume aims to complete the landscape of disciplinary studies by adopting a different perspective. First, it resolutely focuses on the structural (European), rather than individual (country), level. Contributions veer away from individual autobiographies to focus on describing the broad processes that affect the discipline. This analytical focus comes with a diversification of author profiles, as contributors come from different countries and continents, generations, levels of seniority, genders, and ethnic backgrounds. This volume thus hopes to offer an analytical take on the discipline that is diverse enough to feel inclusive and ring true to its equally diverse potential readership.

Second, this volume bridges the gap between the social and intellectual sides of disciplinary history. Thus, it situates itself in line with the social history of social scientific ideas (inter alia Heilbron, Guilhot, & Jeanpierre, 2008). Such bridging is done within individual contributions: for example, the history of shifts in the objects that political science studied over time is shown to be partly linked to broader evolutions in society, particularly in social movements, and the story of professional associations is told in relation to that of paradigm and methods debates. This choice is also made tangible by the structure of the book, which comprises three parts. The first puts the emphasis on intellectual debates by situating political science in Europe in relation to the rest of the world at the level of concepts, objects, and methods. The second focuses chiefly on professional developments by assessing the professional structure and inclusiveness of the discipline. The third broadens the analysis to go beyond internal dynamics and study disciplinary evolutions from the angle of the relationship between the discipline and its social and political environment.

Third, the book departs from country studies to compile chapters focused on studying specific processes. Contributions tackle such diverse questions as the distinctive intellectual character of European political science, its impact on society in general, the threats and tensions it is subjected to, and its inclusive character as a profession. While one contribution focuses on a specific region—Central and Eastern Europe—it is not to highlight local idiosyncrasies, but to acknowledge the fact that bridging the East-West gap is one of the key challenges facing European political science today. In order to further highlight the ambition to produce a coherent volume with a measure of dialogue between contributions, authors were brought together for a collective discussion of their chapters during a workshop held in June 2019 at the European University Institute. While there are still and inevitably blind spots in this collective assessment of the discipline, we believe that the contributions still provide rich material to answer three key questions for political science in Europe: *Is there a distinctive European blend of political science? Is political science in Europe cohesive as a profession? What is the current status of the relationship between the discipline and its environment?* In the following, we discuss each of these questions in turn while presenting the various contributions to this volume and its overreaching structure.

2. IS THERE A DISTINCTIVELY EUROPEAN BLEND OF POLITICAL SCIENCE?

Political science developed at contrasted time and pace across world regions. The discipline became institutionalized at a relatively late stage in Western Europe compared to its development in the United States, but relatively early compared to its institutionalization in Eastern Europe, Asia, and Latin America. This diversity in trajectories is further fueled by the fact that not all Western European countries followed the same road to institutionalization. These discrepancies beg the question of whether the discipline is intellectually unified internationally or best portrayed as an aggregate of relatively different national traditions. Given the existence, in Europe, of continental political science journals and associations, the underpinning question in part I is twofold: Is there a measure of intellectual integration between European political scientists and, if so, to what extent is their work different from the political science of other parts of the world? The chapters in part I depict "European political science" as a broad church, characterized by a historical and ever-increasing diversity of objects, approaches, and methods, fed by the diversity of European political systems and lives themselves. Diversity, however, goes together with tensions and the challenge of keeping this heterogeneous community together.

In chapter 2, Yves Mény takes this question head-on to reflect on whether there is a "European touch" in political science, notably in relation to the United States. The chapter argues that one of European political science's key distinctive features lies in the diversity of political systems on the old continent, which has generated conceptual innovations and distinctive research agendas. The historical proximity between European political science and neighboring disciplines such as law, sociology, history, economics, and philosophy—in unequal measures across the continent—has also contributed to giving the discipline a distinctive European "flavor." Thus, the key point is that European political science is characterized by pluralistic traditions, which make it both less cohesive and more diverse than its U.S. counterpart.

The internal diversity of European political science also has to be understood in relation to the ever-expanding scope of the objects that the discipline studies. In chapter 3, Terrell Carver analyzes this gradual expansion in detail. He argues that this expansion is in part driven by the diversity of European political systems, and by what he calls "democratic challenges" of the discipline—namely, the role of social movements in turning into "political" issues questions that were before outside the realm of "the political." Carver highlights that the extension of the realm of "the political" has been fueled by theoretical innovations that were not exclusively, and even sometimes predominantly, European in nature—such as the linguistic and visual turns in the social and human sciences.

The diversity of European political science also comes with tensions. In chapter 4, Virginie Guiraudon looks at the tensions that arise between competing theoretical and methodological approaches within the discipline. She portrays the discipline as being, historically, characterized by a high degree of internal diversity, linked to its roots in multiple neighboring disciplines. Internal diversity has persisted, but its nature has changed over time: in spite of ambitions, from the 1960s onward, to find a "common ground" notably around the comparative method, political science has become increasingly "balkanized" and fragmented between several subfields. Meanwhile, a common "scientific habitus" has emerged, as peer-review processes have led to "more conformism in the format of research and templates of publication." However, such common ground, Guiraudon argues, does not come without setbacks, as they provide less room for "eccentrics" or minority positions. In other words, they tend to lead to a decline of pluralism.

Expansion and increasing diversity are also what characterize methodological developments in the discipline. In chapter 5, Russell Dalton looks back at the development of behavioralism, and the tremendous rise in the production and availability of empirical data that it prompted. While this evolution stimulated an unprecedented in the number of cross-national studies in various subfields (electoral studies, political parties, social movement studies, etc.), it also implied a growing quantification of political processes that has proven to be a long-lasting point of contention for the discipline.

3. IS EUROPEAN POLITICAL SCIENCE A COHESIVE AND INCLUSIVE PROFESSION?

The intellectual structure and diversity of political science in Europe cannot be fully explained without looking at the social dynamics that shape the discipline. Like other disciplines, political science can be analyzed as a profession. As such, it has to meet the challenges of being organized by a set of norms (such as intellectual standards, hierarchies, evaluation, and advanced criteria) and regulatory bodies (such as professional associations and evaluation boards), in a way that complies with law and the dominant norms of inclusiveness, probity, meritocracy, and so forth. It is also marred by struggles and inequalities that have to do not only with intellectual debates, but also with organizational (e.g., between universities, departments, associations, and journals) and individual competitions (between scholars), in a context of limited financial resources. Part II questions the extent to which European political science is cohesive as a profession and inclusive as a scholarly community. It portrays a profession that is challenged at several levels. The case of associations shows the extent to which intellectual differences may jeopardize the discipline's cohesiveness. European political science also suffers from strong national divides, most notably between Western and Eastern Europe, and from difficulties in integrating scholars from diverse gender, race, ethnic, religion, sexual preference, and class backgrounds.

In chapter 6, Thibaud Boncourt answers these questions through a comparative study of European political science associations: the ECPR, the European Political Science Network (EpsNET), the European Confederation of Political Science Associations (ECPSA), and the European Political Science Association (EPSA). Boncourt shows that the international divisions in the discipline have resulted in the inception of four main professional associations in Europe. Professional associations are seen as precious resource to gain weight in academic, intellectual, and political struggles. Divisions also have an impact on associations' membership. Their institutional structures and intellectual orientations trigger issues in attracting a large membership across all the regions of Europe, disciplinary subfields, and methodologies. As a result, political scientists from different countries, subfields, and methods background are unevenly represented across the different associations, which in turn affects the capacity of the profession to foster unity.

Drawing on a worldwide survey of political scientists, Pippa Norris investigates, in chapter 7, the implication of internationalization for the profession. The global community of political scientists is shown to share common features: across all regions, most scholars hold PhDs, subfields and methods are relatively evenly distributed, and political scientists hold remarkably similar views about the recent changes in the profession. Political scientists across the world share concerns about deteriorating working conditions and potential threats to academic freedom, increasing pressure to publish, teach, and growing administrative duties. Political scientists also share similar enthusiasm for global collaboration and knowledge exchange. There are, however, marked differences between regions with regard to academic migration: as long as they offer open job market conditions, established and wealthy academic systems in Northern and Western Europe are more likely to attract foreign talents than Central and Eastern Europe, Latin America, or Africa.

The differences between Western and Eastern Europe are further explored in chapter 8. Luciana Alexandra Ghica retraces the evolution of "European" over time as perimeter for research and the formation of scholarly community. While the dismantling of the Iron Curtain has allowed for the expansion of political science, Ghica shows that we are still not at the stage of an integrated community across Europe. European political science continues to be Western and Northern European regarding the geographical scope and the distribution of power and privileges across the community. Scholars from Central and Eastern Europe remain underrepresented in European conferences and academic outlets. Despite their knowledge and skills, they have fewer financial opportunities to present their work to an "international" audience (aka Western and Northern European), they publish less often in the major journals of the field, and they almost never access positions of power in the European profession. Ghica contends that it is about time European political scientists foster an integrated scholarly community that will show solidarity with national scholarly communities which are under increasing political and/or financial pressure.

The last two chapters of part II question further the inclusivity of European political science as a profession. In chapter 9, Isabelle Engeli and Liza Mügge assess the patterns of gender inequality in European political science. Echoing Pippa Norris's findings that women remain largely underrepresented in the profession (almost two-thirds of political scientists being men in Europe), they show that while progress has been made at the level of entry positions in the discipline, senior ranks remain overwhelmingly male dominated. Engeli and Mügge argue that, far from being solved, the leaky pipeline has remained, and this at every stage of the academic career. While blatant cases of direct discrimination are becoming more rare, gender inequality in the profession still takes place through a number of mechanisms that reinforce one another across all aspects of academic life: the institutional barriers in career progression go hand in hand with gender gaps in citations, publications, marks of esteem, and leadership positions. To become gender inclusive, the profession does not need to fix the women scholars but rather fix the system.

The picture is even bleaker in terms of race and ethnicity. In chapter 10, Shardia Briscoe-Palmer and Kate Mattocks contend that the investigation of marginalization in the discipline should go beyond the inclusion of women to assess the extent to which the increasing calls for more diversity in academia have had effects on the discipline of political science. In spite of a telling lack of data, they show that the issue of race is still largely ignored in European political science. While the student body is increasingly diverse, the profession has remained largely dominated by white scholars. Even when scholars of color reach institutional positions, their work tends to be marginalized. Reflecting on the irony for a discipline about power to forget the social organization of privileges, Briscoe-Palmer and Mattocks plead for a profession that finally takes stock of its racialization and acts toward reflecting in its composition the diversity of the world out there.

4. EUROPEAN POLITICAL SCIENCE IN A CHANGING ENVIRONMENT?

Managing its internal diversity is not the only challenge facing the discipline. European political science also faces a series of external incentives and pressures. These chiefly come from public authorities, whose funding is increasingly conditioned upon evaluation schemes that assess the quality of research and teaching against quantitative performance benchmarks. Such evaluations take into account the impact within academia of the knowledge produced (e.g., Is it published in well ranked journals?) but also within society at large (e.g., Are scholars engaged in diffusing their work to laypersons?). Together with the increasing pressures to secure funding from private actors, these evolutions mean that European political scientists increasingly need to be concerned with the "impact" and "relevance" of their work. To an extent, the survival of the discipline depends on its ability to strike the right balance between internal and external relevance. This is especially true given the threats that political science has been subjected to in European states that veer away from democracy. Part III tackles these questions at its core: To what extent is the very existence of European political science threatened? How does it cope with the pressures it is subjected to? What are the challenges that come with the ambition of being "relevant" to power and society? The four chapters in part III reflect on issues of *impact* and *relevance* from different angles. The picture that emerges is that of a profession that is nowadays increasingly able to offer advice to and even exert an actual *impact* on its object(s) of study. However, its heightened *relevance* outside the academic realm comes with challenges as well—mostly originating from those actors targeted by the profession on the basis of its established normative and theoretical underpinnings.

In chapter 11, Ivar Bleiklie, Marleen Brans, and Svein Michelsen discuss the advisory role of political science. Through a set of survey data based on responses by a large sample of European political scientists on their professional roles and four country case studies derived from this survey, the chapter assesses the scale and scope of policy advice activities, the major pathways for the provision of policy advice as well as its normative framework. Importantly, Bleiklie, Brans, and Michelsen move beyond the idea that policy advice equates with formalized roles in public administration. Indeed, they show that European political scientists support and engage in various types of policy advice, and they do so primarily as opinion makers and experts. Members of the profession would seem to share important attitudes vis-à-vis policy engagement and the way in which the two roles (academic and advisory) should be balanced. However, and again, institutional differences make a difference into the exact extent to which this balance varies across European countries.

In chapter 12, Diego Garzia and Alexander Trechsel contend that the growing interest in the discipline for digital transformations and the emerging potential of "civic technology" has led to novel forms engagement. They concentrate on a concrete example of engagement with parties, candidates, and voters: Voting Advice Applications (VAAs). VAAs are popular information-providing tools that help voters find their way around the electoral offer. These tools—originating in Europe in the late 1980s and by now prominent throughout all continental democracies—have catapulted political scientists to co-shapers of public opinion formation processes. For one thing, Garzia and Trechsel provide a timely and telling example of the ways in which European political science can engage with the citizenry in the digital age. At the same time, their case study of VAAs sheds precious light on the ethical implications of "doing impact" on our objects of study and calls for a careful reflection about the rapidly changing role of political scientists in the *online* era.

In chapter 13, Anton Hemerijck reflects on comparative welfare state research and the involvement of some of its leading scholars (including Hemerijck himself) in European Union (EU) social investment reforms of the late 1990s and early 2000s. He forcefully argues that academic engagement with policymakers has ultimately prepared the ground for the diffusion of social investment reform across the European continent between the late

1990s and the early 2000s. By offering firsthand insights into the practicalities of academic engagement, this (partly) autobiographical chapter conveys the idea that engagement originates from specific intellectual paradigms and specific corners of the political field coming together in favorable circumstances. In doing so, Hemerijck pinpoints the bidirectionality of the engagement relationship and specifies further the conditions under which academic engagement is likely to have bearings on policymaking.

Finally, in chapter 14, David Paternotte and Mieke Verloo move beyond actual engagement practices to dive into the complexity of the relationship between political science and its social, political, and economic environment. Paternotte and Verloo call for paying urgent attention to the risks that political science and political scientists run into in the current "turbulent" political times. This exemplary chapter does an inventory and categorization of the current threats that political science faces, the existing responses to these threats, and those that could/should be put in place. Hostile public debate, acrimonious politics, and structural changes in academic systems cumulate to put political science in a dangerous position with regard to its capacity to speak truth to power and to thrive. Indeed, the threats currently faced by political science in Europe cannot be dissociated from broader debates on academic freedom in the region and elsewhere. It cannot be dissociated from the threats against the safety and freedom of individual political scientists either.

In the postface, Kris Deschouwer reflects on what he sees as the overarching theme of the book's chapters: that of the boundaries of the discipline (i.e., both its internal divisions and its external limits), which he sees as constantly shifting and challenging political science and political scientists.

5. THE FUTURE OF POLITICAL SCIENCE IN EUROPE: CHALLENGES AND PROSPECTS

To an extent, this collection of chapters is a tribute to the success of the European blend of political science over the last fifty years. European political scientists have contributed to generating a wealth of theoretical, conceptual, and methodological tools that have enhanced the breadth and depth of our knowledge about European and global politics. They have succeeded in ensuring that the discipline's internal diversity remains a major asset to this breadth of understanding. Beyond national and regional borders, the discipline appears to have a measure of internal cohesiveness and coherence. It is also more institutionalized than it has ever been, with transnational dialogue and mobility more organized and frequent. Faced with the pressures for relevance, European political scientists have also engaged with a large variety of actors within civil society, the third sector, and the policymaking sphere. In this perspective, it makes sense to talk about "European political science" as a coherent whole, rather than simply "political science in Europe." However, these chapters also raise awareness of the many challenges that the discipline currently faces and call for individual political scientists and professional bodies to take action.

Intellectual diversity and specialization as well as organizational and individual competitions come with threats to the discipline's unity and professional inclusivity. We believe it is up to professional associations to ensure that all schools and subdisciplines, as well as every scholar regardless of their gender, race, and institutional affiliation, find empowering conditions to push further the boundaries of knowledge, though history proves that this is not easily achieved. At the same time, however, one should remain cautious about the potential challenges stemming from the hyper-diversification of the discipline and its paradigms—which ultimately puts at risk the possibility for political scientists to actually talk to each other.

Another pressing issue to be addressed is the pervasive epistemological hybridization of the "political" with other branches of the social sciences with very little connection to it. Computational social science methods, in particular, have opened up an entirely new frontier for political science. As aptly illustrated by Russell Dalton in this volume, however, the ready availability of an almost infinite amount of data and the increasingly sophisticated nature of the analytical methods (and technological devices) available to virtually every graduate student nowadays open up for the potential rise of atheoretical, fully data-driven approaches to knowledge production and development. Against this background, the emergence of preregistration processes is a welcome development: up-front decisions regarding data collection methods and analytical techniques can reduce biases that would may otherwise occur once the data (or the results) are in front of the researcher. The development of similar tools, which put scientific before technological prowess, should be one of the main topics of current ethical debates.

As far as social diversity goes, its generalized lack within political science remains distressing. The hierarchy of privileges within academia has taken its toll on political science. While steps have been taken to reduce the gender gap and to increase the presence of Central and Eastern scholars within European political science, much more needs to be done. In this respect, there is need for more data collection, more reflection on the intersectional character of the exclusion processes within the political science profession, and concrete action on the part of professional associations and academic departments against marginalization and invisibilization. Women, people of color, and other scholars in vulnerable situations deserve their place in the discipline, and a central one. The issue of inclusivity is made all the more acute by the rise of precariousness. The growing number of PhDs in political science conferred over the last thirty years all over the continent is far from being matched by the increase in the number of permanent academic positions. The road to tenure is becoming ever more uncertain, with obvious long-term consequences at individual, professional, and institutional levels. Political science associations and departments face an immense task in ensuring that such tense climate does not result in deep divisions between scholars of different generations and statuses. Collective reflections on the ethics and objectives of professional mentoring are perhaps more needed than ever.

The pressure for quantified academic performance calls for collective reflection. Should political science keep meeting the increasing demands of academic capitalism, as defined by grant capture, publication, and citation performance—or should it rather push forward a "slow science" approach to the understanding of an increasingly complex social and political world? An important step along these lines is the San Francisco Declaration on Research Assessment (DORA), signed in 2012. The DORA declaration openly tackles the pervasive "publish or perish" approach of contemporary science by means of a number of recommendations. Most notably, it pushes for the elimination of journal-based metrics in funding, appointment, and promotion considerations, and for the corresponding need to evaluate the quality of research on its own merits rather than on the basis of the journal in which the research is published (impact factor). If science is to retain meaning for its practitioners and its public, such initiatives should be encouraged and followed upon not only by statements of intent, but also by concrete changes in funding, appointment, and promotion practices.

The pressures for relevance and impact also prompt the discipline to engage with its social and political environment. Such endeavors are socially situated. They are normatively driven. And they are financially constrained. While the ethics of engagement has triggered debates and sometimes led, as in the case of VAAs, to the crafting of charters of good conduct, much more remains to be done. The desirability of engagement (Under what conditions should political scientists engage with society?), the ethical implications of funding (Does the need to "get money from where it is" justify engagement with any and all actors?), and the scientific implications of engagement (What does engagement do to the content, structure, and professional practices of science?) are in need of further reflection.

Pressure from the environment calls for scholarly solidarity. Paternotte and Verloo provide a worrisome account of the severity of the threats against the political science and social sciences in an increasing number of national contexts across Europe and beyond. Hungary, Poland, Turkey, and Brazil are examples that come first to mind. Indeed, concrete steps have already been taken to threaten political science's objects of study, if not its very existence. Attacks against academic knowledge go increasingly hand in hand with attacks against the job security, the safety, and the freedom of social scientists. Gender studies programs have been defunded in Hungary by governmental decision. The Central European University had to relocate in Austria to be able to pursue its educational mission. When students protest in Hong Kong to protect democratic acquis, they are teargassed, beaten, and arrested. Colleagues have been or are currently prosecuted—or even imprisoned—in Poland, Turkey, Iran, China, and elsewhere. Others have lost their jobs and fled. Giulio Regeni was murdered in Egypt while doing fieldwork for his PhD dissertation. Perhaps political science has never been so "political," at least not in that deadly way. This is a matter of emergency for reflection and action. How can we show solidarity and provide support and assistance to fellow scholars in peril? What structures can we collectively put in place to resist these threats? In this regard, we welcome the fact that the ECPR has recently launched a "Scholars at Risk" program that aims at supporting those colleagues whose academic freedom has been infringed and calls for the development of long-lasting actions. In these perilous political times, academic solidarity takes a new meaning that deserves new forms of actions.

Only a structured collective reflection will be able to pave the way for European political science to face the many, and to an extent unprecedented, challenges ahead. The more modest aim of this book, if anything, is that of raising awareness about such challenges and highlighting the need for political science to adapt to a changing environment much in the same way it repeatedly (and so far successfully) did over the last half century.

REFERENCES

Adcock, R., Bevir, M., & Stimson, S. C. (Eds.). (2007). *Modern political science: Anglo-American exchanges since 1880*. Princeton and Oxford: Princeton University Press.

Bach-Hoenig, B. (2017). Competing for status: Dynamics of scientific disciplines in the European transnational field. *Serendipities. Journal for the Sociology and History of the Social Sciences, 2*(1), 90–106.

Daalder, H. (Ed.). (1997). *Comparative European politics: The story of a profession* (pp. 227–40). London: Pinter.

Dahl, R. (1961). The behavioral approach in political science: Epitaph for a monument to a successful protest. *American Political Science Review, 55*(4), 763–72.

Easton, D., Gunnell, J., & Graziano, L. (Eds.). (1991). *The development of political science: A comparative survey*. London: Routledge.

Goodin, R. E., & Klingemann, H.-D. (Eds.). *A new handbook of political science.* Oxford: Oxford University Press.

Heilbron, J., Guilhot, N., & Jeanpierre, L. (2008). Toward a transnational history of the social sciences. *Journal of the History of the Behavioral Sciences, 44*(2), 146–60.

Krauz-Mozer, B., Borowiec, P., Kulakowska, M., & Scigaj, P. (Eds.). (2015). *Political science in Europe at the beginning of the 21st century.* Krakow: Jagiellonian University Press.

Rose, R. (2014). *Learning about politics in time and space.* Colchester: ECPR Press.

Sapiro, G., Brun, E., & Fordant, C. (2019). The rise of the social sciences and humanities in France: Institutionalization, professionalization, and autonomization. In C. Fleck, M. Duller, & V. Karady (Eds.), *Shaping human science disciplines. Institutional developments in Europe and beyond* (pp. 25–68). London: Palgrave Macmillan.

Part I

EUROPEAN POLITICAL SCIENCE

Chapter 2

Is There a European Touch?

Yves Mény

1. INTRODUCTION

The place and role of European political science is not a new issue. Many reports, stimulated by individuals' or working groups' initiatives, have periodically attempted to assess the "state of political science," first in America, then in Europe, followed by the rest of the world (Newton & Vallès, 1991). From World War II until the 1990s, the dominant (and realistic) view put forward by these studies was that there was an elephant in the room of the political science condominium: the hegemony of American universities and research centers was beyond discussion. Indeed, the United States is and long has been the leader of political science, with Europe its sole competitor for the role. In other regions of the world, political science is still too weak in quantitative (Australia) or qualitative terms (the rest of the world, in spite of promising developments in Latin America or Asia, for instance). However, the overall balance has shifted. The United States is less hegemonic, and political science is more diversified and pluralistic. Europe is playing a major role in this rebalancing game.

Until the 1920s, the domain today considered the playground of political science was occupied by other, more traditional and entrenched disciplines such as law, philosophy, history, and sociology. Politically, the discipline was very much dependent on the development and consolidation of "democratic" regimes. Authoritarian or dictatorial regimes have little appetite for the "science of government" and more generally for humanities and social sciences. It has meant that European countries where political science could tentatively develop were very few: Britain, the Nordic countries, Belgium, the Netherlands, France, and Switzerland. It was only in the 1950s that this narrow group extended to Germany (which had lost most of its potential after

1933), and, later on, to Italy. Very little could be done in countries controlled by authoritarian regimes such as Spain, Portugal, and Greece, and the situation was similar in the countries under Soviet domination.

Therefore, up until the 1990s, "Europe" in political science still had a very narrow meaning. This situation raises several questions and issues.

First are the questions of what "Europe" means beyond its geographical definition and what we mean by referring to a European "touch." In political terms, the concept of Europe has gone through rather dramatic changes: first with the constitution of the European Economic Community (EEC) in 1958, then its successive enlargements during the 1970s and 1980s, and, finally, the fall of the Berlin Wall in 1989. Each of these periods has marked a transformation of Europe and a new development in political science. The establishment of the European Consortium for Political Research (ECPR) in 1970 and, later on, the decision by the European Union (EU) to finance certain applied and cooperative research, followed by the launch of a pan-European research organization (the European Research Council), have also been crucial factors. Talking about a "European" touch implies looking at the variations resulting from the changes in the object of reference. It also requires looking beyond the concept of Europe and questioning if it is able to fully encapsulate the plethora of traditions and practices which survive from one country to the other, in spite of the growing harmonization and standardization of the discipline, both as a specialized field and a profession characterized by its methodologies, its training capacities, its differentiation, and its specialized meetings and journals. Drawing a frontier between what is European and the rest of the world might even be in some cases a futile exercise: Is a contribution by a European working in Canada or Australia still European or not? Or should we consider that anything produced by non-Europeans becomes "European" from the moment it is born on the European continent?

Second, the wording might introduce an initial bias to the analysis. "Touch" suggests something light, specific, added to the main way of doing something or to the substance itself, and a slight variation in the use of approaches and methodological and theoretical tools in contrast with core or mainstream practices. For instance, it might imply that one implicitly accepts that the dominant or mainstream research is done outside Europe, that European political science either follows or imitates. That might be true, but, as a starting point, one should avoid accepting it as an undisputed fact. It might also be interpreted in a different way: the socialization of approaches and methods across the Atlantic divide and throughout the world does not fully erase national or regional nuances, which persist in spite of growing standardization. And finally, it implies that there is a "European" political science reality, not only in contrast to the dominant American discipline, but beyond fragmented and piecemeal national communities.

2. DEFINING THE FIELD

The purported differentiation of European political science might be interpreted in various and somewhat opposing ways: it can be seen as a manifes-
tation of backwardness, or rather as a product of historical differentiation; it
can also be considered, from an evolutionary perspective, testimony of an
ongoing process of emancipation. Finally, a reassessment of the European
contribution might help to revise the relative influence of the two poles.

2.1. Backwardness?

First, such purported differentiation might be seen as a mere reflection of
the gap between two sets of institutions, rules, and academic production.
On the one hand, there is a leader who sets the tune and the rules of the
game, while, on the other hand, the remaining actors adjust more or less
willingly and speedily to the trends and innovations produced, in this case
by the American community. This mode of interpretation is rather obvious
in the report produced by Gabriel Almond (Almond, 1998), in the *Handbook of Political Science*, where he divides the history of the discipline into
four phases: the historical part, mainly dominated by European minds from
Aristotle up to World War I, and three successive phases, presented as exclusively American. There were what Almond refers to as "three rising blips
in the 20th-century curve." There was, he writes, "the Chicago blip in the
interwar decades (1920–1940), introducing organized empirical research . . .
and demonstrating the value of quantification"; a second, much larger blip in
the decades after World War II, characterized by "the spread of behavioral
political science throughout the world" as well as by the professionalization of the discipline; and the third blip, which turned around "the entry of
deductive and mathematical methods, and economic models in the 'rational
choice/methodological individualist' approach" (Almond, 1998, p. 36). What
was labeled by its initiators as a "revolution" has, however, produced mixed
results (Gunnell, 2009). If one accepts that this evolutionary perspective was
characterized by "methodological progress," there is no doubt that Europe
has been left behind. In particular, the "rational choice revolution" had a
rather limited impact on European political science. Any impact was mostly
through economists becoming interested in using political data. However,
this progress in terms of data collection, treatment, and analysis has also
shown its limits when the accumulation of hard data went hand in hand with
indifference to context, institutional differentiations, diversity of cultures,
and heterogeneity of behavior. From this perspective, European distinctiveness cannot be simply equated with backwardness. The "backwardness"
assessment has been vigorously contested by Philippe Schmitter in his 2002

"*J'accuse*" against the "transatlanticized" perspective and the potential future it envisages. According to the mainstream view, which Schmitter vigorously challenges, "It is merely a matter of time before national and regional resistances are overcome and the entire discipline will converge upon an identical set of concepts, assumptions and methods" (Schmitter, 2002).

2.2. Deeply Rooted European Diversity

A second, more lenient, interpretation construes the European peculiarity of the discipline as a result of its historical and variegated development alongside the persistence of eclectic traditions. An illustration of this situation is offered by handbooks on the "state of political science in Europe," usually characterized by an introduction attempting to offer a synthesis of the common trends across countries, followed by twenty or more chapters on individual countries, each of them presenting a diverse narrative about the state of the art in each political/academic setting. From the perspective of convergence and progressive indifferentiation of theoretical and methodological approaches, this can again be interpreted as a negative feature contributing to the "backwardness" assessment. On the flipside, some might see it as a sign of pluralistic richness and an indicator of the failure of the behavioral revolution to accomplish its initial dream to become an encompassing and exclusive method of analysis for the political reality. As underlined by Liisi Keedus, the disciplinary revolution "succeeded in the short run due to its effective self-promotion, but failed in the long-run because of the over-ambitious promises it had made" (Keedus, 2018). Pippa Norris takes a different perspective in underlining the paradox that increasing cooperation between European countries after decades of insulation might be an impediment to a more "cosmopolitan" political science (Norris, 1997).

Partly for historical or political reasons, partly because of the lack, up until recently, of a common language facilitating the circulation, discussion, and cross-fertilization between national systems, there is very little to allow Europe to compete on an equal footing with what happens in the American academic arena. Granted, European fragmentation is less pronounced than fifty or even thirty years ago, but the transnational European debate is still circumscribed to "privileged" places, institutions, journals, and networks (Boncourt, 2015). And, even in the best possible scenario, many political scientists or publications still remain "invisible." A glance at national journals or journals published in English (which by definition are becoming more "European" and international) is telling about how much the profession and the discipline are separated into insulated compartments: those publishing in their national language refer only occasionally to publications in English, while publications in English tend to consider the various national language publications as "terra incognita," except, sometimes, in the fields of area and comparative studies.

2.3. A Reassessment?

2.3.1. Transnationalization

While the European peculiarism has long been associated with negative connotations, since it was perceived as a situation of inferiority vis-à-vis the United States, the landscape has little by little evolved and changed. Initially, the movement of travel was unidirectional, from Europe to America in every dimension: from training and collaboration to having a professional career. This lasted at least up until the 1970s when European universities started to reform themselves and tried to catch up with and emulate the American model, particularly in northern Europe.

In 1970, a few senior academics launched the ECPR and, in 1976, the European University Institute (which had been set up in 1972 after fifteen years of diplomatic stalemate by rather reluctant partners) began its operations with a rather unique—at the time—PhD program, followed twenty-five years later by postdoc programs.

However, these rather hesitant reforms, largely based on trial and error, had the merits of opening new avenues and ways of doing things. First of all, alternatives to the American experience started to be offered to a new generation of doctoral students. The Erasmus program, funded by the EEC, had tremendous merits, in spite of its intrinsic limitations: for the first time, young students had the opportunity to "taste" and try different systems of teaching and research and to look beyond national borders. They had more "options" to experience different and better training without the financial and human costs of crossing the Atlantic. Pippa Norris poses the hypothesis that "there are plausible reasons to suppose that, in recent decades, European political science may have strengthened multilateral links within its borders, yet this very development may have severed some of the older ties linking Europe and the United States" (Norris, 1997, p. 17). This is a fair assessment, but actually the westward road was reserved for a rather small group of students and scholars. For a limited, but growing, number of students, Europe was becoming the new frontier, while training and the profession at the national level were becoming only one option among others. In other words, one could observe the shift from segmented and separated arenas to a "single market" in the making. Countries such as Great Britain and the Netherlands were at the forefront of this evolution. In addition, most, if not all, countries introduced curricula in English at masters and doctoral levels. It was obviously true in small countries whose national language was not used beyond their borders, but also in universities and schools in countries such as Spain, Portugal, and France which attract a large number of Hispanophone, Lusophone, and Francophone students. The magnitude of this de-nationalization and the constitution of a European space have still to be thoroughly evaluated, but it is certainly an element of the specific "touch" characterizing the recent evolution. In other words, education and research are slightly less national and more international, most of the time meaning more European, since European universities are not usually in a position to compete with American universities in the academic market.

2.3.2. Passeurs and Reverse Fertilization?

Until now, we have implicitly assumed that any possible "European touch" results from a divergence between American developments and various forms of European differentiation. Actually, all past assessments, whether done by APSA (American Political Science Association), IPSA (International Political Science Association), or ECPR, support this hypothesis, in spite of some nuances and minor divergences (Boncourt, in this volume). Most of the time, a kind of black-and-white picture prevails, posing the strong American side and the much weaker and left-behind European junior partner as opposites. This assessment, however, does not take into consideration the important contribution provided by Europeans between the two world wars and after 1945. Considerable input was given before, during, and after World War II, by European academics moving westward, where they could get better and more attractive positions than in Europe. In many ways, American political science has been "Europeanized." Would American political science be the same without the contribution of scholars such as Hannah Arendt, Hanna Pitkin, Henry Ehrmann, Carl J. Friedrich, Albert Hirschman, Otto Kircheimer, and Ernst Haas, to mention just a few refugee names? Many political scientists who are not part of the dominant school have brought to the United States a "European touch." The marked opposition between the two sides of the Atlantic might be somewhat overemphasized.

Even more important, perhaps, than their contribution to the American political science scene, these expatriates, together with some of their "local" colleagues, have often played a key role in linking the two continents and playing the role of go-between. One can never emphasise enough the positive contribution of American colleagues who, through monographies or comparative research, have developed new methodologies, concepts, and approaches that have then contributed to the fertilization of the field in Europe.

2.3.3. Funding and Publications

Finally, in trying to better characterize the meaning of a possible "European touch," the issue of funding and publication of research is crucial. There is no systematic analysis of the divergences and convergences in funding research and publishing between the two sides of the Atlantic, but there are a few studies attempting to assess the degree of reciprocal interaction and influence. During the period from the 1950s to the 1980s, the funding structure in Europe and the United States was quite at odds. In the United States, research was funded through federal funds, allocated by the Social Science Research Council (SSRC) according to programs sometimes influenced by political concerns, such as the stimulus given to comparative research in the 1960s after the launching of the Sputnik satellite by the Soviet Union. Abundant funding supporting research abroad was also made available, and this overhaul was complemented by all the major American foundations which provided fellowships or research grants (Ford, Rockfeller, Fulbright, etc.).

On the European side, research funding had two major characteristics: it was exclusively national and the role of private foundations was marginal. The few exceptions were, for instance, the German Marshall Fund or, at the margins, a few foundations exclusively serving their national constituencies (for instance, the Wellcome Trust in the field of biology and medical research in Great Britain; the Volkswagen Stiftung, set up in 1961, exclusively for German applicants; the Agnelli foundation, set up in 1966; the Olivetti foundation, created in 1962; the Wallenberg foundations created in Sweden, in 1917; and the Gulbenkian foundation in Portugal, created in 1956). While some of these charities were crucial sources of funding in some disciplines (the Wellcome Trust) or in small countries (Sweden and Portugal), they played a marginal role in other countries that had little interest for social sciences in general and for political science in particular. While the United States was supporting American research abroad and foreign fellows visiting the United States, there was no parallel avenue in Europe, with a few minor exceptions (the Marshall Fund).

There is no doubt that political science in Europe has a special flavor, a specific touch. But has this peculiarity had any impact on the development of the discipline?

3. THE CONSTITUTIVE ELEMENTS
OF THE EUROPEAN TOUCH

The so-called American revolutions, the behaviorist and the rational choice innovations, were made possible thanks to a number of peculiar factors, including the sheer size of the discipline, its professional organization, and its relations with related disciplines. The decisive factor, however, might have been the structure of the political environment which favored a pluralist and critical approach to the study of politics and a privileged approach based upon methodological individualism. While the ancillary and dependent position of political science vis-à-vis other social sciences has receded in most European countries, the discipline is often too weak to take advantage of its new independence. In many countries, not only have the parent disciplines managed to keep some control of their offspring, but, more importantly, they maintain a strong influence in term of theoretical and methodological approaches. Moreover, since political science was birthed from different sources (sociology, public law, etc.) across Europe, these genetic influences contributed to differentiating the discipline along national lines. In other words, by contrast to America, where the "revolutions" of the past have had a deep and long-standing effect on research production, publications, theoretical, and methodological debates, and internal divisions of the profession; political science in Europe was busy with making a place of its own under the sun and was divided along lines which often had more to do with ideology than methodology. For instance, Marxist or constructivist theories were more prevalent in the debates in Europe than behaviorism, which was adopted by some while others manifested an attitude of benign contempt or indifference. Actually, we might argue that the behaviorist American revolution was used in Europe as an instrument of differentiation from the "mother-disciplines" which were still in positions of domination and control (Newton & Vallès, 1991).

In considering the impact of the so-called European touch, one has to disentangle two constitutive elements. On the one hand, it means that political science has become less national and more "European." On the other hand, and in relation to the "elephant in the room," that is, the United States, one may wonder if the European community of political scientists differentiates itself or has any impact upon its mentor and main competitor?

3.1. The Europeanization of Political Science

3.1.1. The European Consortium for Political Research

As already mentioned, the creation of the ECPR was a decisive factor in the birth of a European dimension. With the benefit of retrospective analysis, it is striking how much this initiative has been successful, in spite of much resistance, and has transformed a loose network into a lasting "European" organization. This success story might be explained by several factors: the first one is the reputation and prestige of the founding fathers; the second one is the type of network which was opted for, that is a network of institutions (universities, schools, departments) rather than an unstable and fragile network of individuals. In other words, the institutionalization process started from the very beginning and was reinforced by the fact that this could guarantee stability and continuity on the one hand and secure stable funding on the other (since the annual contribution was rather minimal, at least for major universities). And since collective membership was required to allow individuals to benefit from networking activities, it transformed every political scientist, even in small organizations/communities, into a lobbyist pleading and pressing to join the "club" in order to be able to participate and enjoy its benefits. Finally, its success has also been linked to the pragmatic approach chosen in setting up the new organization with a light structure based in Essex, set up as a charity benefiting from the support and professionalism of a British university; a decentralized system of meetings and workshops stimulated by bids from local hosts; and no official language policy, which meant that, after a few years and without saying it, English became the lingua franca of this nascent European organization. The structure was not without defects: The British grip was sometimes a bit heavy, but actually there was no real alternative. The attempt to set up an alternative organization focusing on teaching issues, in 1996, in the form of a thematic network sponsored and funded by DG XII of the EU Commission, was short-lived. The inability to transform the network (EpsNET) into a lasting institution and the termination of financial support by the EU brought the initiative to an end. Fortunately, the misunderstandings and tensions which accumulated at the end of the 1990s between the two organizations concluded in cease-fire and collaboration. A still fragmented and fragile discipline escaped the fatal risk of internal conflict. A milestone on the road to this new unity in the making was the launching of *European Political Science* (EPS), the professional journal which has successfully emulated *Political Science* (PS), the journal of the American Political Science Association.

However, the situation is not as rosy as it could be. First of all, there is a strong imbalance between countries, and it is not only related to the size of the country. Two countries dominate (Britain and Germany) and the statistics are biased by the fact that in many countries international relations (IR) is included in "political science," while in Great Britain IR is under the umbrella of its own organization. Secondly, the participation and involvement of Eastern European countries has been rather slow and reluctant (two members in 1992, around forty since 2013), reflecting in many ways the late development of political science in these new democracies. Thirdly, the actual participation of individual members is somewhat disconnected from the number of registered institutional members. The yearly workshops, a core and remarkable activity of the ECPR, set up by Rudolf Wildermann in 1973, are heavily attended by northern Europeans but less by others, even when the location of the meeting takes place, for instance, in southern Europe. And participation is imbalanced in favor of doctoral students or junior academics while senior members are less prone to be involved, a somewhat regrettable trend. However, the overall balance is very positive as it allows the strengthening of socialization and cooperation between political scientists from various European countries, traditions, and cultures. At any point in time, the organization has been able to anticipate and adjust to new challenges: growing from 50 members in 1975 to more than 350 today; launching new journals; electing an American member of the Executive Council in 2012; cutting the umbilical cord with Essex in 2014; and becoming in many ways more international. The biggest challenge ahead might result from Brexit, which would isolate the headquarters from the rest of Europe. It would not be an inextricable Gordian knot, but would handicap the operations of an organization which has always tried to minimize the negative consequences of political divisions over its pan-European goals and mission.

3.1.2. The EU and the European Research Council

Another crucial factor of Europeanization has been the intervention of the EU in promoting research across borders in all fields, including political science. This substantial contribution to research funding has radically modified the landscape in two successive phases. The first one, through the so-called framework programs, brought mixed results. This development has been beneficial in favoring (or rather, forcing) collaboration through a kind of "affirmative action" strategy. However, there were many drawbacks: a poor system of evaluation, a certain level of "bureaucratic" bias, an extremely cumbersome mode of management and control, and an insistence on "relevant" rather than basic research.

The second major development is related to the launching of the European Research Council, in 2007, in order to finance basic/frontier research run by junior or senior individuals and their team (assistants, PhDs, and postdocs). After an initial start that frustrated many candidates and even more so the evaluators, due to the cumbersome bureaucratic requirements, the process has become more fluid and user-friendly. It has become *the* major source of basic research in Europe and beyond (€13 billion over the period 2013–2020), erasing the numerous political requirements in the thematic frameworks and favoring spontaneous, rather than forced, cooperation within Europe and beyond. Major players (Israel, the United States, Switzerland, etc.) are part of the "research area" and the grants obtained by applicants, from any part of the world, are "portable" to any research institution in the area. Out of 65,000 applications, 9,000 projects have been funded. Out of the 7,000 grantees, 537 were non-Europeans (representing 69 nationalities) and 218 were Americans. These figures are still modest but the trend is new and positive. Each project involves, on average, six researchers. In many ways, the ERC program has become a functional equivalent of the SSRC or major private foundations in the United States by creating a unified European instrument overarching national funding institutions. A positive side effect has emerged from the spillover consequences triggered by the ERC process. A number of European countries (seventeen), which often lack the human resources for an independent and unbiased evaluation of national projects, have decided to rely on ERC evaluations to finance projects assessed by the ERC as excellent but rejected due to insufficient funding.

3.1.3. Political Science Journals

"Europeanization/internationalization" (Crewe & Norris, 1991; Norris, 1994) has been encouraged by the incremental decoupling of publications from national settings. First, an increasing number of national journals publish in English or accept submissions both in English and in the national language. Another element might have contributed to further Europeanizing the publications strategy and to overcoming national borders: the launching of journals based in Great Britain that were decisively nonnational in spirit and purpose. The *Journal of Common Market Studies*, set up in 1962, was a forerunner which long remained a unique case; it was followed in the 1970s by the launch of *EJPR* and later on by *West European Politics* (1978). Notable additions in the 1980s/1990s included the *Journal of Public Policy* (1981) and the *Journal of European Public Policy* (1994). Similar initiatives were undertaken in other subfields due to both internationally minded scholars and publishing houses keen to expand their share and consolidate their oligopolies. These innovations have without any doubt contributed to denationalizing research and research outputs. However, one should introduce two caveats: first, the new publication opportunities have probably (there is no study of the situation) been used as much or more by non-European researchers as by academics from Europe; secondly, beyond publication in European/international journals, the largest number of publications are still to be found in national-language journals. A recent study of four countries (Spain, Portugal, Ireland, and Norway) by a European team analyzed publications in European/international journals and showed that "national" publications still make up the majority, especially in southern Europe, and on average represented 73 percent of the total (with a peak of 85% in Spain), while "European" publications (8%) were less than those in international journals (19%). The results of this research are noteworthy as they give a good idea of the overall situation, despite being drawn from a small sample (Camerlo, Doyle, Garcia Diez, & Marsteintredet, 2018).

3.2. The Distinctiveness of European Political Science

The European touch, by contrast with the other main actors worldwide, particularly the United States, might be identified according to several criteria, for instance methodology, theory, or research domains.

The first obvious differentiation derives from differences in institutions, situations, or the salience of political issues. If one considers, for instance, the study of institutions in the United States and in Europe, the divergence is rather marked given the structural differences between the two continents. The party systems in the European parliamentary regimes, their organization, and their ideological underpinnings, alongside the functioning of the parliaments and the regulation of political campaigns, trigger different set of questions for political scientists. There is not much interest in Europe about the behavior of parliamentarians as in most cases it is conditioned and channeled by party whips or disciplinary rules which impose a straightjacket on MPs. The same contrast is observable in relation to the behavior of judges, given the autonomy and the origin of the judiciary both at the state and federal levels in the United States, while in Europe, judges are never appointed through popular vote nor nominated along political lines, except in a few cases and tribunals. The United States and European research agendas are quite distinct since the key issues are so different. In short, the blending of institutionalism with behaviorism or rational choice (Shepsle, 2006), which blossomed in judicial and legislative studies in the United States, rarely took off in Europe (a rare example is Tsebelis's study of European institutions). By contrast, the rediscovery of the role of institutions, in the 1990s, by the historical or sociological institutionalist schools in America, was not on the European agenda, since the study of institutions had never been marginalized. It benefited, however, indirectly from this American rediscovery by considering institutions not only as independent variables, but by emphasizing the influence of institutions on: individual or collective behavior, the organization of interests, and the structuration of expectations and actions. The fact that similar institutions could provide or frame very different outcomes aided the construction of "models" and families contrasting American and European developments and clustering various national traditions according to their structural features.

Beyond these structural differences, another historical factor played a big role. The late, fragmented, and variegated development of political science in national arenas across Europe contributed both to its relative weakness and to the dependency of the field on related disciplines such as philosophy, history, law, and sociology. The proximity between political science and these older and more powerful disciplines had negative effects, such as difficulty in building up an independent and professionalized discipline. On the other hand, it has permitted a more relaxed attitude to the borrowing of concepts, theories, and contributions by a discipline more open to neighbor disciplines. Philosophers have influenced normative theory; historians and lawyers, the study of institutions; sociologists, political sociology; ethnologists and anthropologists, the research on micro-cases and issues or comparative historical analysis. European political science has borrowed heavily from sociologists as diverse as Max Weber, Émile Durkheim, Pierre Bourdieu, Ralf Dahrendorf, Irving Goffmann, Georg Simmel, Anthony Giddens, and Charles Tilly; historical sociologists such as Barrington Moore, Norbert Elias, and Immanuel Wallerstein; philosophers such as Habermas, Michel Foucault, and Norberto Bobbio; historians such as Eric Hobsbawn and Fernand Braudel; economists such as Schumpeter, Keynes and Hirschman; and lawyers such as Duverger and Cassese. These borrowings and influences also help to explain how qualitative methods, borrowed from these related disciplines, continue to blossom in complement or as alternatives to quantitative methods.

4. DOES EUROPEAN POLITICAL SCIENCE HAVE ANY IMPACT BEYOND ITS BORDERS ?

The first impact Europe might have is by exploring fields neglected by the United States or other countries due to their lack of interest or incentives. It has already been observed that political science can develop only if power structures are sufficiently democratic and allow the freedom that research needs. However, this should not prevent the study of nondemocratic systems by researchers enjoying the benefits of liberty in their own countries. Democratic systems cannot be the only objects of political science. Dictatorships and authoritarian regimes are at least as important. Obviously, their study is much more difficult, as it requires not only mastering domestic languages but also access to data under the control of suspicious authorities. It often requires the active involvement of scientists who were forced to leave the country and/or reliance on qualitative methods, since data collection or surveys are nearly impossible to put in place. Given this state of affairs, Europeans have exploited a niche resulting from the past colonial heritage of their countries. Research on the Maghreb or the Machrek is undertaken mainly by French researchers or academics from the region who migrated to France or were educated there. The same can be said for sub-Saharan Africa, where research is mainly organized and sponsored by British and French centers. Some German or Swiss institutes (such as those at the Humboldt or Freie Universities in Berlin or at the Graduate Institute in Geneva) also contribute, thanks to multidisciplinary centers set up around a mix of disciplines including anthropologists, economists, and political scientists. Great Britain has maintained strong linkages with its former colonies, particularly those where European populations overtook the locals (e.g., Canada, New Zealand, Australia), and has remained a major influence on Asian studies. This part of the world has also triggered a growing interest in the United States, in particular toward major countries such as Japan, India, and China. In addition, local research is emerging in India and Singapore, for instance, while it remains under tight control in countries such as Saudi Arabia and the UAE, where researchers from foreign universities need to be "cleared" by political authorities. In most cases, the contribution of natives living abroad conditions research capacities that have, and still, give ex-colonial powers a structural advantage over former colonies in terms of education, training, cooperation, and publications. If these factors are taken into consideration, the quantitative and qualitative American superiority might be slightly reassessed.

Finally, one might consider areas or fields where differentiated emphasis has been placed on some issues, by using distinct theoretical approaches, on both sides of the Atlantic. One might find several illustrations of this methodological and theoretical discrepancy in various fields, and notably in areas such as the relationship between central and local institutions, the study of political parties, research on welfare systems, and, more broadly, the role and place of institutions in politics. And the list is far from exhaustive.

The relations between federal government and states/local government have been at the heart of political studies in the United States in many areas, including normative theory, party politics and legislative studies, group action, public policies, and so forth. Key concepts such as steering and control, compliance, implementation, and intergovernmental relations have been the backbone of the field. However, in Europe the greater emphasis has been on the tensions between the "center and periphery," since many claims were based on economic, social, and cultural subordination rather than perceived as a problem of hierarchy, power allocation, and reciprocal cooperation. In Europe, dependence theories, derived from colonial or minorities studies, were preferred over the institutionalist and policy-oriented theories used in the American context. The two approaches ran in parallel for a long time, both cultivating their mutual *"splendide isolement."* A rapprochement, a reciprocal cross-fertilization, only came about when both American and European scholars became aware that the Europeanization process and growing globalization trends could be better explained and understood by combining the contributions of both sides. Multilevel governance theories put aside the neo-Marxist approaches that prevailed in Europe in the 1960s and 1970s, but kept the center–periphery paradigm as elaborated, for instance by Stein Rokkan, and combined it with the contribution of American and German studies on federalism and "intergovernmental relations." The fact that many American scholars work on the EU, and that their European counterparts are well aware of the empirical and theoretical American research on intergovernmentalism, has contributed to developing a rather intense conversation between the two sides. It is probably the area where the exchange of ideas, theories, and people is most intense, but also rather balanced. One cannot say that one side prevails over the other. By contrast, there is a constant flow of exchange, debate, and mutual influence. It is a small research community where political borders do not have much impact, which is as it should be throughout the discipline.

On both the American and European sides, the study of political parties, as core institutions of the democratic fabric, has been at the center of political science interests and development from V. O. Key to Michels to Duverger. However, the genetic structural differences in terms of ideology, organization, and role in the legislative process, as well as the radical differences between parliamentary and presidential systems, have contributed to research being on two parallel tracks. While American research was organized around the key institution (the legislature) focusing on both the environment (party and elections regulations, gerrymandering, corruption) and the behavior of loosely bound representatives; European research was more concerned with ideology, electoral systems, internal workings of the party, factions, coalitions, parties of government versus extreme parties, and so forth. Not only has there been little cross-fertilization but sometimes reciprocal sheer ignorance.

The same diagnosis applies to the field of welfare state studies; in this case, it might be argued that Europe woke up the United States and pushed it toward the discovery of social policies as a key component of developed political systems. There was not much interest in the field in the United States until a study by Hugh Heclo (Heclo, 1974) in 1974. Then came Esping-Andersen's seminal study on "The Three Worlds of Welfare Capitalism" (Esping-Andersen, 2006), which, with its follow-up of discussions, criticisms, and revisions, triggered further interest in the United States with the development of the historical institutionalist approach. Hall and Soskice's edited volume in 2001 (Hall & Soskice, 2001) and the celebrated and much debated "manifesto" (Evans, Rueschmeyer, & Skocpol, 2002) "Bringing the State Back In" in 2002 (following Skocpol's innovative research on the origins of social policies in the United States) (Skocpol, 1992) were milestones in that process. Paul Pierson (Pierson, 1994, 2001) and Ann Orloff (Orloff, 1993) also contributed to this rebirth of interest in social policies and welfare states.

These limited, but promising, developments found some coherence and convergence with the rediscovery of institutions by American researchers from the 1980s, under the influence of a few researchers who re-legitimated the study of institutions that the behaviorist revolution had considered as formalistic, old-fashioned and with little explanatory capacity for political phenomena. Such was the contempt vis-à-vis the "old institutionalism" that those who considered themselves "institutionalists" kept a low profile, trying to protect themselves from marginalization in many universities and political science departments. These fights were almost entirely concentrated in the

United States since the so-called old institutionalism had never disappeared in Europe. Actually, the rediscovery of institutions, the rise of the "new institutionalist" flag, came as a surprise on this side of the Atlantic where the behaviorist revolution was incorporated but without the excesses which characterized its sweeping developments in the United States. As is often the case, the American revolutions were incrementally and slowly digested in Europe. In addition, the frequent radical presentation of new approaches and theories in the United States and a less encompassing and/or theoretical approach by Europeans tend to emphasize oppositions or differences which are often less dramatic than it first seems. For instance, the description of old institutionalism as merely legalistic, descriptive, and formalistic does not pay fair tribute to the many institutionalists who went much further than this simplistic depiction: researchers such as Hayward and Wright in Britain; Suleiman and Tarrow in the United States; Crozier, Thoenig, and Grémion in France; and von Beyme and Scharpf in Germany did not fit into the kind of black-and-white opposition between avant-garde and laggards.

It has been the task of the American–European duo to attempt to overcome the permanent division in political science between the "hard" type of analysis aiming at universal laws—as in behavioralism and rational choice—and the "soft" historically oriented analysis of political events and lines of cultural development. In 1984, March and Olsen launched not so much a counterrevolution as an attempt to reconcile innovation and tradition under the label of "new institutionalism." The debate went on for twenty years or more, while the initial impulse diversified into various branches (historical, sociological, constructivist, etc.). In 2002, Pierson and Skocpol could proudly claim: "We are all institutionalists now" (Pierson & Skocpol, 2002). As ironically pointed out by von Beyme, "many movements and theories have called themselves 'new'. As in other fields—such as art—they quickly ended in 'post'-movements." In the best case, "this leads to a development 'from post to neo'" (von Beyme, 2006, p. 753).

5. CONCLUSIONS

In conclusion, one can underline the elements of certainty and uncertainty about the so-called European touch: there is no doubt that political science in Europe has finally become more "European" under the twin contributions of Pan-European organizations and policies such as ECPR within the discipline and outside the EU, thanks to its deliberate policies and funding on the one hand and the successive waves of democratization since the 1970s on the other hand. The discipline has become less parochial, less national, and, at the same time, less cohesive and standardized than its American counterpart. The methodological and theorical domination of the United States has not been able to erase the pluralistic traditions stemming from the emergence of the discipline in individual European countries. In spite of the quasi-monopoly of English as the vehicle of communication research and publication, the traditional saying "Two peoples divided by a common language" seems to find application in the political science field as well. It is both regrettable and probably unavoidable as long as Europe is mainly concerned by its own construction and most U.S. political scientists ignore European (or foreign) contributions (Klingemann, 1986). Unfortunately, Pippa Norris's evaluation, stated more than twenty years ago, does not seem to have changed much: "We have easier means to communicate, for sure, but whether we can actually surmount and break down the boundaries of national political science remains under doubt" (Norris, 1997, p. 33). If one takes a slightly more optimistic view, one could argue that borders have started to crumble in Europe and that the task on both sides of the Atlantic is to seek to improve a mutual understanding and conversation. On the occasion of the ECPR's fortieth anniversary in 2010, Colin Hay emphasized the "acknowledged interdependence" of the world and argued that, given its specific tradition, European political science was better placed than its "narrowly disciplinary Northern-American counterpart in responding effectively to those challenges" (Hay, 2010, p. 121). Ten years later, I will not attempt to assess the validity of this assertion, but I am convinced that the task of better understanding a world in flux requires everyone's contribution beyond disputes about convergence, divergence, and blending of the national segments of our discipline. Paradoxically, while the world is becoming more global, it also seeks a more diversified and pluralistic way of researching. The recent successes and failures of economics, organized around a single dominant paradigm, have triggered an appetite for diversity and served as a reminder that this discipline was and should still be a "social" science. Perhaps a harbinger of the future for political science?

REFERENCES

Aldrich, J. H. (2006). Political parties in and out of legislatures. In R. A. W. Rhodes, S. A. Binder, & B. A. Rockman (Eds.), *The Oxford handbook of political institutions* (pp. 555–76). Oxford: Oxford University Press, New York.

Almond, G. (1998). Political science: The history of the discipline. In R. E. Goodin & H.-D. Klingemann (Eds.), *A new handbook of political science*. Oxford: Oxford University Press.

Ball, T. (1993). American political science in its postwar political context. In J. Farr & R. Seidelman (Eds.), *Discipline and history: Political science in the United States*. Ann Harbor: The University of Michigan.

Boncourt, T. (2015). The transnational circulation of scientific ideas—importing behavioralism in European political science (1950–1970). *Journal of the History of the Behaviorist Sciences, 51*(2), 195–215.

Camerlo, M., Doyle, D., Garcia Diez, F., & Marsteintredet, L. (2018). The European social science agenda: A multilevel analysis from a country perspective. *EPS, 17,* 1, March.

Crewe, I., & Norris, P. (1991). British and American journal evaluation: Divergence or convergence? *PS: Political Science and Politics, 24*(3), 524–31.

Evans, P., Rueschmeyer, D., & Skocpol, T. (Eds.). (1992). *Bringing the state back in.* Cambridge, MA: Cambridge University Press.

Esping-Andersen, G. (2006). *The three worlds of welfare capitalism.* Princeton: Princeton University Press.

Goodin, R. E., & Klingemann, H.-D. (1998). *A new handbook of political science.* Oxford, Oxford University Press.

Gunnell, J. (2002). Handbooks and history: Is it still the American science of politics? *International Political Science Review, 23*(24), 339–54.

Hall, P., & Soskice, D. (2001). *Varieties of capitalism.* Oxford: Oxford University Press.

Hay, C. (2010). The changing nature of European political science: The discipline in an age of acknowledged interdependence. In B. Martin, L. de Sousa, J. Mosses, & J. Briggs (Eds.), *Forty years of European political science* (pp. 121–31). Special Issue, EPS: ECPR Press.

Heclo, H. (1974). *Modern social politics in Britain and Sweden.* New Haven, CT: Yale University Press.

Keedus, L. (2018). The poesis of a disciplinary metamorphosis: Rhetoric and ambition in American political science after World War II. *Trames, 22*(722–67), 1.

Klingemann, H.-D. (1986). Ranking the graduate departments in the 1980s: Toward objective qualitative indicators. *PS, 19*(3), 651–61.

Klingemann, H.-D. (2007). *The state of political science in Western Europe.* Opladen and Farmington Hills: Barbara Budrich Publishers.

Klingemann, H.-D., Kuleska, E., & Legutke, A. (Eds.). (2002). *The state of political science in central and Eastern Europe.* Ed. Sygma, Berlin.

Newton, K., & Vallès, J. M. (Eds.). (1991). Political science in Western Europe, 1960–1990 [Special Issue]. *European Journal of Political Research, 20,* 227–38.

Norris, P. (1994). Political science in Britain and in America: The decline of the special relationship? *PSA News, 6,* 15–17.

Norris, P. (1997). Towards a more cosmopolitan political science? [25th Anniversary Issue]. *European Journal of Political Research, 31,* 17–34.

Orloff, A. S. (1993). Gender and the social rights citizenship: The comparative analysis of gender relations and welfare states. *American Sociological Review, 58,* 303–28.

Pierson, P. (1994). *Dismantling the welfare state? Reagan, Thatcher and the politics of retrenchment.* New York: Cambridge University Press.

Pierson, P., & Skocpol, T. (2002). Historical institutionalism in contemporary political science. In Ida Katznelson & H. V. Miller (Eds.), *Political science: State of the discipline.* New York: Norton.

Pierson, P. (2001). *The new politics of the welfare state.* Oxford: Oxford University Press.

Qermonne, J.-L. (Ed.). (1991). *The state of political science in Europe, introduction.* Colchester: ECPR Press.

Schmitter, P. (2002). Seven (disputable) theses concerning the future of "trans-atlanticised" or "globalised" political science. *EPS, 1*(2), 23–40.

Shepsle, K. A. (2006). Rational choice institutionalism. In R. A. W. Rhodes, S. A. Binder, & B. A. Rockman (Eds.), *The Oxford handbook of political institutions* (pp. 23–38). Oxford: Oxford University Press.

Skocpol, T. (1992). *Protecting soldiers and mothers: The political origins of social policy in the United States.* Cambridge, MA: Belknap Press of Harvard University Press.

von Beyme, K. (2006). Political institutions, old and new. In R. A. W. Rhodes, S. A. Binder, & B. A. Rockman (Eds.), *The oxford handbook of political institutions* (pp. 743–58). Oxford: Oxford University Press.

Chapter 3

"The Political" in European Political Science

Terrell Carver

European political science has taken a variety of social processes for its objects of study, but since the mid-twentieth century the definition of "the political" has not remained constant. Thus, the types of social processes to be studied as political objects have changed over time for political reasons, often unpredictable. Moreover, the generation and importation of increasingly complex and diverse methodologies have necessarily altered the scope and definition of the objects of study. And since the late-twentieth century, a reconceptualization of science itself has challenged the self-definition of the discipline, thus realigning "political studies" in relation to "political science." The concept of "the political" has been highly contentious as to its scope and therefore its content, and will doubtless remain "in play," particularly in European political science, for reasons that will be explained below.

Because there have been new developments in organizational political practice—notably social movements addressing what are commonly known as identity issues, such as sex, gender, sexuality, race, ethnicity, religion, language, and so forth—the discipline has extended beyond the study of its classical objects, which were governmental institutions, public opinion and elections, interest groups, and political parties in synchronic, diachronic, and formal terms. Over these decades, supranational institutions, great-power interventions, and unregulated migrations have become salient features of the European political landscape. Because political life has become even more diverse and conflictual in complex ways, "the political," in relation to European political science, has expanded to include new objects for investigation and new challenges in doing this. Many of these extensions are controversial within the discipline itself, and with respect to the boundaries set by other disciplines in the social sciences. Over fifty years European political science has been constituted in and through processes of inclusion and exclusion that are ever-present.

Moreover, philosophical and linguistic theories, developed predominantly and distinctively in European understandings of post-structuralism and allied perspectives, have enabled some students of politics to reformulate the conception of science through which "the political" can be studied (Shapiro, 1985–1986). The "linguistic turn" in philosophy, and the "visual turn" in discourse theory, have argumentatively and controversially redefined the basis from which "the political" is understood such that studies can proceed (Howarth, 2000). The relationship between the premises through which politics is most appropriately and informatively studied, and the principles and protocols through which knowledge is defined and registered, have been debated urgently in Europe. What is or is not political science, and how methodologically inclusive or exclusive it should be, are matters of ongoing practice and engagement, more so in Europe than elsewhere.

Political developments in social life, and in how "the political" is conceived and studied, have promoted the acquisition of increasingly varied analytical tools derived from interdisciplinary resources. The other disciplines and subdisciplines involved in methodological transfer include international relations (IR), law, history, economics, sociology, philosophy, feminist studies, critical race studies, media studies, cultural studies, Indigenous studies, and other frameworks, as well as distinctively European traditions in Marxism and post-Marxism. Owing to the depth and variety of political perspectives and practices that have developed over many centuries in Europe, the imbrication of political projects and movements with academic, even philosophical and methodological disciplinary definitions and demarcations, is perforce an experiential feature of European political science. Cultural, linguistic, intellectual, and political diversity are the impetus for the ongoing pluralism that is a distinguishing feature of European political science.

1. "THE POLITICAL" IN MID-TWENTIETH-CENTURY EUROPEAN POLITICAL SCIENCE

Political science as a systematic study has a heritage dating back to classical Greek sources, ca. fifth to fourth century BCE. Those texts detailed life in the *polis* or city-state, presented typologies of constitutions and regimes, developed a concept of citizen participation as "sharing in ruling and being ruled," and posited an "other" to "the political," for example, the realm of manual labor and its constitutive public/private hierarchies (Aristotle, *Politics* 1283b, p. 42–1284a4, 1278a, p. 8–25). Modern political science developed in a Euro-American context in the early twentieth century, absorbing those ideas as foundational and updating them to contemporary regime types and political practices. Notably in that context there were constitutional monarchies and republics, with their concomitant socioeconomic relationships, extending to voters and officeholders, and property/taxation/employment and sometimes welfare systems. By the mid-twentieth century, "the political" had expanded beyond the legal and administrative studies appropriate to the restricted capacities and ambitions of earlier constitutional states. Thus, it came to embrace the widening realms of citizen participation, interest group and civil society organizations, and socioeconomic demands on governments that were characteristic of postwar democratization (Hay, 2002).

The constitutive "others" to the increasingly well-organized and self-defining discipline of political science were other social sciences, such as economics and sociology, and systematic studies, such as law and IR. Historical studies were taken as necessary context, presuming a boundary line, not often contested, between academic interest in the past and present interest in "the political," even if pursued theoretically and methodologically through retheorizing the ideas and theories of past thinkers (Hampsher-Monk, 2015). Distinctive national traditions in the formalization of intellectual life into academic departments and curricula, together with linguistic and cultural variations between and within nation-states, have necessarily played a very large part in the highly varied interdisciplinarities that have developed in the European context. This of course applies very directly to the "Cold War" division of Europe (1946–1991), through which a geographical, intellectual, and political "constitutive other" in the "East" functioned on numerous levels to define European political science as a study in and of the "West."

Through the twentieth century, the self-definition of political science has thus—but variously over time—identified subject matter for study, and excluded or marginalized other areas of social activity as outside "the political," or at least not central to it. Methodologically, the discipline was rooted in factual description, legal and philosophical studies, and logical and historical analysis pursued in narrative form. The knowledge generated was factual and analytical, and/or classificatory and explanatory, often typological. Voting studies, whether of electorates or within other institutional bodies through which "the political" was made visible, were necessarily quantitative in arithmetical and statistical terms, keeping pace with advances in mathematics (Budge, Crewe, & Fairlie, 2010; Daalder, 2011).

The objectivity of such knowledge in relation to ongoing political concerns, and problem-solving ambitions and usages, has generated continuous controversy and epistemological debate. Political science has thus been at the heart of numerous philosophical and methodological variations on the fact/value distinction, the subjectivity or objectivity of knowledge, and the ethics of professional engagement with, or disengagement from, political activities.

While the positioning of political science in educational institutions and civil service colleges or policy institutes varies from country to country, European political science has sometimes taken on roles and garnered prestige that are commonly lacking elsewhere. The scientific study of politics in Europe has thus harbored intensive and recurring tensions over "for whom, to do what?" questions about knowledge production (Berg-Schlosser, 2012).

Those developments, interests, and tensions are features of the global discipline, within which European political science plays a very large role, overlapping, borrowing, innovating, and collaborating (Blondel, 1981). In order to understand how this works, and why it is important globally, it is first necessary to understand what is distinctive about being in Europe, and working together as Europeans, in order to see how political science positions "the political" as a result.

2. DIVERSITIES IN EUROPEAN POLITICS AND "THE POLITICAL"

Exactly where Europe begins and ends, and exactly what one is talking about in invoking that geographical descriptor, are well-debated questions. However, what is much less debateable in global political science is that commonplace conceptualizations of "Europe" and "Europeanness" are firmly located in northwest Europe (i.e., north of the Pyrenees and west of former "Iron Curtain") and that southern Europe and eastern Europe (post–Cold War) are in a zone of integration. In respect of their own terms and traditions, they are something of an epistemological limit, lying beyond the Anglophone, Francophone, and German-speaking zones of influence that extend from France northward to Scandinavia, and from Ireland eastward to Germany and Austria. As a consequence of imperial conquest and colonial politics, English- and French-speaking settler societies in the Americas and Oceania functioned at first as an extension to northwest Europe, and then, particularly in the case of the United States, as a potent source of reverse knowledge production and transfer, especially in twentieth-century political science. This American influence, even "Americanization" of the discipline, has extended not only to former "mother countries" but also through the former Spanish and Portuguese empires south of the United States in Latin America (Ravecca, 2019).

The European Consortium for Political Research (ECPR) was founded in 1970 not only to push back against the centripetal force and global impact of the North American political science community but also to integrate West European political scientists as a distinctive bloc into global political science as an intellectual force to be reckoned with. Moreover, this framework provided venues and "voice" for a considerable number of "small" European nations, whether judged by population numbers or territorial size (or in some cases, both), in relation to the dynamics of "great-power" politics and consequent marginalizations. In undertaking this from the northwest, the object was to perform a Europeanness in political science that would be equal to any rival and distinctive in ways to be determined.

However, that integrative project is to some degree in productive tension with the challenge to the larger rival across the Atlantic: Does an integration of European academic establishments and intellectual traditions presuppose conceptions of "the political" that are already globally hegemonic, particularly those emanating from the United States? Does this integration of political studies within a zone of Europeanness challenge transatlantic conceptions of "the political" from one or more alternative perspectives? The former project results in piecemeal absorption, and brain-drain in both directions, rather than the emergence of opposing intellectual challengers; the latter project is pushing toward a distinctiveness that may or may not be found and intellectual challenges that may or may not be understood. However, there are important contextual facts that bear on the question of distinctiveness, from which indicative clues can be developed (Kauppi, 2014).

The United States and Europe are not cognate entities in at least one crucial respect: Europe simply has more resources in political phenomena—constitutions, administrations, institutions, ideologies—from which to construct "the political," than does the United States. Diversities among the fifty states in the union are massively dwarfed by the much longer and far-less uniform histories of the forty-odd countries of Europe. And therefore—crucially—Europe has more varied and decentralized political resources to draw on. Thus, the study of politics in various ways, pursued under the sign of Europeanness, has a potential for global applicability unrivaled by any other region (Rokkan, 2009; Sartori, 2016). Of course, global variety and diversity dwarfs even that of Europe, and thus works against the presumptions and reductionisms generated in the more uniform, and markedly less diverse, American context.

On the one hand, the zones of knowledge production produced by imperial conquest and settler colonialism have expunged and marginalized a considerable variety of social systems and cultural practices through which alternative or expanded conceptions of "the political" might have arisen. On the other hand, zones of knowledge production embedded within national and local cultures outside Europe lack, for the most part, regional structures for academic communication such that rival and complementary conceptions of "the political" can be explored. The mid- to late-twentieth-century histories of cooperation and integration in Europe, originating in the northwest Benelux and Franco-German zones, and proceeding east and south through post-Soviet and other formerly marginalized countries and regions, are very well known (Killingsworth, 2012). By any geographical standards, the variety of intellectual traditions, distinctive languages, cultural practices, educational norms and similarly diverse social phenomena in Europe—Reykjavik to Nicosia, St. Petersburg to Cadiz—is exceptional.

Whether this vast array of negotiable political differences conceals an essential Europeanness, or whether Europeanness consists essentially in the exploration of diverse perspectives on politics, poses contrasting questions, but without the need to make a choice. The former question—whether or not there is an essential Europeanness—has been regularly but inconclusively debated; the latter question—whether or not European diversity has generated truly distinct perspectives—has been answered variously, but not in ways that really make the case. Or, in other words, ongoing knowledge production in political science—whether local, regional, national, or meso-constitutional within the European Union (EU) and, moreover, within an array of allied European structures—has effectively expanded the boundaries of "the political."

European countries now have, and have had, a wider variety of nation-building experiences, forms of rulership, constitutional variations, dictatorial regimes, political ideologies, external and internal colonialisms, population management policies, party systems, legislative morphologies, extra-parliamentary interventions, legal codes, judicial structures, property systems, economic schemes and projects, civil service structures, marriage and family laws, religious establishments, secularisms, electoral rules, party political configurations, governmental norms, linguistic workarounds, nationalist-irredentist-secessionist conflicts—the list goes on—than any other region of any size in the world (van Deth, 2013). In effect, political science, doing its job in Europe, is already a challenge to presumed or declared universalisms, or at least uniformities, in defining "the political" and in generating "science." That challenge is owing to the startlingly diverse character of what there is, prima facie, to be considered.

At this point, the relationship between "the political," as characteristically conceived within the mid-century, postwar political hegemony of "the West," and the political character of regime-type classifications as understood within political science comes sharply into focus. "The political" most easily coincides with democratic practice in constitutional regimes, either on the parliamentary or on the republican institutional models, and, indeed, the former are often interpreted to some degree through the latter, rather than the other way around. Notable postwar constitutions were in any case written at various points as hybrids, taken from American and northwest European exemplars. And it would seem obvious that in authoritarian/totalitarian regimes there is simply less politics to be observed, whether conceptualized in narrative or quantitative modes, and, in any case, there would be difficult or insuperable barriers to doing this. Moreover, suggesting that there was ongoing politics in "the East" under Soviet-controlled regimes, and thus presuming that "the political" covered administrative, legal, judicial, electoral, and party-political practices there, itself presented a political threat to the Cold War orthodoxies of East/West great-power politics. Threats of that character were thus threats to knowledge production, and perforce to the liberal values of fearless enquiry and free publication that "the West" purported to defend and "the East" purported to critique. Political science defended northwestern Europeanness, notably in the early history of the ECPR and into the post-1991 political transitions in eastern Europe. These studies reconciled value freedom and objectivity with liberal values and political virtues by researching and celebrating democratic systems, rather than the so-called people's democracies, within "the political" (Mair, 2014). That demarcation posited and defended a disciplinary boundary with Soviet and East European studies, sometimes conceived as comparative communisms, subfields related to political science, but ambiguously, and kept peripheral by presumption.

Within the national and political reorganizations and socioeconomic transformations of the 1990s though, this problem with "the political" has receded for European political science. However, on a global scale, and even at times within Europe, the conceptual issue remains: in authoritarian, dictatorial, one-party regimes, lacking an independent judiciary and thus rule of law, where democratic structures are largely or wholly sham and "for show." Does "the political," taken as the objects of study for political science, actually exist? Does even a presumption that it might exist compromise the national and international credentials of any political scientists who might be able to undertake such studies? If the answer to those questions is negative, does it follow that political science globally, and European political science in particular—however ultra-diverse its conception of "the political" may be—is necessarily confined to regimes that qualify, at least minimally or perhaps transitionally, as democracies (Dolenec, 2013)? Authoritarian challenges to democratic orders have not gone away, and may indeed be rising anew within Europe and around the globe. European political scientists are seasoned experts in confronting the political and intellectual issues that characterize the struggles that define modernity.

3. DEMOCRATIC CHALLENGES TO "THE POLITICAL" IN EUROPE

The character of mass electorates, incorporating women, and ethnic or other minorities, to a greater or lesser degree at highly various points in the last 120 years, has posed challenges to European political science. Political scientists have had to consider how those people "got there" in political systems, rather than simply "what they are" after their incorporation. Pressure groups, already conceptualized as constituents of well-understood processes of institution formation and renewal, were reconceptualized as constituents of "the political," thus falling easily within the discipline of political science. But in the case of feminist activisms, women and the household entered "the political"; in the case of sexuality activisms, sexual identities and bodily morphologies entered "the political"; in the case of racial/ethnic/religious activisms, rights for recognition, inclusion, and representation entered "the political." These groups and interests were accepted (as much as they are) within the discipline of political science, with varying degrees of receptivity and resistance. Those various activisms, rather than belonging as objects of study exclusively to sociology, the major disciplinary "other" to political science, were conceptualized as social movements within "the political," though oftentimes with intra- and interdisciplinary dialogues and boundary disputes (Modood, 2019). Those developments were further refracted through controversies over inclusion and tokenism within the profession itself and cognate academic structures.

Perhaps most notably among all the disciplines within the social sciences, political science was the (albeit reluctant) vehicle for incorporating into the public sphere what had formerly been excluded from "the political" as sacredly private and/or personal, namely women and many female-identified activities and values. In that sphere, political speech and action had been for many theorists and politicians the quintessentially gendered highpoint of masculine/male endeavor, hence a well-defended gender-barrier enforcing female exclusion. Political science, rather than economics, sociology, historical studies, or legal studies and practice, was put into this position as a result of female suffrage, inaugurated in the later nineteenth century and advancing swiftly in the postwar constitutional settlements of 1918 and 1945. Given that electoral studies within democratic frameworks, as discussed above, were foundational to twentieth-century political science, it followed that political scientists could not ignore or marginalize women (Irvine, Lang, & Montoya, 2019). Secret ballots and "one person/one vote" ensured that women joined this crucial object of study on a gender-neutral citizen basis, however much the gender hierarchy operated to their disadvantage elsewhere in the public realm, and in political science as a profession.

Thus, "the political" has extended to processes of "becoming political" in institutional terms, for example, political parties' efforts at self-definition; identity politics in voter behavior; legal and moral challenges and protests. That extension is necessarily an open-ended and interdisciplinary process, but often in tension with the exigencies of disciplinary demarcation, professionalization, institutional hierarchy, and methodological purity or eclecticism. Methodologies are thus not simply applied to "the political" but effectively define it as a domain of study. The less eclectic and the more reductionist the methodological mix of techniques and associated presumptions, the narrower the field of study becomes, and the more the discipline risks hermetic exclusions and nonspecialist incomprehension. Alternatively, the more eclectic the methodological mix, and the wider the field of study, the more the discipline risks subject overlap, boundary disputes, and intellectual incoherence (Bruter & Lodge, 2013). Owing to the diversities described above, Europeanness positions European political science more on the side of pluralism and methodological eclecticism, though the virtues of methodological purity and discrimination remain in significant and productive tension with this.

Methodologically, the inherited tools of descriptive accuracy, logico-historical analysis, and evidential observation of behavior have been operative in studying politics, albeit with somewhat different emphases often ascribed to national cultures and academic empire building. In the later nineteenth century, political studies—only sometimes identified as political science, and even then working within varying conceptions of science—began to develop as a distinct discipline, in contradistinction to philosophy, public law and jurisprudence, political economy, political history, and the like. Definitions of science varied from *wissenchaftlich* conceptions modeled on natural philosophy and idealist histories in German-speaking traditions, to logico-empiricist formal reductionisms in some British and French conceptions. Broadly speaking, Anglophone cultures in political studies also highlighted history of political thought, but rather separately from public administration and constitutional studies. The Germanic tradition (extending to Scandinavia, Italy, and Spain) was rather more rooted in, and broadly focused on, legal and administrative studies relevant to the state, treated conceptually and practically. Francophone studies have notably focused on class-based partisan politics and ideologies, with highly significant contributions in political theory from philosophers and sociologists (McNay, 1994).

The introduction of empirical premises and quantitative methods in the mid-twentieth century, principally from North American sources, developed more hegemonically—if in tension with older traditions—in Germany, Scandinavia, and the Netherlands than in the United Kingdom and Australia. Notably, the professional organizations in the latter two countries are denominated associations for "political studies," reflecting suspicions toward the kinds of "science" embraced elsewhere. Nonetheless notable contributions to political science, particularly in electoral studies in first-past-the-post parliamentary systems, originated in the United Kingdom, and elsewhere in Europe in relation to proportional-representation systems, which are more common there than anywhere else (Bartolini & Mair, 2007).

Following the development of the natural or physical sciences away from natural philosophy and explanatory narrative and toward much more quantitative data collection and formal mathematical reductions, political science has also been augmented with more abstract constructions and techniques. Those approaches and "tool kits" were very largely derived from axiomatic schemata developed within economics, such as rational actor and strategic interaction modeling, including stylized "games," presuming strategic interaction among self-interested individual agents. Those tools could be applied just as well to social movements as to already-recognized interest groups, and also to political actors seeking inclusion and legitimacy, as well as to officeholders (Laver, 1997). However, the extent to which those presumptions, inputs, and outputs did or did not reflect uniform, average, or particular individual psychologies has posed recurrent questions as to the utility of the models and reliability of their predictions. The reductions through which history, culture, and individuality were made to disappear have generated analytical elegance, though arguably at the expense of verisimilitude. However, those reductions have also generated usefully predictive insights into well-defined strategic interactions observable in political conflicts. Notably, for European political science this was a highly successful American import.

Of course, this interdisciplinary borrowing also implies a reverse dynamic, namely disciplinary splitting. In this regard, the major challenge facing European political science has come from IR as an increasingly influential disciplinary rival. While this bifurcation in "the political" dates only from the 1920s, and constantly poses definitional questions to itself about "the international," the scholarly community has grown enormously since the late twentieth century and has become increasingly professionalized through the North American-based International Studies Association. The ECPR, however, has developed a substantial European presence in global IR within its organizational structures, following a pattern of pluralist inclusion and flexible accommodation.

More broadly, geographers have notably moved in on voting studies, deploying quantitative techniques of data analysis and graphical representation (Johnston, Pattie, & Dorling, 2010). Political scientists, by contrast, have not been such important contributors to social geographies concerned with mapping political power indexed to measurable factors and proxies. While political scientists are generally concerned with policy formulation and offering advice and predictions, economic policy in that advisory respect has been somewhat ceded to "experts." Studies of economic and social inequality, political and economic development, social class and mobility, generally fall into economics, political science, and sociology about equally. Political economy has been significantly challenged by the recondite mathematical modeling of econometrics, though notably European political scientists have challenged that situation very effectively through more conventional quantitative studies (Hay & Wincott, 2012). Studies of the labor market and employment grounded in social class are a zone where sociology has picked up traction over a political science that was for a time rooted in the politics of social class (Wilkinson & Pickett, 2010). There are some confrontations that do not seem to happen: political science and psychology (whether experimental, neural, or psychoanalytic) are very often pursued in parallel universes, despite the fact that both have roots in individual agency and behavioral regularities. Public administration, constitutional law, judicial politics, and administrative sciences have sometimes been marginalized from the political science mainstream, generating separate but parallel professional structures.

European distinctiveness is particularly notable in respect of gender equality policies and theorizations, where European political science has fostered feminist studies that address women's politics and women's issues within an unusually varied set of structures. From the later twentieth century, the so-called mainstreaming programs and policies have developed at the level of EU legal and administrative systems which have, in turn, been an arena from which European political scientists have addressed similar national, intergovernmental (IGO) and nongovernmental (NGO) strategies for inclusion and equalization. And working from and on particular European countries, political scientists have initiated research *within* these policy objectives, and also critical *of* these policy objectives—on feminist and other grounds—that cannot be rivaled elsewhere (Lovenduski, 2015). This has not been uncontroversial within the discipline, since these studies are also commonly assigned elsewhere, particularly to sociology. Moreover, the politics involved itself challenges the gender neutrality and public/private distinctions through which the discipline defined itself as the science of "the political." Elsewhere the policies and programs are simply not in place, except perhaps as aspirations, or—as in the United States—those ambitions and interests operate more through legal/judicial, rather than through political/administrative, circuits of power.

For European political science, "the political" has remained eclectic in content and method, pluralistic rather than monistic, thus facilitating a useful variety of studies, themselves inflected with a diversity of national, cultural, and hybridized objects for observation, and with a similar diversity in target audiences of academics, "users," and students. That eclecticism has reflected the ongoing cooperative tensions through which Europeans maintain their identities, academic and otherwise, in productive modes of interchange and communication. Those interchanges eschew—for the most part—hegemonic ambition on the part of some and withdrawal to defensive noncommunication on the part of others. Moreover, the coinage of "the political" as a term of art through which to understand the meaningful activities studied by political scientists is itself a European development.

However, to understand the further ways that Europeans have developed distinctive and challenging conceptions of "the political," we must turn to the innovatory reconceptualization of science developed within the post-structuralisms and allied perspectives that have arisen in Europe. This largely European intellectual upheaval is characterized by reversals and inversions of very familiar premises.

4. THE SCIENCE IN POLITICAL SCIENCE

Two important developments, through which the "science" in political science was constituted, date approximately to the later 1950s, and relate particularly to American political science. Those two were the protocols of "behaviorism," typically applied to explaining and predicting phenomena associated with political activities broadly conceived, and the formal protocols, typically used to generate explanatory and predictive models for strategic interaction between self-interested human individuals. That conjunction constituted the self-styled and widely accepted scientific core of the discipline, conceived as "mainstream," precisely because of this conjunction of certainty and rigor. Both those constituents were borrowed from the defining core of post-seventeenth-century science, a union of observation, data collection, and mathematical analysis, which departed from the Aristotelian premises of natural philosophy in striking and important ways. The apparent success of marginalist economics in conceptualizing observable interactions as "economic" patterns of human behavior was a powerful motivator. Economics was an exemplar because its concepts were quantifiable regularities that could be captured in formulaic mathematics.

Those formulae were cast in highly abstract, symbolically manipulatable terms, and premised on individualized though uniform human actors whose "behavior" could be observed and modeled. Unsurprisingly, voting was conceived by some political scientists as an intrinsically or analogously economic transaction based on strategic pursuit of self-interest, easily aligned with the marginal utility curves through which market transactions between buyers and sellers had been conceptualized as predictable regularities. Self-interested activity by individuals was then understood paradigmatically as the kind of human interaction through which politics itself is, or should ideally be, constituted and studied (Olson, 1965).

What holds that view of science together—whether natural/physical or social/political—is an empiricism, that is, a view of the world as comprised of human individual subjects, such as political scientists, who "know," and objects of knowledge, conceptualized as human "behavior," which are "to be known." In philosophical terms, this is an ontology, an account of what exists in the world, which in this case are discretely different objects. That account of "what is" also presupposes an epistemology, a formalization of the ways through which objects—which are "what is"—can be known with accuracy and certainty. The understanding of what an object "is" thus determines, in circular fashion, the kinds of ways through which it can "be known."

Human social action and interaction is in that way conceived as behavior that, through observation and analysis, can be reductively understood as discrete objects. That reduction is by means of conceptual abstraction and symbolic representation, so then the methods used to understand nonhuman physical objects, whether inanimate or animate, can be applied in explanatory and predictive ways. Thus, the ontology and epistemology of scientific materialism is complete, forming a methodological unity within a comprehensive concept of science, applicable in principle to physical sciences and social sciences alike. In that way, scientific studies are said to be empirical, and subject–object ontology and epistemology are said to be empiricist (Benton & Craib, 2011).

Late twentieth-century developments in philosophy, literary studies, IR, linguistics, and psychoanalysis, as well as feminist-inspired activisms and analyses, have contributed to a "linguistic turn" in the social sciences. That development has challenged prior presumptions about science itself, thus posing a definitional issue quite different from the developmental expansion discussed so far. The "linguistic turn" rejects empiricism, and indeed subject–object epistemologies and ontologies altogether, from which conventional definitions of science had previously proceeded. Rather than a world constituted "for us" of knowable objects that can be "mirrored" as knowledge, post-structuralists posit instead a world of human meaning-makers engaged in social activities. Those activities are both repetitive and innovatory (Belsey, 2002).

These later twentieth-century developments challenge the empiricism described above, precisely by positing human language, social interaction, practical activities, and meaning-making, taken altogether, as a substitute for both ontology and epistemology. The "linguistic turn" thus represents a subversion of the subject–object/knower-known structure through which empiricism is defined. Post-structuralism constitutes a revisioning of the human world, including sciences, technologies, and all forms of human "being-in-the-world" as meaning-making. Moreover, it posits that scientists, researchers, and, indeed, all human "knowers" therefore function wholly within that environment. There is thus no "view-from-nowhere" or otherwise disembodied or necessarily privileged point from which truth arises (Yanow, 2014a).

Post-structuralism is a critique of structures that, following the protocols of empiricism, were presumed by structuralists to be "there" in the objects of knowledge, such that explanatory and predictive generalizations were validated as accurate reflections of how such objects "really are." Rather, on the post-structuralist view, that situation is one of projection: human "knowers" are finding what is "to be known" as already "there" in object-structures and, so, evidently discoverable. That process is obviously circular, but virtuously so, and anyway inescapable (Carver & Hyvärinen, 1997). On the post-structuralist view, then, objects of knowledge are themselves human conceptual constructs, not "things" which have a discernible structure or fixed nature in themselves "to be known." In that way, structuralists were said to have been supplanted by a philosophical view or methodological outlook that was "post."

Post-structuralists have argued that objects of whatever kind cannot be presumed to be constituted in themselves in terms that map to human conceptual constructs. Rather the process of knowledge creation must be working the other way around. Knowledge is necessarily humanly derived and socially driven, rather than "there" in structures to be "discovered," as scientists were said to be doing. For that to be so, objects would have to have already come into existence in ways that do—or will—map to human conceptions. Thus, for structuralists certain knowledge of things as they really are—even if only gradually and asymptotically approached—requires a metaphysical presumption of coincidence. That coincidence would be between the human mind and everything else. Or it would have to have come from a creator-God, Himself humanlike, who made a universe that was founded on, but was mysteriously concealing of, determinate truths that can be mirrored in human conceptual constructions (Rorty, 1989).

The origins of post-structuralism and allied post-empiricist views lie in German intellectual achievements of the mid-nineteenth century through which the truths of biblical revelation of God's creation and His will were undermined, and religion was explained as a projection of human concepts and capacities onto imaginary beings (Zimmermann, 2015). Those origins also lie in mid-twentieth-century French methodologies of deconstruction (Glendinning, 2011), developed in sociological and historical studies, and in British "ordinary language" philosophies of about the same time, particularly a theory of "speech acts" (Finlayson & Valentine, 2002), as well as in studies of scientific practice (Latour, 1999).

The "material-semiotic" approach in "actor-network" theory holds, somewhat analogously, that material objects and processes, as well as ideas and concepts—and so not just observable human behavior—are foundational to social and thus political systems. This approach releases scientific method from causal factor explanation, yet argues that networks, as descriptively mapped, constitute "the political" over and above, yet in and through, human-centric meaning-making activities (Law, 1994). While derived from sociological theorizing, methods of network analysis—with or without the presuppositions of empirical political science—now regularly appear in the political science "tool kit."

Physical and natural sciences do not escape the post-structuralist and allied critiques: the truthful and certain coincidence between what material objects are and the human capacities and conceptions that enable knowledge construction cannot be presumed at the outset or in finality. Rather, human knowledge construction arises and proceeds within socially communicative practices of meaning-making. Of necessity, those meaning-making activities include the varying protocols through which standards of validity are socially set in ongoing ways. Thus, the use of the natural/physical "hard science" model in the social sciences, through which certitude could be obtained, has been challenged (Hawkesworth, 2019).

From the mid-twentieth century, and particularly with the dissolution of the Soviet bloc and Yugoslav communist regimes, these processes have accelerated and placed Europe and Europeanness in something of a defensive position with respect to defining both "the political" and the "science" in political science. And in the twenty-first century, vast stretches of the world that were formerly allocated in academic terms to area studies or "(third) world politics" are generating political interventions, particularly in Europe—given its geographical proximity to northern Africa and the Middle East, as well as histories of colonization and postcolonial diversities—with far-reaching intellectual consequences. Those developments are challenging established modes of knowledge production, such that universalisms, formulated in northwest Europe, especially those of political science, are now subject to sustained decolonizing critique from inside and outside the academy. Those critical projects are directed at both content and method, and at exclusions and under-representations, within the profession and cognate disciplines (Tuhiwai Smith, 2012).

5. THE "VISUAL TURN" AND INTERPRETATIVE METHODS

Meaning-making does not have to come to humans only from other humans via speech and text as described above. Rather, meaning-making within human social activities is done in conjunction with further physical objects and phenomena. Images and sounds do not merely represent concepts, albeit defectively and imprecisely. Nor are they merely vehicles for conveying meanings that are necessarily only verbal. Rather, images and sounds convey conceptual and emotional messages, which may or may not be easy to put into words. As communicators of concepts through which we experience sociality as meaning-making, they are indispensable to being human. That understanding of meaning-making extends even more to the built environment. That is because the instantiation of concepts, such that meanings are communicated more or less effectively and then read and interpreted variously by individuals, is a constituent of architectural theory and practice, and similarly with respect to art and design (Yanow, 2014b). Political theory in Europe readily absorbed the work of European philosophers in aesthetics and other academic approaches to art, but as we see below, North Americans have been key in orienting studies of art and politics, traditionally conceived, to twentieth-century technologies of representation and persuasion. Because this approach, and these methods, has gained their traction from European "turns" to post-structuralism, interpretative methods represent something of an intercontinental hybrid.

Images, still and moving, are important meaning-makers, though they need not, and in many cases do not, occur in conjunction with written or spoken words. Modern cultures are logocentric in conflating writing and speech with concepts and thus finding images problematic as meaning-makers in communicating ideas. Like written and spoken texts, images mean different things to different people. Like words, images can be denotative or representational, and connotative or associational. Similarly, they evoke feelings and emotions. And rhetorically they can persuade or dissuade. Like people they "want" to be looked at, to be engaged in dialogical meaning-making, and to be social creatures and political agents (Mitchell, 2005). Of course, that view is a projection of humanness into physical objects, but then that post-structuralist and actor-network trope licenses an interpretative analysis of nonverbal communications. Nonverbal communications, perhaps because of their ubiquity and potency, are often even more effective meaning-makers than conventional verbal media, especially in politics (Chandler, 2017).

The "visual turn" thus opens political science up to a very wide range of methods, derived from very diverse disciplinary resources, including concepts and techniques of picture space, geometry, composition, color, light, perspective, symbolism, culture, audience, intention, circulation, reception, and any number of similar categories previously developed in European art history and aesthetics (Bleiker, 2018; Rose, 2016). For photography, many of those apply similarly but with additions of "the gaze," viewer camera positioning, framing and cropping, the window-on-reality effect, and similar technical considerations (Hand, 2012). For moving images, whether cinematic, animation, or amateur video, a grammar of narrative meaning-making has been derived from literary studies to which technical terms are analogous. Reading a film is thus portraying it rhetorically as a meaning-maker (Monaco, 2009). Following through on this research agenda thus aligns political science with political studies of popular culture, an approach already well developed within IR, and of particular relevance to studies of electoral politics and public opinion formation (Caso & Hamilton, 2015). Crucially, as outlined above, the appropriation of new methods introduces new objects to be studied and thus expands the concept of "the political."

6. REDEFINING "THE POLITICAL" IN POLITICAL STUDIES

As a term of art, "the political" is also programmatic, particularly in developing lines of critique that post-structuralists can draw in opposition to the empiricisms through which political science defines itself. Unsurprisingly, then, the riposte from many political scientists is that post-structuralist premises imply a nihilistic skepticism or a judgmental vacuum, the antidote to which lies precisely in the truths that arise when scientific methods are properly deployed. On post-structuralist premises, however, science itself is a practice rather than a protocol. It resolves into human communities operating within vocabularies of inclusion and exclusion. In turn, those power hierarchies operate politically in relation to interests and resources (Kuhn, 2012). Thus, ideas that are considered to constitute "the political" have no referential or validatory basis other than in the citational, repetitive performances through which those activities themselves are recognized and understood as meaningful (Butler, 2011). So, on post-structuralist and allied perspectives premises, "the political" is itself an open-ended realm of meaning-making.

It would seem that on post-structuralist and similar nonempiricist presumptions "the political" will encompass any meaning-making activity whatsoever and will exclude nothing as an object of study. That is, of course, the reverse of the disciplinary history of political science, which has seen a variety of centrifugal and centripetal contestations pitting coherence against coverage. Post-structuralism and allied perspectives do not themselves offer a demarcatory boundary line dividing "the political" from anything else. Indeed, any suggestion that something is itself "non-political" almost always raises skeptical comments such as "Is it really?"

However, distinctive and substantive content has been given to "the political" as a term of art in ways derived from post-structuralist rereadings of Marx and Marxist political theory by Europeans, with debts to post-structuralist feminist and other social movement theorizing. Most notably, a principle of "agonism," as opposed to antagonism, has been introduced from within European theorizing in order to demarcate "the political" proper from what is merely conflictual and violent, thus providing a different kind of conceptual "lens." That lens is different from conceptual demarcation by objects of knowledge, between a disciplinary "inside" and "outside." An agonistic set of presumptions about "the political" presumes that human social relations are inherently conflictual in all kinds of ways but can nonetheless be factored abstractly by a distinction between friend and enemy. The former signals a generous acknowledgment of continuing and irreconcilable difference as an inescapable condition of social relations; the latter comprehends a reprehensible intolerance and will-to-extinction of the "other."

Agonistic interactions are said to presume friend/enemy as a constitutive distinction, given irreconcilable differences among human social actors. That outlook is thus opposed to consensus as a presumptive political norm, founded on the view that differences among human social actors are divisive but reconcilable and should thus be expunged. Misrecognition of that crucial presumption and distinction, so it is argued, licences and unwittingly encourages destruction of the "other" and thus a violent negation of "the political," within which the friend/enemy distinction is critically lodged. Moreover, unlike more abstract accounts of "the political" as ideally rational or hypothetically moral, and characteristically presuming consensus as a goal, the agonism principle embraces, rather than excludes, considerations such physicality, emotion, desire, and power seeking (Mouffe, 2006).

Thus, an agonistic account of "the political" does not so much posit a view of what to study as offer a critique of consensus as an assumption in considering the general nature of human interaction, and therefore the kind of political institutions that would fit with this and enhance the "human" qualities that political scientists generally endorse. That viewpoint takes us back to the congruence, explained above, between—on the one hand—political science conventionally conceived, together with the conventional value positions most commonly evinced by political scientists, and—on the other hand—the institutions and values of representative democracies founded on liberal principles, but bearing in mind the commonplace slippage between high-minded avowal and hypocritical action (Offe & Preuss, 2016). That congruence, as previously argued, somewhat limits the "reach" of political science, in theory and practice, in its application in full to nondemocratic regimes.

The agonistic view does not challenge the values and institutions of liberal democracies as such but rather the explicit or implied conjunction of liberal democratic practices with accounts, whether idealized or evidential, of humans as inherently consensus-seeking. This apparently bland and benign presumption conceals, from the agonistic perspective, not just a set of ideological presumptions, but a powerful teleology. And given that both are concealed, it follows that both may be exploited as cover for political projects about which opinions will differ, sometimes in very conflictual ways. In some cases, political scientists have deliberately or naively aligned themselves personally and/or professionally with governments and movements (Freeden, 2013). On occasion, "the political" conceived as inherently aligned with democracies and democratization, for example, has generated charges of collusion and hypocrisy—as well as awards and medals.

Studying politics from an agonistic perspective thus broadens out "the political" to cover any configuration of values and institutions without the blind spots as to regime type in terms of subject matter, and without the commitments, overt or covert, declared or suspected, on the part of research-ers that might overdetermine any findings. Working from post-structuralist premises obviates the ontology/epistemology binaries through which politi-cal science and political studies are so often—and arguably rather unpro-ductively—set against each other. Disarticulating political studies from philosophies of "hard science," and from epistemologies of certainty, could well have advantages. Reconceiving the premises through which knowledge is understood as such could well disarm interdisciplinary and methodological boundary disputes and professional rivalries. Political scientists may at some point have to choose or find a way to make each side of a contradiction work effectively.

7. CONCLUSION

The global politics of science, through which political science has been conceived, and through which the profession identifies itself as a reliable knowledge producer, is underpinned by economic competition, imperial great-power dynamics, and market-driven strategies for capital accumulation. It is very much to the credit of Europeans that critical perspectives on "the political" have been generated, not in national zones of isolation, but within international/interregional structures of cooperation. Whether post-structural-ism and allied perspectives herald a paradigm shift such that the empiricisms, through which political science has constructed its objects and validated knowledge of them as scientific, will fall away, or whether such alternatives will fail to gain professional traction and eventual hegemony in knowledge production remains to be seen; and certainly there is a lively dissensus. But it is a very good bet that this exciting episode in making sense of modernity will play out more effectively and transparently in the European context—not least in the pluralism and eclecticism that the ECPR encourages—than elsewhere.

REFERENCES

Aristotle. (2017). *Politics* (C. D. C. Reeve, Trans.). Cambridge: Hackett.

Bartolini, S., & Mair, P. (2007). *Identity, competition and electoral availability*. Colchester: ECPR Press.

Berg-Schlosser, D. (2012). *Mixed methods in comparative politics*. London: Palgrave Macmillan.

Belsey, C. (2002). *Poststructuralism*. Oxford: Oxford University Press.

Benton, T., & Craib, I. (2011). *Philosophy of social science* (2nd ed.). London: Red Globe.

Bleiker, R. (Ed.). (2018). *Visual global politics*. Milton Park: Routledge.

Blondel, J. (1981). *The discipline of politics*. London: Butterworth.

Bruter, M., & Lodge, M. (2013). *Political science research methods in action*. London: Palgrave Macmillan.

Budge, I., Crewe, I., & Fairlie, D. (2010). *Party identification and beyond*. Colchester: ECPR Press.

Butler, J. (2011). *Bodies that matter*. Milton Park: Routledge.

Carver, T., & Hyvärinen, M. (1997). *Interpreting the political*. London: Routledge.

Caso, F., & Hamilton, C. (Eds.). (2015). *Popular culture and world politics*. Bristol: E-International Relations.

Chandler, D. (2017). *Semiotics*. Milton Park: Routledge.

Daalder, H. (2011). *State formation, parties and democracy*. Colchester: ECPR Press.

Dolenec, D. (2013). *Democratic institutions and authoritarian rule in Southeast Europe*. Colchester: ECPR Press.

Finlayson, A., & Valentine, J. (Eds.). (2002). *Politics and post-structuralism*. Edinburgh: Edinburgh University Press.

Freeden, M. (2013). The morphological analysis of ideology. In M. Freeden & M. Stears (Ed.), *The Oxford handbook of political ideologies* (pp. 115–37). Oxford: Oxford University Press.

Glendining, S. (2011). *Derrida*. Oxford: Oxford University Press.

Hampsher-Monk, I. (2015). *Concepts and reason in political theory*. Colchester: ECPR Press.

Hand, M. (2012). *Ubiquitous photography*. Cambridge: Polity.

Hawkesworth, M. (2019). *Gender and political theory*. Cambridge: Polity.

Hay, C. (2002). *Political analysis*. Cambridge: Polity.

Hay, C., & Wincott, D. *The political economy of European welfare capitalism*. Basingstoke: Palgrave Macmillan.

Howarth, D. (2000). *Discourse*. Milton Keynes: Open University Press.

Irvine, J. A., Lang, S., & Montoya, C. (2019). *Gendered mobilizations and intersectional challenges*. Colchester: ECPR Press.

Johnston, R., Pattie, C., & Dorling, D. (2010). *From votes to seats*. Manchester: Manchester University Press.

Kauppi, N. (Ed.). (2014). *A political sociology of transnational Europe*. Colchester: ECPR Press.

Killingsworth, M. (2012). *Civil society in communist Eastern Europe*. Colchester: ECPR Press.

Krook, M. L., & Childs, S. (Eds.). (2010). *Women, gender and politics*. Oxford: Oxford University Press.

Kuhn, T. (2012). *The structure of scientific revolutions* (50th ann. ed.). Chicago: Chicago University Press.

Latour, B. (1999). *Pandora's hope*. Cambridge, MA: Harvard University Press.

Laver, M. (1997). *Private desires, political action*. Thousand Oaks, CA: Sage.

Law, J. (1994). *Organizing modernity*. Oxford: Blackwell.

Lovenduski, J. (2015). *Gendering politics, feminising political science*. Colchester: ECPR Press.

Mair, P. (2014). *On parties, party systems and democracy*. Colchester: ECPR Press.

McNay, L. (1994). *Foucault*. Cambridge: Polity.

Mitchell, W. J. T. (2005). *What do pictures want?* Chicago: Chicago University Press.

Modood, T. (2019). *Essays on secularism and multiculturalism*. Colchester: ECPR Press.

Monaco, J. (2009). *How to read a film*. Oxford: Oxford University Press.

Mouffe, C. (2006). *The return of the political* (Rev. ed.). London: Verso.

Offe, C., & Preuss, U. (2016). *Citizens in Europe*. Colchester: ECPR Press.

Olson, M. (2009). *The logic of collective action* (Rev. ed.). Cambridge, MA: Harvard University Press.

Phillips, A. (1995). *The politics of presence*. Oxford: Oxford University Press.

Ravecca, P. (2019). *The politics of political science*. Milton Park: Routledge.

Rokkan, S. (2009). *Citizens, elections, parties*. Colchester: ECPR Press.

Rorty, R. (1989). *Contingency, irony and solidarity*. New York: Cambridge University Press.

Rose, G. (2016). *Visual methodologies* (4th ed.). Thousand Oaks, CA: Sage.

Sartori, G. (2016). *Parties and party systems*. Colchester: ECPR Press.

Shapiro, M. J. (1985–1986). Metaphor in the philosophy of the social sciences. *Cultural Critique, 2*, 191–214.

Tuhiwai Smith, L. (2012). *Decolonizing methodologies* (2nd ed.). London: Zed.

van Deth, J. W. (Ed.). (2013). *Comparative politics*. Colchester: ECPR Press.

Wilkinson, R. G., & Pickett, K. (2010). *The spirit level*. Harmondsworth: Penguin.

Yanow, D. (2014a). Neither rigorous nor objective? In D. Yanow & P. Schwartz-Shea (Eds.), *Interpretation and method* (pp. 97–119) (2nd ed.). Armonk, NY: M.E. Sharpe.

Yanow, D. (2014b). How built spaces mean. In D. Yanow & P. Schwartz-Shea (Eds.), *Interpretation and method* (2nd ed.). Armonk, NY: M.E. Sharpe.

Zimmermann, J. (2015). *Hermeneutics*. Oxford: Oxford University Press.

Chapter 4

Methodological Pluralism in European Political Science

Virginie Guiraudon

1. INTRODUCTION

This chapter reflects on the diversity of approaches in political science and its associated challenges, comparing them with the risks of conforming to a single *doxa* and *praxis*. Alongside the fashionable and ubiquitous term "diversity," I will use the concept of "pluralism." It refers to the desirability of multiple opinions, even if they are not equally valued. John Stuart Mill powerfully argued that science would be "dead dogma" if it dismissed eccentrics and defenders of unpopular minority opinions (Lloyd, 1997). He insisted on the importance of pluralism and the pursuit of liberty, not just for political debate, but also for scientific progress.

First, I will establish whether there is a dominant paradigm, as defined by Thomas Kuhn, with an aligned ontology and methodology (Hall, 2003), or parallel "research programmes," a term coined by Imre Lakatos to designate concomitant scientific inquiries, each with a hard core of theoretical assumptions and auxiliary hypotheses. This implies distinguishing two levels of analysis: first, the existence of a consensus on the *scientific method*, the boundary work on what constitutes political science and what does not; second, the multiplicity of more specific theories that may be context-bound and fleeting in nature—what the "epistemological anarchist," Paul Karl Feyerabend, referred to as scientific "fads" in *Against Method* (1975). There are plenty in political science: "the cultural turn," the "neo-institutionalist" decade, the return of political psychology, and so forth. In the first instance, we are referring to an exclusionary process of defining the rules of the game and its players and, in the second, the introduction and confrontation of different perspectives, which is a big part of the game itself. It is integral to the scientific method to set up "straw men" to claim theoretical innovation or to test alternative explanations. As pointed out by Pierre Bourdieu: "An authentic scientific field is a space where scholars agree on what they can disagree about and on the instruments that will allow them to come to terms with their disagreements and nothing else" (1992, p. 152).[1]

Empirically objectifying the existence of a plurality of research programs, as opposed to establishing a consensus on what "science" means in political science, is a daunting task given the lack of data. We do not have a comprehensive view of all national academic systems in the discipline, let alone of local PhD courses or criteria for recruitment. Regarding pedagogy, it would be interesting to know how students are socialized into the discipline by studying syllabi and textbooks, yet this research has yet to be conducted. Similarly, there are few relevant questions in surveys of the discipline (see Pippa Norris's chapter).

Bibliometric analysis might appear to be a quick-and-easy tool to measure the relative dominance of scientific paradigms since journals are funnels or sieves that instruct us on what is acceptable or legitimate. Its heuristics are limited because of the so-called "straw man" strategy, whereby isolated or minority stances are cited profusely to better criticize them. Some call it the "Mearsheimer effect": John Mearsheimer, arch-Realist, is often taught in international relations courses and also widely quoted, only often to be dismissed as irrelevant. In some national traditions, including France, one never mentions the "enemy," as it would be granting them too much honor, so it is difficult to identify *Methodenstreit*. There are also many self-referential journals. Authors submit articles referencing themselves or others already published in the same outlet, thus signaling their allegiance to a particular chapel and creed. Discussing bibliometrics as a potential source for data analysis reveals the variety of views on the scientific method, for example, testing alternative models to understand an empirical phenomenon versus accumulating knowledge to test only one particular model.

Faced with a dearth of aggregate data and the difficulty of mapping the tenets of the discipline across the European space, I have tried more modestly to assess whether pluralism has increased or decreased, focusing on the period since 1970, when the European Consortium for Political Research (ECPR) was established. I provide a meta-analysis of texts that discuss the contours of the discipline and its internal divides, including "anniversary" pieces, such as Colin Hay's in 2010, and this one, in a palimpsest-like fashion. I also discuss widely quoted publications that try to define the "scientific method" in key fields of political science, for example, comparative politics. Other sources include inaugural statements of political science schools, and the mission statements of journals and professional associations, with a particular attention to the editorials of new journals and new sections or networks.[2]

My goal, through an imperfect examination of the historiography of the discipline, is not so much to provide robust answers as relevant hypotheses.

Building on the history and sociology of science, I start from the premise that both endogenous and external factors drive trends toward unity or diversity. To understand how fields of knowledge are structured, we need to observe the internal dynamics as the discipline gained institutional autonomy and the number of scholars expanded and sought recognition as a profession. External dynamics imply that we study interactions with other disciplines, academic institutions, and the outside world, such as funders, and "stakeholders" like governments (the research-policy nexus). This includes paying attention to *instruments* that may have their own logic and effects such as research assessment exercises, Shanghai ratings, and European Union (EU) calls for tender (Kauppi & Erkkilä, 2011). Throughout the chapter, I will also emphasize the broader political context or *Zeitgeist* in which scholars live and work.

Regarding internal dynamics, I have identified two sets of contradictory pressures. There is a tension between national histories of political science that are plural and transnational (or transatlantic), dynamics that go beyond the European context yet homogenize or at least simplify ontological debates. This rather banal statement, which points to methodological nationalism and its limits, needs to be embodied in scholars' trajectories and embedded in particular settings. The pressure to stick to the national *doxa* or conform to a more global "mainstream" may not be felt the same way by scholars, depending on their individual position (micro-level) and that of the discipline within a national space (meso-level), and, finally, the position of his or her country in the European and global landscape (macro-level). This latter level speaks to core–periphery relations, to use terms well known in political science. One particular sequence regards the post-1989 era when countries in Central and Eastern Europe became subjects of attention. The few older scholars that survived changes in the universities and the younger generations took part in the frenzy of transitology studies during the so-called third wave of democracy (Gans-Morse, 2004). They were focused on postcommunist party systems or EU enlargement depending on their linguistic and empirical knowledge of certain countries. Yet, somehow this precluded the opening up of new modes of thinking, alternative research agendas or counternarratives to the "end of history."

Finally, I formulate a hypothesis that bridges internal and external dynamics, namely the alignment between the position of scholars in society and their professional practice. Many political scientists are likely to be "pluralists" for sociological reasons: their socioeconomic characteristics and, in many European countries, their nominally "collegial" professional milieu make them prone to encourage political pluralism (see the chapter on academic liberties in this volume). This does not mean that they are naïve about the struggles for dominance or the monopoly of authoritative knowledge, the concentration of power and capital in their institutions, and discipline. Pluralism is an aspiration. Whether it is a pious vow or a reality in scholars' experience is another issue. Recent movements in social science to "decolonize," or include gender perspectives, also studied in this volume, have reinforced the pluralist bias in our field. It is thus interesting to examine the arguments of those in favor of nondiversity today and those that self-exclude from a "mainstream" they abhor, both groups are establishing autonomous subfields, new journals, and competing professional associations.

In a dialogue with other chapters in the first part of the volume, including Yves Mény's, I am interested in the specificity of European approaches to political phenomena. The plan of the chapter is chronological: covering the birth of the modern discipline, its expansion and growing autonomy in the second part of the last century, and its current state as an established field. I argue that, in spite of transnational influences, the very diverse intellectual origins and academic locations of political science endure and contribute to methodological pluralism. This is not just an argument about "path dependence" but an embodied story of legacies and transmission. In any case, in each historical period, there are internal struggles and external drivers that influence the unity versus plurality of political studies.

The first section reflects on the diverse origins of European political science, starting in 1870. The second section focuses on the postwar and Cold War period up to the early 1970s. I analyze the debates in comparative politics at that time, and, more precisely, the comparative study of democracies and party systems, a subfield where European scholars—Duverger, Sartori, Rokkan, and Lijphart—set global standards. Compared to the United States, the paradigm wars of the 1970s and 1990s seem less bloody and the triumph of formal modeling and econometrics was localized and not widespread. It thus makes sense to focus on 1970 as a watershed year when scholars had to choose between sociological and economic camps: between behavorialists and functionalists and the proponents of social or rational choice. In the third, and last, section, I assess the current state of the discipline in Europe compared to the 1970s. I track signs of an agreement on how to disagree, seeking a dominant view on what constitutes political science. I can also observe diverging trends: on the one hand, the Balkanization of the discipline as a kind "exit" from "the mainstream," and, on the other, a growing homogenization of research projects and publications driven by external funding requirements and the global competition between universities.

2. *"E PLURIBUS UNUM"?* PLURALISM
AS A HISTORICAL LEGACY

In institutional and professional terms, political science has only recently become an independent discipline compared to other social sciences such as law, history, and economics—it was once called "political economy" by Jean-Baptiste Say and others. The American Political Science Association (APSA) was only founded in 1903. One can always invoke an anachronistic manly pantheon—that includes Thucydides and Aristotle, Machiavelli and Tocqueville—to claim that "political scientists" existed prior to the field being established. Notwithstanding, political science has long been a subfield, an afterthought in other disciplines. For instance, this was the case with public and constitutional law, and many political science departments and programs are still located in faculties of law in France, Belgium, and the Netherlands.

Conversely, in certain historical circumstances, the science of politics or political administration is hard to locate. As Yves Mény underlines in this volume, when, after the 1870 French defeat against Prussia, Emile Boutmy created the institution we know now as Sciences Po, it was a school of political sciences, the "s" included geography and history. In fact, Boutmy was the first "historical institutionalist," as he asserted that history was the "natural home of political studies" and any study without a historical dimension "was blind empiricism or vague ideology, in both cases foreign to a scientific approach" (Boutmy, 1889). Sidney and Beatrice Webb, two of the Fabians who founded the London School of Economics (LSE), met Boutmy in Paris. They also observed business schools and chose a multidisciplinary name for their institution: London School of Economics and Political Science. In Germany and parts of Scandinavia, we have an older example with cameralism (Laborier, Audren, Napoli, & Vogel, 2011; Lindenfeld, 1997). The Prussian sciences of the state were also plural and included economy, public finance, and *Polizei* (public policy).

What is interesting is that, early on, political studies expanded the realm of disciplines that are deemed relevant to understanding the world of politics. It was not enough to examine laws and constitutions, the "old institutionalism." To analyze—not only describe—political phenomena, it was argued that they had historical, spatial, and social dimensions. André Siegfried, who published *Tableau politique de la France de l'Ouest sous la Troisième République*, in 1913, is considered to have inspired electoral sociology. To understand the vote, he went back to the geology of the soil (granite or limestone) in Western France, and its effects on the spatial organization of rural areas (isolated farm or dense villages) and ultimately on social interactions and the church and landowners. In brief, to understand a political outcome, Siegfried resorted to geography, history, and sociology—the three disciplines listed on the plaque one can read on the building where he lived in Paris. He did so, however, to devise a parsimonious explanation of voting patterns based on a series of observable variables. No matter what, one century later, one may think of his book, the approach deserves attention: taking into account the complexity of the world to come up with a simple explanation.

We must keep in mind that, at the birth of political studies, the aim was to embed politics in wider socioeconomic processes, and, thus, demanded of political scientists' knowledge, if not command of, a range of social sciences. The context in which the French authors, that I have mentioned, worked is important: Boutmy and Siegfried were in a particular state of mind. France had been defeated by the Prussians in 1870, and the Third Republic was at best fragile. There was a yearning for comprehension and thus the will to cast a wide analytical net.

The trajectory of Italian political science is exemplary of the parallel paths of the development and autonomy of the discipline and the advent of the modern nation-state, bureaucracies, and mass politics. As early as the 1850s, Angelo Messedaglia, professor at the university of Pavia, a supporter of the *Risorgimento*, argued that an organic plan of studies in politics and administration within law faculties should be urgently introduced. In 1875, Carlo Alfieri founded the "School of Social Sciences" in Florence, inspired in part by Boutmy, to train the civil servants of the newly unified Italian state. But the project for an independent faculty of political sciences with dedicated degree courses only came into being in 1925, at the University of Rome La Sapienza. The same year started with Mussolini's speech in Parliament that marked the beginning of the fascist regime.

The impact of the wider political context on the development of the discipline was most acute with the rise of totalitarian regimes that had profound effects on the lives of many political scientists, on the profession, and ultimately on the questions that the discipline sought to answer. In the interwar period, a special kind of "school" was founded that merits attention. In 1930, thanks to the generosity of a wealthy Marxist student, Max Horkheimer inaugurated the Institute for Social Research in Frankfurt. In his speech, he set the agenda: "investigations stimulated by contemporary philosophical problems in which philosophers, sociologists, economists, historians, and psychologists are brought together." He underlined that "with this approach, no yes-or-no answers arise to the philosophical questions. Instead, these questions themselves become integrated into the empirical research process; their answers lie in the advance of objective knowledge, which itself affects the form of the questions" (1930). This "critical" endeavor is based on the integration of various disciplines and a focus on methods of empirical enquiry. Horkheimer explicitly praises the development of American survey questionnaires, that, in his view, allow scholars to be "connected to real life," "verify insights," and "prevent errors." The philosopher also demonstrated the need to connect to the "real world" through a partnership with the International Labour Organization (ILO) in Geneva.

The Frankfurt school is not a school of political science, yet the "philosophical problems" that Horkheimer and his colleagues addressed were eminently political. After the failure of the 1918 November revolution in Germany, the quashing of the Spartacist uprising and the rise of Nazism, they wanted to understand why the laboring classes in several industrial capitalist societies supported reactionary forces and endorsed authoritarian regimes and how "mass politics" replaced the "class struggle." The enlightenment led to darkness. Why? How? Sixty years on, on the other side of the Rhine, the context was radically different from the time and place when the Paris Free School of political science was founded, at the epitome of what Frankfurt scholars referred to as the "liberal phase of capitalism." However, the means and tools were remarkably similar in satisfying academics' yearning for knowledge. In the 1870s and the 1930s, groups of well-off university professors, overwhelmed by the political manifestations of modernity, devised relatively similar intellectual strategies. In both cases, understanding politics required a collective reflection of the old "humanities" and new social science disciplines and the best methods to study empirics.

In the Frankfurt school's first generation, theoretical novelty lay in the development of psychology and Freudian psychoanalysis, and methodological advances involved U.S.-inspired survey research that helped them focus on individual subjectivities. Today's political science students will probably come across Theodor Adorno's work on "authoritarian personality" and Otto Kircheimer's postwar article on the "catch-all party." They are exemplars of the ways in which this generation of scholars sought to explain the political developments of their troubled times. They not only integrated new sciences like psychology but also expanded the objects of study of political science. Notably, Adorno explored the role of cultural industries in "manufacturing consent" and sought to understand how Fascism and Nazism tried to create a political aesthetic using propaganda films and orchestrated marches. Herbert Marcuse, who coined the famous sentence "the medium is the message," studied the media. Political communication is now an established subdiscipline, but it is interesting to recall its link to those who experienced firsthand the power of images and state propaganda. To understand "real-world" politics, scholars expanded both the range and the remit of their expertise.

One way of understanding the plurality of approaches in political science is to see it first as a "problem-driven" discipline, as opposed to theory- or method-driven. History is an example of a method-driven discipline: studying the past through all sorts of archives from carbon dating samples to old manuscripts and oral testimonies. With this method, you can study anything and everything. Today's neoclassical economics is an example of trying to apply a small set of theoretical assumptions to all aspects of life. For the first generations of political scientists, the logic was different: selecting from all available theories and methods to understand one sphere or aspect of life, the political. Thus, methodological pluralism is not an accident but constitutive of the discipline.

Yet, this implied that politics should not be an afterthought in another discipline, typically law. In the last century, a number of scholars were frustrated to see political science as merely an addendum to teaching programs or politics as a "theme." For those seeking a specific voice, the ongoing quest for identity has involved defending positions on ontology and methodology. We will now focus on the postwar period when the discipline expanded and sought autonomy and when the ECPR was founded in order to reexamine the debates in the discipline by focusing on comparative politics.

3. COMPARATIVE POLITICS: EUROPEAN SCHOLARSHIP BEYOND THE BEHAVIORIST/ RATIONALIST PARADIGM WARS

When discussing debates on ontology and methodology, in the European context, an obvious case study is the comparative study of democracy and party systems, with key work by European men, in Europe or in exile (like Otto Kircheimer), setting the international research agenda, and defining concepts that are still used today. This stands in contrast to other fields, such as legislative or electoral studies, in which studies of the United States, undertaken by Americans, generated analytical templates that were exported globally. Some of them have become so influential as to become adjectives: just like "Keynesian," "Rokkanian" is a semantic shortcut to define an entire approach, derived from Stein Rokkan, a Norwegian political sociologist trained in philosophy. It is interesting to note that, in the case of the Rokkan/ Lipset matrix, there is a continuity with previous generations. They were inspired by the German sociologist Max Weber's concept of *Schicksalgemeinschaft* as a space of contrasted and hierarchized identities and based their argument on a wealth of historical data on "critical junctures." They lay out a scheme of classification rather than a causal narrative.

Many of these scholars put their country on the map by devising a concept or a typology that "traveled" across other cases, a form of "home-grown" theorizing. For instance, Arend Lijphart first published a book on the Dutch political system and then developed the concept of consociationalism in *Democracy in Plural Societies*, demonstrated when he studied thirty-six consensus and majoritarian democracies characterized by ten variables and their correlations with nineteen indicators of "government performance" (1999). He is perhaps the ultimate functionalist, whereby phenomena are explained by their consequences, but he is only one of many in the postwar era who embarked on taxonomic projects based on a holist ontology whereby causation is defined as constant conjunction (when one finds x, one also finds y). On closer inspection, these European scholars started with a specific national case but sought generalizations that could be tested in many others.

To account for this dynamic, one could argue that this nomological approach was dominant after the war, inspired by the work of sociologists Talcott Parsons and Robert Merton. In addition, there was a propitious ideological context to this search for common ground after the demise of Weimar, Nazism, and Fascism, and with Cold War–era U.S. "soft diplomacy" in full swing sponsoring cross-national research on democracy, modernization, and party systems (e.g., the Social Science Research Council (SSRC) Committee on Comparative Politics and the Ford Foundation investment in the ECPR). The comparative method, as defined in the 1960s and 1970s, was also conducive to forging a common language and hence a dialogue among scholars from different countries, certainly more so than prewar studies that considered each set of political institutions as an idiosyncratic result of national histories. For a nascent social science, this basic agreement on method enabled it to increase the number of scholars in the field via multicountry research cooperation. In other words, during the emergence and expansion of a field, dynamics are more consensual than after their institutionalization, when logics of distinction are more likely.

Nonetheless, the aforementioned scholars were aware of the fragility of a consensus based on a method and they were invested in institutionalizing the discipline, including by founding the ECPR. In 1971, Arend Lijphart published a defense of the comparative method in the *American Political Science Review*, only one year after Giovanni Sartori's famous article on concept misinformation, preempting critiques that were building in and outside the field. For Lijphart, the comparative method is a *technique* that can be substituted with the statistical method, and that can be improved by expanding the number of cases, aggregating variables and performing "critical tests" to avoid the "small n" and "omitted variable bias" problems. He was aware of what he called the "weakness" of the method. In a telling passage, he makes reference to John Stuart Mill's methods of agreement and difference and acknowledges that Mill never believed that they could not be applied in the social sciences, yet argues that his objections "are founded on too exacting a scientific standard" (1971, p. 688). This attitude may seem offhand. Yet it was representative of the progressive mentality of the time: it is important to plow on, harvest, and sift empirical material, albeit with imperfect methods based on shaky logical foundations. The research program is the priority and research tools will improve over time. And, while scathing criticisms of consociationalism proliferated (including by Brian Barry in 1975), Lijphart's views on the comparative method "exemplify what became the dominant understanding in the field setting the tone for much of the subsequent debate" and the use of statistics (Hall, 2003, pp. 380–81).

Another key text on the logic of scientific inquiry at the time is Giovanni Sartori's seminal article on "Conceptual misinformation in comparative politics" (1970).[3] Sartori's piece is a nice counterpoint to the above discussion. For him the priority was not to devise new techniques of case selection or measurement but to address the increasingly elastic use of concepts and search for functional equivalents in the many cross-national taxonomies of democracies and party systems at the time. The question was not "how to study" democracy or other phenomena but "what it is that we are studying," and not "how to compare" but "what is comparable." The challenge is known in philosophy of science as "incommensurability" and Sartori proposed ways to form concepts that are heuristic across cases moving up and down "the ladder of abstraction" (1970).

In the end, Sartori's mission was not so different from Lijphart's: to legitimate and defend the state-of-the-art. He is also an example of "a rigorous optimist" (Collier & Gerring, 2009), utilizing what Gabriel Almond termed a "progressive-eclectic" approach (1998). It is interesting to note how his American colleagues viewed his thought processes as "European," in particular his attachment to etymology and history. In a volume dedicated to his work, David Collier and John Gerring describe Sartori teaching Columbia students "wearing tailored Italian suits and clutching his worn briefcase under his arm. With old-world charm and a dry sense of humor," expressing "his dismay over their ignorance of Latin and Greek, which limited their capacity to grasp the historical and etymological roots of concepts under discussion" (2009, pp. 8–9). It may seem quaint that the recipe in 1970 to defend a research program was "old world charm" and a love of the classics. Yet, it was a clever consensual move. It is difficult to be against "better" concept formation and this call can be heard in various contexts beyond Europe. Moreover, it dodges the ontological question about the drivers of political phenomena (functionalist or not?).

How did this message somehow survive the trials and tribulations of the following decades? The 1970s was a period when efforts to institutionalize political science bore fruit, involving many protagonists in the subfield of democracy and party politics. Many were fully integrated in international academe but they also cofounded and/or worked in more generalist West European institutions, such as the ECPR (1970) and the European University Institute (EUI) (1976), which were largely sheltered from the paradigm wars that raged in the United States.

The trajectories of some of the protagonists positioned in cross-European academic nodes tell a story of intergenerational transmission, illustrated by interpersonal relationships that spanned decades. Hans Daalder, yet another cofounder of the ECPR and involved in the U.S. Committee on Comparative Politics, also known for his work on consociational democracy, held the first chair in comparative politics at the EUI when Stein Rokkan was the department chair. He was a close friend of Peter Mair, who was a key figure in the study of political parties also thanks to his works on "cartel parties" with Richard Katz and on the evolution of party systems with Stefano Bartolini. Peter Mair was very active in the ECPR summer school on party politics. He later became an editor of *West European Politics*, a journal founded in 1978. One of his doctoral students was none other than Cas Mudde, a former editor of the *European Journal on Political Research*, known for his work on the radical right, who was awarded the Stein Rokkan Prize in Comparative Social Science Research in 2008, a prize awarded in 1990 to both Peter Mair and Stefano Bartolini. This example of lineage in political science is not just about interpersonal relations but also about how they were consolidated by the development of professional associations and conferences, peer-reviewed journals, prizes, and transnational training institutions and schools, allowing for the legitimation and transmission of the canon.

What stands out is continuity in this research program. Generations after generations plow the same furrow. The world around them is changing—with European integration, the fall of the Berlin Wall—universities and funding schemes evolve, and social science is rife with ontological battles, including the intestine wars among the motley crew of post-structuralists, neo-Marxists, postpositivists, postcolonialists, and feminists and the offensives of deductive social scientists keen on game theory, rational choice, and formal modeling. In the "scientific community" that studies democracy and political parties, there has been no revolution and no one has killed their father(s). The research program is on track, adapting to new contexts by incorporating empirical developments into its existing frameworks within the field, notably in postcommunist regimes that emerged in East and Central Europe after 1989 and the so-called new cleavage between the losers and haters of globalization and European integration, as argued by Liesbet Hooghe and Gary Marks. When models are contested and amended, the implicit rule is not "to throw the baby out with the bathwater." References to the Lipset/Rokkan matrix of functional and territorial cleavage structures still abound.

This section described the "normal" process whereby a scientific community organized itself to self-perpetuate. I highlighted one factor: the definition of the field by a rather inclusive method delinked from a precise ontology or, at least, relatively open in terms of its theoretical micro-foundations, focusing on mid-range concepts or models that could be heuristic to infer from empirical phenomena. You do not have to buy into an entire worldview as you would if you practice rational choice or radical constructivism. There are no "–isms" needed to enter this large subfield. The question is whether this case study applies to political science as a whole today.

4. GROWING PAINS SINCE THE 1990S: BETWEEN "EXIT" STRATEGIES AND THE PRESSURE TO CONFORM

In this section, I argue that European political science has no dominant ontology, as in economics, or only a couple of identified theory-driven research programs, as in physics. There is instead a kind of Balkanization of knowledge with a very large number of thematic subfields, each with a different set of theoretical inspirations, sometimes at odds, sometimes leading to a form of syncretism. Yet, there are strong internal and external forces that pressure political scientists to conform to a particular standard of knowledge production.

In the previous section, we saw that, in Europe, central subfields in the discipline were not so much pluralist as inclusive by default. They did not directly engage in the clash of paradigms described by one of its rare European protagonists, Brian Barry. In *Sociologists, Economists and Democracy* (1970), he contrasted the "sociology" of Parsonian functionalists and the "economic" school, best represented by the now-classic works of Anthony Downs and Mancur Olson. For Barry, choosing between sociology and economics was a litmus test for the location of political studies.

Today, in fact, the import of each social science depends on the subfield of the discipline. Think of political mobilization, an important subject of inquiry in political science. Many scholars who study social movements work in sociology departments that have sections in major sociology professional associations such as the American, European, and International Sociological Associations (respectively, ASA, ESA, and ISA). We can think of other subfields not directly rooted in sociology, such as political economy or social policy, where sociologists have been influential in defining the terms of the debate—such as Gøsta Esping-Andersen and his typology of welfare states (see Hemerijck, in this volume). Conversely, in other subfields in European political science, such as legislative studies, scholars have embraced U.S. research that emphasizes rational choice and quantitative methods.

So, the reality is a discipline split into small pieces of a puzzle where you can publish in self-referential specialized or "niche" journals that have a homogeneous approach to politics. This may be a normal development given the growth of the field and the trend toward specialization that happens in all types of professions. In political science, there are more and more subdisciplines, institutionalized for instance in the sections or research groups of associations (the ECPR standing groups), where scholars do not necessarily talk to one another and only cross paths at a few conference plenaries. Ten years ago, as Colin Hay reflected on the fortieth anniversary of the ECPR, he underlined that "contemporary political challenges ... expose some of the limitations of our discipline—in particular, its tendency to disciplinary and sub-disciplinary parochialism" (2010, p. 130). Parochialism moots the possibility of pluralism, which presupposes discussion between groups in one agora, not in a variety of oligarchic sub-arenas. We have even seen a form of internal exit from the intellectual home of political science, with the creation of separate associations, such as EPSA, as mentioned in Thibaud Boncourt's chapter.

Another form of "exit" from political science is worth discussing with respect to scientific pluralism. It regards the institutionalization of "international relations" (IR) as a separate department in many universities and distinct large associations, such as the International Studies Association. No one is a prophet in his own land, and it is tempting to build another intellectual home where political scientists can act as apostles vis-à-vis other disciplines. Typically, in my recollection of ISA meetings, under the broad notion of IR constructivism, political science scholars cohabited with postmodernists from the humanities or neo-Gramscian political economists and thus escaped the dominant (positivist) paradigm in their discipline.

In 1995, the first issue of the *European Journal of International Relations* (*EJIR*) was published. One of the reasons was frustration with *International Organization*, seen as formatted for scholars from the United States, where rationalist approaches had come to dominate certain subfields, such as international political economy. When a new editorial board in Amsterdam took over from their Sussex-based predecessors, they published an editorial that stressed "the European roots" of the journal and the "European tradition in IR" (EJIR, 2018). *EJIR* is also biased (vs. rational choice), but it is interesting to see how the journal is presented on its web page.* This includes "blurbs" from senior scholars such as "'An antidote for parochialism of all kinds—geographic, methodological, theoretical, and ideological.' *David A Baldwin*; '. . . EJIR* has demonstrated to the rest of the world that the power of ideas is separate from the power of power.' *Takashi Inoguchi.*" While this is just illustrative, the arguments to promote the journal read as a more general criticism of political science, as serving the ideology of the "power of power" and

---

* The journal web page is available at this URL (consulted on October 15, 2019): https://us.sagepub.com/en-us/nam/journal/european-journal-international-relations#description

not being diverse. The editors invoke both scientific and political pluralism as European values to legitimate the need for the new journal and define their position.[*]

It seems that while North American debates were imported to Europe with some delay—academic time is slow—they still created tensions. What I would underline here is that the argument does not claim the superiority of a particular approach but presents Europe as superior in moral and (geo) political terms. In fact, the "other camp" rarely resorts to normative or moral arguments to justify their stance. I found a reference to the intrinsic "value of unification and the necessity of universalism in science" in an article by rational choice scholars John Ferejohn and Debra Satz (1995, p. 71), but it seems to be a minority view. Robert Bates, a leading figure in the application of rational choice theory, did not share this "universalist" view and wrote that "anyone working in other cultures knows that people's beliefs and values matter, so too do the distinctive characteristics of their institutions" (1990).

Scientific and political pluralism is used by some scholars, who see or portray themselves as "underdogs," as a tool for self-distinction and legitimization. In its extreme form, they suggest that imported paradigms are "imperialist," what the French simply term "Americanization." The response by European associations, such as the ECPR, has been to include and recognize them (*EJIR* is an ECPR journal). In other words, the ECPR's stance is oecumenical, hosting in its midst various parishes with different interpretations of what political science is. I think here it is important to explain the congruence of interests and a form of "opportunistic pluralism." For the ECPR, the point is to encourage reluctant potential members hailing from different traditions, despite its American roots. For scholars in minority positions, it may be a way of placing their students in the mainstream job market, rather than relying on interpersonal relations with like-minded scholars.

So, we observe the fragmented structure of political studies, and yet there is a strong pressure to conform to a particular way of doing science, regardless of the subdiscipline. The rules of the game are more precise and spread internationally, notably through review processes. As in other sciences, political scientists' careers increasingly depend on publishing in peer-reviewed journals—increasingly in international outlets and in the lingua franca of research, English. At some stage, young scholars may need to emerge from the noncompetitive cocoon of academia to apply for jobs. Later, they may be pressured into applying for European Research Council or national grants where they will be exposed to international and interdisciplinary panels and

---

[*] "Theoretical pluralism" is also a criterion to win the prize of the best article in *EJIR*.

need to please economists or the like that will mock their "impressionistic" research design or their "small n."

These review processes, which are part of a professional's practice, resemble a form of the Eliasian "civilizing process," and short of creating a common *habitus* for the European *homo academicus*, they lead to some form of standardization. Through this incremental diffusion of norms, we conform to a particular format, acknowledging previous work in "state-of-the-art" sections, trying to show the theoretical relevance of empirical findings. This is exactly what Gabriel Almond described as the "progressive-eclectic" version of political science, far from maximalist views on epistemology affirmed by public choice or Marxist theorists, and equally far from postmodern or postpositivist contempt for methodologies that emphasize the observation of facts. There is a real risk, however, that national research assessments and new research funders (EU) that affect local and national academic battles for distinction and survival, provide less room for "eccentrics" or minority positions, which Mill—and Popper—considered key to pluralism. More conformism in the format of research and templates of publication equals nondiversity. While major research funders use the "innovation" buzzword, this does not apply to social science where they are happy with the not-so-innovative.

This state of play represents the tip of the iceberg. Underneath the iceberg, political scientists are not concerned with ontology. Scientific principles involved in assessing students rely on the notion of a "track record" as a synonym for "excellence" to fund projects and positions. Business as usual. Depending on the subfield, there are always new elections, social movements, or policy reforms to study. This is the time to either replicate tried analytical frameworks or test new tools, for example, "big data" mining. This is what Kuhn calls "normal science."

This lack of ambition is reinforced by the asymmetrical relationship between scholars and policy stakeholders. Few institutions in Europe have the material means to be fully independent from their political objects of study, in contrast to the "ivory towers" of the ivy league in the United States. This is obvious for those who study public policy. Typically, economists evaluating the efficiency of policies, their costs, and their benefits, are more likely to be heard than political scientists critically assessing the how and why of policy choices and questioning structures and systems. The evaluation of policies, part of the "policy cycle" as taught in management schools, has long been derided by American constructivists. Yet, there is financial pressure to engage in "applied research," even where is there is little room to engage critically. In all subfields, projects now have to be "policy relevant" and "socially impactful," and many of us are required to participate in public debates. Yet, this is not the same thing as adopting a narrow "technocratic" agenda.

This could lead to corseted social science, which goes to the heart of the notion of pluralism: the capacity to engage independently with the dominant paradigm both scientifically and politically, that is, to "falsify," in a strong Popperian sense, hegemonic views. However, political scientists are not in the same situation as historians feeding nationalist narratives, or biologists catering to the lobbyists of big pharma. Yes, in 1970, the ECPR was funded by U.S. foundations, as part of "soft power" diplomacy during the Cold War, but this seems less dramatic than the position of nuclear physicists in the same context. Still, our capacity to speak truth to power is part of our reflection on ontology and the scientific method. To quote the facetious Michel Foucault, "truth is a thing of this world: it is produced only by virtue of multiple forms of constraint" (1979, p. 131).

European political studies showed its capacity to adapt to new contexts when European studies evolved from a boutique to a boom field in the 1990s. Transnational politics was a challenge for comparative politics that still thought of states as bunkers in a strong form of methodological nationalism. Interestingly, as Adrian Favell and I have underlined (2011), this challenge was met by revisiting early sociological work by U.S. pioneers on European integration on the social bases of this process and its effects on socioeconomic practices, but this time with European scholars hailing from different Weberian and Durkheimian traditions and the diffusion of country-specific inspirations such as Bourdieusian field theory or Habermassian studies of the public sphere. In parallel, rational choice approaches focused on EU political institutions, as exemplified in journals such as *European Union Politics*. The effervescence of research in addressing the "deepening" of integration, in the 1990s, is an example of the fruitfulness of methodological pluralism.

5. CONCLUSION: SHADOWS OVER SCIENTIFIC PLURALISM

There is an obvious need for more research and data mining on disciplinary practices. Nevertheless, I will sum up what I see as common trends in contemporary political science with respect to the scientific method.

First, in spite of a long-term wish to become an autonomous "science," scholars studying politics continue to borrow ontologies and methodologies from other disciplines. We have seen imports from sociology, economics, and, even beyond social science, from evolutionary biology and mathematics (via game theory). Regarding methodologies of empirical investigation, a whole array of observational techniques are not specific to the discipline: the testing of models based on statistics, thick descriptions grounded in ethnography, the discourse analysis of archives and interviews, and so forth. In this context, political studies is a "weak field" that is submerged into other fields that are mapped out and constituted more firmly (Topalov, 1994, p. 464). In other words, it is situated at a crossroads, where one can observe the respective import of different imported paradigms. If we use the field as a metaphor, in the United States, the discipline has been a battlefield with belligerents seeking unconditional surrender and many foot soldiers vying for survival. In Europe, it is more like a playing field with many matches involving teams in different leagues.

In the end, when discussing various approaches, the issue is whether they can address important puzzles or only serve to legitimize the method they use. Ultimately, the question is: Do the analytical preoccupations of contemporary political science and their substantive content help us understand "real world developments"? If the answer is negative, the discipline is irrelevant. To be clear, few will notice, since there are other social sciences that speak to current trends that may affect politics: growing inequalities and new social insecurities, linked to changes in work patterns, spatial dynamics, and technology. Political scientists must identify what they bring to the debate, and how they can make sense of the political dynamics that accompany multiple transformations in an interdependent world. There is also the resurgence of known political phenomena—such as populism, nationalism, polarization, democratic backsliding, political unrest—that affect Europe as well as other regions of the world. We have tested tools of analysis. Yet, it begs for an ontology, a vision of politics that is much more global geographically and transversal and reintegrates the so-called area studies and world systems theory. European political science remains West-European-centric. Adapting our lenses to the "real world" also requires a less narrow vision of what falls within the remit of political science and what its legitimate objects of study are. One significant and welcome move forward is all the chapters in this volume that interrogate the boundaries of the political.

NOTES

1. *"un champ scientifique authentique est un espace où les chercheurs s'accordent sur les terrains de désaccord et sur les instruments avec lesquels ils sont en mesure de résoudre ces désaccords, et sur rien d'autre"* (1992, p. 152).

2. The last part of the chapter, which focuses on the discipline as of the 1990s, is perhaps influenced by my own experience. My viewpoint is transatlantic, as I trained in the United States before working in France, and at the EUI I sat on the board of professional associations (CES, EUSA) that originated in the United States, although they boasted a strong number of European attendees. It is also transdisciplinary, as I was happy to "bring politics back" into sociology when I helped found the political sociology network of the European Sociological Association and, conversely, to bring

sociology back into EU studies when it became dominated by political scientists! Yet, most of the research for this chapter focuses on periods that I did not experience (1870–1990) filled with characters that I cannot identify with. So, there is de facto more critical distance than subjectivity or normativity in this account.

3. Both also spent time in the United States (at Columbia) and are ECPR cofounders.

REFERENCES

Almond, G. (1996). Political science: The history of the discipline. In Robert E. Goodin & Hans-Dieter Klingemann (Eds.), *A new handbook of political science* (pp. 50–96). Oxford: Oxford University Press.

Barry, B. (1970 [1985]). *Sociologists, economists and democracy* (New ed.). Chicago: Chicago University Press.

Barry, B. (1975). The consociational model and its dangers. *European Journal of Political Research, 3*(4), 393–412.

Bates, R. (1990). Macropolitical economy in the field of development. In James Alt & Kenneth Shepsle (Eds.), *Perspectives on positive political economy* (pp. 31–54). Cambridge: Cambridge University Press.

Bourdieu, P. with L. Wacquant. (1992). *Réponses. Pour une anthropologie réflexive.* Paris: Seuil.

Boutmy, E. (1889). *Des rapports et des limites des études juridiques et des études politiques.* Paris: Armand Colin. Retrieved from (consulted on September 10, 2019) https://fr.wikisource.org/wiki/Des_rapports_et_des_limites_des_%C3%A9t udes_juridiques_et_des_%C3%A9tudes_politiques

Cohen, M. (2015). *Paradigm shift: How expert opinions keep changing on life, the universe and everything.* Imprint Academic.

Collier, D., & Gerring, J. (Eds.). (2009). *Concepts and method in social science. The tradition of Giovanni Sartori.* London: Routledge.

EJIR editors. (2018). European journal of international relations March issue: From the editors. *European Journal of International Relations, 24*(1), 3–7.

Favell, A., & Guiraudon, V. (Eds.). (2010). *Sociology of the European Union.* Basingstoke: Palgrave.

Ferejohn, J., & Satz, D. (1995). Unification, universalism, and rational choice theory. *Critical Review, 9*(1–2), 71–84.

Feyerabend, P. ([1975] 2010). *Against method* (4th ed.). New York: Verso Books.

Foucault, M. (1979). *Power/knowledge: Selected interviews & other writings from 1972–1977.* Pantheon Books.

Fuller, S. (2003). *Kuhn vs. Popper. The struggle for the soul of science.* Cambridge: Icon Books.

Gans-Morse, J. (2004). Searching for transitologists: Contemporary theories of postcommunist transitions and the myth of a dominant paradigm. *Post-Soviet Affairs, 20*(4), 320–49.

Hall, P. A. (2003). Aligning ontology and methodology in comparative research. In J. Mahoney & D. Rueschemeyer (Eds.), *Comparative historical analysis in the social sciences*. Cambridge, UK and New York: Cambridge University Press.

Hall, P. A., & Taylor, R. (1996). *Political science and the three new institutionalisms*. MPIfG discussion paper, No. 96/6. Köln: Max-Planck-Institut für Gesellschaftsforschung.

Hay, C. (2010). The changing nature of European political science: The discipline in an era of acknowledged interdependence. *European Political Science, 9*, 12–131.

Kauppi, N., & Erkkilä, T. (2011). The struggle over global higher education: Actors, institutions, and practices. *International Political Sociology, 5*, 314–26.

Laborier, L., Audren, F., Napoli, P., & Vogel, J. (Eds.). (2011). *Les sciences camérales. Activités pratiques et histoire des dispositifs publics*. Paris: PUF.

Lamont, M. (1987). How to become a dominant French philosopher: The case of Jacques Derrida. *American Journal of Sociology, 93*(3), 584–622.

Lijphart, A. (1971). Comparative politics and the comparative method. *American Political Science Review, 65*(3), 682–93.

Lindenfeld, D. F. (1997). *The practical imagination: The German sciences of state in the nineteenth century*. Chicago: Chicago University Press.

Lloyd, E. A. (1997). Feyerabend, mill, and pluralism. *Philosophy of Science, 64*(December issue), 396–407.

Lustick, I. (1997). Lijphart, Lakatos, and consociationalism. *World Politics, 50*(1), 88–117.

Sartori, G. (1970). Concept misformation in comparative politics. *The American Political Science Review, 64*(4), 1033–53.

Topalov, C. (1994). Le champ réformateur, 1880–1914: un modèle. In C. Topalov (Ed.), *Laboratoires du nouveau siècle. La nébuleuse réformatrice et ses réseaux en France, 1880–1914* (pp. 461–74). Paris: Édition de l'EHESS.

Vauchez, A. (2008). The force of a weak field: Law and lawyers in the government of the European Union (for a renewed research agenda). *International Political Sociology, 2*, 128–44.

Chapter 5

The Expansion of the Political Science Dataverse

Russell J. Dalton

The scientific method consists of observation, measurement, experiment—and the formulation, testing, and modification of hypotheses.

—Sheldon Cooper

The former mayor of New York City, Michael Bloomberg, says that one cannot evaluate policies or the performance of government without empirical evidence. Historically, academic scholarship provided a rich base for discussing human values, the role of institutions, the evolution of democracy, and the relationship between states. This literature left us theoretically rich, but with little way to objectively evaluate competing theories—such as the contrasting views of Jefferson, Bagehot, Toqueville, Schumpeter, and Lippmann on citizens and democracy—other than choosing the one we preferred or we thought applied. If one of the main goals of academic research is to understand how the political process actually functions, we had an abundance of ideas but uncertain answers. Moreover, large portions of the political science world appeared as medieval maps, with large voids and only lacking the "there be dragons here" demarcation.

This situation has changed fundamentally with the behavioral revolution that began in the 1960s. The *behavioral revolution* was part of the *scientific revolution* in political science. The collection of empirical, intersubjective evidence, theory-testing, and statistical methods became more central to the research process. In addition, technological advances led to an explosion of empirical evidence on citizens' opinions, the patterns of electoral politics, the functioning of political institutions, and the characteristics of governments. Scholarship also expanded internationally to include emerging democracies and the developing world. The collapse of the Soviet Union enabled rigorous social science to develop in the successor nations. As a discipline, we have gone from being data-poor to data-billionaires in a few decades.

My career as a political scientist has spanned this development. My first presentation as an aspiring political scientist (a PhD student) was at a 1974 European Consortium for Political Research (ECPR) workshop on political cleavages chaired by Stein Rokkan (Dalton, 1974). Most of the workshop papers utilized and described an election or a single data source (a survey or electoral statistics) from one nation. Today, political scientists have ready access to a volume and cross-national diversity of information on voters, parties, and election campaigns that would amaze Stein Rokkan or Warren Miller.

The collection of data, per se, is less important than how this has changed the field of political behavior, and the value of political science research that merges theory, systematic data collection, and scientific theory-testing. The electoral studies field, for example, has changed from a small set of scholars doing an ad hoc project in one nation, to large research groups, with an institutionalized infrastructure, doing complex data collections to address major topics, and often spanning national borders. Research becomes more cumulative in such settings, providing continuing investigations into central interests in the field, while also providing the seed capital to extend the boundaries of research. And the skills and knowledge brought to bear on a topic in such an environment typically goes beyond what a single scholar or ad hoc project is likely to achieve.

This chapter describes the evolution of electoral behavior research to illustrate the expansion of the political science dataverse over the past five decades. I also discuss parallel developments in research on political parties and political participation. One chapter cannot fully describe the evolution of political science as a whole, because there are currents and subcurrents within our discipline. However, I believe that many of the same patterns extend to parliamentary studies, policy research, and other areas of political science. Finally, the chapter discusses some of the implications of this data explosion for our understanding of citizen political behavior and the democratic process, as well as implications for the social science research community.

1. THE BEHAVIORAL REVOLUTION IN ELECTORAL RESEARCH

One of the classics of modern electoral research is David Butler's (1952), *The British General Election of 1951*. Butler's first sentence boldly stated: "Until recently General Elections have been surprisingly neglected in academic research." He then focused on the supply aspects of elections: candidates, parties, and the media. Much less attention was devoted to citizens' political views and choices.[1] Data from the British Institute of Public Opinion briefly described a few basic traits of 1951 voters. My, how things have changed. In the next several decades, academic election research focused on the public, their engagement in the electoral process, and the factors shaping voting choices.

One of the wellsprings of the behavioral revolution was the University of Michigan election studies (now the American National Election Studies) (Campbell, Converse, Miller, & Stokes, 1960; Converse, 1987). *A technological innovation*—the development of area-probability survey sampling—created the opportunity to scientifically sample public opinion for a large population. Research no longer had to rely on unrepresentative samples, anecdotal evidence, or the insights of expert observers to assess public opinion on political issues and how citizens made their electoral choices.

This technological advance had a magnified research impact because it was paired with the *theoretical innovation* of the Michigan model of voting behavior. Psychological concepts of party identification, candidate images, and party images became central tools in electoral research—moving the field beyond the sociological framework of most previous research. As research progressed, this model incorporated the research of cognitive scientists, political economy scholars, and public choice research.

The Michigan team's conscious goal of international collaboration also benefited electoral research projects outside the United States. Warren Miller (1994, p. 256) stated, "The Michigan contribution to the international effort was guided—if not driven—by a particular view of the intellectual discipline of political science. That view held that the essential uniqueness of the discipline was to be found in the need to understand the contributions, the roles and the impact of institutions of politics and government."

National election studies in Britain, the Netherlands, Norway, Sweden, and other nations built upon this new methodology (Curtice, 1994; Holmberg, 1994; Valen & Aardal, 1994; Van der Eijk & Niemöller, 1994). In other nations, collaboration with the Michigan group was less extensive or built on existing national initiatives (Kaase & Klingemann, 1994; Schmitt-Beck, Rattinger, Roßteutscher, & Weßels, 2010; Thomassen, 1994).[2] I am surprised when some Europeans refer to this as the Americanization of electoral studies; rather, it was the combination of technological and theoretical innovation that happened to occur in the United States with the involvement of many emigres from Europe (Mény, this volume; Schmitter, 2002).[3]

Electoral research then expanded in methodological sophistication. Panel studies (pre/postelection or interelection) became more common to track the dynamics of electoral choice. Data collections periodically include surveys of the candidates running for office. Other projects examine media coverage of elections; recent projects add a social media component. This rich array of evidence has pushed forward the quantity and quality of electoral research. For example, the 2017 German Longitudinal Election Study (GLES) collected over thirty-five million data units in their public opinion surveys, along with parallel data on party elites and the media election content; the 2017 British Election Study (BES) was slightly larger.[4]

Another major advance is the *institutionalization of a research infrastructure*. Instead of the traditional individualistic style of scholars collecting and analyzing evidence on their own, national election research centers were created, and their expertise disseminated to regional and local centers. Surveys are relatively high-cost activities, requiring facilities, principal investigators, research assistants, and interviewers. When done within universities, this creates a framework for recruiting, funding, and training graduate students on a large scale.

National election study teams also developed training programs in the new research approach. Summer schools in survey and statistical methods formed in the Interuniversity Consortium for Political and Social Research (ICPSR) program in Michigan and the ECPR summer schools in Essex and Grenoble. Another component was the creation of data archives to collect, prepare, and disseminate empirical data. This often overlapped with the home institutions of the election study teams in Ann Arbor, Essex, Bergen, Cologne, Gotenberg, and other locations. For example, the U.K. Data Archive celebrated its fiftieth anniversary in 2017; its dataset collection grew from 450 studies in 1975 to almost 7,500 studies in 2018. The Zentralarchiv in Cologne merged into the GESIS network; its holdings increased from about 500 studies in the mid-1970s to more than 7,000 datasets in 2017.

A further development has been the growing collaboration among national research groups. The creation of the ECPR was, in part, an effort to provide an institutional setting for cross-national exchange among empirically oriented researchers who were a distinct minority in European academia (Mény, in this volume). Data collections also developed from these international networks. The Cross-National Election Project (https://u.osu.edu/cnep/) began with election studies in five nations in the early 1990s. The Comparative Study of Electoral Systems (www.cses.org) is now in its fifth wave and includes thirty to forty elections in each wave.[5] The European Election Studies (www.europeanelectionstudies.net) are a valuable vehicle for studying EU elections (Dalton, 2018; Schmitt & Thomassen, 1999). This is only a partial list of examples. International agencies and foundations also regularly conduct cross-national opinion surveys on a wide variety of political topics.

The value of these international networks was apparent after the democratic transitions in Eastern Europe in the 1990s. The infrastructure for scientific polling was understandably limited in most of these nations. Technology and resource transfers from Western Europe and North America assisted in creating academic surveys in the East. For example, the Wissenschaftszentrum Berlin coordinated six national surveys in Eastern Europe in 1990–1991 (Barnes & Simon, 1998). Richard Rose instituted the New Democracies Barometer in 1991 (Rose, Mishler, & Haerpfer, 1998). Foundations in the West provided funds for surveys and institution building in the East. Postcommunist democracies were rapidly integrated into international survey projects such as the World Values Survey, the Comparative Study of Electoral Systems, and eventually the European Election Studies (Schmitt, 2010).[6] The behavioral revolution took root in a decade rather than a generation as in the West.

Not only do electoral researchers collect public opinion data, but the empirical approach provides a common methodological and theoretical paradigm that facilitates discourse and collaboration among researchers. This research community also expanded beyond electoral studies. The same survey research networks began investigating sociological themes. For example, the International Social Survey Program (ISSP; www.issp.org) began in the early 1980s as a collaboration between social surveys in three nations (the United States, the United Kingdom, and Germany). These modules expand research to topics such as social inequality, family and changing gender roles, work orientations, environmental attitudes, national identity, and health care. Now the typical ISSP module includes several dozen nations on a global scale. Other projects, such as the European Values Survey (https://european-valuesstudy.eu) and the European Social Survey (www.europeansocialsurvey.org), provide platforms for other research on European public opinion. The Eurobarometers are an invaluable resource for tracking the evolution of European opinions with several hundred surveys since the 1970s (www.gesis.org/eurobarometer-data-service/home/). Innumerable ad hoc research projects examine the opinions of European publics on diverse themes.

This data explosion greatly expanded our knowledge of citizen political behavior. I would argue that we now know more about political psychology, political thought, and political behavior since the advent of behavioral research than in previous scholarship. Instead of experts' speculation about the opinions of citizens, we can consult the citizenry directly. Of all the things "we know" are true, empirical research helps to determine which of these are accurate. For example, I believe that a political party competing in a contemporary election with the extant knowledge of the 1950s would be severely disadvantaged in comparison to a party drawing on the current state of electoral research. The same applies to research on political participation, citizen policy preferences, their images of government, and many other areas of social science.

Even more important, public opinion studies and other empirical research has changed the dynamics of democratic politics. Surveys give citizens a greater voice in the policy process. This is especially true in relatively closed societies where the opportunities for public voice are limited. This also applies to established democracies where public opinion has a policy impact (Bevan & Jennings, 2013; Soroka & Wlezien, 2010). Public opinion results can affect contemporary policy debates—and empirical studies give the overall public an opportunity to voice their views and preferences.

In short, in the span roughly matching the history of the ECPR, electoral studies and public opinion research more broadly have undergone a transition from a data-poor field to a large-data scientific enterprise. A theory-rich field with long-standing philosophical debates about the mass public can finally discuss these theories in light of empirical evidence.

2. RESEARCH ON POLITICAL PARTIES

Some of the classic works in modern political science research involve political parties (Durverger, 1954; Michels, 1962; Reiter, 2006; Sartori, 1976). Parties deserve this attention because they are so central to the democratic process. They recruit candidates for elected office, their actions structure political campaigns, their members are often the foot soldiers for electioneering, elections focus on party choice, party elites are primary actors in the political process, and parties structure the organization of democratic governance. So this attention to the various facets of political parties is well deserved.

Albeit to a lesser degree, I see research on political parties as following the same trajectory of expanding empirical and comparative analyses over recent decades. Earlier research primarily offered descriptive or anecdotal information about a specific party or family of parties. Larger studies comparing parties often required collaboration between individual specialists. As political science research became more comparative and empirical, party research followed these trends.

A founding work was Kenneth Janda's (1980) International Comparative Parties Project that collected evidence on 158 parties in 53 nations. A large part of the research agenda was drawn from earlier theorizing on political party organization, the centralization of power, party behavior, and the involvement of its members. This was an incredible effort when party records were dispersed, unorganized, and followed different reporting standards. Janda produced one of the first systematic studies of parties' structure and behavior embedded their respective political environments (Harmel & Janda, 1982). Their reach for evidence may have been beyond their grasp, because they were so ambitious in the range of nations they studied and the information they wished to capture. But this pushed forward the boundaries of our knowledge.

Another major milestone was the Katz/Mair project on party organizations, their funding, and their actions (Katz & Mair, 1995a).[7] The rich conceptual writings on parties—such as the iron law of oligarchy—were examined with systematic comparative evidence. In addition, Katz and Mair (1995b) added to our theories of parties through this project.

Building on this tradition, the Political Parties Data Base (PPDB) is an ongoing collection of information on party organizational structures, internal decision-making processes, and party funding (Scarrow, Webb, & Poguntke, 2017). As evidence of the expanding dataverse, the Katz/Mair study included 68 parties in 11 nations; Round 2 of the PPDB is collecting data from nearly 300 parties in over 40 established and developing democracies.

A challenge in studying political parties is their involvement in so many diverse aspects of the democratic process. Consequently, additional data collections exist in many distinct areas. For example, Ian Budge and his colleagues established the Manifesto Research Group in 1979 to collect and code the content of party manifestos (Budge, Robertson, & Hearl, 1987; Budge, Klingemann, Volkens, Bara, & Tanenbaum, 2001; Klingemann et al., 2006; Volkens et al., 2016). The international scale of the project expanded to include the postcommunist democracies in Central-Eastern Europe and emerging democracies in the developing world. At present, the project has coded the content of nearly 2.5 million quasi-sentences and roughly half of the manifestos are available in digital form.

Other new studies rely on academic experts to describe party policies and other party traits. After several early starts, most notably by W. Ben Hunt and Michael Laver (1992), the Chapel Hill Expert Survey (CHES) now asks academic experts for information on party positions for a growing set of nations (Bakker et al., 2015; www.ches.org). Rohrschneider and Whitefield's (2012) expert surveys provide information on European parties' positions, internal structure, and other organizational traits. New voter advice applications (VAAs) are designed to help voters to make electoral choices; they also provide extensive information on the party positions that are the foundation of the VAA (Garzia & Marshall, 2019). Moreover, the policy of open access leads to extensive use of these data to study spatial models of party competition, political representation, the electoral strategy of political parties, political agenda-setting, democratic responsiveness, and numerous other topics.

Another party subfield focuses on party candidates/officeholders (Best & Higley, 2018). These began as ad hoc single-nation surveys of elites that often built upon the national election studies platform (e.g., Aberbach, Putnam, & Rockman, 1981; Miller et al., 1999). Several nations, such as Germany, the

Netherlands, and Sweden, now survey MPs over time, which provides a valuable resource for studying topics such as the changing social composition of elites, the expansion of women's representation, and changing styles of representation. Building on the 1994 and 2009 European Election Studies surveying citizens' EP candidates (Katz & Wessels, 1999), the Comparative Candidate Survey (CCS) has created an international network collecting coordinate information from candidates in several dozen nations (http://www.comparativecandidates.org). Studies of party members and party activists are also more common, ranging from the Reif, Cayrol, and Niedermayer (1980) survey of elites in thirty-nine parties in the 1970s to a set of surveys in the 1990s that collected data on members of fifty-seven parties (van Haute & Gauja, 2015). A new study of party members in European democracies includes nearly forty parties (www.projectmapp.eu). These projects provide exciting opportunities to test long-standing theories of elite political behavior (Rodriguez-Teruel & Daloz, 2018).

In short, after a long history of experts describing how parties function and the mechanisms of electoral change based on individual observation of a limited number of parties, scholars now have access to rich evidence that allows us to test these ideas systematically and cross-nationally. Imagine if Duverger or Michels began their studies of political parties with access to the systematic evidence now available to every PhD student in political science.

3. RESEARCH ON PARTICIPATION AND SOCIAL PROTEST

A third example of the expansion of empirical resources comes from the study of political participation and social protest. The vitality of democracy is often equated to the public's political involvement. In affluent democracies, participation has expanded beyond voting to direct and often contentious forms of action. Often the stimulus for change and innovation comes from nonelectoral efforts by social groups, social movements, and reformist interests.

Verba, Nie, and Kim's (1978) seven-nation survey operationalized a theoretical model of who participates and then applied this to a diverse set of nations. It provides the benchmark for later participation research. Today, ongoing cross-national studies—the International Social Survey, the European Social Survey, the European/World Values Survey, and other projects—periodically include a battery of participation questions. As the extent of cross-national data has increased over time, this has produced a series of comparative studies focusing on voting (Blais, 2000; Franklin, 2004; Gallego, 2014), nonelectoral participation (Micheletti & McFarland,

2011; Vráblíková, 2017), and related topics (Dalton, 2017; van Deth, 2007). This literature provides in-depth knowledge of who participates, why people participate, and the changing nature of participation in democracies today, which often conflicts with popular impressions of public activity based solely on voting turnout statistics.

The study of protest illustrates the challenge in collecting evidence for an activity that is episodic and not highly institutionalized. The protest movements of the 1960–1970s stimulated the first systematic cross-national study of unconventional political action (Barnes, Kaase, et al., 1979). The Political Action project assembled evidence on who were protesting, the values underlying these new forms of action, and the relationship between conventional and unconventional action. Since then, cross-national studies routinely include examples of contentious action in their general battery of political activities (Quaranta, 2016). The Data Harmonization project has taken these efforts a step further. It has merged the survey questions on protest activity from over 1,700 national surveys and into a database of over 2.25 million respondents (Słomczyński et al., 2016). An innovative project collects comparable information from individuals in the act of protesting (Stekelenburg, Klandermans, & Verhulst, 2012; www.protestsurvey.eu). The novelty was not interviewing protesters per se, but in recognizing the value of comparison and systematic measurement across different protests and national experiences.

Another method of studying protest collects information on individual protest events from media sources. This began in the early waves of the World Handbook data. More recently, J. Craig Jenkins assembled a cross-national (ninety-seven countries) and cross-temporal (1994–2004) database on protest events (Maher & Peterson, 2008).[8] These data include rich information on the types of protest, the major actors, the government response, and other characteristics. Similarly, other projects have collected longitudinal data on specific protest actions for a set of European democracies (Hutter, 2014; Kriesi, 2012). New projects, such as ICEWS and Google's GDELT, use AI methods to create a database on political events on a daily basis.[9] With refinement, these data may provide an exceptional resource for tracking the ebb and flow of protest activity over time and across countries.

As patterns of citizen participation change, research has evolved to examine the use of new political tools, such as Twitter, Facebook, and social media postings (Anduiza, Jensen, & Jorba, 2011; Cantijoch Cunill & Gibson, 2019). Such postings include valuable information on the flow of political information, the content of these posts, the networks of interaction, and their shifting currents over time.

In summary, with expanding systematic evidence, our understanding of how citizens think about politics, make their political decisions, and participate in politics is much richer. Researchers have objective evidence of what parties promise in the campaign, thus generating the potential to see who and why parties fulfill these promises. Scholars can determine the most common paths to becoming a successful politician, and how the class and gender diversity of elites is changing. We can learn more about how institutional structures shape party actions, and thus the democratic process. We know who participates in politics and why, and what factors produce political inequality. Data for data's sake is not the goal; the goal is to use empirical evidence to address such questions.

4. THE CHANGING RESEARCH DATAVERSE

The expansion of research in electoral politics, political parties, and participation has followed different courses. Electoral research benefited from the regularized and publicly visible nature of elections, and thus grew most dramatically and became highly institutionalized. Party research lacks the organizational and financial stimulus that comes from studying elections. Thus, this field has followed a more varied course in gradually developing large projects, databases, and collaborative networks. In addition, party research is more differentiated because parties are active in so many different elements of democratic politics and most projects focus on one subsection. Participation research has expanded, but through a less structured process. Survey data on participation grew dramatically because of the frequency of public opinion surveys. As the modes of participation changed, the methods of research also shifted toward more detailed and large-scale projects. In each field, however, our empirical and cross-national knowledge base has expanded exponentially in the past five decades.

Some might question my conclusions, and so I sought empirical evidence to substantiate the trends described in this chapter—focusing on *the use of such data and methods* over time. Several studies have tracked the evolution of political science research by classifying journal articles over time, including the *European Journal of Political Research* (*EJPR*) (Norris, 1997; also Boncourt, 2008).[10] The *EJPR* is part of the international research community described in these pages, and thus its articles can illustrate how scholarly research has evolved over time. I categorized *EJPR* articles from 1973 to 2019 at five-year intervals. The anomalies of a single year or changes in EJPR editors might affect journal content in a specific year, but the pattern over four-plus decades should reflect long-term patterns in scholarship.

Figure 5.1 shows the changes in the methodology of articles over time. In the *EJPR*'s first years (1973–1974), the journal published a diverse mix of methodologies as others have shown (Boncourt, 2008; Norris, 1997).[11]

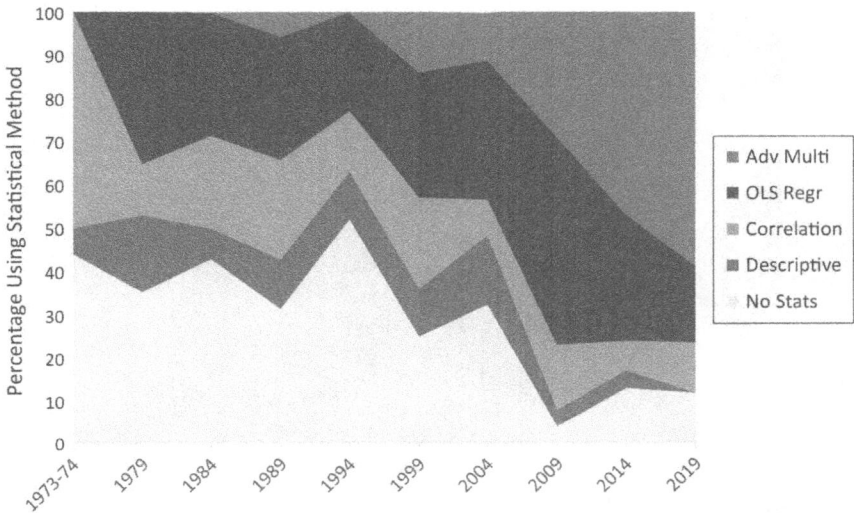

Figure 5.1   Methodology Used in EJPR Articles Over Time. *Source*: Author coding of EJPR journal articles by year.

A conceptual piece on the nature of political power appeared alongside an empirical study of government coalition behavior or the correlates of protest activity. The research methodology gradually shifted toward empirical analyses and then more advanced statistical analyses. Hypothesis-testing correlational or multivariate analyses grew from a small share of articles to the majority in the 1990s.[12] Then more articles began utilizing advanced multivariate methods, such as time-series models, hierarchic multilevel analyses, or structural equation models. Not a single article in the 2014 issue lacked some empirical evidence, and nearly all were hypothesis-testing empirical studies. There is a similar trend toward statistical methodologies in the *American Political Science Review* up through the most recent evidence (Sigelman, 2006).

I have also described the expansion of cross-national analyses as an increasingly rich research infrastructure created new research opportunities. Early in my career, access to even a single national survey was often rare outside the individual principal investigators, and "comparativists" were often a group of single-nation experts. The proliferation of data sources, open access to data, and the dissemination through archives create a rich resource environment that facilitates cross-national comparison.[13]

Figure 5.2 illustrates the expansion of cross-national research in *EJPR* articles. In 1973–1974, nearly three-quarters of the articles considered only a single nation or presented a conceptual discussion without focusing on any

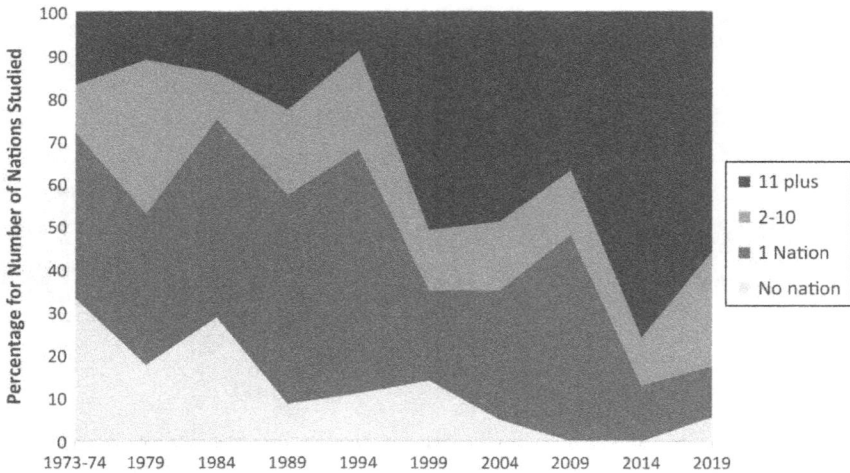

Figure 5.2   The Number of Countries in EJPR Articles over Time. *Source*: Author coding of EJPR journal articles by year.

nation national experience. By 1999, single-nation articles are a minority, and the largest proportion includes ten or more nations. Some of these articles utilize cross-national opinion surveys, but a substantial number study political economy topics across Organization for Economic Co-operation and Development (OECD) nations or other international topics. Single-nation studies can illuminate general theory, but increasingly research seeks to place nations into a larger context.

Admittedly, these research trends have sometimes divided our discipline. From the outset, preexisting academic communities criticized empirical political behavior studies. Jean Converse (1987, p. 252) described reactions to the first wave of survey research in the 1950–1960s:

> Quantitative work was criticized for many sins—for being antitheoretical and barren of intellect ("dustbowl empiricism"); for triviality ("If you can count it, it isn't worth counting"); for illiteracy, deliberate obscurantism, and mumbo jumbo; for malicious or mindless "scientism"; for mechanical reductionism; for displacement of the individual scholar; for pretentious explication of the obvious; for prodigal waste of money. (1987, p. 252)

I have heard these sentiments throughout my academic career, although often less elegantly phrased. They existed when I first attended large political science conferences and have continued through my last political science department meeting. Such sentiments were a factor encouraging the formation of the ECPR at a time when many national associations in Europe were heavily oriented toward humanities, legal studies, and qualitative research. I see this methodological debate as a natural part of the research process, as a new paradigm challenges traditional scholarly ways. And as empirical research has grown in volume and stature, it is still being questioned from new (or sometimes old) quarters.

If anything, the pace of empirical data collections is likely to increase as new technological developments open up additional research frontiers. Big Data is rapidly developing massive data sources bringing together diverse information in analyzable forms (Dalton, 2016; Hersch, 2015). Artificial intelligence methods, such as the ICEWS and Google's GDELT projects, enable researchers to process unprecedented masses of data and examines the patterns in these data. As the digital world develops, so also will the data on voting patterns, consumer behavior, political activity, and other aspects of our lives. High school coders are now collecting and analyzing data that go beyond the skill set of most political science faculty. I suspect that at the seventy-fifth anniversary of the ECPR, scholars can look back at today as the rudimentary nature of political behavior research.

Rather than reengaging in a methodological debate on empirical research, I want to conclude by discussing some of the possible consequences of these trends toward empirical and cross-national political science research.[14] A primary consequence is the increased specialization of knowledge by individual scholars. In virtually every field of political science, there has been an explosion in research output that challenges our ability to keep current beyond our field of specialization. This follows from more research funds flowing into political science, more scholars active in the discipline, the expanding topics of study, more published research, and the publish-or-perish demands of academia.

Another potential problem is that specialization may narrow our research horizons. Public opinion studies sometimes focus on narrow questions or methodology, or are not driven by significant theoretical interests. Similarly, often social movement research examines a single protest or a single-movement organization, without understanding the need for variance and comparison. But the same can be said of many academic fields. Indeed, at one time or another, all of us probably feel that we are learning more and more about less and less. And this issue is not limited to empirical social sciences.[15]

At the present state of our discipline, I would suggest that a focus on *theory-based empirical testing* of mid-level theories seems appropriate. We have a large storehouse of grand theories from historical sources, it is time to take stock of which ideas best fit reality. Moreover, a critique of political behavior research often misunderstands how cumulative, scientific research progresses. In our cognate field of economics, the Nobel Prize is often given for a lifetime of research, building the evidence behind a new principle—and seldom for a single grand theorem that transforms the field. Many more economists are testing these ideas in different contexts or with different assumptions to address the same principle (without winning the Nobel). Specific knowledge that is theoretically guided is more likely to cumulate into scientific progress, even if the steps are small and uncertain.[16]

At about the time of the ECPR's twenty-fifth anniversary, Gabriel Almond (1988) expressed a related concern that specialization means that researchers are increasingly sitting at separate tables and not discussing their findings and the connections between separate parts of political science. I understood his concerns, but was more optimistic about the future (Dalton, 1991). I still am. My general optimism flows from observing how political science research has built bridges between related islands of theory and research. The growth of empirical and cross-national research applies to media studies, elite studies, and policy analyses. Electoral research projects often include these other sources—and vice versa. Social movement scholars coordinate data collections with researchers studying similar movements in other nations and then use multiple methods of data collection (participant interviews, events coding, media reports, etc.). This is less a top-down framework for building an understanding of the world, and more a bottom-up approach. It results in building connections between many diverse specializations in political research.

Another concern is that the expansion of large-scale cross-national research may diminish country-specific knowledge. Others raise legitimate concerns that some important islands of potential scholarship will remain uninhabited because of the focus on other areas. However, the expansion in the number of journals and publications across topics and methodologies has increased and diversified views of the field and the world rather than narrowed it. A hundred flowers are blooming, although they vary in size and relevance.

These questions about research deserve our attention, and this discussion has continued for several decades now. I have become more sanguine as research has developed. In international projects, the principal investigators inevitably bring their own national experience to the project. Now they benefit by comparing their theoretical expectations to other national experiences. And the cross-national project benefits from the insights of national participants. In terms of diversity, the research topics have expanded to include inequality, gender, race, gay rights, and other diversity themes—now with a discussion linked to research findings rather than debating opinions. In addition, research foundations and universities demonstrate a tendency to seek out new targets of opportunity, rather than doubling-down on past investments. And new large-scale institutes for social research provide a foundation for further advances.[17]

Finally, some skeptics argue that empirical research naturally supports the existing social paradigm and is anti-progressive and conservative by nature.

Thus, the empirical method is questioned by certain subfields of the discipline. To me, this is the weakest point that critics have voiced. As Stephen Pinker (2018) has recently stated:

> If there's anything the Enlightenment thinkers had in common, it was an insistence that we energetically apply our faculty of reason to understanding our world, rather than fall back on generators of delusion like faith, dogma, revelation, authority, superstition, charisma, mysticism, divination, visions, gut feelings, or the hermeneutic parsing of sacred texts. . . . To the Enlightenment thinkers, the escape from ignorance and superstition showed how mistaken our conventional wisdom could be, and how the methods of science—skepticism, fallibilism, open debate, and empirical testing—are the paradigm of how to achieve reliable knowledge about the world.

This logic applies as much to understanding the political issues of our times as it did to shape the course of civilization during the Enlightenment.

Intersubjective evidence and a diversity of ideas are essential to scientific inquiry. The diversity of ideas has a long history in the social sciences. But only in the past generation has empirical evidence begun to evaluate these long-established theories. The quality and quantity of evidence is still evolving and remains imperfect, but it has generated major advances in scientific knowledge. To its credit, the ECPR has played a major role in promoting the intellectual discourse behind this development.

5. ACKNOWLEDGMENTS

I want to thank Stefano Bartolini, Diego Garzia, Hanspeter Kriesi, Hersh Mann, Ekkehard Mochmann, Rüdiger Schmitt-Beck, Tony Smith, Jacques Thomassen, Emilie van Haute, Andrea Volkens, Stefaan Walgrave, and the editors of this book for their assistance in developing this chapter.

NOTES

1. Data from the British Institute of Public Opinion polls were briefly cited in Butler's study. However, these surveys were methodologically limited and were not focused on understanding and modeling electoral choices.

2. Germany followed a different path (Kaase & Klingemann, 1994). The post–World War II occupation forces established a survey research capability as a policy tool during the reconstruction period. Residence cards provided an alternative to area probability sampling. This led to the establishment of the Allensbach Institut in 1947 and the German Institute for Population Surveys (DIVO) in 1951.

3. For example, when astronomers changed their conception of the solar system because of Galileo's discoveries, we would not call this the Italianization of astronomy. Or perhaps some would?

4. Data units are the number of survey respondents multiplied by the number of items collected on each person. In addition, there were nearly half a million data units in the GLES candidate survey. My thanks to Rüdiger Schmitt-Beck for these estimates. By comparison, the three separate surveys of the 1961 election study had only 900,000 data units.

5. An ICORE conference launched the CSES drawing on the Michigan "network" (Thomassen et al., 1994).

6. For example, the initial wave of the CSES included Belarus, the Czech Republic, Hungary, Lithuania, Poland, Romania, Russia, Slovenia, and the Ukraine.

7. A predecessor was *The Future of Party Government* project that connected many of the participants and provided a theoretical foundation for the Katz/Mair project (Castles & Wildenmann, 1986).

8. These data are available from https://sociology.osu.edu/worldhandbook.

9. The respective project websites are ICEWS (https://dataverse.harvard.edu/dataverse/icews), POLCON (www.eui.eu/Projects/POLCON), and GDELT (www.gdeltproject.org)/.

10. The ECPR has a more empirical research profile because of its origins. Boncourt's (2008, 2010) comparison of the *EJPR* to *Political Studies* in Britain and the *Revue Française de Science Politique* finds a higher percentage of comparative and quantitative studies in the EJPR. I suspect each journal's identity produces such patterns. *Political Studies* has highlighted political theory articles in contrast to the more comparative and empirical *British Journal of Political Science*. In the United States, *Comparative Political Studies* is more empirical than *Comparative Politics*. The value of using the *EJPR* as a base is also illustrated by the 2017 ISI journal citation impact rankings: *EJPR* #6, *BJPS* #9, *CPS* #16, *Political Studies* #54 and *Comparative Politics* #73. Also see Klingemann (2007) on the divergent paths of national political sciences.

11. I followed a more detailed definition of methodology than Norris or Boncourt, so the results are not fully comparable. In addition, the figures span an additional twenty-five years. The 2019 data are based on the first three issues of the journal.

12. The 1994 *EJPR* shows a drop in statistical analyses, but this is because a special issue was devoted to the history of national election studies. These articles described these empirical projects but without statistical analyses.

13. Since 2000, a majority of the articles dealing with citizens, political organizations, national governments, or IR/EU studies use multivariate analyses or more sophisticated statistics.

14. This section draws upon my earlier discussion of the evolution of comparative politics research in industrial democracies (Dalton, 1991).

15. For example, in discussing British historians, Bagehot (2019) recently stated that "some historians almost seem to be engaged in a race to discover the most marginalised subject imaginable."

16. Another skeptical question asks whether easy access to so much information may lead to misuse or naïve use of the data by some analysts. If this implies that we should limit access, this solution would be worse than the initial problem. Scientific

research should be an open process with minimal limits on access, whether it is a data archive or a document archive. An insightful example of the negative consequences of limited access in another field involves the Dead Sea Scrolls (Collins, 2012). A double-blind review process with access to intersubjective evidence exists to make quality judgments, even if requests for reviewing manuscripts fill our email inbasket.

17. This involves the development of large social science research institutes, such as the Institute for Social Research in Ann Arbor, GESIS in Germany, the National Centre for Social Research in London, the Varieties of Democracy and Quality of Government projects in Sweden, or the Wissenschaftszentrum Berlin.

REFERENCES

Aberbach, J., Putnam, R., & Rockman, B. (1981). *Bureaucrats and politicians in western democracies*. Cambridge, MA: Harvard University Press.

Anduiza, E., Jensen, M., & Jorba, L. (Eds.). (2012). *Digital media and political engagement worldwide*. Cambridge: Cambridge University Press.

Bagehot. (2019, July 18). The study of history is in decline in Britain. *Economist*.

Bakker, R., de Vries, C., Edwards, E., Hooghe, L., Jolly, S., Marks, G., Polk, J., Rovny, J., Stegenberger, M., & Vachudova, M. (2015). Measuring party positions in Europe: The Chapel Hill expert survey trend file, 1999–2010. *Party Politics, 21*, 143–52.

Barnes, S., Kaase, M., et al. (1979). *Political action: Mass participation in five western democracies*. Beverly Hills: Sage Publications.

Barnes, S., & Simon, J. (Eds.). (1998). *The postcommunist citizen*. Budapest: Erasmus Foundation.

Best, H., & Higley, J. (Eds.). (2018). *The Palgrave handbook of political elites*. New York: Palgrave.

Bevan, S., & Jennings, W. (2013). Representation, agendas and institutions. *European Journal of Political Research, 53*, 37–56.

Blais, A. (2000). *To vote or not to vote? The merits and limits of rational choice*. Pittsburgh, PA: University of Pittsburgh Press.

Boncourt, T. (2008). Is European political science different from European political sciences? *European Political Science, 7*, 366–81.

Boncourt, T. (2011). *L'internationalisation de la Science Politique: Une Comparison Franco-Britannique* (1945–2010) (PhD Thesis). Institut d'études politiques de Bordeaux, University of Bordeaux.

Budge, I., Robertson, D., & Hearl, D. (Eds.). (1987). *Ideology, strategy and party change: Spatial analyses of post-war election programmes in 19 democracies*. Cambridge: Cambridge University Press.

Budge, I., Klingemann, H.-D., Volkens, A., Bara, J. & Tanenbaum, E. (Eds.). (2001). *Mapping policy preferences: Estimates for parties, electors, and governments, 1945–1998*. Oxford: Oxford University Press.

Butler, D. (1952). *The British general election of 1951*. London: Macmillan.

Campbell, A., Converse, P., Miller, W., & Stokes, D. (1960). *The American voter*. New York: Wiley.

Cantijoch Cunill, M., & Gibson, R. (2019). E-participation. In *Oxford Research Encyclopedia: Politics*. Oxford: Oxford University Press. Retrieved from https://oxfordre.com/politics

Castles, F., & Wildenmann, R. (1986). *The future of party government vol. 1: Visions and realities of party government*. Berlin: de Gruyter.

Collins, J. (2012). *The dead sea scrolls*. Princeton: Princeton University Press.

Converse, J. (1987). *Survey research in the United States*. Berkeley, CA: University of California Press.

Curtice, J. (1994). Great Britain: Imported ideas in a changing political landscape. *European Journal of Political Research, 25*, 267–86.

Dalton, R. (1974). *Regional variations in the political attitudes of Italians*. Paper presented at the annual meetings of the European Consortium for Political Research, Strasbourg.

Dalton, R. (1991). The comparative politics of advanced industrial democracies. In W. Crotty (Ed.), *Political science: Looking to the future* (pp. 5–43). Evanston, IL: Northwestern University Press.

Dalton, R. (2016). The potential of "Big Data" for the cross-national study of political behavior. *International Journal of Sociology, 46*, 8–20.

Dalton, R. (2017). *The participation gap: Social status and political inequality*. Oxford: Oxford University Press.

Franklin, M. (2004). *Voter turnout and the dynamics of electoral competition in established democracies since 1945*. New York: Cambridge University Press.

Gallego, A. (2014). *Unequal participation worldwide*. Cambridge: Cambridge University Press.

Garzia, D., & Marschall, S. (2019). Voting advice applications. *Oxford Research Encyclopedia*. doi:10.1093/acrefore/9780190228637.013.620.

Harmel, R., & Janda, K. (1982). *Parties and their environments: Limits to reform?* New York: Longman.

Hersch, E. (2015). *Hacking the electorate: How campaigns perceive voters*. Cambridge: Cambridge University Press.

Holmberg, S. (1994). Election studies the Swedish way. *European Journal of Political Research, 25*, 309–22.

Hunt, W. B., & Laver, M. (1992). *Policy and party competition*. London: Routledge.

Hutter, S. (2014). *Protesting culture and economics in Western Europe*. Minneapolis: University of Minnesota Press.

Janda, K. (1980). *Political parties: A cross-national survey*. New York: Free Press.

Kaase, M., & Klingemann, H.-D. (1994). Electoral research in the Federal Republic of Germany. *European Journal of Political Research, 25*, 343–66.

Katz, R., & Mair, P. (Eds.). (1995a). *How parties organize: Change and adaptation in party organizations in western democracies*. Beverly Hills, CA: Sage Publications.

Katz, R., & Mair, P. (1995b). Changing models of party organization and party democracy: The emergence of the cartel party. *Party Politics, 1*, 1–58.

Katz, R., & Wessels, B. (1999). *The European parliament, the national parliaments, and European integration*. Oxford: Oxford University Press.

Klingemann, H.-D. (Ed.). (2007). *The state of political science in Western Europe*. Berlin: Barbara Budrich.

Klingemann, H.-D., et al. (2006). *Mapping policy preferences II: Estimates for parties, electors and governments in Central and Eastern Europe, European Union and OECD, 1990–2003*. New York: Oxford University Press.

Kriesi, H., et al. (2008). *West European politics in the age of globalization*. Cambridge: Cambridge University Press.

Kriesi, H., et al. (2012). *Political conflict in Western Europe*. Cambridge: Cambridge University Press.

Kritzinger, S. (2018). National election studies: Valuable data machineries and their challenges. *Swiss Political Science Review, 24*, 565–74.

Maher, T., & Peterson, L. (2008). Time and country variation in contentious politics: Multi-level modeling of dissent and repression. *International Journal of Sociology, 38*, 58–81.

Micheletti, M., & McFarland, A. (Eds.). (2011). *Creative participation: Responsibility-taking in the political world*. Boulder, CO: Paradigm.

Michels, R. (1962). *Political parties: A sociological study of the oligarchical tendencies of modern democracy*. New York: Free Press.

Miller, W. (1994). An organizational history of the intellectual origins of the American National Election Studies. *European Journal of Political Research, 25*, 247–65.

Norris, P. (1997). Towards a more cosmopolitan political science? *European Journal of Political Research, 31*, 17–34.

Norris, P., & Inglehart, R. (2019). *Cultural backlash: Trump, Brexit, and authoritarian populism*. Cambridge: Cambridge University Press.

Pinker, S. (2018). *Enlightenment now: The case for reason, science, humanism, and progress*. New York: Viking.

Quaranta, M. (2016). *Political protest in Western Europe*. Berlin: Springer.

Reif, K., Cayrol, R., & Niedermayer, O. (1980). National political parties' mid-level elites and European integration. *European Journal of Political Research, 8*, 91–112.

Reiter, H. (2009). The study of political parties, 1906–2005: The view from the journals. *American Political Science Review, 100*, 613–18.

Rodriguez-Teruel, J., & Daloz, J.-P. (2018). Surveying and observing political elites. In Heinrich Best & John Higley (Eds.), *The Palgrave handbook of political elites* (pp. 93–113). London: Macmillan.

Rose, R., Mishler, W., & Haerpfer, C. (1998). *Democracy and its alternatives: Understanding post-communist societies*. Oxford: Polity Press.

Sartori, G. (1976). *Parties and party systems*. Cambridge: Cambridge University Press.

Scarrow, S., Webb, P., & Poguntke, T. (Eds.). (2017). *Organizing political parties: Representation, participation, and power*. Oxford: Oxford University Press.

Schmitt, H. (2010). *European parliament elections after eastern enlargement*. London: Routledge.

Schmitt, H., & Thomassen, J. (1999). *Political representation, and legitimacy in the European Union*. Oxford: Oxford University Press.

Schmitt-Beck, R., Rattinger, H., Roßteutscher, S., & Weßels, B. (2010). Die deutsche Wahlforschung und die German Longitudinal Election Study (GLES).

In F. Faulbaum & C. Wolf (Eds.), *Gesellschaftliche Entwicklungen im Spiegel der empirischen Sozialforschung* (pp. 141–72). Wiesbaden: VS-Verlag.

Schmitter, P. (2002). Seven (disputable) theses concerning the future of "transatlanticised" or "globalised" political science. *European Political Science, 1*, 23–40.

Sigelman, L. (2006). The coevolution of American political science and the "American Political Science Review." *American Political Science Review, 100*, 463–78.

Słomczyński, K., et al. (2016). *Democratic values and protest behavior: Harmonization of data from international survey projects*. Warsaw: IFiS Publishers.

Stekelenburg, S. W., Klandermans, B., & Verhulst, J. (2012). Contextualizing contestation: Framework, design and data. *Mobilization, 17*, 249–62.

Thomassen, J. (1994). Introduction: The intellectual history of election studies. *European Journal of Political Research, 25*, 239–45.

Thomassen, J. (Ed.). (2005). *The European voter*. Oxford: Oxford University Press.

Thomassen, J., Rosenstone, S., Klingemann, H.-D., & Curtice, J. (1994). *The comparative study of electoral systems*. Paper presented at the International Committee for Research into Elections and Representative Democracy (ICORE) Conference, Berlin, Germany. Retrieved from http://cses.org/plancom/module1/stimulus.htm

Valen, H., & Aardal, B. (1994). The Norwegian programme of electoral research. *European Journal of Political Research, 25*, 287–309.

Van Deth, J., et al. (Eds.). (2007). *Citizenship and involvement in European democracies: A comparative analysis*. London: Routledge.

Van der Eijk, C., & Niemöller, K. (1994). Election studies in the Netherlands: Pluralism and accommodation. *European Journal of Political Research, 25*, 323–42.

Van Haute, E., & Gauja, A. (Eds.). (2015). *Party members and activists*. London: Routledge.

Verba, S., Nie, N., & Kim, J.-O. (1978). *Participation and political equality: A seven-nation comparison*. Cambridge: Cambridge University Press.

Volkens, A., Bara, J., Budge, I., et al. (2013). *Mapping policy preferences from texts III: Statistical solutions for manifesto analysts*. Oxford: Oxford University Press.

Vráblíková, K. (2017). *What kind of democracy? Participation, inclusiveness and contestation*. New York: Routledge.

Ysmal, C. (1994). The history of electoral studies in France. *European Journal of Political Research, 25*, 367–85.

Part II

THE PROFESSION OF EUROPEAN POLITICAL SCIENCE

Chapter 6

Interpreting Scientific Regionalization

Where European Political Science Associations Come From and How They Shape the Discipline

Thibaud Boncourt

Academics tend to take the existence of transnational professional scientific associations for granted. Implicitly, we assume them to be a mechanical by-product of disciplines reaching a critical mass, as though as disciplines grew in size and sophistication and spread internationally, they increasingly needed such organizations to regulate intellectual exchanges.

There might be, of course, an element of truth in this explanation. But the history of European political science associations suggests that more complex dynamics are at work. The development of a transnational professional infrastructure for European political science is indeed, at first sight, quite puzzling. After World War II, European political studies were little developed at the organizational level. Over the first half of the twentieth century, professional associations had been created only in the United States (1903), Canada (1913), India (1938), China (1942), and Japan (1948). The only such organization to be located in a European country was the Finnish one, founded in 1935 (Trent & Coakley, 2000). There were no interactions between these associations, and transnational exchanges remained scarce. The discipline was also weakly institutionalized in the European university system, and chairs dedicated to the study of politics remained rare until the end of the 1950s (Stein, 1995). In addition to this limited institutionalization, European political studies also had rather weak intellectual foundations. There was little agreement upon the idea that political activities should be a subject for scientific studies. In most countries, different agents based in either academic or nonacademic institutions were engaged in an "ideational struggle" in which they promoted competing views of the political and how to study it (Adcock, Bevir, & Stimson, 2007; Bevir, 2001; Favre, 1989). The debate, which had begun in the late nineteenth century, took different shapes in each specific national context (e.g., Collini, Winch, & Burrow, 1983; Dammame, 1987), but, in spite of national differences, competitions between rival intellectual traditions resulted in a similar situation in all European countries: in the late 1940s, the study of politics was subordinate to other more established academic disciplines—such as law, history, and philosophy—and had little autonomy from the political sphere itself.

Such frailty made the subsequent professionalization of the discipline in Europe hard to foresee. In 1949, the creation of the International Political Science Association (IPSA), a transnational federation of national associations, triggered the foundation of professional political science organizations in France (1949), Poland, the United Kingdom, Sweden (1950), Austria, Greece, Belgium (1951), Germany, Italy, Yugoslavia (1952), Holland (1953), Norway (1956), Spain (1958), Switzerland (1959), Denmark (1961), and, sometime later, in a range of Eastern European countries—Czechoslovakia (1964), Bulgaria, Hungary, and Romania (1968). Organizations with an explicitly European ambition followed from the 1970s onward. The European Consortium for Political Research (ECPR) was created in 1970, the European Political Science Network (EpsNet) in 1996, the European Confederation of Political Science Associations (ECPSA) in 2007, and the European Political Science Association (EPSA) in 2010.

The fact that IPSA and early national associations were created at a time when there was no discipline to speak of (Gaïti & Scot, 2017) shows that the professionalization of European political science cannot be described as a mechanical consequence of its growth. The fact that European-wide organizations were created at different times also suggests that there is more to this process than the simple rise of the discipline's numbers. This chapter aims, firstly, at identifying and understanding the dynamics that lead up to the creation of transnational European political science organizations: How can we explain the emergence of a regional organizational infrastructure for political science?

The coexistence of several European associations also indicates that disciplines are not simply there to act as a neutral platform for intellectual exchanges. This chapter therefore aims, secondly, at understanding the effect of this professional infrastructure on the shape of the discipline: How do European political science associations structure the profession and its intellectual productions?

By answering these questions, the chapter contributes to our understanding of the past and current structure of the discipline, as well as to broader debates on the internationalization and professionalization of sciences.

1. UNDERSTANDING THE DEVELOPMENT OF TRANSNATIONAL DISCIPLINARY INFRASTRUCTURE

The introductory overview shows that European political science associations are a relatively recent invention. Political science is not an exception in this regard, as transnational professional associations came relatively late in the history of all scientific disciplines. Although scholarly associations appeared as early as the seventeenth century at the national level, it was only from the late nineteenth century that international scientific organizations were founded (Feuerhahn & Rabault-Feuerhahn, 2010; Rasmussen, 1995). Initially quite slow, the rhythm at which these organizations were created increased considerably from 1945, with 70 percent of them set up in the second half of the twentieth century (Schofer, 1999). These new organizations varied in their geographical ambitions: some established themselves at a global level (internationalization), while others pursued regional or continental attachments (regionalization). This second tendency was particularly visible in Europe (Europeanization). In the social sciences, Europeanization occurred from the 1960s onward and in different periods for different disciplines (Boncourt, 2016).

Understanding how Europeanization occurs in political science implies tackling three debates in the sociology of the sciences. The first has focused on whether changes in the intellectual and professional shape of sciences originate from dynamics internal or external to disciplines themselves. What is at stake is the question of the relative autonomy of sciences vis-à-vis external influences. While seminal works in the sociology of science have placed a strong emphasis on internal factors and described sciences as autonomous communities (Merton, 1973), historians of the social sciences have largely focused on analyzing the impact of political actors, contexts, cultures, and systems—liberal democracies, colonial empires, communist regimes, postwar reconstruction, the Cold War, and so forth—on the development of disciplines, thereby portraying the social sciences as porous fields (inter alia Solovey, 2012; Steinmetz, 2013).

The second debate has focused on the way in which scientific internationalization should be interpreted. One branch of the literature has described it as a particular "stage" in the national development of sciences. The rhythm and shape of the internationalization of the social sciences has been understood as the consequence of the combination of the quantitative growth of these disciplines at the national level, the diversity of national "scientific traditions," the unequal international distribution of "research capacities" (UNESCO, 2010), and the linguistic characteristics of different countries. Internationalization therefore comes after national development in chronological terms (Guilhot, 2014). By contrast, another branch of the literature has emphasized the transnational dynamics which shaped scientific development from a very early stage (Adcock et al., 2007; Heilbron, Guilhot, & Jeanpierre, 2009). Disciplinary fields have therefore been analyzed as intrinsically transnational (Gemelli, 1998; Guilhot, 2014), and the emergence of a transnational scientific infrastructure has been seen as the completion of the institutionalization of preexisting circulations of researchers and knowledge.

The third debate has focused on the study of the effects of internationalization, and on the processes of scientific harmonization that are associated with it. Two interpretations coexist here, which differ in the degree of unilateralism and conflict that they associate with these dynamics. The first considers internationalization as linked to an incremental homogenization of intellectual knowledge and practices. The process is thus understood as an ensemble of localized interactions that produce different forms of harmonization in different contexts: the local appropriation of scientific ideas developed elsewhere gives rise to heterogeneous hybridizations (Bourdieu, 2002; Rodríguez Medina, 2014). The second interpretation focuses instead on the hegemonic nature of these phenomena. Internationalization is seen as linked to relations of domination between scientific "centers" and "peripheries," and harmonization reflects the imposition of the dominant orientations of the center, rather than a melting pot of national scientific cultures (Alatas, 2003; Keim, 2010; Mosbah-Natanson & Gingras, 2014). From this perspective, internationalization and Europeanization are thus often seen as a synonym of Americanization, and this process comes with tensions as much as it generates rapprochements.

In what follows, I take a nuanced stance on these three debates. In part II, I argue that the creation and development of European political science associations may only be accounted for by mapping a set of alliances and competitions that involved factors both internal and external to the scientific field and processes unfolding at both the national and international level. I portray scientific Europeanization as a consequence of academics seizing funding provided by political actors, in order to gain weight in intellectual and organizational competitions. In other words, Europeanization worked as a resource used as a means for actors to distinguish themselves in competitive spaces. In part III, I argue that European professional associations do not fulfill their "European" ambition in similar ways. While some place the emphasis on the building of trans-European bridges, others are more on connecting Europe to North America and, in some cases, the Global South. Thus, Europeanization is shown to be a plural and conflicted process. I back this argument with material drawn from the archives of the political science associations under study (ECPR, EpsNet, ECPSA, IPSA) and organizations that played a role in their development (Ford Foundation, UNESCO), as well as interviews with some of their founding members and past officers (see table 6.5 in appendix).

2. HOW EUROPEAN POLITICAL SCIENCE ASSOCIATIONS WERE CREATED

European political science organizations were set up in different contexts (during and after the Cold War). They were initiated in different countries (the United Kingdom, France, Germany), they relied on funds from diverse sources (philanthropic foundations, national governments, the European Union (EU), etc.), and they structured themselves around different types of membership and organizational set-ups (table 6.1). They also pursued different objectives: while ECPR, EpsNet, and EPSA focus on organizing scientific activities, ECPSA focuses on lobbying and aims to "promote the discipline's interests" and "make [it] more meaningful in public debate and policy-making."

Closer examination of the conditions in which these organizations were set up provides material to take sides in the first two debates outlined in part I. The foundation of European associations constituted a resource that was mobilized in the framework of scientific (competition between tenants of different paradigms and methods), academic (rivalries between universities), and/or political struggles (interstate opposition or cooperation) (first debate), in different competitive transnational and national environments (second debate). The weight of scientific, academic, and political stakes varied greatly depending on the particular structure of the field of European political science at the time when a given association was created.

2.1. European Associations as a Means to Influence Scientific Debates

In at least two of the cases under study, the creation of a new European association served a clear intellectual purpose. Rather than simply advocating transnational dialogue between different national traditions, the founding

Table 6.1   Characteristics of European Political Science Associations

Name	Date of creation	Initial funding	First president	Type of membership	Number of members
ECPR	1970	Ford Foundation University of Essex	United Kingdom	Institutions	338
EpsNet	1996	European Union Sciences Po	France	Institutions	N/A (dissolved in 2007)
EPSA	2010	Personal capital of founders	United Kingdom	Individuals	548
ECPSA	2007	National political science associations	Germany	National associations	19

members of ECPR and EPSA took a stand in scientific debates. Specifically, they adopted American political science as a point of reference and sought to work from it. Held up as a model, the American example was assimilated to its most positivist elements while its internal complexity and diversity was glossed over. The founding members' discourse was that of Europe's intellectual (in terms of the degree of methodological sophistication) and institutional (in terms of the academic structuring of disciplines) delay compared to America. The objective was thus to reduce this gap by working on importing deductive reasoning based on the use of sophisticated statistical methods, while also contributing to the integration of a European community of researchers, essentially around western European countries.

This logic can be seen in the foundation of ECPR. Its founders were a group of academics essentially based in western and northern Europe (the United Kingdom, Germany, the Netherlands, Sweden, Norway, France) who had spent time in the United States over the course of their careers. These researchers saw the scientific refinement of European political studies as held back by the weight of legal, historical, and philosophical approaches to the subject. Their goal was to import the quantitative and behavioralist political science developed on the other side of the Atlantic, in order to make European political studies "more scientific." They advocated a shift to a more empirically grounded discipline, driven by deductive reasoning, the comparative method, sophisticated statistical techniques, and a focus on the study of the behavior of political actors. To this end, they set up ECPR after the model of the Michigan-based Interuniversity Consortium for Political Research (ICPR). Like the latter, ECPR focused on the diffusion on new intellectual standards, notably via the organization of an annual summer school in statistical methods and the setting up of a European "data bank," whose mission was to provide a platform for quantitative and comparative studies by centralizing and standardizing the data produced around Europe (Boncourt, 2015).

Paradoxically, the same logic was behind the creation of EPSA, forty years later. Although the ECPR was already established and successful (large membership base, numerous activities, etc.), EPSA emerged around a specific objective of emulating, again, the American example. Its founders, a group of mostly British and German political scientists, said that they were guided by the impression that the ECPR had somewhat "lost its soul" as it has increased in size. They regretted the fact that the Consortium, formerly concerned with importing American political science perceived as specifically scientific, had progressively welcomed a wider variety of approaches:

> Gradually the European ECPR networks have kind of died for me. . . . When it was originally set up . . . ECPR was an exit from national political studies associations dominated by historians and philosophers. And so, this was people

who had a more European perspective and more kind of modern political science deductive type stuff. . . . ECPR grew gradually to become a victim of its success. You look at ECPR, it's like all the sociologists and historians are back! All the other people have been pushed off to the margins so now we have to set up our own bloody thing again. So, we now set up . . . the European political science association, opting out of ECPR. (Simon Hix, interview with the author, 2013)

This importation was therefore not disinterested. In the case of ECPR and EPSA, the founding members saw themselves as the minority in the European field of political science in which other approaches, presented as nonscientific and normative, dominated. For marginalized currents (or those who saw themselves as such), the goal was to influence European scientific hierarchies by claiming, in their words, an alternative "modern" approach to social phenomena inspired by a particular branch of American political science (Jean Blondel, "Letter to Serge Hurtig," Hurtig archives, box 18, July 4, 1969).

To a certain extent, the creation of EpsNet may be analyzed as a reaction to this process. While ECPR focused on importing certain American intellectual standards into Western Europe, EpsNet presented itself chiefly as European in outlook, with an emphasis on building bridges between western and southern and eastern Europe. In contrast to ECPR and EPSA, whose creation had been mostly driven by scholars based in western and northern Europe, EpsNet was significantly based in France. The emphasis was placed more on the expression of and the dialogue between the diversity of approaches being developed in Europe, rather than the diffusion of a single international norm. Seen in this light, Europeanization appears as an attempt to bend knowledge exchanges in different ways, with the United States playing either the role of the model to be imitated or that of the dominant power to be resisted.

2.2. European Associations as a Means to Gain Weight in Academic Competitions

The connections between European associations and particular countries (fourth column, table 6.1) also call for an analysis of the links between organizations and the national contexts in which they were created.[1] While their founders saw these associations as means to promote certain ideas and professional activities, they were also designed to gain new symbolic resources on the national stage—a form of prestige that they could then attempt to convert and use locally (Dezalay & Garth, 2002) and in academic competitions: for universities, hosting an international organization was a way to legitimize themselves in relation to more established institutions. The creation of associations was thus connected to institutional ambitions.

This is tangible in two cases. The creation of ECPR in 1970 has to be understood in relation to the University of Essex's ambition to rival top social science faculties in the United Kingdom, in spite of its relatively recent creation (Boncourt, 2015). Founded in 1964, the University was one of the new institutions created in the framework of the rise of mass higher education. These new universities were quickly faced with the task of attracting enough good students and funding to exist in an academic landscape that had for a long time been dominated by Oxford and Cambridge, as well as the London School of Economics (LSE) (Grant, 2010). In the framework of this competition, Essex and its department of government followed an internationalization strategy: the department organized a summer school in quantitative methods, recruited researchers with international backgrounds, and developed partnerships with foreign institutions (Blondel, 1997; Boncourt, 2015). The creation of a European consortium of political science was in line with these choices (Budge, 2006). Interestingly though, the process did not go smoothly, as the department's international partners also made a case to host the new organization. While these attempts were unsuccessful and Essex became the seat of the consortium, they signal the fact that ECPR was seen as a potential resource for universities.

EpsNet was created along similar objectives, although the idea was for its promoters to enhance their reputation on the international stage, rather than the national one. The creation of the new network was indeed part of Sciences Po Paris's bid to become more internationalized and to find its place on the international scientific map, along with French political science as a whole. Notwithstanding the intellectual agenda outlined above, Europeanization also appears to be a way for academic institutions to distinguish themselves on an increasingly competitive and international landscape of higher education.

2.3. European Associations as a Resource in Political Struggles

The third column of table 6.1 shows that the founders of social science associations often relied on external grants. As they sought to gather support and funding for their projects, they were led to collaborate with political actors such as philanthropic foundations and the EU. This shows the weight of political actors and agendas in the creation of European political science associations.

The influence of philanthropic foundations on the development of the social sciences is well documented. In the context of the Cold War, these foundations sought to influence European cultural developments, with a view of contributing to the strengthening of transatlantic ties and to the containment of Soviet influence (Berghahn, 2001; Solovey & Cravens, 2012). Social sciences were a key part of this project, as foundations invested money into the development of European economics, political science, social psychology, international relations, and public administration, among other areas. By funding these disciplines, they sought to support the development of social knowledge in order to improve human welfare in the long run. Investing in Europe and other continents, such as Latin America, rather than in the United States, was a way to help local social scientists catch up to their American counterparts, to deepen transatlantic connections, and to strengthen European democracies (Guilhot, 2011; Moscovici & Markova, 2006; Saunier, 2003; Tournès, 2011).

Behavioralism was a key paradigm in this process. With its emphasis on individual agency, it was seen as a potential counterweight to the Marxist focus on structures. Philanthropic foundations therefore invested heavily in the development and diffusion of this paradigm in the 1960s and 1970s. The Ford Foundation, especially, played a central role. The Foundation first focused on funding the development of behavioralism in the United States (Hauptmann, 2012) and gradually changed its policy to encourage its diffusion beyond national boundaries (Gemelli, 1998; Magat, 1979).

This transnational policy took different shapes, which all played a role in the creation of ECPR. First, the Ford Foundation and other philanthropic organizations funded research fellowships in prestigious American universities for European political scientists, thus contributing to the structuring of transatlantic and transnational networks around behavioralist approaches. These networks were later instrumental in assembling founding members for the consortium. The Ford Foundation also provided more direct support by supplying the initial grant that sustained the creation of ECPR and its first decade of operation. The political objectives of the Foundation are made visible by the political clause that it inserted into ECPR's statuses: subscription to the consortium was to be restricted to universities based in democratic countries and free from political influences. This principle, which was in line with the Foundation's Cold War agenda, was also welcome by those of those of the ECPR founding fathers who had directly suffered from the war and were suspicious of communism (Daalder, 1997; Kaase & Wildenmann, 1997).

Philanthropic foundations were not the only political actors to intervene in the creation of European political science associations. From the 1990s onward, the EU also took an interest in funding such organizations, as it sought to promote the structuring of a "European Research Area" (ERA). Rather than pushing for the development of specific paradigms—be they of European or American origins—EU officials followed a geographical objective as they aimed at building scientific bridges between Eastern, Western, Southern, and Northern Europe. The main idea behind the funding of the European Political Science Network was thus to support the development of an organization that would be more closely connected to Eastern and Southern Europe than the existing ECPR was. Significantly, this did not come without critiques from ECPR directors, who saw the new organization as imbued with a political agenda:

> The Thematic Network (TN) is politically biased—its goals are in correspondence with the general EU "ideology." Not all members of ECPR will agree. This is, however, a minor point. More important: the conditions for proposing and succeeding within TN are written in such a way that bureaucrats can be in complete and happy control throughout. (Mogens Pedersen, "Note on the 'thematic networks' issue," ECPR archives, box "EpsNet files," 24 June 1996)

The EU also had more indirect effects on the European infrastructure of political science. Just like national governments had, historically, been the subject of lobbying from national political science associations (with such action leading, for example, to the creation of an autonomous *agrégation* for the discipline in France), the growing importance of EU institutions for research funding and regulation fueled the idea that these institutions should be subjected to active lobbying from political scientists. In the eyes of its founding members, the creation of ECPSA was motivated by the perception that the ECPR was unwilling to develop its activities in this direction. ECPSA may thus be seen as a response to a change in opportunity structures (Tarrow, 2005).

This complex combination of intellectual, academic, and political motives led to multiple organizations coexisting in the structuring of exchanges in European political science. The following section examines the consequences of this coexistence for the discipline.

3. HOW EUROPEAN POLITICAL SCIENCE ASSOCIATIONS SHAPE THE DISCIPLINE

While it is relatively easy to evaluate the "success" of associations from a purely organizational point of view (Do they have an important membership? Stable sources of funding?), their impact on the general structure of the discipline is more difficult to assess (Do they contribute to the circulation of the ideas? Do they stimulate a form of Europeanization of political science research?). It is possible, however, to use proxies that provide partial answers to these questions. The geographical scope of associations' membership is one such indicator. The following tables compile basic data on the current membership of ECPR and EPSA (thus excluding EpsNet, which ceased to exist as an independent organization in 2007, and ECPSA, whose activities are of a different nature) and compare it to the membership of two associations that also play a role in fueling transnational exchanges in political science: the American Political Science Association (APSA), whose membership goes beyond U.S. borders, and IPSA. The data is imperfect in more ways than one. First, because it compares individual memberships (APSA, IPSA, EPSA) with institutional membership (ECPR). Second, because numbers are in IPSA's case relatively context dependent: to an extent, they tend to fluctuate along with the locations of its world congresses. Thus, Spain is overrepresented in 2012 (Madrid world congress) and Australia in 2018 (Brisbane world congress). To account for these imperfections, the analysis compares IPSA membership at two different dates (2012 and 2018) and takes into account organizational differences between associations when interpreting the data. When possible, the data is also put in historical perspective.

3.1. Europeanization Shaped by Country Characteristics

The data firstly reveal national logics of internationalization that run through the organizations studied. Some countries are indeed quantitatively dominant in most, if not all, cases: the United States, Germany, and the United Kingdom systematically count among the most represented countries. "Small" countries such as the Netherlands, Norway, and Switzerland also appear to be more represented than their demographical weight could lead one to expect. By contrast, demographically "big" countries such as France and Spain are underrepresented (table 6.2).

If we follow one branch of the literature (see, for example, Gingras & Heilbron, 2009; Klingemann, 2008), these figures can be interpreted as revealing aspects of scientific internationalization that are transversal to the associations studied. The processes seem not so much linked to the characteristics of

Table 6.2   Ten Most Represented Countries in European Political Science Associations, by Decreasing Order

ECPR (2018)	EPSA (2013)	IPSA (2012)	IPSA (2018)	APSA (2018)
United Kingdom	*United States*	*United States*	*Australia*	*United States*
Germany	*United Kingdom*	*Spain*	*United States*	United Kingdom
United States	Germany	*Germany*	*Japan*	Canada
Italy	Switzerland	*Brazil*	*India*	Germany
Sweden	Ireland	*United Kingdom*	Canada	Japan
Norway	Italy	*Canada*	*Germany*	Switzerland
Canada	Spain	*France*	United Kingdom	Australia
Netherlands	Netherlands	Italy	South Korea	China
France	Canada	Japan	Brazil	Sweden
Spain	Norway	Australia	France	Denmark

Notes:
-Countries highlighted in italic bold represent, together, at least 50 percent of members.
-EPSA has not responded to requests for more recent data.

these organizations as to those of different European countries, in linguistic, cultural and institutional terms. The strong presence of the United Kingdom and Germany and the relative overrepresentation of small western and northern European countries (Scandinavia, the Netherlands, Switzerland) could be considered symptomatic of their strong connection to the Anglo-Saxon world. Conversely, the relative absence of France, Spain or Portugal can be understood as the consequence of alternative areas of internationalization, Francophone, Hispanophone, and Lusophone, respectively—such as the international congresses organized by Francophone political science organizations, for example—a counterargument being that German-speaking venues also exist. The data can also be analyzed in light of the specificities of higher education and research in each of the countries considered. The strong presence of British researchers overseas can be seen as linked to the substantial budgets British universities have long had for professional mobility—although this has tended to be reduced in recent years. They could also be connected to the development of frameworks for evaluating research, which, like the Research Assessment Exercise (RAE) and its successor, the Research Excellence Framework (REF), value the internationalization of academics, and indeed make it a condition for the attribution of funding in their establishments (Camerati, 2014). By contrast, the injunctions to internationalize and the means available to do so appear less substantial for academics in other countries. In France, for example, these injunctions have little concrete impact on the funding of research centers, or on the careers of academics, whereas in the United Kingdom they can lead—in the most extreme cases—to threats to close departments (Boncourt, 2017). The interplay of academic resources and constraints is also associated with linguistic and cultural factors and results in an internationalization that is, all else being equal, unevenly distributed between countries.

3.2. Europeanization Shaped by Organizational Strategies

Beyond these shared points, the associations cover geographic territories that are markedly different. These variations can be felt at two levels. The number of countries represented in the membership bases of organizations varies significantly depending on the case, from 28 countries (EPSA) to 122 countries (IPSA in 2018). Moreover, the organizations differ in the geographical distribution of their members. Table 6.3 clearly shows this disparity: EPSA and APSA are almost exclusively composed of Western Europeans and North Americans, albeit in unequal measures; ECPR is the most "European" association of the sample. This said, Eastern European members are markedly underrepresented compared to their Western counterparts, but less so at ECPR than in EPSA and APSA. IPSA is the less Western organization of the

Table 6.3 Membership of Political Science Associations (Percentages)

	ECPR (2018)	EPSA (2013)	IPSA (2012)	IPSA (2018)	APSA (2018)
Europe	80.5	59.2	51.6	26	9.4
- Western Europe only	*70.7*	*57.9*	*43.4*	*19.6*	*8.9*
- Central and Eastern Europe only	*9.8*	*1.3*	*8.2*	*6.4*	*0.5*
North America	10.4	38.6	18.4	18.3	83.7
Latin America	1.2	0.2	13.2	6.1	1.2
Asia	5.9	1.6	12.1	25.2	4.3
Africa	0.0	0.0	1.8	4.7	0.9
Oceania	2.1	0.4	2.8	19.3	0.6
No. of members	338	548	4,044	3,684	11,000
No. of countries	42	28	108	122	96
Ratio Western / Eastern Europe	7.2	44.5	5.3	3.1	17.8
Ratio Europe / North America	7.7	1.5	2.8	1.4	0.1
Ratio Europe / Global South	13.6	40	2.3	0.9	2.1
Ratio Global North / Global South	15.9	89.4	3.4	2.6	21.2

sample, with Eastern Europe and the Global South slightly more represented in relative terms, both in 2012 and 2018 and in spite of world congresses then being held, respectively, in Spain and Australia.

These variations can be explained not so much by the characteristics of the specific countries as by the characteristics of the organizations studied—or by the interaction between the two.

A first level of explanation is linked to the geographic perimeter that associations aim to cover, and in the ways that they conceive their transnational vocation. This would sound obvious (it makes sense, after all, for organizations branded "European" or "American" to cover a narrower perimeter than an "international" association) if the organizations under study had not, in fact, embraced increasingly similar international ambitions over time. In the 1950s and 1960s, IPSA's activities revolved heavily around Western Europe, but the association became gradually more concerned with living up to its "international" title and increasingly organized events in various regions of the world (table 6.4). As seen above, ECPR initially chose to only allow institutions situated on the European continent and to exclude Eastern European universities, but from the end of the Cold War it opened its membership to Eastern Europe and even offered reducing subscription rates for

Table 6.4 Locations of Main Scientific Events of Political Science Associations (2005–2019)

	ECPR (Joint sessions)	ECPR (General conference)	EPSA (General conference)	IPSA (World congress)
2001	Grenoble	Canterbury		
2002	Turin			
2003	Edinburgh	Marburg		Durban
2004	Uppsala			
2005	Granada	Budapest		
2006	Nicosia			Fukuoka
2007	Helsinki	Pisa		
2008	Rennes			
2009	Lisbon	Potsdam		Santiago
2010	Munster			
2011	St. Gallen	Reykjavík	Dublin	
2012	Antwerp		Berlin	Madrid
2013	Mainz	Bordeaux	Barcelona	
2014	Salamanca	Glasgow	Edinburg	Montreal
2015	Warsaw	Montreal	Vienna	
2016	Pisa	Prague	Brussels	Poznan
2017	Nottingham	Oslo	Milan	
2018	Nicosia	Hamburg	Vienna	Brisbane
2019	Mons	Wrocław	Belfast	

institutions located in the region. It also created new membership categories to allow non-European, and especially American academics to join. The fact that the consortium organizes conferences in various regions of Europe and even in Montreal once testifies to its increasingly global ambitions. EPSA was from the outset conceived as a global association which—like APSA—claimed both geographical attachment (here European) and universal membership. Contrary to ECPR, most of its congresses are held in Western Europe.

A second level of explanation is linked to the organizational forms chosen by the associations when they were created. Associations varied according to the type of membership upon which they were based: while some functioned on the basis of individual memberships (EPSA, APSA), one opted for a structure as a consortium of institutions (ECPR) and another as a federation of associations (IPSA). They also differed in the types of activities that they proposed. Most of them functioned according to a classical model organizing conferences and journal publications, but one also organized a summer school program (ECPR) and regular research workshops (the ECPR "joint sessions"). The diversity of organizational forms is often mobilized by the actors themselves as an argument to explain the variable geographic distribution of the members of these groups. The "Consortium" format is seen as being less favorable to national diversification of the membership base of these organizations; it is mechanically less likely to increase diversification than an individual membership system, all the more so given that non-Western institutions tend to not have sufficient funds to envisage membership to transnational groups. The training activities (summer schools), generally more costly, are also seen as mechanisms that exclude less privileged universities.

These spontaneous interpretations may help account with the relative lack of geographical diversity of ECPR. However, the argument of the specificity of organizational forms again loses its relevance over time. The development of the organizations under study is indeed characterized by a progressive despecification of their structures and activities. First, new categories of members were introduced, with IPSA now welcoming individual members and APSA institutional ones. Second, organizations diversified their activities along similar lines by publishing new journals (the *European Journal of International Relations*, *European Political Science*, and the *European Political Science Review* in the case of ECPR; *Political Science Research and Methods* in the case of EPSA; etc.) and by organizing additional events and conferences (summer schools, graduate conferences, etc.). Third, associations professionalized their internal structures by establishing and expanding a permanent secretariat and putting in place a division of labor between their officers. The organizational landscape thus became increasingly uniform as membership options, activities, and structures became more homogeneous across associations.

This organizational isomorphism (DiMaggio & Powell, 1991) may be explained by the existence of a competition between organizations. As their organizational environment became denser and more competitive (with the number of professional associations growing over time), political contexts changed (notably in relation to the fall of communist regimes), and economic issues became more pressing (with universities less inclined to fund memberships as they operate with increasingly tight budgets), associations became more acutely aware of their opportunities for growth and their risk of decline. The case of EpsNet shows that these risks were more than just speculative as, after having been funded by the EU, the organization failed to gather enough members to remain independent and was eventually absorbed by ECPR. Therefore, on the basis of strategic reviews produced by internal task forces, associations adapted their rules and activities by importing from other organizations what they identified as "best practices," with the explicit objective of attracting new members. Though some differences still persist (institution-only membership and the joint sessions being, for example, distinctive ECPR features, while national association membership is a specificity of IPSA), the oldest associations of the sample (APSA, IPSA, ECPR) have all achieved long-term stability through such convergence.

3.3. Europeanization Shaped by Scientific Discrepancies

This relative harmonization leads us to consider the influence of other parameters, this time intellectual. As shown elsewhere (Boncourt, 2017), political scientists trained in different national academic contexts tend to feel unequally at ease in the activities organized by international associations. While this is, as seen above, partly a language issue, it is also a scientific one. For example, some French political scientists indicate feeling their research does not fit these international environments, as they see it at odds with the dominant international, American-driven "mainstream"—described as a combination of variable-based reasoning, statistical methods, and rational choice assumptions. Such feelings may be no stranger to some countries being underrepresented in organizations like ECPR and EPSA, originally created around the objective of strengthening transatlantic ties along specific intellectual lines.

While this hypothesis is difficult to verify, it still has a strong impact on the behavior of European associations' officers. Over time, the ECPR indeed sought to soften its initial intellectual stances, to be seen as more open and attract more numbers. Indeed, even though the history of the consortium can be described as a success, it faced problems in the course of its growth. While it had initially been funded by a Ford Foundation grant, it was soon faced with the problem of obtaining sufficient resources to remain viable in the long term. ECPR's intellectual objectives then became a problem for its organizational interests, as its closeness to the American field was seen as an obstacle to its growth:

> It is still the case that both in general and more specifically in some countries we are viewed by many political scientists as being in some fashion slanted towards the "behavioural" school of political science. [Some institutions in Germany, the UK, Finland, France] have been reluctant to become involved in the ECPR because they are convinced that we do not give enough emphasis to some specifically theoretical and in particular normative aspects of political analysis. (Jean Blondel, "Report of the executive director on the fourth year of activity, 1973–74," ECPR Archives, Box "reports of the executive director," April 1974)

This perception, which still had currency in the 1980s, led ECPR's officers to adopt strategies to soften this intellectual stigma: the intellectual perimeter of the consortium's activities (conferences, workshops, summer schools) was widened to include a greater diversity of subfields (such as political theory and intellectual history) and methods (qualitative, in particular). The fact that this diversification coincided with a growth of the organization seems to indicate that this strategy paid off—although the move eventually led, as seen above, to some of its members being dissatisfied with ECPR, opting out of it, and founding EPSA.

It is worth noting that EPSA's breakaway is not the only instance of centrifugal forces at work within political science associations. As subdisciplines grow in size, some of their members may take steps to set up distinctive professional structures that may eventually become autonomous from the generalist association's umbrella. Such dynamics were at work in the creation of the ECPR standing group in international relations in 1990 (Groome, 2010), which gradually led to the foundation of the European International Studies Association in 2013, and they may well be currently at work in other subfields. Such processes are proof of the inherent tensions that associations face as they seek to manage the diversity of their intellectual perimeter and, correlatively, the scope of their membership.

***

This chapter has multiple limitations. As it focuses on the creation of European political science associations, it leaves in the dark many types of transnational circulations of ideas and scholars—journals, books, informal networks, and so forth. While keeping these gaps in mind, two conclusions may be drawn from this short study.

The logics behind the creation of a European infrastructure for political science are more complex than the simple translation of the discipline's growth into professional organizations. Paradigm struggles, academic competitions, and changes in the political environment interplayed to fuel competitions between political scientists, with European associations a resource to gain weight in these oppositions. These dynamics had both national and transnational ramifications, with the founding members of the associations under study often circulating between these two levels and pursuing agendas on various stages. The creation of European political science associations, then, is best portrayed as a conflicted process where professionalization is a result of multilayered professional struggles between actors vying for different kinds of recognition (Abbott, 1988).

These competitive dynamics do not stop with the creation of associations. Rather, these organizations compete and, as they do so, they deploy strategies to expand their membership and activities. This generates a certain amount of isomorphism, but transnational political science associations still do not cover the same geographical perimeters. This suggests that associations play an active role in the asymmetrical diffusion of ideas within the discipline, with a center–periphery model seemingly an appropriate tool to make sense of the channels through which ideas may, or may not, circulate. In spite of their differences, all the organizations under study seem to face the same challenges: as they all heavily lean toward the Western world, the integration of Eastern Europe and the Global South is still a pressing issue; as they sometimes, and for good reasons, convey the impression of being the vectors of an "international mainstream," the question of whether spaces should be opened up for intellectual and methodological diversity regularly tops the agenda.

NOTE

1. One might be tempted to use the site of the first head office of the organizations as a geographical indicator. However, data collected in this way would not have been particularly heuristic given the diversity of what is actually covered by the idea of a "head office" or "secretariat," as some of them existed only on paper. The geographical diversity of organizations is thus included in table 6.1 based on the country where the first president of each organization was based. This indicator has the merit of revealing the national field most closely connected to the dynamic of the creation of each new organization. However, given its clear limitations, it must not be over interpreted—for example, by assimilating EPSA and ECPSA to British and German organizations, respectively.

REFERENCES

Abbott, A. (1988). *The system of professions: An essay on the division of expert labor.* Chicago: The University of Chicago Press.

Adcock, R., Bevir, M., & Stimson, S. C. (Eds.). (2007). *Modern political science: Anglo-American exchanges since 1880.* Princeton and Oxford: Princeton University Press.

Alatas, S. F. (2003). Academic dependency and the global division of labor in the social sciences. *Current Sociology, 51*(6), 599–613.

Berghahn, V. R. (2001). *America and the intellectual cold wars in Europe.* Princeton: Princeton University Press.

Bevir, M. (2001). Prisoners of professionalism: On the construction and responsibility of political studies. A review article. *Public Administration, 79*(2), 469–89.

Blondel, J. (1997). Amateurs into professionals. In Hans Daalder (Ed.), *Comparative European politics: The story of a profession* (pp. 115–26). London: Pinter.

Boncourt, T. (2015). The transnational circulation of scientific ideas. Importing behaviouralism in European political science (1950–1970). *Journal of the History of the Behavioral Sciences, 51*(2), 195–215.

Boncourt, T. (2016). La science internationale comme ressource. Genèse et développement comparés des associations européennes de sciences sociales. *Revue française de sociologie, 57*(3), 529–61.

Boncourt, T. (2017). Gouvernement des carrières académiques et diffusion d'un *mainstream* scientifique. Les politistes français et britanniques face aux injonctions à l'internationalization. In Martin Benninghoff, Jean-Emile Charlier, Cécile Crespy, & Jean-Philippe Leresche (Eds.), *Le gouvernement des disciplines académiques. Acteurs, dynamiques, instruments, échelles* (pp. 121–40). Paris: Editions des archives contemporaines.

Bourdieu, P. (2002). Les conditions sociales de la circulation internationale des idées. *Actes de la recherche en sciences sociales, 145,* 3–8.

Budge, I. (2006). Jean Blondel and the development of European political science. *European Political Science, 5*(3), 315–27.

Camerati, F. (2014). *Les universitaires britanniques face aux instruments d'évaluation et de financement de la recherche* (PhD diss.). Sciences Po Paris.

Collini, S., Winch, D., & Burrow, J. (1983). *That noble science of politics: A study in the nineteenth century intellectual history.* Cambridge: Cambridge University Press.

Daalder, H. (1997). A smaller European's opening frontiers. In H. Daalder (Ed.), *Comparative European politics: The story of a profession* (pp. 227–40). London: Pinter.

Dammame, D. (1987). Genèse sociale d'une institution scolaire. L'Ecole libre des sciences politiques. *Actes de la Recherche en Sciences Sociales, 70,* 31–46.

Dezalay, Y., & Garth, B. G. (2002). *La mondialisation des guerres de palais.* Paris: Seuil.

DiMaggio, P., & Powell, W. (1991). The iron cage revisited: Institutional isomorphism and collective rationality in organizational fields. In P. DiMaggio & W. Powell, *The new institutionalism in organizational analysis* (pp. 63–84). Chicago: University of Chicago Press.

Favre, P. (1989). *Naissances de la science politique en France 1870–1914.* Paris: Fayard.

Feuerhahn, W., & Rabault-Feuerhahn, P. (Eds.). (2010). La fabrique internationale de la science. *Revue germanique internationale, 12,* 1–240.

Gaïti, B., & Scot, M. (2017). Une science sans savants: Les paradoxes de l'émergence de la science politique en France entre 1945 et 1968. *Revue française de science politique, 67*(1), 13–42.

Gemelli, G. (1998). *The Ford foundation and Europe (1950's–1970's): Cross-fertilization of learning in social science and management.* Brussels: European Interuniversity Press.

Gingras, Y., & Heilbron, J. (2009). L'internationalisation de la recherche en sciences sociales et humaines en Europe (1980–2006). In G. Sapiro (Ed.), *L'espace intellectuel en Europe* (pp. 359–79). Paris: La Découverte.

Grant, W. (2010). *The development of a discipline: The history of the political studies association.* London: Wiley-Blackwell.

Groom, A. J. R. (2010). The formation of the standing group on international relations. In K. Newton & T. Boncourt (Eds.), *The ECPR's first forty years 1970–2010* (p. 34). Wivenhoe: ECPR Press.

Guilhot, N. (Ed.). (2011). *The invention of international relations theory: Realism, the Rockefeller foundation, and the 1954 conference on theory.* New York: Columbia University Press.

Guilhot, N. (2014). The international circulation of international relations theory. In W. Keim, E. Çelik, C. Ersche, & V. Wöhrer (Eds.), *Global knowledge production in the social sciences. Made in circulation* (pp. 63–86). Dorchester: Ashgate.

Hauptmann, E. (2012). The Ford foundation and the rise of behavioralism in political science. *Journal of the History of the Behavioral Sciences, 48*(2), 154–73.

Heilbron, J. (2008). Qu'est-ce qu'une tradition nationale en sciences sociales? *Revue d'histoire des sciences humaines, 18*, 3–16.

Heilbron, J., Guilhot, N., & Jeanpierre, L. (2009). Vers une histoire transnationale des sciences sociales. *Sociétés contemporaines, 73*, 121–45.

Kaase, M., & Wildenmann, R. (1997). Rudolf Wildenmann: German scholar, institution builder, democrat. In H. Daalder (Ed.), *Comparative European politics: The story of a profession* (pp. 40–53). London: Pinter.

Keim, W. (2010). Pour un modèle centre-périphérie dans les sciences sociales. *Revue d'anthropologie des connaissances, 4*(3), 570–98.

Klingemann, H.-D. (2008). Capacities: Political science in Europe. *West European Politics, 31*(1–2), 370–96.

Magat, R. (1979). *The Ford foundation at work: Philanthropic choices, methods and style*. New York and London: Plenum Press.

Merton, R. K. (1973). *The sociology of science: Theoretical and empirical investigations*. Chicago: The University of Chicago Press.

Mosbah-Natanson, S., & Gingras, Y. (2014). The globalization of social sciences? Evidence from a quantitative analysis of 30 years of production, collaboration and citations in the social sciences (1980–2009). *Current Sociology, 62*(5), 626–46.

Moscovici, S., & Markova, I. (2006). *The making of modern social psychology*. Cambridge: Polity Press.

Rasmussen, A. (1995). *L'Internationale scientifique (1890–1914)* (PhD diss.). Ecole des Hautes Etudes en Sciences Sociales.

Rodríguez Medina, L. (2014). Bounding Luhmann: The reception and circulation of Luhmann's theory in hispanic America. In W. Keim, E. Çelik, C. Ersche, & V. Wöhrer (Eds.), *Global knowledge production in the social sciences. Made in circulation* (pp. 39–62). Dorchester: Ashgate.

Saunier, P.-Y. (2003). Administrer le monde ? Les fondations philanthropiques et la public administration aux Etats-Unis. *Revue française de science politique, 53*(2), 237–55.

Schofer, E. (1999). Science associations in the international sphere 1875–1990. The rationalization of science and the scientization of society. In J. Boli & G. Thomas (Eds.), *Constructing world culture* (pp. 249–66). Stanford: Stanford University Press.

Solovey, M., & Cravens, H. (Eds.). (2012). *Cold war social science. Knowledge production, liberal democracy and human nature*. New York: Palgrave Macmillan.

Stein, M. B. (1995). Major factors in the emergence of political science in western democracies: a comparative analysis of the United States, Britain, France, and Germany. In D. Easton, J. Gunnell, & M. B. Stein (Eds.), *Regime and discipline: Democracy and the development of political science* (pp. 165–95). Ann Arbor: The University of Michigan Press.

Steinmetz, G. (2013). A child of the empire: British sociology and colonialism, 1940s–1960s. *Journal of the History of the Behavioral Sciences, 49*(4), 353–78.

Tarrow, S. (2005). *The new transnational activism*. Cambridge: Cambridge University Press.

Tournès, L. (2011). *Sciences de l'homme et politique. Les fondations philanthropiques américaines en France au XXe siècle*. Paris: Editions des Classiques Garnier.

Trent, J. E., & Coakley, J. (2000). *History of the international political science association 1949–1999*. Dublin: International Political Science Association.

UNESCO. (2010). *World social science report*. Paris: Unesco.

APPENDIX

Table 6.5   Interviews Conducted

	Interviewees	
Association	*Name*	*Position*
ECPR	Jean Blondel	Founding member, first director
	Hans Daalder	Founding member, second chair
	Serge Hurtig	Founding member
	Ian Budge	Second director
	David McKay	Third director
EPsNET	Gérard Grunberg	Founding member, first president
	André-Paul Frognier	Founding member
EPSA	Ken Benoit	Current executive director
	Simon Hix	Founding member

Chapter 7

The World of Political Science

Internationalization and Its Consequences

Pippa Norris

How far has the political science profession been transformed by contemporary processes of internationalization? It is timely to reflect on this issue in the light of two major milestones: the seventieth platinum anniversary of International Political Science Association (IPSA) and the fiftieth golden anniversary of the European Consortium of Political Research (ECPR). Following an initiative by UNESCO, IPSA was founded in 1949. The association gradually expanded until today it connects over fifty national associations and thousands of individual members worldwide. IPSA seeks to create an inclusive and global political science community in which all can participate, building academic networks linking East and West, North and South (Bardi, 2011). The ECPR was established in 1970, designed to foster scholarship within the region. Within a few years of its founding, the ECPR had developed a range of activities—the summer training school, annual joint workshops, research projects, publications, and data archiving networks—which sought to foster multinational links among political scientists throughout Europe (Newton, 1991; see Mény, chapter 2, and Boncourt, chapter 6). But these international organizations, along with sister bodies such as the International Studies Association, International Communication Association, the World Association for Public Opinion Research, and International Society for Political Psychology, reflect just the tip of the iceberg. Engagement by political scientist in numerous transnational meetings, conferences, and workshops has also expanded through the proliferation of more specialized organized thematic sections within subfields, as well as the growth of more informal social networks among colleagues scattered across the globe (Kendall, Woodward, & Skrbis, 2009).

Growing international linkages of peoples, communications and labor within the political science profession are part of much broader cosmopolitan trends widely observed in higher education during recent decades (Altbach,

Reisberg, & Rumbley, 2009; Bok, 2015; Deardorff, de Wit, & Heyl, 2012; Wihlborg & Robson, 2017). The impact of these developments on political science continues to be debated. If we have indeed become a truly cosmopolitan profession, this implies that colleagues in Lagos and London, Moscow and Mumbai, or Sydney and Stockholm can be expected to read much the same canonical books and articles, teach similar foundational texts and concepts, and share common academic norms, analytical methods, role priorities, and intellectual agendas. Place and nation of origin become less significant as an academic identifier. On the other hand, if political science still bears the legacy of path-dependent historical traditions, enduring cultural traditions, and diverse regimes, then distinct national and local idiosyncrasies can be expected to persist—even contrasts among colleagues living, studying, and teaching in neighboring states. In which case, meaningful distinctions would still be observed among, say, European and American political scientists (see Mény, chapter 2). Despite discussion about these matters, hard data to establish a convergence of national cultures of political science has been elusive.

Using empirical evidence from a new study of over 2,000 political scientists—the ECPR-IPSA World of Political Science (WPS-2019) survey—this chapter addresses several questions. Firstly, are there similar background characteristics, qualifications, and career profiles among political scientists employed in higher education in different countries around the world, such as by birth cohort, gender, work status, institutional affiliation, and academic rank? Secondly, do political scientists in diverse societies share common perceptions about their work roles, and thus the relative importance of teaching and mentoring, research and publication, university and professional service, and real-world policy impact? Thirdly, is there a similar balance in the proportion of colleagues in each region studying the major subfields or, for example, are there more theorists in Europe and more behaviorists in America? Fourthly, have doctoral training programs and summer schools generated a common set of methodological skills, approaches, and analytic techniques shared among early career scholars, so that a broad epistemological agreement exists about the nature of empirical evidence? Finally, if globalization has indeed gradually transformed political science as a discipline, as many believe, then this process is likely to have generated both winners and losers (Castells, 2000; Knight, 2013; Wihlborg & Robson, 2017). So how do colleagues evaluate changes in recent years and what is thought to have been lost—and what gained?

Part I discusses three mega-trends expected to contribute toward transforming the discipline of political science, focusing upon the accelerated flow of people, communications, and labor. Part II describes the evidence used to examine these propositions, presenting the first results of new survey data from the ECPR-IPSA WPS survey (WPS-2019). Part III uses the cross-national data to describe regional political science communities in their social background and career profiles, role perceptions, methodological techniques, and subfields of expertise. The conclusion in section 4 (see page 152) summarizes the key results and considers their implications.

1. THEORETICAL FRAMEWORK

1.1 A Cosmopolitan Political Science?

Since Aristotle, the aim of cosmopolitans has been to develop scientific generalizations based on concepts, theories, and empirical generalizations which travel beyond the national boundaries of any particular society. This is often regarded as the sine qua non of any mature science. Cosmopolitanism can be understood to celebrate the politics of "everywhere," where political science flowing across national borders is thought to expand the scope of general theories applicable across diverse contexts and societies, deepening international interchange and multiculturalism within the discipline (Kendall, Woodward, & Skrbis, 2009; Norris, 1997; Norris & Inglehart, 2009).

One of the primary drivers of change in higher education has been processes of globalization, accelerating the scale, density, and velocity of economic, social, and political interconnectedness around the world (Held, McGrew, Goldblatt, & Perraton, 1999). This is far from a novel phenomenon; globalization has occurred historically in periodic waves, whether driven by free trade, population migrations, military conquests, technology, or religious conversions (Chanda, 2007). The long arc of history steadily expanded the modern era of globalization from the 1970s until 2015, after which annual growth stalled (Gygli et al., 2019). Globalized political science is reflected in the growth of regional and international organizations like the ECPR and IPSA, as well as the accelerated movement of *people* (academic mobility providing opportunities for younger scholars to study, train, and work in foreign countries), *communications* (technological developments which expedite global information sharing and sustain geographically dispersed collaboration in research networks), and *labor* (growing neoliberal competition in more open employment markets). All these trends may be expected to generate a growing convergence of the political science profession, eroding national boundaries.

1.2 People: Global Academic Mobility

Academic mobility among students is a phenomenon observed on all continents around the world; for example, today five million tertiary students are enrolled outside their country of citizenship, rising from two million in 1999, and expected to surge further to seven million by 2030 (OECD, 2018). In terms of numbers, shifting economic power and the growth of the middle classes in Asia, especially in China and India, has been critical to these developments (OECD, 2019). Until relatively recently, the inflow of foreign students enrolled in higher education abroad was highest in the United States (host to 25% of the total) and the United Kingdom (12%), followed by China (10%), France (8%), and Australia (7%) (IIE, 2017).

Human mobility across borders has grown with more affordable transport and communications, along with the international market in higher education. STEM subfields—science, technology, engineering, and mathematics—have been at the vanguard of these developments. But other disciplines have also been swept up in this tide (OECD, 2018). The impact has been most dramatic at graduate level; international students now represent around one-quarter of all contemporary enrollments in doctoral programs (Bauder, 2015). Some may subsequently return home after graduation, but many younger scholars choose residency abroad; three-quarters of foreign doctoral graduates were still in the United States one year after graduation and 60 percent remained there a decade later (Altbach, Reisberg, & Rumbley, 2009; Bauder, 2015). And some become transnational citizens, building professional teaching, research, and fellowship resumes with professional qualifications and institutional affiliations in several countries. The spread of English as the lingua franca of scientific discourse has fueled connectivity and also reinforced the attractions of study abroad in leading Anglo-American universities (Lublin, 2018; OECD, 2018).

1.3 Communications: Global ICTs and Transnational Collaboration

Transnational connectivity and digital information technologies have also obviously played a major role in transforming the pace of scientific dissemination. Recent decades have witnessed a rapid growth in international scientific collaboration, where colleagues increasingly work together across borders. For example, Wagner (2018) compared a half-dozen diverse scientific fields, documenting remarkable growth in the breadth of collaborative projects and publications; reporting that the number of multiauthored scientific papers with scholars from more than one country more than doubled from 1990 to 2015, from 10 percent to 25 percent. Access to the growing range of off-the-shelf global datasets and indices in political science has facilitated large-N cross-national and time-series comparative analysis (Cooley & Snyder, 2015; see Dalton, chapter 5). The discipline's publications have followed the natural sciences by adopting the collaborative model of multiauthorship

(McDermott & Hatemi, 2010). Programs by scientific foundations supporting innovative research projects, like the European Union (EU)'s Horizon 2020, expand resources for international collaboration and require multicountry partnerships.

1.4 Labor: Diversity, Inclusion, and Competition in the Academic Workforce

In addition, working conditions in higher education have been transformed through increasing social diversity, inclusion, and competition in the global labor market. Higher education has also seen gradual shifts toward greater gender equality and expanded opportunities for women, although many challenges remain in achieving gender parity and greater inclusion of racial and ethnic minorities (see Engeli & Mügge, chapter 9, and Briscoe-Palmer and Mattocks, chapter 10). IPSA's *Gender and Diversity Monitoring Report 2017* reported that women were around one-third of the membership of the largest national political science associations, such as in the United States, Korea and the United Kingdom, with parity almost achieved in a few exceptional cases, notably in Russia and Iceland (Abu-Laban, Sawer, & St-Laurent, 2018). Associations have also seen the active and growing engagement of women at all levels of the profession, including in the leadership roles, with diversity taskforces, caucuses, and executive committees routinely monitoring positive trends. Several associations have also seen increased concern about other dimensions of social diversity among their membership, such as in race/ethnicity, language, disability, and indigeneity, although reliable cross-national data remains more scattered.

The European University Association reports that the social sciences have also agreed to implement more rigorous standards of technical skills, and professional and technical training for PhD students, with the Salzburg principles recognizing the importance of internationalization and mobility experiences, both geographic and interdisciplinary (EUA, 2010). National labor markets have become more open for early and mid-career scholars, as recruitment programs seek to tap into the international pool of talent, universities compete in global league table rankings, and countries have dismantled residual barriers to the free movement of peoples (Bok, 2015). More competitive labor markets in higher education have also been associated with the growing casualization of teaching and research contracts, along with a loss of tenured security, collective bargaining, and growing inequality among faculty in levels of pay, academic status, and working conditions (Currie, Deangelis, deBoer, Huisman, & Lacotte, 2003). In the United States, for example, where these trends may be most advanced, the American Association of University Professors (AAUP) estimates that the proportion of full-time tenured and tenure track faculty fell from 45 percent in 1975 to 30 percent in 2015, with almost three-quarters of the academic labor force now made up of contingent appointments, such as adjuncts, postdocs, TAs, part-timers, or instructors lacking job security and the protection of academic freedoms.[1]

In response to global market competition, many universities are thought to have developed an increasingly bureaucratic managerial corporate culture, eroding the traditional value of scholarly autonomy. This process is exemplified by the use of research selectivity exercises by policymakers in the United Kingdom and Australia, tying institutional status and funding to formal evaluation processes of research performance (Harley, 2010).

1.5 The Implications for Political Science as a Discipline

The implications of growing global mobility, communications, and labor for the profession of political science deserve examining. If pressures dismantle academic protectionism within national borders, does this facilitate a genuine interchange of theories and methods—or foster a one-directional center–periphery flow which threatens indigenous approaches, localized understandings, and non-Western cultural values? Is there a process of "Americanization"—or the growth of regional hegemonic powers in a multipolar world, where Eastern European students chose to study in Moscow, South East Asians in Sydney, and Francophone Africans in Paris? Do some subfields of the discipline, like certain basic concepts in political philosophy or sociology, travel more easily without the need for translation than others, such as institutional analysis? And what has been the effect on work satisfaction in the discipline of contemporary changes in the academic workforce, like growing casualization and the loss of job security?

2. DATA AND RESEARCH DESIGN

We can explore some of these issues empirically with new survey data. If transnational convergence has been occurring in the discipline of political science, as widely assumed, then we might expect to see growing commonalities among political scientists across world regions, exemplified by the employment of faculty with similar background experiences, training, technical skills, and formal qualifications, as well as shared role perceptions, methodological, subfields of research, and perceptions of academic change.

What methods would allow us to examine whether political science has evolved into a truly internationalized profession? Bibliometric studies have commonly been conducted over the years to develop a profile of political science, whether examining journal outputs (see, for example, Lima,

Morschbacher, and Peres, 2018; Teele and Thelen, 2017; Camerlo, Doyle and Diez, 2018) or analyzing the "h-index" to measure publication records and citation impact among colleagues working within American departments of political science (Kim & Grofman, 2019; Masuoka, Grofman, & Feld, 2007). Two decades ago, on the occasion of the twenty-fifth anniversary of the ECPR, the *European Journal of Political Research (EJPR)* published my study of transatlantic convergence and divergence in political science publications (Norris, 1997). This analyzed the contents of three leading journals in the profession from 1971 to 1995, including in the *EJPR*, the *American Political Science Review (APSR)*, and *Political Studies*, the official periodicals of the ECPR, APSA, and PSA U.K., respectively (see also Dalton, chapter 5). To test claims of growing transatlantic convergence, the study scrutinized evidence for several empirical indices from analyzing the types of articles published in these journals for each decade during this period. The results suggested that, in fact, political scientists in the United States and Europe were no closer in the mid-1990s on several dimensions than in the early-1970s, and perhaps methodologically even further apart. Multilateral links had strengthened within Europe. Yet it was more common during this era for colleagues to publish research about the politics of their own country—the decline of class voting in Sweden, changes in Austrian corporatism, or the growth of the extreme right parties in France—rather than cross-national research. Bibliometric analysis provides useful insights into publication trends (e.g., see Dalton, chapter 5), especially where the data can be disaggregated by subfield, gender, cohort, and institutions. Yet this approach is limited unless coupled with other types of evidence. Moreover, which types of publications included in any study, and the boundaries concerning who is and isn't counted as a "political scientist," can prove arbitrary, generating a systematically skewed bias, for example, by focusing on articles at the exclusion of books, or by American studies arbitrarily excluding political scientists located in interdisciplinary departments, research centers, or schools of public policy (cf Kim & Grofman, 2019).

By contrast, surveys of scholars facilitate more fine-grained analysis of background and attitudes, disaggregated at individual level, exemplified by the series of TRIP survey of international relations faculty (Maliniak, Oakes, Peterson, & Tierney, 2011; Maliniak, Peterson, & Tierney, 2019).[2] National professional associations also routinely conduct surveys of their members and departments, such as to monitor training and employment opportunities.

Accordingly, the WPS survey (WPS-2019) was implemented to establish a representative profile of the political science profession across the world.[3] Invitations asking political scientists to participate were distributed through social media notifications (Facebook, emails, and Twitter), the ECPR Newsletter list and IPSA lists, and through several national associations (CPSA,

PSA U.K., Australian PSA, and Russian PSA) from 3 February to 7 April 2019. Overall, 2,446 responses were collected from respondents currently studying or working in 102 countries. These can be categorized into eight global regions, including North America (the United States and Canada), Western, Northern, Southern, and Eastern Europe, Latin America and the Caribbean, Asia-Pacific, and continental Africa. Unfortunately, there were too few responses to permit reliable analysis of the Middle East and North Africa, where political science departments are also least well represented. We can also focus more intensively upon the countries with larger national samples, comparing diverse cases such as Italy (79), Australia (70), Russia (73), Canada (78), the Netherlands (87), Nigeria (116), the United Kingdom (238), Germany (246), and the United States (281).

One important qualification should be noted, however, namely that by tapping into those members already relatively actively involved in the ECPR and IPSA, the survey may oversample those most likely to be globalized, while underrepresenting colleagues who have not joined or become active in these international networks. It was possible to double check this issue by examining how actively respondents said that they attended meetings of the ECPR, IPSA, and their national association. The overwhelming majority of survey participants reported that they "Never" or "Not very often" attended the ECPR (70%) or IPSA (84%) meetings, while the majority (62%) said that they were "Fairly" or "Very" active in their national association meetings. Thus, the survey may overestimate the most globally engaged, but respondents are likely to provide a reasonably representative sample of the profession as a whole.

3. CROSS-NATIONAL COMPARISONS

The flow of data, scholars, and publications around the globe may be expected to facilitate the ability of political scientists from different countries to share a common body of knowledge, methodological approaches, and intellectual concerns. If political science has converged, then cross-national and cross-regional similarities should be evident today, especially among early career scholars.

3.1 The Social Profile of Political Scientists in Academic Posts

To start to describe the survey evidence, table 7.1 provides a profile of the political science professionals who are in full or part-time academic employment by gender, education, age, migrant status, and religion, broken down by global region.

Table 7.1 Social Profile of Political Scientists in Academic Employment (% Within Region)

		Total	North America	Western Europe	Northern Europe	Southern Europe	Eastern Europe	Latin America and Carib	Asia-Pacific	Africa
Gender	Men	**65**	64	63	63	61	67	72	62	88
	Women	**35**	36	37	37	39	33	28	38	12
Highest degree	Doctoral degree or equivalent	**85**	93	73	92	88	91	78	85	76
	Master's degree or equivalent	**14**	7	27	8	11	7	17	12	21
	Undergraduate degree	**1**	0	0	0	1	2	5	3	3
Decade of birth	1940s	**3**	9	0	2	2	4	4	1	0
	1950s	**9**	15	5	7	6	12	11	9	5
	1960s	**19**	20	12	20	26	15	19	22	27
	1970s	**30**	29	24	33	32	26	36	31	46
	1980s	**34**	26	47	35	29	39	26	32	22
	1990s	**6**	2	13	4	5	5	4	5	0
Cohort of birth (4-cat)	Interwar or boomers (1964 or earlier)	**19**	30	10	19	19	22	24	22	10
	Gen X (1965–1979)	**41**	42	31	43	47	35	46	41	67
	Millennials (1980 or later)	**40**	28	59	39	34	43	30	37	22
Field of highest degree	Political science	**62**	81	58	66	50	49	63	52	64
	International relations	**12**	6	15	10	9	12	7	20	18
	Sociology, political, sociology	**6**	2	8	6	13	5	5	4	0
	Public administration/policy	**4**	4	4	4	10	3	2	3	6
	Philosophy, political theory	**4**	1	3	3	7	15	5	3	2
	All others	**12**	5	13	11	12	16	19	17	11

(Continued)

Table 7.1 Social Profile of Political Scientists in Academic Employment (% Within Region) (Continued)

		Total	North America	Western Europe	Northern Europe	Southern Europe	Eastern Europe	Latin America and Carib	Asia-Pacific	Africa
Academic migrant:	Migrant	33	28	39	49	28	11	20	38	5
	Native	67	72	61	51	72	90	80	62	96
Religious denomination, if any	Protestant	13	16	16	19	2	5	5	4	36
	Catholic	17	14	22	10	25	17	30	5	28
	Orthodox	5	1	2	1	11	30	0	2	3
	Jewish	3	12	2	1	0	1	3	6	0
	Muslim	4	1	1	1	2	0	1	18	21
	Hindu	1	0	0	0	0	0	1	5	0
	Buddhist, Confucian, or other Asian religion	1	1	0	0	1	0	0	4	0
	Other (please specify)	4	7	4	1	4	5	7	4	8
	Do not belong to any religious denomination	52	47	55	67	56	42	53	51	5
Number of respondents		1335	206	310	286	122	102	90	152	67

Note: Column % (within region). The table only includes those currently in full- or part-time academic employment, excluding retired, those employed in nonacademic work, and graduate students.

Source: ECPR-IPSA World of Political Science survey (Norris), Spring 2019.

A discipline is characterized by common standards and norms, transmitted through minimal professional competencies acquired and accredited in graduate training programs (Goodwin & Klingemann, 1996). In terms of the highest qualifications, therefore, an important sign of a profession concerns the proportion of political scientists with a doctoral degree or equivalent, as an indication of training, skills, and mentoring. Overall, 85 percent of political scientists in academic jobs had completed a doctoral degree or equivalent, with the proportion highest in North America and Northern Europe, and lowest in Latin America and Africa. In terms of subfields, 62 percent had studied political science for their highest degree, with the proportion dropping to around a bare majority in Southern and Eastern Europe as well as Asia-Pacific. The next most common highest degree was international relations (12%), followed by sociology, public administration, and philosophy. Transfers into political science from colleagues with PhDs in other disciplines, such as law, history, psychology, and economics, were far less common, with less than 1 percent drawn from any of these subfields.

In terms of social diversity and inclusion, overall women are estimated to constitute around one-third (35%) of the profession, similar to the proportions reported in several associational memberships (Abu-Laban, Sawer, & St-Laurent, 2018). All the regions are similar except for Africa, where women are the most underrepresented (12%). The age profile of the profession is fairly evenly distributed across a normal curve, with Millennials (40%) forming the largest cohort of the profession, followed by Gen X (41%). The religious profile of political science largely reflects the predominant type of faith and the strength of religiosity in each region (Norris & Inglehart, 2011), with predictable patterns of Catholicism strongest in Southern Europe and Latin America, Protestantism in Northern Europe, Orthodox Christianity in Eastern Europe, and Muslim political scientists in Asia-Pacific and Africa. Overall, half the profession is secular, as expected, while religiosity proved strongest in Africa.

3.2 Academic Mobility

The survey also facilitates the analysis of migration and pathways toward academic mobility, including the country of birth and of citizenship, country of undergraduate and postgraduate training, and current country of residency for work and study. Given geographic fluidity, the "current" country of study or work may prove a temporary or a permanent home. Overall, if we define "migrants" most simply as the difference between country of birth and current country of work or study, migrants constitute one-third of political scientists in academics jobs, testimony to the impact of globalization and open labor markets. Some substantial contrasts were evident by region, however, with a high share of foreign scholars studying and working in affluent postindustrial societies in Northern and Western Europe, states which are highly globalized by other indices—such as in Switzerland, the United Kingdom, Belgium, Ireland, France, Australia, and the Netherlands (see figure 7.1). By contrast, very few foreign political scientists are currently studying or working in Latin America and Africa. Middle- and low-income economies such as in Nigeria, Uruguay, and Guatemala are more likely to export students and scholars to better-paid positions in more affluent societies. Overall, therefore, as expected, global mobility is not a two-way process; instead, political scientists typically flow across national borders from poorer developing societies toward opportunities to study and work in more affluent nations with open labor markets. This strengthens opportunities for talented scholars, and it can

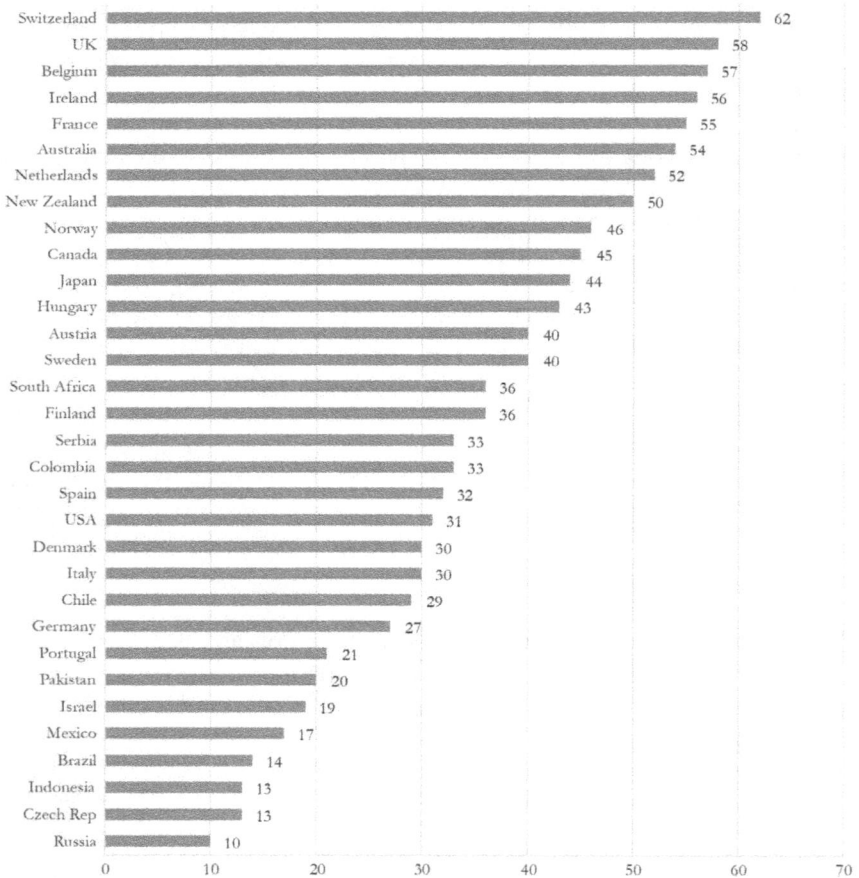

Country	Value
Switzerland	62
UK	58
Belgium	57
Ireland	56
France	55
Australia	54
Netherlands	52
New Zealand	50
Norway	46
Canada	45
Japan	44
Hungary	43
Austria	40
Sweden	40
South Africa	36
Finland	36
Serbia	33
Colombia	33
Spain	32
USA	31
Denmark	30
Italy	30
Chile	29
Germany	27
Portugal	21
Pakistan	20
Israel	19
Mexico	17
Brazil	14
Indonesia	13
Czech Rep	13
Russia	10

Figure 7.1   Proportion of Foreign-Born Political Scientists by Current Country of Work or Study. *Source*: ECPR-IPSA World of Political Science survey (Norris), Spring 2019.

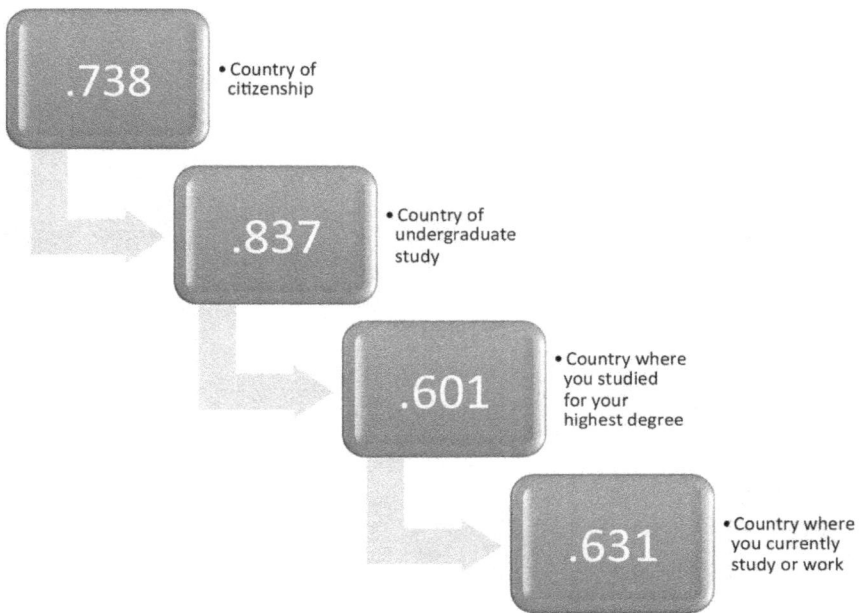

Figure 7.2 Academic Mobility Paths: Correlations with Country of Birth. *Source*: ECPR-IPSA World of Political Science survey (Norris), Spring 2019.

also expand local capacity if migrants eventually return home for permanent employment after postgraduate training and research fellowships, but it can also represent a brain drain for developing societies.

The pathways of migrants can also be analyzed by comparing the correlations between country of birth and any of the subsequent stages of academic studies and careers. As figure 7.2 illustrates, there is a strong correlation between the country of birth and subsequent citizenship, as well as the country of undergraduate studies. It is at the stage of the highest degree of postgraduate study, and then subsequent work abroad, where the correlations weaken with the country of birth. As discussed earlier, the move abroad to study and train for postgraduate qualifications is one which may prove temporary, but it can often lead to scholars finding permanent academic employment as teachers and researchers in their new country of residency.

3.3 The Employment Profile of all Political Scientists

Neoliberal reforms in labor markets, and the dismantling of protections for job security, are expected to lead toward greater casualization in the workforce. Table 7.2 describes the employment profile of all political scientists

Table 7.2 Employment Profile of all Political Scientists in the Survey (% Within Region)

	Total	North America	Western Europe	Northern Europe	Southern Europe	Eastern Europe	Latin America and Caribbean	Asia-Pacific	Africa
Work status									
Full-time academic employment	**72**	70	75	80	70	67	57	71	72
Part-time academic employment	**6**	5	6	3	6	12	12	7	5
Nonacademic employment	**5**	6	4	1	9	3	15	6	5
Postgraduate study	**12**	8	13	13	13	15	14	11	18
Other	**4**	10	4	4	2	2	2	4	1
Job security									
Continuous contract (tenure line)	**64**	36	58	46	48	60	51	79	52
(if in academic									
Fixed-term contract	**30**	60	36	44	43	24	36	16	41
employment)									
Temporary post (no contract)	**6**	4	6	10	9	15	14	4	8
Academic status									
Senior management	**4**	3	3	3	5	5	9	6	5
Professor	**22**	34	20	25	14	18	22	18	6
Associate professor	**12**	20	5	11	11	21	17	15	4

Assistant professor	**11**	16	11	5	16	13	14	11	4
Lecturer or senior lecturer	**15**	6	9	25	8	9	4	18	56
Research fellow	**20**	7	32	15	29	20	17	18	14
Graduate student	**16**	15	19	15	18	14	17	16	12
Department									
Political science	**47**	64	42	49	41	43	41	38	57
International relations	**12**	13	9	13	9	23	10	15	7
Public policy	**9**	7	11	5	10	8	9	10	18
Social sciences	**21**	7	25	21	32	19	27	23	10
Other	**11**	9	13	13	7	7	13	14	8
Department size									
50 or more FTE academic staff	**28**	16	29	38	37	39	21	18	18
30–49 FTE academic staff	**21**	21	21	26	21	17	14	19	18
20–29 FTE academic staff	**18**	20	18	20	12	14	22	17	16
10–19 FTE academic staff	**20**	24	20	13	18	15	24	26	34

(Continued)

Table 7.2 Employment Profile of all Political Scientists in the Survey (% Within Region) (Continued)

	Total	North America	Western Europe	Northern Europe	Southern Europe	Eastern Europe	Latin America and Caribbean	Asia-Pacific	Africa
9 or fewer FTE academic staff	**13**	20	12	2	13	16	19	21	13
Institution									
50,000 or more FTE students	**13**	20	12	2	13	16	19	21	13
30,000–49,000 FTE students	**20**	24	20	13	18	15	24	26	34
20,000–29,000 FTE students	**18**	20	18	20	12	14	22	17	16
10,000–19,000 FTE students	**21**	21	21	26	21	17	14	19	18
9,000 or fewer FTE students	**28**	16	29	38	37	39	21	18	18
Sector									
Public	**79**	64	89	90	87	84	53	70	79
Private	**13**	25	6	2	10	8	35	16	16
Nonprofit	**8**	12	5	8	3	8	12	14	5
Number respondents	2446	359	511	462	235	188	219	281	145

Source: ECPR-IPSA World of Political Science survey (Norris), Spring 2019.

who responded in the survey (i.e., including graduate students and the retired, not just those currently academic employment) by region, including their work status, job security, academic status, department, and institution.

Overall, almost three-quarters (72%) of survey respondents worldwide were in full-time academic employment, while 6 percent were in part-time academic posts, with 12 percent in postgraduate study. These proportions did not vary substantially by region except in Latin America, where only 57 percent were in full-time academic employment. Overall, two-thirds were in positions with continuous contracts (tenured or tenure line), while one-third (30%) worked with fixed-term contracts without job security. This situation was reversed in North American universities, however, where only 36 percent of political scientists now hold continuous contracts, fewer than in any other world region. As previous reports suggest (AAUP, 2015; Currie, Deangelis, deBoer, Huisman, & Lacotte, 2003), casualization of the academic work-force, and the use of adjuncts, postdocs, and instructors, has gone furthest in American higher education.

When these figures were broken down by gender, more women were found to be in the early stages of the academic career pipeline; thus, in the survey, women are 44 percent of graduate students and 37 percent of lecturers and senior lecturers, dropping to 28 percent of full professors, and only 22 percent of more senior academic leadership positions, such as deans and pro vice-chancellors. Among women in academic employment, slightly more are in part-time (39%) than full-time positions (35%). A higher proportion of women are also working on fixed-term contracts (44%) rather than on continuous contracts with tenure (30%). The profile by birth cohort also shows a similar profile, with women one-quarter (26%) of the baby boomers, 35 percent of Gen X, but 43 percent of the Millennials. This suggests that processes of demographic change may gradually strengthen gender equality in the profession, but only if women graduates do not subsequently drop out from the leaky pipeline due to structural barriers experienced in recruitment, working conditions, research awards, publications, promotion, and retention. Further analysis elsewhere in this book examines the gendered analysis further (see Engeli & Mügge, chapter 9).

The distribution of academic ranks by region varies, but this may be due to lack of uniform nomenclatures even among English-speaking nations; for example, the terms "Lecturer and Senior Lecturer" are traditionally commonly used to describe academic ranks in the United Kingdom, while "Assistant and Associate Professor" are standard in the United States. Overall, one-fifth of respondents were full professors, but this proportion rose to one-third in North America. Only 47 percent of respondents were working or studying in a Department of Political Science, although this was more common in North America, while fully one-fifth of political scientists were based in Departments of Social Science, with a more multidisciplinary organizational structure. There was a broad distribution across regions by departmental size (measured by the number of full-time equivalent (FTE) academic staff) and by institutional size. Lastly, 79 percent of respondents were studying or working in public-sector institutions, especially in Europe, although again the labor market in North American differed, with more private and nonprofit sector universities.

3.4 Evaluating Changes in the Profession

There are both positive and negative consequences from the way that higher education has been transformed in recent years. Potentially these developments may be expected to erode job security and increase pressures on academic productivity, while also expanding opportunities to network and collaborate more widely with colleagues around the world. To see how political scientists responded, the WPS survey asked participants to evaluate a wide range of twenty-one items in terms of whether they thought that academic life has changed during the last five years for better or worse. The mean scores on the five-point evaluative scales are shown in figure 7.3. Overall, there are several aspects which colleagues rated poorly, believing that things had got a lot or somewhat worse, including job security, pay, and working conditions, administrative duties within the university, and pressures to publish and teach. Yet these were the exceptions, and in general colleagues evaluated changes more positively on fifteen items, notably in methodological and technical skills, social diversity within the profession, and opportunities for collaboration and networking. The growth of gender equality and developments in methods training are regarded as welcome developments.

The twenty-one items in figure 7.3 were subject to Principal Component factor analysis with varimax rotation, and the analysis suggested that these fell into four underlying dimensions. Accordingly, the items were summed and converted into standardized 100-point scales, where a higher score reflects a more positive assessment. The results in table 7.3 confirm that working conditions were seen most negatively, with the results fairly similar across regions with the exception of Africa, which regarded changes in working conditions as improving. The scales on professional standards, academic opportunities and skills, and relevance in political science were positive across all world regions but especially so again in Africa, which is a welcome sign of progress. In general, the reactions to change suggest that developments have been global in impact and there are reasons for optimism in welcoming expanded opportunities and skills in the profession.

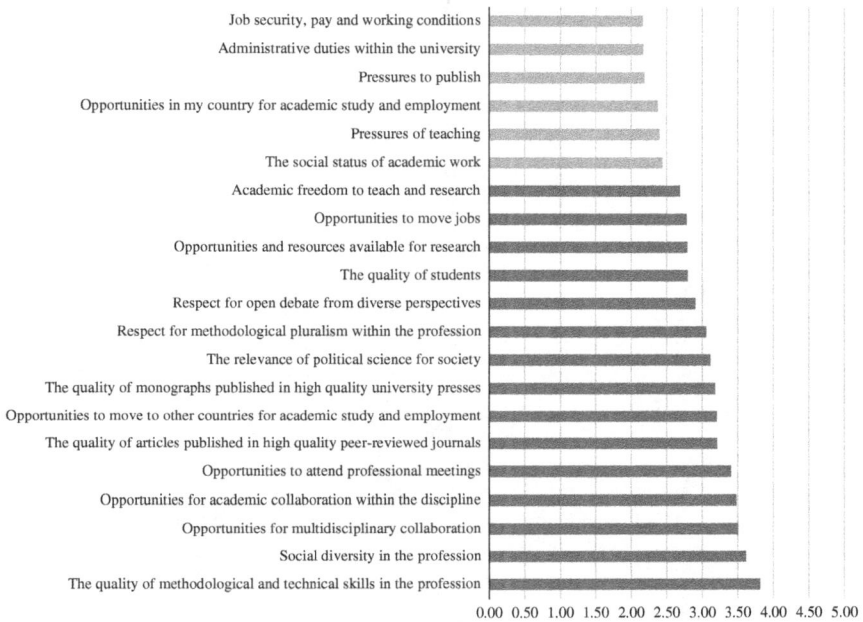

Figure 7.3 shows a horizontal bar chart with the following labels from top to bottom:

Job security, pay and working conditions
Administrative duties within the university
Pressures to publish
Opportunities in my country for academic study and employment
Pressures of teaching
The social status of academic work
Academic freedom to teach and research
Opportunities to move jobs
Opportunities and resources available for research
The quality of students
Respect for open debate from diverse perspectives
Respect for methodological pluralism within the profession
The relevance of political science for society
The quality of monographs published in high quality university presses
Opportunities to move to other countries for academic study and employment
The quality of articles published in high quality peer-reviewed journals
Opportunities to attend professional meetings
Opportunities for academic collaboration within the discipline
Opportunities for multidisciplinary collaboration
Social diversity in the profession
The quality of methodological and technical skills in the profession

0.00 0.50 1.00 1.50 2.00 2.50 3.00 3.50 4.00 4.50 5.00

Figure 7.3 Evaluating Changes in the Profession during the Last Five Years. *Note*: Q10–11: *"Academic life is often thought to be in a state of change. Using the following scale, based on your experience, please indicate whether you think the quality of the following aspects of academic life have changed over the last five years. Got a lot worse (1), got somewhat worse (2), no change (3), got somewhat better (4), got a lot better (5)."* Mean scores. *Source*: ECPR-IPSA World of Political Science survey (Norris), Spring 2019.

3.5 Roles

What of role perceptions? Some suggest a decline over time has occurred in the policy-relevant work of political scientists, such as providing policy advocacy and advice designed for a broad public affairs audience, in favor of more technical pure scientific research published in specialist academic journals. On the basis of time-series trends in articles published in the *APSR*, some claim that the American profession has opted for rigor, such as formal models and quantitative techniques, at the expense of relevance and policy recommendations (Desch, 2019). To explore role priorities, respondents were asked to rate the importance of nineteen roles using five-point Likert scales. Figure 7.4 illustrates the relative importance of roles, which displays a mix of priorities, as expected in academic life where there are many competing tasks and responsibilities to be juggled. The abstract goal of "advancing scholarly knowledge" was regarded as most important, but other roles which were also rated highly include the more pragmatic aim of achieving a life–work balance, encouraging students to learn and having a well-paid and secure

Table 7.3 Evaluating Changes in the Profession

	Total	North America	Western Europe	Northern Europe	Southern Europe	Eastern Europe	Latin America and Caribbean	Asia-Pacific	Africa
Working conditions	47	47	47	44	46	51	49	48	58
Academic opportunities	63	57	67	62	63	66	59	62	61
Professional standards	55	66	66	66	65	64	69	66	71
Skills and relevance	63	60	64	63	63	62	64	62	71
Number of respondents	2446	359	511	462	235	188	219	281	146

Notes: Q10–11: "Academic life is often thought to be in a state of change. Using the following scale, based on your experience, please indicate whether you think the quality of the following aspects of academic life have changed over the last five years. Got a lot worse, got somewhat worse, no change, got somewhat better, got a lot better." Principal Component factor analysis was used to determine the dimensionality of all the items listed in figure 1. These items were then summed and converted into standardized 100-point scales, where a higher number represents a more positive assessment of change.

Working conditions: for example, changes in job security, pay, status, pressures to teach and publish, academic freedom

Academic opportunities: for example, changes in opportunities to study and work abroad, to attend professional meetings, to collaborate, to move jobs

Professional standards: for example, changes in the quality of articles, methodological skills, books, students, and social diversity in the profession

Skills and relevance: for example, methodological pluralism, relevance to society, multidisciplinary collaboration

Source: ECPR-IPSA World of Political Science survey (Norris), Spring 2019.

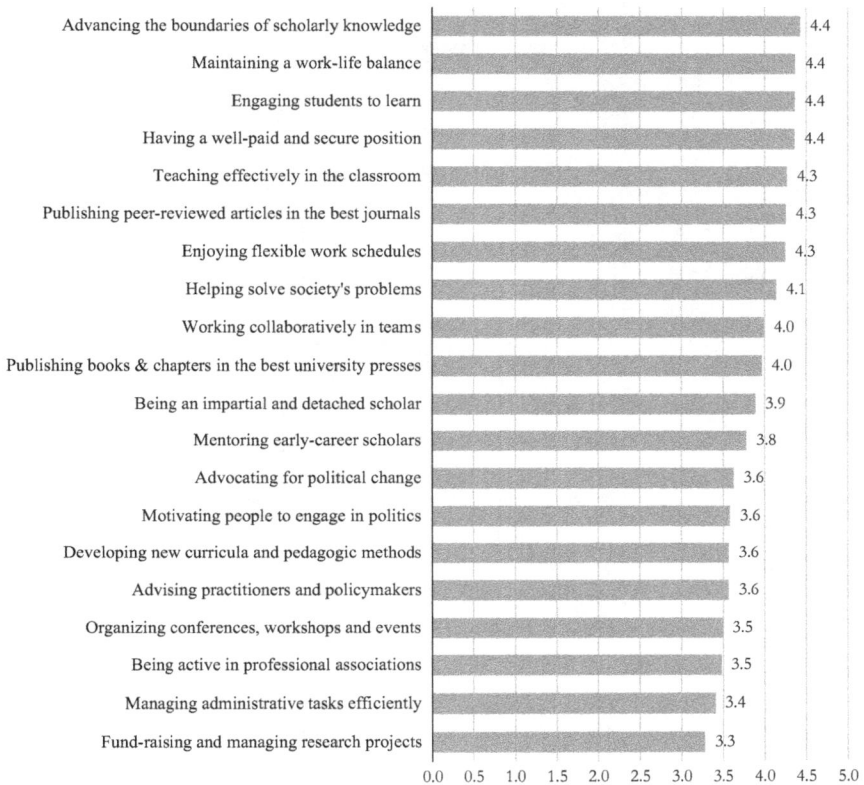

Figure 7.4 The Importance of Roles. *Note: How important are each of the following to you personally?* The importance of different role scales are measures using 1–5 scales, where a higher score represents greater importance. The bars reflect the mean scores. *Source*: ECPR-IPSA World of Political Science survey (Norris), Spring 2019. N. 2,466.

position. The roles regarded as least important concern fund-raising and management research projects as well as handling administrative tasks efficiently. To reduce these items for comparison, Principal Component factor analysis showed that responses fell into five broad dimensions, including the saliency of research management, policy advocacy, teaching, publishing, and work–life balance. Table 7.4 shows that there was a broad consensus about role priorities across world regions, with a great deal of emphasis on work–life balance and publishing, closely followed by teaching and policy impact.

3.6 Subfields and Methods

Finally, what is the focus of the profession in terms of subfields of interest, what are the methods commonly used in political science, how have subfields

Table 7.4 Perceived Importance of Roles by Region

	Total	North America	Western Europe	Northern Europe	Southern Europe	Eastern Europe	Latin America and Caribbean	Asia-Pacific	Africa
Research management	71	65	68	69	73	72	73	73	87
Teaching	80	79	77	80	81	79	84	82	89
Publishing	84	80	83	84	85	85	82	86	92
Policy advocacy	75	73	71	73	75	72	79	78	88
Work–life balance	86	86	84	85	87	85	85	87	90
Number of respondents	2446	359	511	462	235	188	219	281	146

Note: "*How important are each of the following to you personally?* The importance of different role scales is constructed as standardized 100-point scales from the items in figure 4, where a higher score represents greater importance.
Source: ECPR-IPSA World of Political Science survey (Norris), Spring 2019.

and methodological skills changed over time, and has there been growing transatlantic convergence in methods (Rihoux, Kittel, & Moses, 2008)? Table 7.5 illustrates the proportion of political scientists across a range of major subfields in the discipline. The table shows a fairly balanced and equal distribution across nearly all areas, rather than concentration in just one or two sectors. The one exception is normative political theory, which appears to be confined today to a very small minority of scholars. Moreover, there is a fairly even spread of subfields across regions rather than any clear contrasts between North and South, East and West.

Similar observations can be made if we compare the main methods most commonly used in the profession. Table 7.6 shows that qualitative and historical methods prevail, used by 28 percent of political scientists, along with normative, analytical, and conceptual methods (20%) but behavioral methods rank third most common (18%). There was little difference by region, for example remarkable similarities between North America and Europe. Despite fears that formal modeling may have taken over in the *APSR* (Desch, 2019), a broader comparison demonstrates that rational choice and formal models remain the least commonly used methods in political science worldwide, while qualitative approaches predominate.

We are unable to compare trends in the profession over the time, without equivalent prior survey data. Instead, however, cohort analysis by decade of birth can be used as a proxy to analyze convergence or divergence over time. This gives a sense of the contrasts between older and younger generations, which are likely to have long-term consequences if they are sustained through new appointments, retirements, and thus turnover in the workforce. Figure 7.5 shows that two subfields have grown in popularity among the younger cohorts, namely political behavior and methods. The 1960s may have been seen as the birth of the "behavioral revolution" but the evidence here suggests increased interest in this subfield which may be due to the growing availability of survey and experimental data, and the skills needed for analysis, along with the perennial interest in topics in mass political behavior and attitudes such as issues of participation, public opinion, and voting choice (see Dalton, chapter 5). By contrast, the study of political economy and public policy are both more popular among the older than younger cohorts in the profession. If we turn to similar comparisons to understand cohort changes in methods, shown in Figure 7.6, the techniques used for econometrics show a substantial gain in popularity among younger cohorts of scholars, suggesting that the techniques used for large-N regression analysis have grown in popularity, even if the study of political economy has declined, while policy analysis techniques also saw a fall among younger cohort.

Table 7.5 Subfields by Region

	ALL	North America	Western Europe	Northern Europe	Southern Europe	Eastern Europe	Latin America and Caribbean	Asia-Pacific	Africa
Political institutions	15	13	14	16	18	14	17	13	16
Political behavior	15	14	18	16	17	14	15	15	9
International relations	14	17	12	12	10	16	11	16	22
Comparative politics	13	17	14	14	12	13	14	13	10
Public policy	12	9	12	12	14	10	13	10	13
Social movements	11	10	9	12	13	14	9	15	9
Methods	10	10	12	9	9	11	11	8	6
Political economy	8	10	8	7	6	5	8	7	11
Normative political theory	2	1	2	2	2	3	3	3	3
Col percent (%)	100	100	100	100	100	100	100	100	100
Total responses	5967	875	1292	1108	569	465	572	729	357

Note: Q:4: "Which of the following best describes your subfields of interest. Check as many as appropriate." Multiple response items. Percentages and totals are based on 5,667 responses.

Source: ECPR-IPSA World of Political Science survey (Norris), Spring 2019.

Table 7.6 Methods by Region

	ALL	North America	Western Europe	Northern Europe	Southern Europe	Eastern Europe	Latin America and Caribbean	Asia-Pacific	Africa
Qualitative and historical	28	25	26	28	26	27	28	31	32
Normative, analytical and conceptual	20	14	15	17	20	24	18	24	25
Behavioral	17	18	19	18	20	14	17	14	15
Policy analysis	13	12	12	11	15	17	12	15	12
Econometrics	9	13	11	12	7	7	12	6	4
Experimental	6	8	7	8	4	5	5	4	4
Big data	5	5	7	5	4	5	5	4	3
Rational choice and formal models	3	4	3	2	3	2	4	3	4
Col percent (%)	100	100	100	100	100	100	100	100	100
Total responses	2446	790	1020	893	446	384	346	511	214

Note: Q: "Which of the following methods do you commonly use? Check as many as appropriate." Multiple response items. Percentages and totals are based on 4,604 responses.

Source: ECPR-IPSA World of Political Science survey (Norris), Spring 2019.

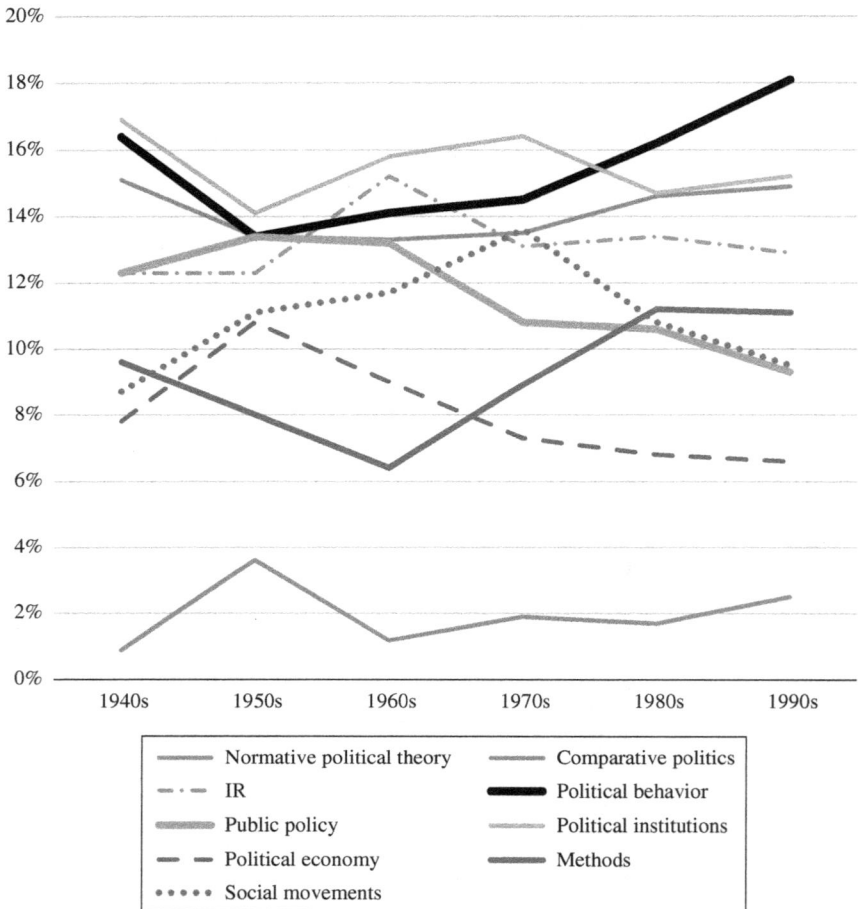

Figure 7.5 Subfield by Decade of Birth. *Note*: Multiple responses. Percentages are based on 4346 responses. *Source*: ECPR-IPSA World of Political Science survey (Norris), Spring 2019. N. respondents 2,466.

4. CONCLUSIONS AND IMPLICATIONS

There are many reasons to believe that internationalization—and the accelerated flow of peoples, communications, and labor—has transformed the academic world of higher education. The discipline of political science is not immune from these broader developments. Bonds from collaboration, networking, and knowledge exchanged across national and even regional borders appear increasingly common. Both IPSA and the ECPR have made an invaluable contribution toward this process, through innumerable activities including organizing international conferences and workshops, sharing

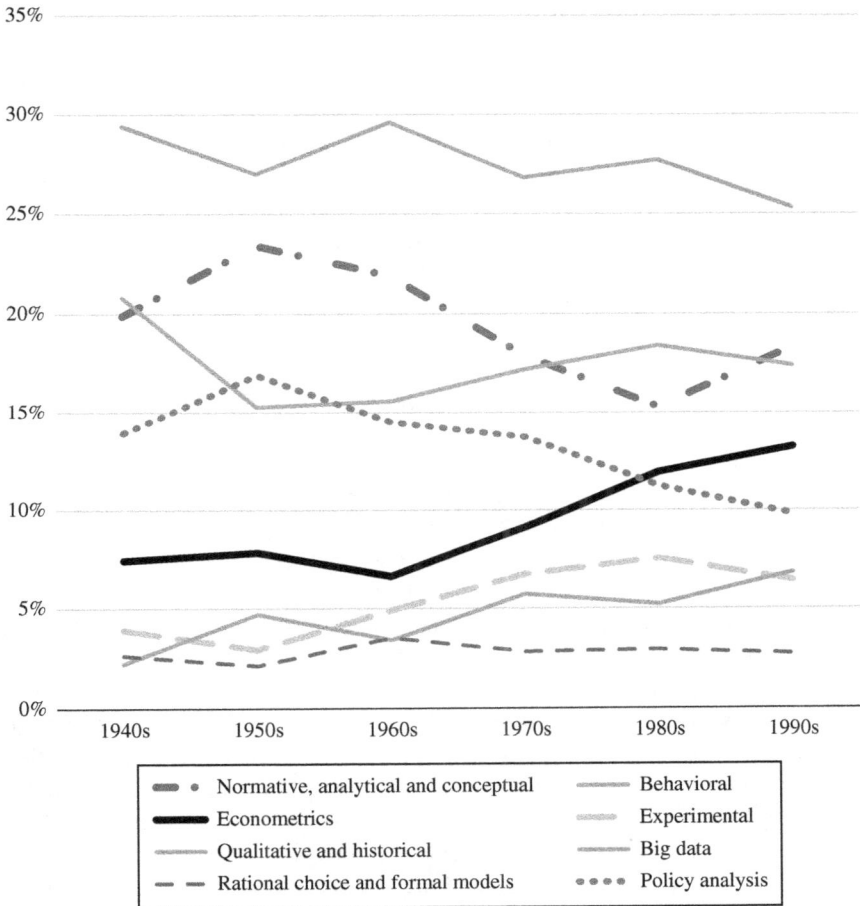

Figure 7.6   Methods by Decade of Birth. *Note*: Multiple responses. Percentages are based on 4,543 responses. *Source*: ECPR-IPSA World of Political Science survey (Norris), Spring 2019. N. respondents 2,466.

information about the profession, and providing training and mobility programs expanding opportunities for early career scholars.

This chapter contributes survey evidence with global coverage from thousands of political scientists working and living in over 100 countries in an attempt to understand some of the consequences of these developments for the profession. The results suggest several major findings, which can be regarded as both the best of times and perhaps the worst of times.

First, *considerable similarities in political science as a profession exist in regions around the world*, from shared working conditions and professional qualifications to attitudes toward academic change, role priorities, research subfields, and methods. Yet not everywhere is identical, by any means, and important path-dependent differences continue to color the culture and ethos of political science around the world.

Secondly, some developments during the last five years are regarded negatively by political scientists, including concern about worsening working conditions (job security and pay), the burden of administrative duties within universities, and growing pressures to publish and teach. Yet the overall picture which emerges is one where colleagues remain fairly buoyant about several other important developments, including expanded opportunities for academic mobility and collaboration, growing social diversity, and the improved quality of methodological and technical skills in the profession. Finally, cohort analysis comparing older and younger generations indicate the increased popularity of the subfields of political behavior and survey methods, but less focus on public policy analysis. Methods have also changed, as well, with growing use of the techniques of econometrics and big data among early career scholars, and less use of policy analysis methods.

How these developments should be interpreted remains a matter open for debate, however, and indeed shifts may be regarded as both better *and* worse (Knight, 2013). Proponents of "slow political science," analogous to the slow food movement, emphasize the value of preserving intellectual heterogeneity and path-dependent local traditions. The normative tensions concerning the desirability of fast and slow political science continue to reverberate in the discipline. In the past, deep-rooted intellectual traditions and ideological differences were thought to divide political scientists in different regions of the world, including within Europe (McKay, 1988, 1991). Critics argue that internationalization may generate uniformity or "one-size-fits-all," accompanied by a loss of local cultures, depth, and diversity within the discipline, losing the distinctive flavor of European political science. Moreover, on a more anecdotal basis, anyone attending international, regional, or national meetings can casually observe that, despite numerous common linkages, even today the flavor and ethos of political science continue to differ from one place to another, whether in terms of concepts and languages, the focus and methods of research topics, or the roles and rewards of academic life. In short, Cambridge (Massachusetts) is not Cambridge (the United Kingdom). Therefore, the effects of globalization should not be exaggerated; many scholars still choose to focus on "somewhere," not "everywhere," with concerns are rooted in what happens within their local community and nation-state.

Neoliberal reforms in higher education can also be blamed for worsening inequality between institutions, by reinforcing the power and reputation of prestigious and well-endowed university centers of excellence located in wealthy Western nations, which can attract talent and human resources at the expense of institutions located in developing societies at the "periphery."

Open labor markets and pressures on academic productivity can also be rightly regarded as exacerbating inequality among sectors and individuals within the profession, generously rewarding international stars who can take advantage of expanded opportunities for global impact while penalizing adjuncts, temporary instructors, and part-time research assistants struggling to gain a foothold in teaching and publishing on the starting rungs of academic careers. Some issues of genuine concern are highlighted by this study, particularly deteriorating working conditions and the loss of job security, with new potential threats to academic freedom of expression on the horizon.

Alternatively, however, the consequences of developments can also be regarded more positively. For those favoring cosmopolitanism, the future of political science where national barriers are eroded suggests growing multiculturalism and openness, a more welcoming climate for social diversity and gender equality, and stronger technical skills in the profession. Cosmopolitanism promises substantial gains for international scientific knowledge, collaborative intellectual advances, and the multicultural exchange of peoples, evidence, and ideas. This seems more important than ever at a time when nationalist forces and isolationist walls appear resurgent in politics, when the evidentiary basis of factual information is under challenge, and when scientific expertise and impartiality in the social and natural sciences are criticized as irrelevant and dismissed as partisan. The profession should repeat the ECPR-IPSA WPS survey in future years to monitor developments, expand country coverage, explore additional themes, and replicate the analysis. This process can help us to understand more fully how to respond to the profound trends transforming the discipline and higher education around the globe.

NOTES

1. https://www.aaup.org/sites/default/files/Academic%20Labor%20Force%20Trends%201975-2015.pdf.
2. See https://trip.wm.edu/.
3. The ECPR-IPSA World of Political Science questionnaire and dataset is available from https://doi.org/10.7910/DVN/FXKVXJ.

REFERENCES

Abu-Laban, Y., Sawer, M., & St-Laurent, M. (2018). *IPSA gender and diversity monitoring report 2017*. Montreal: IPSA.

Altbach, P., Reisberg, L., & Rumbley, L. E. (2009). *Trends in global higher education*. Paris: UNESCO.

Bardi, L. (2011). Forty years of political science in Europe: The European consortium for political research celebrates its ruby anniversary. *PS: Political Science & Politics, 44*(1), 93–95.

Bauder, H. (2015). The international mobility if academics: A labor market perspective. *International Migration, 53*(1), 83–96.

Bok, D. (2015). *Higher Education in America*. Princeton, NJ: Princeton University Press.

Brady, H. E., & Collier, D. (2004). *Rethinking social inquiry: Diverse tools shared standards*. Maryland: Rowman & Littlefield Publishers.

Camerlo, M., Doyle, D., & Garcia Diez, F. (2018). The European political science agenda: A multilevel analysis from a country perspective. *European Political Science, 17*(1), 1–9.

Castells, M. (2000). *The networked society*. Oxford: Blackwell.

Chanda, N. (2007). *Bound together: How traders, preachers, adventurers, and warriors shaped globalization*. New Haven: Yale University Press.

Currie, J., Deangelis, R., deBoer, H., Huisman, J., & Lacotte, C. (2003). *Globalizing practices and university responses: European and Anglo-American differences*. NY: Praeger.

Deardorff, D. K., de Wit, H., & Heyl, J. (Eds.). (2012). *The SAGE handbook of international higher education*. Thousand Oaks, CA: SAGE Publications.

Desch, M. C. (2019, February 29). How political science became irrelevant. *The Chronicle of Higher Education*.

EUA. (2010). *Salzburg II recommendations*. Brussels: European University Association.

Goodin, R. E., & Klingemann, H.-D. (1996). Political science as a discipline. In *A new handbook of political science*. New York: Oxford University Press.

Harley, S. (2010). The impact of research selectivity on academic work and identity in UK universities. *Studies in Higher Education, 27*(2).

Held, D., McGrew, A., Goldblatt, D., & Perraton, J. (1999). *Global transformations: Politics, economics, and culture*. Stanford, CA: Stanford University Press.

IIE. (2018). *A world on the move: Trends in global student mobility*. New York: Institute of International Education (IIE) Center for Academic Mobility.

Kendall, G., Woodward, I., & Skrbis, Z. (2009). *The sociology of cosmopolitanism: Globalization, identity, culture and government*. London: Palgrave MacMillan.

Kim, H. J., & Grofman, B. (2019). The political science 400: With citation counts by cohort, gender, and subfield. *PS: Political Science and Politics, 52*(2), 296–311.

King, R. F., & Marian, C. G. (2008). Defining political science: A cross-national survey. *European Political Science, 7*(2), 207–19.

Knight, J. (2013). The changing landscape of higher education internationalization: For better or worse? *Perspectives, Policy and Practices in Higher Education, 17*(3).

Lima, E., Morschbacher, M., & Peres, P. (2018). Three decades of the International Political Science Review (IPSR): A map of the methodological preferences in IPSR articles. *International Political Science Review, 39*(5), 679–89.

Lublin, D. (2018). The case for English. *European Political Science, 17*(3), 358–65.

Maliniak, D., Peterson, S., & Tierney, M. J. (2019). Policy-relevant publications and tenure decisions in international relations. PS-*Political Science & Politics, 52*(2), 318–24.

Maliniak, D., Oakes, A., Peterson, M. S., & Tierney, M. J. (2011). International relations in the U.S. academy. *International Studies Quarterly, 55*, 437–64.

Masuoka, N., Grofman, B., & Feld, S. (2007). The political science 400: A 20-year update. *PS: Political Science and Politics.*

McDermott, R., & Hatemi, P. K. (2010). Emerging models of collaboration in political science: Changes, benefits, and challenges. *PS: Political Science and Politics, 43*(1), 49–58.

McKay, D. (1988). Why is there a European political science? *PS: Political Science and Politics, XXI,* Fall, 1051–56.

McKay, D. (1991). Is European political science inferior to or different from American political science? *European Journal of Political Research, 20,* 459–66.

Mény, Y. (2010). Political science as a profession. *European Political Science, 9*(SI), 11–21.

Newton, K. (1991). The European consortium for political research. *European Journal for Political Research, 20,* 445–58.

Norris, P. (1997). Towards a cosmopolitan political science? *European Journal of Political Research, 30*(1), 17–34.

Norris, P., & Inglehart, R. (2009). *Cosmopolitan communications.* New York: Cambridge University Press.

Norris, P., & Inglehart, R. (2011). *Sacred and secular.* New York: Cambridge University Press.

OECD. (2018). *Education at a glance 2018: OECD indicators.* Paris: OECD Publishing.

OECD. (2019). *Trends shaping education 2019.* Paris: OECD Publishing.

Rihoux, B., Kittel, B., & Moses, J. W. (2008). Methodology: Opening windows across Europe . . . and the Atlantic. *PS: Political Science and Politics, 41*(1), 255–58.

Rose, R. (1990). Institutionalizing professional political science in Europe: A dynamic model. *European Journal of Political Research, 18,* 581–603.

Savigny, H. (2010). Looking back to move forward: Historicizing the construction of disciplinary narratives in European political science and international relations. *European Political Science, 9*(1), S99–S110.

Teele, D. L., & Thelen, K. (2017). Gender in the journals: Publication patterns in political science. *PS: Political Science and Politics, 50*(2), 433–47.

Wagner, C. (2018). *The collaborative era in science.* NY: Palgrave Macmillan.

Wihlborg, M., & Robson, S. (2017). Internationalization of higher education: Drivers, rationales, priorities, values and impacts. *European Journal of Higher Education, 8*(1), 8–18.

Chapter 8

From Imagined Disciplinary Communities to Building Professional Solidarity

Political Science in Postcommunist Europe

Luciana Alexandra Ghica

When the European Consortium for Political Research (ECPR) was established in 1970 as the first professional association on the continent explicitly aiming to foster cooperation among political scientists beyond national academic communities, *European* referred to a very small place: a group of just eight universities from six countries situated in Western and Northern Europe—France, Germany, the Netherlands, Norway, Sweden, and the United Kingdom (Blondel, 1973). In September 2019, at the end of the last full academic year before its fiftieth anniversary, the ECPR listed on its website (www. ecprnet.eu) 329 members in 46 countries from all continents except Africa and the small island states of Oceania. Despite this global expansion, European institutions still make up 85 percent of its members. More significantly, the consortium continues to be largely Western and Northern European, both geographically and symbolically. In 2019, 46 percent of its members were from the original six countries, with British and German universities accounting for about two in three members within the original group, and one in three members overall. Also, in the three decades since the organization expanded beyond its initial geographical locus, it attracted more members from just four Organization for Economic Co-operation and Development (OECD) countries (i.e., the United States, Canada, Australia, and New Zealand) than from all the twenty-four European former communist states or inheritors of such states (with seven of them never having been represented in the ECPR).[1] Furthermore, none of the current four ECPR journals has ever had managing editors based in Central or Eastern European institutions. The number of articles published in the ECPR journals that have at least one Europe-based author outside Western or Northern Europe is also still significantly limited, although this is increasing.

Similar situations can be found within other European scientific infrastructures. For instance, at the European Confederation of Political Science Associations (ECPSA, est. 2007), an organization comprised of national political science associations, where membership fees have been mostly symbolical, membership from Central and Eastern European countries has been sporadic. Likewise, at the European Political Science Association (EPSA, est. 2010), where membership is individual and fees are significantly lower than for participation in ECPR events, the voices from postcommunist countries have been rarely heard, a fact that can be easily noticed in the programs of the organization's scientific events. The scarcity of authors and editors from Central and Eastern Europe can also be noticed in highly ranked Europe-based journals in other sub/transdisciplinary areas, such as policy studies and international relations (e.g., *Journal of European Public Policy*, *European Journal of International Relations*). In short, three decades after the beginning of the largest wave of democratization on the continent, political scientists from certain European countries, particularly those from the former communist space, are still largely invisible in mainstream European political science. This democratization wave radically transformed the political dynamics of the continent and provided plenty of food for thought for many political scientists as it involved multiple issues at the core of the discipline. Given the privileged linguistic and empirical proximity that researchers from Central and Eastern Europe had with these objects of study, one might have expected that they would advance quickly and in large numbers to the forefront of European and global political science. This has not happened yet.

In this chapter, I take a closer look at this puzzle, exploring the dynamics of political science in the former communist space in relation to the scope, evolution and institutionalization of European political science. In the first section, I briefly discuss how a narrative on catching up with the "West" has emerged in debates on the evolution of the discipline at the European level. During the Cold War the United States was often imagined as the archetypal institutional model that European political science would/should follow, especially in comparative politics; this linear modernization narrative was later adopted in the literature on the evolution of Central and Eastern European political science and still dominates discussions on the topic. In the second part, I argue that, while isolated from the European institutionalization process of the discipline during the Cold War, the scholarly communities in the region were not fully or equally closed to political science thinking or institutional practices before the collapse of the communist regimes. In fact, before World War II, the intellectual and institutional patterns of scientific development in many of these countries were largely similar to those emerging elsewhere in Europe, including in matters of political thinking. During communism, there was also a large variety of institutional settings through which exposure to "Western" political science was possible. In the last section, I show that after the Cold War this variation increased and that the process of professionalization and institutionalization of the discipline has not been linear, nor is it irreversible. Furthermore, with few exceptions, political science in the region seems to be currently more threatened by economic and institutional/structural vulnerabilities than by open political or ideological interference. Most of these vulnerabilities, such as the lack of adequate and predictable funding for social sciences and humanities, or institutional pressures to unify departments for financial reasons, are acutely present across the continent. Therefore, the time has come to rethink the development of political science in Europe beyond the borders of our imagined communities and include within our agenda on the study of political science as a discipline more consistent discussions on scholarly and professional solidarity.

1. IMAGINING POLITICAL SCIENCE IN EUROPE

During the last fifty years, the debates on the viability and scope of Europe-based political research and political science as a discipline in Europe have expanded within the ECPR and elsewhere. Even if not always explicit, this epistemic ecosystem has operated on two major premises: (1) political science is conditioned by the possibility that political questions are settled by scientific argument rather than tradition or authority (Mackenzie, 1971); and (2) the knowledge and skills that political science offer are fundamental for preserving democracy (Newton & Vallès, 1991). Consequently, the study of democracy itself is central to political science.

Before the Cold War ended, democracy could be found in Europe mostly in its western and northern parts. Therefore, the study of Western and Northern European political regimes became central to the emerging European political research agenda. Since funding and institutional models developed within the already-well-established U.S. political science community had been instrumental to the establishment of this agenda, many of the methodological tools and research questions built initially for the study of U.S. political institutions were also imported to Europe. In this process, the more coagulated disciplinary networks, such as the ECPR, had a major role in framing the debates (Newton & Boncourt, 2010); some research areas, such as policy studies (Geva-May & Pal, 2018), also strongly connected the European and U.S. scholarly communities. Yet, the variety of institutional settings, even within the small set of cases of Northern and Western European democracies, did not fit well with many of the U.S.-generated theories and instruments. This stimulated the study of comparative politics, which then served as a means of emancipation for European political science (De Sousa et al. 2010).

However, the issues of the viability, legitimacy, and scientific autonomy of European political science have remained highly sensitive. While European political scientists seem to be more familiar with U.S. scholarship than U.S. political scientists are with European research (McKay, 1988), European political science started to be represented in the debates on the evolution, scope, and institutionalization of the discipline as rather underdeveloped compared to its U.S. counterpart (Gunnell & Easton, 1991; Hix, 2004). Imagining a linear developmental pattern, many scholars on both sides of the Atlantic assumed that the European political science agenda should/would necessarily follow the allegedly more developed U.S. one (Goodin & Klingemann, 1998). Yet, as both European and U.S. scholars argued well into the 2000s, neither is U.S. political science inherently superior, nor is there necessarily a convergence of European (or global) political research toward the U.S. agenda (McKay, 1991; Schmitter, 2002). Moreover, the perceived differences are centered largely on evaluation tools and procedures (Erne, 2007), while a noteworthy European influence on U.S. scholarship also exists and goes beyond the more obvious (European) political theory tradition (Adcock, 2006; Farr, 2006).

When scholars from outside Western and Northern Europe joined this disciplinary debate, once their countries started to democratize, most of its focus was set around the relation between European and U.S. political science. However, as the disciplinary landscape grew and became more diverse, it also stimulated the development of large-scale assessments of the discipline within Europe, especially after the Cold War. Whether consciously or not, in such overviews *Europe* has most usually been equated with "Western" Europe (Berndtson, 2012; Bull, 2007; Quermonne, 1996; Rose, 1990; Schneider, 2014). Even when the focus was explicitly on *Western Europe*, such as in Klingemann (2007), the label did not designate a clearly defined geographical region, but a rather arbitrary area that was not necessarily physically contiguous and which reflected certain political divisions or constantly changing ad hoc categories. For instance, Turkey was traditionally listed as Western European (Klingemann, 2008) and thus rarely compared with other postauthoritarian cases. Similarly, the surveys of political science in Central and Eastern Europe usually aimed to cover the postcommunist territories, but they did not include all of them and did not treat East Germany as a separate case (Eisfeld & Pal, 2010; Kaase, Sparschuch, & Wenninger, 2002; Klingemann, Kulesza, & Legutke, 2002).

The fact that defining *Europe* as *Western Europe* becomes the dominant narrative, particularly after the Cold War, connects directly to probably the most striking feature of the existing comparative scholarship on the topic; namely that it has been framed primarily by researchers in the "West," many of whom had been actively participating at that time in the larger debate on the autonomy and distinctiveness of European political science vis-à-vis the U.S. counterpart. When scholars from former communist countries started to (re)establish political science institutions in the "Western" canon, thus (re) discovering both academic freedom and the field as it evolved in the United States and around the ECPR agenda, it was the "Western" eye that first presented this process to an international audience. In fact, until Krauz-Mozer et al. (2015), no major comparative overview of European political science originated within the region. Scholars from Central and Eastern European countries and their scientific diaspora contributed to the literature on the evolution of the discipline rather as informants, writing short studies on their respective countries of origin but, in general, they had very little to say on how the comparison was framed across the region.

From the little available data, both "Westerners" and local informants initially told a similar story which reinforced the perceived superiority of "Western" institutions, including those of political science, with a logic not far from Fukuyama's "end of history" enthusiasm: the Central and East European countries would have properly discovered "Western" political science only after the Cold War because most of what had been produced during communism was heavily distorted ideologically. Therefore, the success of the discipline and the presence of researchers from this region in international networks would be just a matter of catching up with the "Western" canon. Similarly to classic modernization theories produced at the height of the Cold War's ideological confrontations, as well as to how European political science was initially represented as underdeveloped compared to the U.S. version, countries outside "Western" Europe were thus implicitly ranked in relation to the degree of closeness to "Western" institutions and research agendas, even if such a canon was not itself stable in time or clearly defined institutionally or intellectually. Within this linear logic, the systematic underrepresentation of institutions and scholars from Central and Eastern Europe in international scientific infrastructures, such as the ECPR, would indicate both chronic scientific underdevelopment and a limited level of success of the democratization processes in the region.

After the fashion of studying the European transitions to democracy faded, when faced with newer or sometimes more rewarding topics, this simple yet powerful storyline also gradually diminished the appeal of international research and network-building for scholars in the region. Fueling a vicious circle, it further contributed to imagining Central and Eastern European scientific communities as internationally isolated both before and after communism. In addition, it diminished the timely access to and exchange of expertise on empirical data relevant for addressing analytically and practically the post-communist contexts, as well as the larger puzzle of vulnerabilities of democratic consolidation that affect even long-established democracies (Bernhard & Jasiewicz, 2015). This isolation not only contradicts the vision of those political scientists who had hoped for a fast and substantial pan-European integration of political research even during the Cold War (Rokkan, 1973), but ultimately contributes to undermining the public reputation and the capacity of political science to provide working and timely solutions to issues at the core of what the discipline is supposed to address. Given the marginality of the reflection on political science as a discipline within the economy of modern political science teaching and research infrastructures, this narrative is also what the new generations of internationalized political scientists in Central and Eastern Europe have most often first discovered about their own scientific communities.

2. THE EVOLUTION OF POLITICAL SCIENCE IN CENTRAL AND EASTERN EUROPE

When modern political science(s) started to emerge in several European countries and the United States as an autonomous discipline in the second half of the nineteenth century, most of Central and Eastern Europe was still divided among three empires. Several territories gradually started to gain independence, usually through violent conflicts, mainly between the 1870s and World War I. Although some scholarly institutions were hundreds of years old (e.g., Charles University in Prague, Jagiellonian University in Krakow), most of the higher education systems in these countries emerged largely in the second half of the nineteenth century, modeled on the Humboldtian university, and their development was strongly connected to the process of nation-state building. In some parts of the region, due to further territorial unifications and separations, these state-building processes were reset several times throughout the twentieth and twenty-first centuries, a fact that slowed down the development of national scientific communities. Political writings, particularly on the nation-state and political parties, as well as some incipient political science institutionalization, similar to what was happening at that time in other parts of Europe, existed in the region before World War II, most notably in Czechoslovakia, Hungary, Poland, and Romania. However, such texts and institutions addressed primarily local puzzles of nation-state building and did not generate the consciousness of distinct national or transnational epistemic communities in the field. Also, like in France, what could be acknowledged as political science expertise resided mostly within law departments (Ghica, 2014; Holzer & Pšeja, 2010; Sasinska-Klas, 2010).

Largely coinciding with the beginning of the behaviorist revolution that subsequently led to the ascendancy of the transatlantic connection in European political science which was briefly presented in the previous section, the instauration of the communist regimes suddenly isolated the local scientific communities. This happened mostly through the dismantling of independent social science research, the prohibition of noncommunist scientific literature, the physical elimination or forced emigration of scientists, and, crucially, through the adoption of pseudoscientific Marxist-Leninist teachings. The communist parties also built their own party schooling systems and distinct research institutions which ideologically controlled academia, while also providing the knowledge framework for the reproduction of the political, social, and economic systems that these regimes created (Tismăneanu, 2003). However, the relation between the party schooling and the rest of the national higher education and research infrastructure varied substantially throughout the region, sometimes even within a country. Such factors had significant long-term consequences on how political science emerged and developed in each of these countries.

An extreme case is Albania, which until about two decades ago had not experienced any significant form of democracy. After its independence in early twentieth century and subsequent state-building struggles, the country also had to construct almost its entire public education system from the ground up. In fact, communist infrastructures were established before the creation of the first modern university in Tirana, in 1957. This may partly explain: why the highly isolated Albanian communist regime survived for so long; why the low level of trust in the public sector initially led to the first generation of postcommunist elites being educated abroad; why the first political science department in an Albanian public university wasn't created until the 2000s; and why private universities were initially more successful in attracting political science candidates (Cami, 2010).

In the rest of the communist bloc, after the Stalinist period, new scholarship from the "West" gradually started to be accessed, even if it was still ideologically controlled. While in Bulgaria, Romania, the USSR, and, to a lesser extent, Czechoslovakia, knowledge about politics was concentrated mainly in the parallel institutions created by the communist party; in Hungary, Poland, and Yugoslavia, political science scholarship was more easily accessible via public universities (Powell & Shoup, 1970; Révész, 1967; Tismăneanu, 2003). This latter institutional setting allowed scientific research, particularly in Poland, to be slightly freer from political interference and allowed social scientists to be more connected to international academia (Sasinska-Klas, 2010). Additional international academic contacts were developed in Czechoslovakia, Hungary, Poland, and Yugoslavia through exchanges with "Western" Marxist scholars or through other disciplinary entry points less prone to ideological bias or political control (Falk, 2003). This strategy ultimately stimulated the international recognition of local scholars beyond the communist bloc or scientific networks (e.g., Zygmunt Bauman, Alfred Bibič). Debates on topics associated with "Western" democracies, such as civil society, as well as substantial empirical research on local administration, also emerged. This happened particularly in Yugoslavia, where the communist party promoted its vision of socialism through science while addressing issues specific to governing the federation and some of its republics (Kasapović, Petković, & Grdešić, 2010; Pavlović, 2010; Zajc, 2010).

These higher degrees of academic freedom allowed the establishment, in Hungarian, Polish, and Yugoslav public universities, of partly autonomous political science departments and research institutes, most of which are still in existence. In Czechoslovakia, during a brief intermezzo of liberalization in the 1960s, political science departments were created in Prague and Bratislava, but they were quickly dismantled after 1968, an experience that made the dialogue with or experiments in "Western" political science more difficult and highly sensitive until the fall of the communist regime (Holzer & Pšeja, 2010). Then again, a similar liberalization period in Romania did not generate the creation of political science departments, but it led to the University of Bucharest establishing probably the first Romanian academic journal in political science defined as an autonomous discipline (*Analele Universității din București. Științe Politice*) in the early 1970s. Articles published there reveal a rather extensive knowledge of many "Western" political scientists and debates of the period, particularly those written/translated in French (e.g., Raymond Aron, Maurice Duverger). However, these texts were heavily biased ideologically and the journal was fully controlled in both authorship and editorial policy by the communist party schooling and research system.

Despite such developments, when the communist regimes collapsed, the existing expertise on politics and political science was ideologically distorted in general, minimally connected to the "Western" scientific world and concentrated within the circles of the communist party elites (Eisfeld & Pal, 2010; Klingemann, Kulesza, & Legutke, 2002). That is why the establishment of new political science departments or curricula based on the "Western" canon, in the 1990s, was strongly perceived, at least initially, as a civic education duty and/or a symbolic triumph of democracy over dictatorship (Markarov, 2010). However, the human resources for building new political science epistemic communities and institutions were often lacking.

Many scholars had already left the region, largely due to political pressures. In exile, some of them contributed significantly to the discipline (e.g., Karl Deutsch, Mattei Dogan, David Mitrany, Karl Polanyi) and/or to the establishment of international academic infrastructures in the field (e.g., Serge Hurtig, Peter E. de Janosi). In general, this scientific diaspora maintained limited contact with their original scientific communities both during and after communism. However, in some cases such as Estonia (Pettai, 2010) what little contact there was had long-lasting effects on how the discipline has evolved in the region. Most significantly, in the 1980s Hungarian émigré George Soros founded and started to financially support the Open Society Institute (OSI), which pushed forward the agenda of democratization in the region through a growing network of foundations, as well as through several international private higher education initiatives, most notably the Central European University (CEU, est. 1991). This has gradually become the most significant university in the region in terms of globally recognized scientific output, especially in political science, as well as a major incubator of democratic, political, and academic elites in postcommunist countries.

Beyond these rather isolated cases of private initiatives, human capacity largely remained limited. Especially in the former Soviet space, many of the previous instructors of Marxist-Leninism, who survived the regime transformation, initially only changed the name of the curricula but not their content (Naumova, 2010). In countries where political science departments had been already created before the Cold War, most of the staff were usually maintained, but this generated tensions about institutional and curricular development, as well as increasingly visible rifts between the old guard and the new generation of scholars (Zajc, 2010). Sometimes the old guard could hold on to power by administratively overloading younger scholars and/or setting and implementing opaque and/or arbitrary criteria for professional advancement. In other countries, teaching staff had to be recruited from other social science and humanities departments, occasionally supplemented with foreign guest lecturers (including from the scientific diaspora); and later expanded with some of these newly established departments' former students, occasionally after these returned from further studies abroad (Ghica, 2014; Rybář, 2010).

In the newly independent Baltic and Caucasian countries, and to a lesser extent in Moldova and Ukraine, the establishment in the 1990s and 2000s of think tanks, as well as of U.S.-inspired political science or international relations departments at both public and private universities, was connected to nation-state building processes and the affirmation of independence vis-à-vis the Russian Federation, a fact that stimulated the development of international contacts outside the Russian-language *oikumene* (Muskhelishvili & Abashidze, 2010). For Bulgaria, Croatia, the Czech Republic, Estonia, Hungary, Latvia, Lithuania, Poland, Romania, Slovakia, and Slovenia, the integration with "Western" political science teaching and research was further enhanced by the need to prepare expertise for their accession to the European Union (EU) and the North Atlantic Treaty Organization (NATO). However, this also led to increased competition to achieve political science institutional autonomy and/or dominance in the field, especially due to the establishment of the separate departments of European studies, public administration, and public policy (Eisfeld & Pal, 2010; Krauz-Mozer et al. 2015). At the same time, in Armenia, Bosnia-Herzegovina, Georgia, Moldova, North Macedonia, Serbia, Ukraine, and, to a lesser extent, Azerbaijan, the Organisation for Co-operation and Security in Europe (OSCE) schools of political studies (Council of Europe, 2006), as well as curricular development support [from the Curriculum Resource Center (CRC) program of OSI/CEU and various U.S.-based universities], contributed substantially to the growth of professionalization in the discipline. Yet in these cases the pace of integration with mainstream political science has been slower due to the particularities of the "triple transition" (Offe & Adler, 2004), most notably the fact that these countries have been involved in intermittent or ongoing political and violent conflicts related to parts of their territories being claimed by separatist groups or neighboring states.

In the Russian Federation, as well as in Azerbaijan and Belarus, after brief periods of liberalization in the 1990s, the rebranding of the old political party system and the establishment of new political science departments gradually transformed into ideological battlegrounds. These served more the new yet also increasingly authoritarian regimes than the purpose of consolidating disciplinary autonomy or academically independent and productive national scientific communities (Naumova, 2010; Popova, 2015; Rizayev, 2004). In the case of Belarus, this also led to the extraordinary situation in which an entire university (European Humanities University) relocated to neighboring Lithuania to provide Belarusian students with social and political science education free from government interference after it was closed by the Belarusian government in 2004 (Naumova, 2010). Recently, similar political pressures appeared even in more democratic environments. For instance, the international powerhouse that is the CEU started relocating from Hungary to Austria, while in Poland several subjects that do not fit with the ideology of the conservative government, most notably gender studies, were deemed improper for academic research and institutionally eliminated or marginalized.

Further hindering a rapid rapprochement with mainstream (i.e., English-language) political science, the relatively large national and regional market for Russian-language scientific exchange, as well as the still limited number of teaching and research staff cognitively socialized in the "Western" canon (Gorbunova, 2012), diminishes the incentives and resources for Russian-speaking scholars from the former Soviet space to participate in international scientific events in English or other languages of international circulation. However, over the last two decades, the less regulated and difficult-to-sanction copyright infringements in the Russian Federation, coupled with the scarcity of academic resources and the scholarly need of exposure to scientific advancements, has also created considerable alternative/black academic markets, especially in digital access of scientific publications. Some of these have become popular in academia and are currently widely used across the world, including by researchers from affluent countries or universities who cannot otherwise reach certain publications due to the increasingly high access fees (Bohannon, 2016).

3. IS THERE A CENTRAL AND EASTERN EUROPEAN POLITICAL SCIENCE (PATTERN)?

Currently, there are political science departments/faculties in all twenty-four European former communist states or inheritors of such states. Political science education is at present structured throughout the region, at least formally, within the logic of the Bologna process, both in public and private universities. In some former Soviet countries, such as Belarus (Naumova, 2010) and Armenia (Markarov, 2010), institutional elements of the Soviet higher education system are, however, still present. The Bologna process and the logic of academic capitalism enhanced the push toward interdisciplinarity, often through institutional competition for limited resources and integration into larger institutional units mostly for reasons of economic efficiency. As in the rest of Europe (Reinalda, 2011), these particularly affected smaller departments, the less financially appealing humanities and social sciences, and/or, more recently, the disciplinary areas recognized as institutionally autonomous. Often meeting all three of these criteria, political science has been especially vulnerable. The scientific output originating from the region is also still below its potential in both quantity and quality, mostly due to pressures related to the time demands of the mass education system, increasing administrative load, and limited access to appropriate, timely, and transparently allocated funding resources (Eisfeld & Pal, 2010; Klingemann, Kulesza, & Legutke, 2002; Krauz-Mozer et al. 2015). Despite limited resources, collective research/authorship is still rare (Jokić, Mervar, & Mateljan, 2019).

The search for alternatives seems to characterize the current dynamics of local markets for academic exchange in the region. Few of the scientific journals for social and political research established during the communist regimes survived or maintained their status after the Cold War. In the absence of incentives and resources to maintain them as long-term projects, independent of their founders, many of the new periodicals also quickly disappeared (Eisfeld & Pal, 2010). Aiming to diminish the arbitrariness of previous forms of evaluation for career advancement purposes in many Central and Eastern European countries, subsequent national reforms on research output assessment roughly followed the mainstream pattern found elsewhere in Europe.

This pattern increasingly favors quantitative over qualitative indicators, publication of peer-reviewed/highly ranked journal articles over volumes, as well as using the number of citations as proxy for scientific impact. This led to various strategies, ranging from stimulating the internationalization of local journals and increasing the pressure to publish abroad to the contestation of the criteria and building international networks of new and often predatory journals that increased their impact factors through mutual citation (Feşnic, 2019). Although there is still little systematic and timely research on local journals and journal authorship in the region, existing scholarship suggests that, in the 2000s, the typical political science author from Central and Eastern Europe published alone, mostly qualitative case studies focused on their own country of origin (Jokić, Mervar, & Mateljan, 2019; Schneider, Bochsler, & Chiru, 2013). However, when skimming through the CVs of those hired over the last decade in political science departments across the region, one may also notice the increasing popularity of quantitative research. This tendency may likewise be discerned in recent scholarship, (co)authored by younger scholars from the region, on the study of political science as a discipline (ibid.) or as a profession (Proteasa & Fierăscu, 2018).

While more research is needed on the topic, financial and institutional sustainability seem to be the main factors behind the limited involvement in collective initiatives. In fact, despite an increasingly professional infrastructure of research granting schemes which are often modeled on the EU-level funding logic, most collective projects in the region seem to be generally highly dependent on national public funding, which in some countries is frequently unpredictable and/or allocated through opaque/noncompetitive criteria and/or only for certain topics prioritized for political/economic reasons. At the same time, most universities in Central and Eastern Europe, including those from EU countries, still seem to lack the institutional capacity to access funds for large international consortia projects, and when they take part in such projects, it is rarely as lead partners. The scientific exchange within traditional national political science associations, as well as in the Central European Political Science Association (CEPSA, est.1994) and other (sub)regional networks, also remain generally weak and are usually limited to periodic scientific events without significant impact on setting collective, national, or transnational long-term research programs. Furthermore, the existence of a professional association does not necessarily imply the existence of a thriving scientific community of political research or vice versa. In 1989, with the exception of Albania, all European communist states (i.e., Bulgaria, Czechoslovakia, the GDR, Hungary, Poland, Romania, the USSR, and Yugoslavia) had national political science associations (*PS*, 1989), affiliated to IPSA, but these had little to do with representing scholars' interests or the genuinely scientific research of politics. Though currently such associations exist in most of the twenty-four postcommunist states, and are still IPSA members, many are de facto inactive or have little impact on setting professional national standards or research programs in the discipline.

4. CONCLUSIONS

Despite sharing the experience of a recent nondemocratic past that started and ended at roughly the same time, the Central and Eastern European countries do not share a common pattern of institutional development of political science. During communism, political expertise was controlled by the communist party elites and instrumentalized for political purposes aiming to legitimize and reproduce the regime. Most of the local scholarly communities were also largely disconnected from the mainstream international infrastructures in the field. Despite these commonalities, significant institutional variations across the region and often within each country or areas of specialization existed, even before the Cold War. Since the 1990s, there has been increasing exposure to the "Western" European and U.S. political science canons and institutional models. Curricula were designed, reformed, and standardized following the Bologna logic. Most significantly, political science teaching and research has advanced largely outside political control.

However, these were not linear, similar, or irreversible processes. Such institutional developments have been highly dependent on the local particularities of the transition to democracy and market economies, as well as on the larger Euro-Atlantic integration context. Many, but not all, countries in the region also experienced significant state-building challenges, sometimes involving violent or protracted conflicts on their territory; this not only slowed the evolution of the field but also, as in the case of Ukraine, shifted national research agendas. The democratic backsliding in countries such as Azerbaijan, Belarus, the Russian Federation, and, more recently, Hungary and Poland triggered significant governmental pressure on independent academic expertise, forcing universities to follow the official political position, eliminate study programs. In extreme cases, universities were also forced to close or move to neighboring countries. In most of the region, however, the recent history of political science has been rather peaceful. Over the last three decades, pressure has derived more frequently from the particularities of the mass education systems, administrative overload, limited funding for research, as well as from the need for international communication while also building local epistemic communities. These are challenges that political science faces throughout the rest of Europe and in many other countries around the world.

Therefore, the story that the evolution of political science in Central and Eastern Europe tells, especially after the Cold War, is more about rebuilding practices, institutions, and networks for conducting genuine scientific inquiry, free from political interference, than about simply catching up with the "West." In fact, political science in the region is currently far from being underdeveloped institutionally or in terms of research agendas, contrary to the mainstream narrative on the region that emerged in the early 1990s. In all twenty-four postcommunist countries there are political science departments. Most of them serve primarily academic purposes and, while the content and quality of teaching may vary significantly, they produce graduates exposed, at least minimally, to the type of political science thinking and research agendas developed elsewhere in Europe and the United States.

Despite being increasingly dynamic and connected, political science in postcommunist countries is far from flourishing. Most significantly, independent scientific research and political science departments remain highly vulnerable to political interference. Although direct political pressure is still limited to a small group of countries where governments have manifested stronger authoritarian traits, several worrying signs are present throughout the entire region, occasionally reported informally in scientific events. First, there is still little tolerance for pluralism and many debates on political issues, including within academia, are still largely held according to a zero-sum logic. Against this background, and, although initially essential for replacing the previous regime, as well as for promoting the "Western" perspective on political science, the anti-communist fight against corruption discourse has become increasingly conservative, often hindering the intellectual progress of the discipline, as well as the professional advancement of colleagues who do not share similar political views. Falsely representing more liberal/leftist concerns as Marxist(-Leninist), such conservative voices have dominated the public debate for most of the last three decades and often have found uncomfortable research outside a usually oversimplified version of the neoliberal paradigm. Ocassionaly, they have used their (political) power to discredit publicly such research by claiming that it is not scientific or even explicitly eliminating it from the curricula. At the same time, irrespective of the right/left or progressive/conservative divides, scientific expertise in political matters has been largely publicly ignored, being frequently shunned in favor of more tabloidized approaches to political analysis, usually in the form of political commentary by nonprofessionals. In addition, politics as a profession and field of inquiry has a mixed reputation, as there is still little public awareness of what political science education can produce.

Beyond the confrontational character and the difficulties that politics faces in new democracies, negative public attitudes toward political science have been helped by the recent memory of the former communist party schooling system. There is also a rather mechanistic public expectation that universities produce clearly defined professions and jobs, in line with both the new academic capitalism narrative on higher education reforms and with the already-familiar communist logic of preparing cadres that have a predetermined role in economy and society. Reinforcing the narrative that social and political research is marginal to economic progress, this perspective also contributed to keeping funds allocated to the field at low levels. Not least, the linear and deterministic representations of political change in the logic of classic modernization narratives, which have dominated the process of (re) discovering political science in the region, further created a false sense of security that progress is irreversible once a certain threshold is achieved. This threshold has been usually operationalized as adoption of/integration into "Western" institutions. Although this process fostered progress in political research, it also created significant cleavages and fragmentation within the local scientific communities, diminishing the levels of trust and professional solidarity.

The fact that Central and East European scholars are still underrepresented in traditional international infrastructures of European political science seems to be due to (1) the integration of these scholars into alternative professional networks and routes of publications either within the region or outside Europe; and (2) the smaller institutional leverage that political science departments and expertise usually have in accessing funds for research and academic exchanges, particularly in the context of increasingly crowded interdisciplinary and scientific markets. A less visible, but significant, alternative route is becoming part of the scientific diaspora. In fact, due to social, economic, and academic pressures related to the nondemocratic character of the Central and East European political regimes throughout much of the last two centuries, exporting brainpower to the "West" has been a major feature of the region. This process has contributed significantly to scientific advancements in the United States and Western Europe, including to the intellectual and institutional development of political science, but the links between diaspora members and the scientific communities of origin have been in general weak, further diminishing the capacity of local academia to resist political pressure and thrive scientifically.

Most of these vulnerabilities, however, are not specific to Central and Eastern Europe. What the experience of the former communist countries can convey to the larger European and global communities in the field is not only that genuinely scientific political research can indeed flourish rather in democratic environments, but also that political science may be highly vulnerable even in democracies. Furthermore, since independent and reliable political expertise is crucial for resisting authoritarian tendencies, professionally weaker political science communities can become liabilities not only to the discipline but to the survival of democracies. Though displaying local specificities, these vulnerabilities are not the result of exclusively local processes. Long-term structural factors, as well as transnational dynamics, are as relevant as the actions of the local stakeholders. Therefore, beyond counting ourselves periodically, we also need to investigate more thoroughly such vulnerabilities and create appropriate structures to diminish them. Given their complexity and implications, such substantial efforts require collaborative research and professional solidarity. As the oldest and largest European network in the field, ECPR has the chance to play a leading role in such efforts and consequently in the advancement of political research and teaching that can support the consolidation of democracy for the next fifty years, in Europe and beyond.

5. ACKNOWLEDGMENTS

For their feedback and support in developing this study, I thank Agnieszka Bejma, Giliberto Capano, Luis De Sousa, Florin Feşnic, Béla Greskovits, Armand Goşu, Virginie Guiraudon, Bogdan Iancu, Yves Mény, David Patternote, Bogdan Mihai Radu, Philippe Schmitter, Laurenţiu Ştefan, Claudiu D. Tufiş, and Mieke Verloo. I am also extremely grateful to the editors of this volume. Their immense patience and graceful comments not only helped me finish writing this text, eventually, but also stimulated me to extend this research into a monograph on the evolution of political science in postauthoritarian environment, currently in progress.

NOTE

1. I thank Helen Cooper (ECPR Communication Office) for providing the digital database with the ECPR membership per year, country and university.

REFERENCES

Adcock, R. (2006). The emigration of the 'comparative method': Transatlantic exchange and the birth of American political science. *European Political Science, 5*(2), 124–36.

Berndtson, E. (2012). European political science(s): Historical roots of disciplinary politics. In J. Trent & M. Stein (Eds.), *The World of Political Science: A Critical Overview of the Development of Political Studies around the World, 1990–2012* (pp. 41–66). Opladen, Berlin, Toronto: Barbara Budrich Publishers.

Bernhard, M., & Jasiewicz, K. (2015). Wither Eastern Europe? Changing perspectives and approaches on the region in political science. *East European Politics and Societies and Cultures, 29*(2), 311–22.

Blondel, J. (1973). European Consortium for Political Research. *European Journal of Political Research, 1*(1), 103–5.

Bohannon, J. (2016, April 28). Who's downloading pirated papers? Everyone. *Science, 325*, 508–12. doi:10.1126/science.aaf5664.

Buchstein, H., & Göhler, G. (1990). After the revolution: Political science in East Germany. *PS: Political Science & Politics, 23*(4), 668–73.

Bull, M. (2007). Is there a *European* political science and if so, which are the challenges facing it? *European Political Science, 6*(4), 427–38.

Cami, S. (2010). Political science in Albania: Creating spaces for the discipline's development. In R. Eisfeld & L. A. Pal (Eds.), *Political Science in Central-East Europe: Diversity and Convergence* (pp. 37–44). Opladen & Farmington Hills: Barbara Budrich Publishers.

Council of Europe. (2006). *Activities of the council of Europe—Democracy department.* OSCE Human Dimension Implementation Meeting—Working session 10 (Democratic institutions), Warsaw 2-13.10.2006, HDIM.IO/270/2006. Retrieved from https://www.osce.org/odihr/21393 (last accessed 3 November 2019).

De Sousa, L., Moses, J., Briggs, J., & Bull, M. (2010). Forty years of European political science. *European Political Science, 9*(S1), S1–S10.

Eisfeld, R., & Pal, L.A. (Eds.). (2010). *Political science in Central-East Europe: Diversity and convergence.* Opladen & Farmington Hills: Barbara Budrich Publishers.

Erne, R. (2007). On the use and abuse of bibliometric performance indicators: A critique of Hix's "global ranking of political science departments." *European Political Science, 6*(3), 306–14.

Falk, B. (2003). *The dilemmas of dissidence in East-Central Europe.* Budapest: Central European University Press.

Farr, J. (2006). Transactions of European-American political science. *European Political Science, 5*(2), 171–82.

Feşnic, F. (2019). *When quantity beats quality in the evaluation of academic work.* Paper prepared for the 6th international interdisciplinary conference of political research *SCOPE: Science of Politics*, Bucharest, 31 May–2 June.

Geva-May, I., & Pal, L. A. (Eds.). (2018). Special issue: Twenty years of the journal of comparative policy. *Journal of Comparative Policy, 20*(1), 1–132.

Ghica, L. A. (2014). Academic bovarism and the pursuit of legitimacy: Canon-building in Romanian political science. *European Political Science, 13*(2), 171–86.

Goodin, R. E., & Klingemann, H. D. (Eds.). (1998). *A new handbook of political science.* Oxford: Oxford University Press.

Gorbunova, E. (2012). Institutionalization of European studies in Russia. *European Political Science, 11*(3), 337–50.

Gunnell, J. G., & Easton, D. (1991). Introduction. In J. G. Gunnell, D. Easton, & L. Graziano (Eds.), *The Development of Political Science: A Comparative Survey* (pp. 1–12). London: Routledge.

Hix, S. (2004). European universities in a global ranking of political science departments. *European Political Science, 3*(2), 5–23.

Holzer, J., & Pšeja, P. (2010). Political science in the Czech Republic: On the edge of maturity. In R. Eisfeld & L. A. Pal (Eds.), *Political Science in Central-East*

Europe: Diversity and Convergence (pp. 103–18). Opladen & Farmington Hills: Barbara Budrich Publishers.

Jokić, M., Mervar, A., & Mateljan, S. (2019). The development of political science in Central and Eastern Europe: Bibliometric perspective, 1996–2013. *European Political Science, 18*(3), 491–509.

Kaase, M., Sparschuh, V., & Wenninger, A. (Eds.). (2002). *Three social science disciplines in Central and Eastern Europe: Handbook on economics, political science and sociology (1989–2001)*. Berlin: Informationszentrum Sozialwissenschaften; GESIS Servicestelle Osteuropa; Collegium Budapest, Institute for Advanced Study.

Kasapović, M., Petković, K., & Grdešić, I. (2010). Political science in Croatia: Dropping the plural. In R. Eisfeld & L. A. Pal (Eds.), *Political Science in Central-East Europe: Diversity and Convergence* (pp. 89–102). Opladen & Farmington Hills: Barbara Budrich Publishers.

Klingemann, H.-D. (Ed.). (2007). *The state of political science in Western Europe*. Opladen & Farmington Hills: Barbara Budrich Publishers.

Klingemann, H.-D. (2008). Capacities: Political science in Europe. *West European Politics, 31*(1–2), 370–96.

Klingemann, H.-D., Kulesza, E., & Legutke, A. (Eds.). (2002). *The state of political science in Central and Eastern Europe*. Berlin: Sigma.

Krauz-Mozer, B., Kołakowska, M., Borowiec, P., & Ścigaj, P. (Eds.). (2015). *Political science in Europe at the beginning of the 21st century*. Krakow: Jagellonian University Press.

Mackenzie, W. J. M. (1971). The political science of political science. *Government and Opposition, 6*(3), 277–302.

Markarov, A. (2010). Political science in Armenia: The challenges of institutionalisation. In R. Eisfeld & L. A. Pal (Eds.), *Political science in Central-East Europe: Diversity and convergence* (pp. 38–60). Opladen & Farmington Hills: Barbara Budrich Publishers.

McKay, D. (1988). Why is there a European political science? *PS: Political Science and Politics, 21*(4), 1051–56.

McKay, D. (1991). Is European political science inferior to or different from American political science. *European Journal of Political Research, 20*(3–4), 459–66.

Muskhelishvili, M., & Abashidze, Z. (2010). Science or ideology? Georgian political science at the crossroads. In R. Eisfeld & L. A. Pal (Eds.), *Political science in Central-East Europe: Diversity and convergence* (pp. 135–48). Opladen & Farmington Hills: Barbara Budrich Publishers.

Naumova, S. (2010). Belarussian political science: On the opposite side of the barricade. In R. Eisfeld & L. A. Pal (Eds.), *Political science in Central-East Europe: Diversity and convergence* (pp. 61–74). Opladen & Farmington Hills: Barbara Budrich Publishers.

Newton, K., & Boncourt, T. (2010). *The ECPR's first forty years 1970–2010*. Colchester: ECPR Press.

Newton, K., & Vallès, J. M. (1991). Introduction: Political science in Western Europe 1960–1990. *European Journal of Political Research, 20*(3–4), 227–38.

Offe, C., & Adler, P. (2004). Capitalism by democratic design? Democratic theory facing the triple transition in East-Central Europe. *Social Research, 71*(3), 501–28.

Pavlović, D. (2010). Political science in Serbia: The struggle for autonomy. In R. Eisfeld & L. A. Pal (Eds.), *Political science in Central-East Europe: Diversity and convergence* (pp. 281–89). Opladen & Farmington Hills: Barbara Budrich Publishers.

Pettai, V. (2010). Political science in Estonia: Advantages of being small. In R. Eisfeld & L. A. Pal (Eds.), *Political science in Central-East Europe: Diversity and convergence* (pp. 119–33). Opladen & Farmington Hills: Barbara Budrich Publishers.

Popova, O. V. (2015). The development of political science in modern Russia. In B. Krauz-Mozer, M. Kołakowska, P. Borowiec, & P. Ścigaj (Eds.), *Political science in Europe at the beginning of the 21st century* (pp. 425–48). Krakow: Jagiellonian University Press.

Powell, D. E., & Shoup, P. (1970). The emergence of political science in communist countries. *American Political Science Review, 64*(2), 574–88.

Proteasa, V., & Fierăscu, S. I. (2018). The institutionalisation of social sciences: Bringing graduates' employment into explanation. *Romanian Journal of Political Science, 18*(1), 79–107.

PS [s.aut.]. (1989). National political science associations. *PS: Political Science and Politics, 22*(2), 317–27.

Quermonne, J.-L. (Ed.). (1996). *La Science Politique en Europe: Formation, Coopération, Perspectives.* Paris: Institut d'Études Politique de Paris.

Reinalda, B. (2011). *The Bologna process revisited.* Paper prepared for the ECPR General Conference, Reykjavik, 25–27 August.

Révész, L. (1967). Political science in Eastern Europe: Discussion and initial steps. *Studies in Soviet Thought, 7*(3), 175–210.

Rizayev, E. (2004). Reflections on political science in Azerbaijan. *PS: Political Science & Politics, 37*(4), 927–28.

Roeder, K.-H. (1989). Political science in the German Democratic Republic. *PS: Political Science & Politics, 22*(3), 753–58.

Rokkan, S. (1973). Data exchanges in Europe: The role of the European Consortium. *European Journal of Political Research, 1*(1), 95–101.

Rose, R. (1990). Institutionalizing professional political science in Europe: A dynamic model. *European Journal of Political Research, 18*(6), 581–603.

Rybář, M. (2010). Political science in Slovakia: Hesitant emergence from elementary problems. In R. Eisfeld and L. A. Pal (Eds.), *Political science in Central-East Europe: Diversity and convergence* (pp. 267–80). Opladen & Farmington Hills: Barbara Budrich Publishers.

Sasinska-Klas, T. (2010). Political science in Poland: Roots, stagnation and renaissance. In R. Eisfeld and L. A. Pal (Eds.), *Political science in Central-East Europe: Diversity and convergence* (pp. 207–20). Opladen & Farmington Hills: Barbara Budrich Publishers.

Schmitter, P. (2002). Seven (disputable) theses concerning the future of "transatlanticised" or "globalised" political science. *European Political Science, 1*(2), 23–40.

Schneider, C. Q., Bochsler, D., & Chiru, M. (2013). Comparative politics in Central and Eastern Europe: Mapping publications over the last twenty years. *European Political Science, 12*(1), 127–45.

Schneider, G. (2014). Nothing succeeds like success: The past and future of European political science. *Political Science Research and Methods, 2*(2), 153–61.

Tismăneanu, V. (2003). *Stalinism for all seasons: A political history of Romanian communism.* Berkeley, Los Angeles & London: University of California Press.

Zajc, D. (2010). Political science in Slovenia: Driving democratization? In R. Eisfeld & L. A. Pal (Eds.), *Political science in Central-East Europe: Diversity and convergence* (pp. 251–66). Opladen & Farmington Hills: Barbara Budrich Publishers.

Chapter 9

Patterns of Gender Inequality in European Political Science

Isabelle Engeli and Liza Mügge

1. THE PROBLEM THAT HAS A NAME: GENDER INEQUALITY

Betty Friedan introduced "the problem that has no name" in the *Feminine Mystique* (1963) with which she referred to the unhappiness and dissatisfaction of women in the 1950s. The book was inspired by the experience of Friedan's former classmates at Smith College—a prestigious women's college in the United States—who reported being unhappy with their lives as housewives. Much has changed since then. Due to the efforts of first- and second-wave feminists, like Friedan, and the first women professors, women can now have academic careers. However, despite legal equal rights and the progress of recent decades, academia—including political science—remains male dominated.

There is room for optimism. Women are entering the profession in increasing numbers and breaking many glass ceilings in leadership positions that traditionally have been dominated by men. Professional associations and universities have become sensitive to gender gaps and actively promote gender equality as a top priority. Some may argue that change takes time and that we will almost naturally achieve a gender-equal profession. Others may even say that gender inequality is "over" and that it is "now an advantage to be a woman" in our discipline. They could not be more wrong. Gender inequality persists. More women enter the system, but their career progression to full professorship is slower and they are likely to be paid less than men. Women remain severely underrepresented in senior leadership. Women are more likely to have part-time positions and to be on fixed-term contract. Sexual harassment takes its toll on women, scholars, and students alike (Sapiro & Campbell, 2018). In short, sexism, prejudice, and bias have remained and thus the leaky pipeline has remained too. This is apparent at every stage of the academic career. While academic life is still structured on a no-childcare duty model, recent studies have shown that in addition to care duty it is the gender patterns of discrimination and prejudice in academia that prevent women from reaching senior ranks at the same pace as men—if they reach them at all (Santos & Dang Van Phu, 2019).

To understand how gender inequality still plays out in political science, this chapter takes stock of empirical evidence on gender gaps regarding institutional, scholarly, and professional recognition. While blatant cases of direct discrimination are becoming rarer, we contend that gender inequality in our profession persists through a number of mechanisms that reinforce one another across all aspects of academic life. The first domain is the institutional environment and barriers that women face in career progression, such as promotion, gender pay gap, teaching evaluations, administrative tasks, and emotional labor. The second domain involves recognition in the wider discipline and its subfields in terms of the canon, citation, and publication. The third domain relates to the profession and the platform that women are given as keynote speakers, panelists, awardees of prestigious prizes, and journal editors.

Our key message is that we should shift our focus from "fix the women" to "fix the system" to enable long-term change (Atchison, 2018). A "fixing"-the-women approach is generally popular in institutions, as it is not conceived as a fundamental critique of how things are managed by those in power. Women are the problem and need to "lean in" to navigate a competitive arena (as examplified in Sandberg, 2013). A "fix the women" approach on its own is problematic for two reasons. First, power structures that cause inequality are likely to remain intact. Second, it suggests that women are the problem; they are simply not good or ambitious enough. Professional associations should take a proactive role regarding gender equality policies and lead by example. There is much that we can do to fix the system. Interventions to redesign the way we work are simple and inexpensive. This change should be a collective effort and the responsibility of all scholars in our discipline, regardless of their gender.

2. ROOT CAUSES OF GENDER INEQUALITY

Women in leadership positions navigate an environment that historically is not designed for them and where the default norm is white and male. This includes a complete package of norms and institutional cultures (Rai, 2015) tied together with implicit and explicit gender scripts of appropriate behavior and expected performance. Think, for instance, about something as ordinary as the faces portrayed on the paintings that have decorated university buildings for centuries: they are predominantly those of white men. These galleries present the legacy of academic institutions. It signals to women—and people of color—that academia is not their natural place; at the same time, it signals the exact opposite to white men. People in power in our profession, university management and professors, produce and reproduce gender stereotypes. Typical female stereotypes such as being affectionate, cheerful, understanding, shy, compassionate, and sympathetic are traits not naturally associated with leadership. On the contrary, stereotypically male characteristics such as aggression, ambition, risk-taking, independence, competition, and decisiveness are traits traditionally associated with leadership (Williams & Dempsey, 2014, p. 13).

Psychologists distinguish a descriptive and prescriptive component of gender stereotypes that lead to sexism. The descriptive component consists of beliefs about the characteristics that women *do* possess; the prescriptive component consists of beliefs about the characteristics that women *should* possess (Burgess & Borgida, 1999, pp. 665–66). Scholarship demonstrates that women who not conform to prescriptive beliefs are penalized (Bowles, Babcock, & Lai, 2007; Okimoto & Brescoll, 2010; Slaughter, 2015). Behavior that disrupts traditional gender norms, such a woman behaving in a directive manner, is devalued. Penalties may include negative evaluation or absence of pay raise or a denied promotion. On the contrary, women leaders who act in a participatory democratic style are positively evaluated (Eagly, Makhijani, & Klonsky, 1992). Women in leadership positions appear to be aware of prescriptions and tend to behave in a manner that is congruent with stereotypic prescriptions (Eagly & Johnson, 1990). Prescriptive patterns of bias maintain power relations as they are (Burgess & Borgida, 1999, p. 666).

Williams and Dempsey (2014) identify four patterns of gender bias in the workplace that also apply to academia: Prove-It-Again!, the Tightrope, the Maternal Wall, and the Tug of War. *Prove-It-Again!* is a descriptive bias that stems from assumptions about the typical woman. It describes how "women have to prove themselves over and over again much more so than men in order to be seen as equally competent" (Williams & Dempsey, 2014, p. 21). One factor that feeds into the mechanism is that men tend to be judged on their potential while women are judged on their achievements. The *Tightrope* prescriptive bias is based on assumptions of how women should behave. It describes a double bind: "Women often find that if they behave in traditionally feminine ways, they exacerbate Prove-It-Again! problems; but if they behave in traditionally masculine ways, they are seen as lacking social skills" (Williams & Dempsey, 2014, p. xxi). Women who follow the feminine script are "good girls," they do not break rules like their male competitors, but play by the book while sacrificing their career. The *Maternal Wall* consists of a combination of descriptive and prescriptive bias. Motherhood triggers "negative competence and commitment assumptions" but at the same there is disapproval of working mothers, as they are deemed to be at home or to work fewer hours. "Women with children are routinely pushed to the margins of the professional world" (Williams & Dempsey, 2014, p. xxi). Women *without* children experience the "no-child penalty" and "are seen to have near-infinite time to spend on their jobs, as well as on care work inside the office" (Williams & Dempsey, 2014, pp. 145–46). At the same time, researchers find that they are seen as "insufficiently nurturing, excessively masculine, and not 'not quite normal'" (Gatrell and Swan cited in Williams & Dempsey, 2014, p. 146). The *Tug of War* refers to clashes between women who each in their own way navigate their path between "assimilating into masculine traditions and resisting them. Women's different strategies divide them [and] often pit against each other; as do workplaces that communicate that there's room for only one woman" (Williams & Dempsey, 2014, p. xxi). This leads to judgments on "what's the right way to be a woman" (Williams & Dempsey, 2014). In popular culture and the media, this pattern is often represented as a "cat fight."

The four patterns that explain gender bias are deeply embedded in the way we work and apply to women in leadership positions in politics, academia, and the corporate world. Nonetheless, these patterns do not necessarily play out in similar ways for all women. Black feminist scholars demonstrate how the specific interaction between race and gender produces different forms of racism and sexism (Crenshaw, 1991). Black women and women of color experience a "double jeopardy" (Beal, 1970) or "matrix of oppression" (Collins, 1990). Barriers based on the specific intersection between race, ethnicity, and gender, as well as other social positions such as sexuality, religion, and ability, are not static but context specific (Smooth, 2016). While all women in political science face, one way or the other, the *Prove-It-Again!*, *Tightrope*, *Maternal Wall*, and *Tug of War* mechanisms, women of color experience these patterns in different and/or more pronounced ways in addition of being subject to other discriminatory patterns (see, for example, Davis, 2016; Gutiérrez y Muhs, Niemann, Gonzalez, & Harris, 2012; Marbley, Wong, Santos-Hatchett, Pratt, & Jaddo, 2011; Sampaio, 2006; and Briscoe-Palmer; see also Mattocks, in this volume).

3. THE GENDER GAP IN EUROPEAN POLITICAL SCIENCE

Studies generally tackle aspects of academic gender gaps in isolation. We develop an integrated model of recognition based on three main pillars:

Career Progression Senior Leadership Pay Teaching evaluation Administration	Conferences Publications Citations Co-authorship PI/Co-PI	Keynotes Speeches Awards Editorship Professional body
Institutional Recognition	**Scholarly Recognition**	**Professional Recognition**

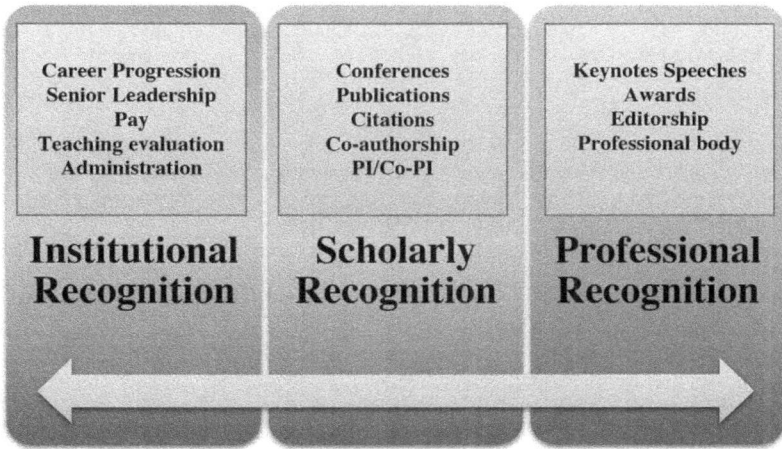

Figure 9.1   The Three Pillars of Academic Recognition. *Source*: Authors' own.

institutional, scholarly, and professional recognition (see figure 9.1). Patterns may differ in intensity across European countries; nevertheless, we contend that assessing the three channels of recognitions is pivotal for moving ahead in solving the "gender" problem in the political science profession. The "gender problem" of our profession is multidimensional. It is a system of established privileges and ways of functioning that do not leave flexibility enough for women and minority groups to evolve at a similar pace as men. The dominant single approach to gender inequality is unlikely to produce significant change and long-lasting effects. The first pillar addresses institutional recognition of women political scientists in their university positions. How do women fare in their departments and their universities? What are the main barriers to the equal treatment of female and male faculty? The second pillar tackles issues in the scholarly recognition of women's contribution to the disciplinary knowledge. What do we know about the gender gap in citations, publications, and co-authorship? The third pillar is linked to the differences in professional standing and covers the main aspects related to professional recognition such the gap in invitations to deliver keynote and speeches, invitations to offer prestigious services such as journal editorship and awards.

The bulk of the scholarship on gender and academic leadership focuses on the United States, collected by the American Political Science Association (APSA). APSA has been actively gathering data and supporting data collection on gender imbalances since the 1970s. There is less data available for Europe. Moreover, existing data often are not comparable across countries. For this chapter, we can rely on the ECPR gender study that has been conducted since 2016 and covers the gender balance in the main ECPR-led

Table 9.1 Gender Composition of Employment Profile across Europe

EU, Iceland, Switzerland, and Norway		Women (%)	Men (%)
Academic Staff		39 (341)	61 (524)
Work status**	Full-time academic employment	37 (254)	63 (437)
	Part-time academic employment	38 (19)	62 (31)
Job security***	Continuous contract (tenure line)	32 (130)	68 (271)
	Other types (fixed term, temporary)	45 (211)	54 (253)
Academic Status***	Senior management	18 (5)	82 (23)
	Full professor	24 (40)	76 (126)
	Associate/assistant professor and lecturer/senior lecturer	41 (129)	59 (183)
	Research fellow	45 (94)	55 (117)
	Graduate student	49 (73)	51 (75)
Department size*	50 or more FTE academic staff	41 (105)	60 (154)
	30–49 FTE academic staff	36 (62)	64 (109)
	20–29 FTE academic staff	33 (43)	67 (89)
	10–19 FTE academic staff	33 (41)	67 (83)
	9 or fewer FTE academic staff	44 (29)	57 (37)
Institution***	50,000 or more FTE students	51 (37)	49 (35)
	30,000–49,000 FTE students	32 (46)	68 (100)
	20,000–29,000 FTE students	29 (44)	71 (109)
	10,000–19,000 FTE students	25 (39)	75 (115)
	9,000 or fewer FTE students	45 (63)	55 (76)

Survey respondents included are currently (1) holding a part-time or full-time academic employment and (2) reporting an academic rank or to be engaged in postgraduate studies.
*** $p<0.001$, **$p<0.01$, *$p<0.05$.
Source: ECPR-IPSA World of Political Science survey (Norris), Spring 2019.

activities and on the survey data from the ECPR-IPSA World of Political Science survey conducted by Pippa Norris in 2019 (see Norris, in this volume).

Table 9.1 displays the gender composition of the employment profile of academics who are currently working in academic institutions based in the European Union, Iceland, Switzerland, and Norway. The gender breakdown of the academic ranks reveals the familiar picture of vertical balance. Women are as well represented as men among graduate students, and only slightly fewer among research fellows. The gap slightly increases in the intermediate ranks to become extremely large at the level of full professors and individuals holding senior leadership positions. Large institutions and, to a lesser extent, large departments seem to have a more balanced academic staff than medium-sized ones. While women are almost equally likely to be in full-time employment as men are, they are more likely to work on fixed-term contracts.

3.1 Institutional Recognition

In a seminal study of the professorial landscape across U.S. institutions in the late 1960s, Schuck (1969, p. 644) concluded that "a woman who is a full professor is almost an exception; tenured positions at all levels appear to be a masculine preserve." While the professorial body is feminizing, recent studies point to several factors that hinder feminization among the higher ranks. The persistent leaky pipeline is alarming (see Abels & Woods, 2015; Akhtar Fawcett, Legrand, Marsh, & Taylor, 2005; Bates, Jenkins, & Pflaeger, 2012; Briggs & Harrison, 2015; Curtin, 2013; Elizondo, 2015; LNVH, 2018; Sawer & Curtin, 2016; Timperley, 2013). Based on an APSA-sponsored survey, Hesli, Lee, and Mitchell (2012, pp. 475–77; see also Burton and Darcy, already in 1985), find that female scholars are less likely to be promoted to associate professor in American institutions than male scholars. To explain this difference in promotion track, they emphasize the potential impact of gender prejudices and unconscious bias on academic judgment. These barriers take their toll even prior to the start of the promotion clock. Tolleson-Rinehard and Carroll (2006) remind us that while the PhD program drop-out rate in American programs does not show any significant difference between men and women, women PhD researchers mention grounds for leaving their PhD program related to the lack of support for career development and to the nongender-friendly environment. Their male counterparts are mostly motivated by scarce employment perspectives. Moving up the career ladder is extremely difficult for scholars of color and indigenous scholars in North America (see Abu-Laban, 2016; Agathangelou & Ling, 2002; Canadian Political Science Association Diversity Task Force, 2012; Monforti & Michelson, 2008). While there is no longitudinal data available across the whole of Europe, there are reasons to believe that the situation for women minority scholars is much worse. For example, there are only twenty-five black women scholars who are currently full professors in the U.K. academic system, all disciplines included (Rollock, 2019; see also Begum & Saini, 2019; Emejulu & Mcgregor, 2019; Mattocks & Briscoe-Palmer, 2016; Mattocks & Briscoe-Palmer, in this volume).

It is often said that women progress slower in their career and receive fewer resources because they ask for less, are less likely to refuse tasks that that are not directly profitable to their career advancement, and do not bargain as much as men do. This well-worn explanation makes women solely responsible. They have to change their behavior in order to become as successful as male scholars. Yet research shows that while women scholars in U.S. institutions seem more likely to be invited to perform services and less likely to refuse, they nevertheless bargain for resources as much as men do (McLaughlin, Lange, & Brus, study, 2013). A Dutch study finds that women do ask, but do not get as much. Compared with men, women report having less access to resources that allow them to carry out their work as academics, such as research funding, a travel budget, assistance, and their own office. Women also have less research time than men, as they spend more time on teaching and other tasks (Van Veelen & Derks, 2019, p. 48).

Timperley (2013) argues that even when women are invited to do services that are considered as potential career boosters, like serving on senior leadership positions, the assessment of these services may be gendered. For example, a head of department role can be perceived as a *position of power* when occupied by a man and as a *service* when occupied by a woman. In a similar vein, an overwhelming number of studies demonstrates student bias against teachers who are not part of the traditional white and male norm (Rollock, 2019). Women, scholars of color, foreigners, and minority scholars are less well assessed than majority teachers.[1] Experiments have been conducted to isolate gender bias (MacNell, Driscoll, & Hunt, 2015). Participants of an online class were given the exact same course delivered by the same instructor. A group of students were informed the instructor was "male," and the other group of students were told the instructor was "female." The performance of the "male" instructor was better assessed than the performance of the "female" instructor. Not only are they not as well assessed on the quantitative metrics, but female teachers also receive different characterization in the qualitative comments (MacNell, Driscoll, & Hunt, 2015). Students were more likely to qualify the "male" performance as "brilliant, awesome, and knowledgeable."

Women and minority scholars are also at higher risk of bullying and sexual harassment in their workplace, at conferences (APSA report on sexual harassment at annual meeting 2018; for the Netherlands, see Naezer & Benschop, 2019), and on social media (Savigny, 2019). A large number of universities, conferences, and professional associations do not have a code of conduct that explicitly prohibits such behavior. And when they do, the complaint process often is not adequate. Procedures are unclear or sanctions are not systematically applied if the code contains any. In politics, women are more likely to have been threatened with death, rape, or physical violence and the numbers are even higher among racial, ethnic, and religious minorities (ILO, 2019; IPU, 2018). The same intersectional phenomenon takes place in academia. A growing number of studies and testimonies underline the isolation of minority scholars in departments which have all remained overwhelmingly white and the racial violence that occurs (Rollock, 2019; Smith, 2017).

Unequal career advancement opportunities and bias in academic assessment severely affect the gender pay gap. Inequalities in academic salaries between men and women are not a recent or unknown phenomenon. In 1971, Jaquette pointed out severe income disparities between female and male faculty in the United States and the gap has not been resolved since then. Over 90 percent of U.K. universities displayed a gender pay gap in 2017, with an average median pay gap at 13.7 percent (BBC, 2017). Unequal pay is not the only outcome of the concentration of female scholars in lower professorial ranks or at earlier career stages. Pay discrimination takes places within ranks as well. A recent Canadian study investigates the differential in pay across professional ranks in Ontario and reports the systematic existence of a gap across all ranks (Momani, Dreher, & Williams, 2019). In the Netherlands, the difference in a full-time gross monthly salary between a male and female academic of the same age is €390 (De Goede, Van Veelen, & Derks, 2016).

3.2 Scholarly Recognition

Gender difference in scholarly recognition is well documented. One key feature is the consistent gender gap in citations (Breuning & Sanders, 2007; Dion, Sumner, & Mitchell, 2018; Teele & Thelen, 2017; see also Maliniak, Powers, & Walter, 2013; and Mitchell, Lange, & Brus, 2013 for the gender gap in citations related to international relations; Williams, Bates, Jenkins, Luke, & Rogers, 2015 for the gender gap in citations in U.K.-based journals).[2] The gap seems to be larger in fields where the underrepresentation of women is the largest (Dion, Sumner, & Mitchell, 2018). The gender citation gap reflects a broader phenomenon of invisibilization of women's scholarly contribution to the discipline. Works authored by female scholars, minority scholars, and scholars based in the Global South are also less likely to appear on syllabi and reading lists (see, for instance, Bonjour, Mügge, & Roggeband, 2016; Colgan, 2017; Medie & Kang, 2018; Mügge, Evans, & Engeli, 2016; Phull et al., 2018). Women are also less visible as experts in the media (Beaulieu et al., 2017; Savigny, 2019). Given the growing importance of metrics for performance evaluation and promotion, the gap in citations and media visibility is highly likely to negatively influence the promotion and salaries of women academics. Initiatives have been launched to make women and minority scholars more visible in the profession. *Women Also Know Stuff* and *People of Color Also Know Stuff* provide online expert directories of female scholars and scholars of color by subfields and topics, and Jane Lawrence Sumner has created an online tool for assessing the gender balance in syllabi.[3]

Drawing on the citation gap, attention has recently turned to potential gender bias in the publishing process as a whole. Again the United States is ahead of the game: a number of American journals and professional associations have played a leading role in assessing any potential discrimination in the editorial process and publishing process more generally (see, for example, the APSA roundtable on gender bias in the editorial process in 2017 and the symposium on gender in publications edited by Nadia Brown and David Samuels in *PS: Political Science and Politics* in 2018). A significant number of journals do not seem to exhibit *direct* discrimination against submissions with at least one female author. These submissions are sent out for review at a largely similar rate to others (Brown, Horiuchi, Htun, & Samuels, forthcoming). The acceptance rate for female and male authors seems also to be similar across a significant number of journals (Samuels, 2018). What transpires from these studies is that there is a severe submission gap. Women submit less scholarly work to peer review across the gamut of leading generalist journals in political science and the lower representation of women in the profession does not really account for this gender gap in submissions (Teele & Thelen, 2017). This gap in submissions affects European journals alike (ECPR Gender Study, 2018): in 2018, 27 percent of submissions to the *European Journal of Political Research* had a female lead author, 20 percent of submissions to *European Political Science* had a female lead, and 22 percent of submissions to *European Political Science Review* had at least one female author.

Addressing the gender gap in submission and citation requires far-reaching changes to the way our profession welcomes, acknowledges, and promotes the contribution of female scholars. While we are still at the stage of identifying the causal mechanism(s) that lead women to submit to journals in lower numbers than men, the scholarship points to a number of avenues. Brown et al. (forthcoming) unveil a *gender perception gap* where women are more reluctant than men to submit to some journals, regardless of the methods of specialization. Key and Sumner (2019) identify that dissertation topics vary across gender and that some of the research topics more likely to be studied by women (such as gender and race) are less preeminent in the work published by top generalist journals in the discipline. A consensus emerges about the implications of methodological orthodoxy for the gender gap in journal publications in a number of top journals in the discipline. Journals that display a strong preference for quantitative work may amplify the methodological divide in the profession which has implications for women who still tend to be underrepresented in quantitative methodology (Barnes & Beaulieu, 2017; Breuning & Sanders, 2007; Teele & Thelen, 2017). Finally, the *American Review of Political Studies* dug into coauthorship patterns and identified a puzzling phenomenon (König & Ropers, 2018). Authoring teams with more than two authors are much more likely to be men-only teams than women-only or mixed-gender teams. The ECPR Gender Study 2018 reports a similar trend for book authoring. From their inception to 2018, 16 percent of the books published by ECPR Press were authored/edited by men-only teams against 4 percent by women-only teams and 15 percent of mixed-gender teams. Also, 44 percent of the books were authored/edited by a single male and 22 percent by a single female. This is again an indication that differentials in publishing are outcomes of a larger system of inequalities between female and male scholars. If this phenomenon of men-only teams persists in the future, closing the gap in submissions will be challenging.

3.3 Professional Recognition

The last pillar refers to professional recognition as the mark of prestige and esteem but also encapsulates positions of power in the profession. Regarding the indicators related to esteem, the main professional associations compile data about the gender breakdown of their awards and flagship activities during their conferences. Marks of esteem were predominantly a male territory until recently, at least for the highest honors. While prestigious recognition is now awarded to women more often than in the past, the pool of female recipients appears to remain small. Several women have received more than one award.

The biennial ECPR Lifetimes Achievement Award celebrates "outstanding contributions to European political science," according to the official description of the prize. To date, it has been awarded six times to a male scholar and for the first time to a female scholar, Joni Lovenduski, in 2017. A similar pattern is found for the IPSA Karl Deutsch Award, which has been awarded to one woman only (Pippa Norris in 2014) since its inception (Abu-Laban, Sawer, & St-Laurent, 2018), while the PSA Sir Isaiah Berlin Prize has been awarded to five women scholars (Joni Lovenduski in 2013, Onora O'Neill in 2014, Pippa Norris in 2017, Anne Phillips in 2016, and Carole Pateman in 2019).[4] Prizes focusing on earlier career stages or of lower scope have seen a higher number of women winners (Rothmayr & Engeli, 2019). The Jean Blondel PhD Prize, for example, has acknowledged the work of eight women and eight men since its inception.[5]

Keynote speeches follow a largely similar pattern (Rothmayr & Engeli, 2019). The plenary lecture at the ECPR General Conference has remained a male bastion to the present day. Since the first conference in 2001, Pippa Norris (ECPR Budapest 2005) and Nonna Mayer (ECPR Bordeaux 2013) are the only women scholars who have delivered the plenary lecture while eleven men scholars have received this honor. Of the plenary roundtables at ECPR General Conferences, 57 percent have been chaired by men and 43 percent by women during the same time period. While the first plenary roundtable that had a woman chair was as late as the ECPR conference in Reykjavik in 2011, the feminization of conference roundtables has clearly accelerated since the ECPR conference in Oslo in 2017. The conferences in Kent (2001), Marburg (2003), Pisa (2007), Potsdam (2009), and Montreal (2015) exhibited the traditional pattern of "all-men-take-all." In Montreal, the chairs of the roundtables were all men, with only three women speakers out of thirteen on the roundtables. Reflecting the new ECPR Gender Action Plan, the ECPR conference in Wroclaw 2019 showcased more than 50 percent female speakers on the plenary roundtables and the four chairs were also women. Similarly to the awards, the invisibility of women in the most prestigious plenary events has been gradually compensated for over time by an increase in the women in plenary events at a lower level. It can be questioned whether this compensation from below is enough to reverse the symbolic invisibility of women at the top.

Professional recognition comes with power. Journal editorship and governance bodies of professional associations are two of the highest gatekeeping positions in the profession. Unsurprisingly, the feminization of powerful positions seems to have taken place at an even slower pace than the feminization of professional esteem. Of the journals that are ranked in the top thirty in the 2017 ISI Journal Citation Reports, 30 percent of the fifty-two lead editors and 34 percent of the eighty-seven associate editors are women. A comparison with a previous study puts this progress into perspective. Stegmaiers et al. (2011) collected similar data from the journals that appeared in the top fifty in 2010. At that time, only 18 percent of the lead editors and 23 percent of the associate editors were women. Equal opportunity to access journal editorship is still not secured for women. While some flagship journals have recently appointed their first female editors—for example, the *American Journal of Political Science* with Kathy Dolan and Jennifer Lawless, the new all-women editorial team of the *American Review of Political Science*, and the *European Journal of Political Research* with Isabelle Engeli and Sofia Vasilopoulou—nine of the top thirty journals still have an all-male editorial team.

Power also remains firmly in male hands within professional leadership in Europe. The ECPR Executive Committee (EC) has only had one female chair since the inception of the ECPR fifty years ago, Simona Piattoni (2012–2015). Since 2000, the representation of women on the executive oscillates between 33 percent (four women out of twelve members) for the good years (since 2018) and 16 percent (two women of twelve members) for the bad years. While it is true that there have been significantly fewer women than men running for the EC elections, women candidates seem to have, overall, a harder time in getting the support of the institutional representatives who are still a male majority. APSA had its first woman president in 1989 and since then nine other women have served in this capacity (Abu-Laban et al., 2018). IPSA's first female president was elected in 1991 (Carole Pateman) and two additional women have reached this leadership position since then (Abu-Laban et al., 2018). IPSA has not had fewer than 23.5 percent women on its EC since 2000, and currently 44.4 percent are women (Abu-Laban et al., 2018).

4. MOVING FORWARD

The implications of the gender gap in academic recognition in political science are multifold. First and foremost, there is the question of justice and fairness. An academic career is a long endeavor with multiple challenges and barriers for both male and female political scientists. Positions are scarce and expectations are increasing and diversifying—long hours are the norm and essential to remain competitive. Gender discrimination, prejudice and stereotypes, and the persistent predominance of a masculine career model where childcare responsibility is assumed by the female partner, create additional barriers for female political scientists. The gender gap in political science accounts for a large share of the system of inequalities in academia. A second argument in favor of acting on gender equality is individual quality. Catalyzing the faster feminization of leadership is an efficient way to achieve academic excellence. Outstanding scholars are currently sidelined even though they have the knowledge and the skills to contribute to the healthy development of the discipline and the profession. The third argument concerns the future of the discipline. Classrooms in political science programs are full of female students and students who do not identify with a binary gender. While the faculty has significantly diversified, the positions of power are still occupied predominantly by men. What kind of model are we offering to our students to inspire them in their future endeavors? What kind of perspectives are we offering to our early career colleagues for the development of their careers?

Making our profession more equal involves cultural and structural change—moving from a discipline that is male dominated and where research that is conducted by men is the golden standard, to a discipline where quality and not gender comes first. In this final section, we offer a number of recommendations for actions to contribute to achieving gender equality in the discipline. Women political scientists experience the *Prove-It-Again!*, *Tightrope*, *Maternal Wall*, and *Tug of War* patterns at all levels of their work. To fix the system, institutions need to shape the new normal: a gender-equal environment. In a reflective piece about gender inequality in American political science, Beckwith (2015) underlines three dimensions that are vital for making a significant difference: conductive structures, sympathetic leadership, activists, and allies.

To achieve change, we need data to understand whether and why there is gender inequality. These data arm us with information to develop policies that aim at closing the gap across the entire system. The APSA infrastructure of data collection, monitoring, and lobbying can serve as a model, and APSA has been a pioneer in data collection related to gender in the profession at the individual and departmental levels (Atchison, 2017). APSA appointed the Committee on the Status of Women in the Profession in 1969, and one of its first actions was to send a questionnaire about women in political science to departments of political science and graduate schools (Schuck, 1969). Additionally, APSA's official report on the status of women (APSA, 2005) was a major landmark in raising awareness about gender inequalities and launching a series of actions. *PS: Political Science and Politics* regularly publishes pieces on the gender status of the profession (with the first piece appearing as early as 1992), and many of these pieces rely on data collected by or with the support of APSA. While the task of collecting data in Europe is likely to be complex given the diversity in European academic systems, there is nevertheless no other way to identify patterns in gender inequalities. For the moment, only a handful of national associations collect (a limited) amount of gender data (Abu-Laban et al., 2018). The ECPR has an opportunity to play a leadership role in the promotion of gender equality in political science in Europe and expand the efforts in data collection about gender dynamics in the profession at the ECPR level and across national professional structures.

We recommend regular data collection over time across the three dimensions of academic recognition with the goals to (1) identify and monitor progress over time in career progression, pay gap, and institutional recognition as well as assess barriers linked to discrimination and harassment, (2) identify patterns in scholarly recognition and potential explanations for gender differentials in collaboration, submission, citation, and dissemination, and (3) keep collecting data on conference participation, invited speeches and keynotes, and positions of power. This could be done at least for the scholars who attend ECPR events and the departments which are institutional members of the ECPR in a first stage.

Moreover, it is also crucial to start data collection about minority groups and scholars in vulnerable positions. While we have acquired sufficient knowledge about gender dynamics to safely state that the profession has remained unequal up to the present day, the dire situation of minority scholars in European political science has remained largely undocumented. Women of color face an almost infinite number of barriers to access our profession in Europe. ECPR conferences and workshops taking place in Europe (including workshops on gender research) have remained overwhelming white. The inclusivity movement is expanding in European academia and political science remains largely absent for the time being.

The lack of generalizability is often put forward as an argument against the implementation of measures to solve gender inequality. Building an evidence base of European-wide data on gender inequalities in the profession will provide invaluable support toward designing actions in favor of gender equality. Communicating about gender equality in the profession across Europe and monitoring progress is a first step toward building collective action. National professional associations also have a pioneer role to play in European political science. The ECPR is in the position to take the lead and draft a Gender Equality Charter that institutional members can endorse. The charter should include a mandate to collect systematic gender data and to produce joint efforts in promoting gender equality on the ground, such as, for example, expanding the ECPR ban on all-men panels to the national professional associations and institutional members of the ECPR, promoting women's access to journal editorship, and implementing gender quotas for professional boards. Collective action is the only way forward to make sure that this chapter will not need to be rewritten for the ECPR sixtieth anniversary in 2030. After all, it is the system that needs to be fixed, and not women scholars.

NOTES

1. See the resources collected and assessed by Mirya Holman Ellen Key and Rebecca Kreitzer (2019). "Evidence of Bias in Standard Evaluations of Teaching": http://www.rebeccakreitzer.com/bias/.

2. Another key feature is the gap in research funding. While studies for political science are scarce, there is a growing scholarship pointing out gender patterns in research grant applications (see Ranga et al. 2012 for a review; European Commission 2009). Women apply less to research funding and for lower amounts, and their research profile as principal investigators seems to be less well evaluated than their male counterparts.

3. The expert directories can be accessed at https://womenalsoknowstuff.com/ for WomenAlsoKnowStuff and https://sites.google.com/view/pocexperts/home?auth user=2 for Scholars of Color Also Know Stuff. The Gender Balance Assessment Tool is accessible here: https://jlsumner.shinyapps.io/syllabustool/.

4. The annual Stein Rokkan Prize in Comparative Social Science Research has been awarded to six women scholars and sixteen men scholars since 1996, and the Mattei Dogan Foundation Prize in European Political Sociology has acknowledged the scientific contribution for the advancement of political sociology of four men scholars and two women scholars since its launch in 2007.

5. All the ECPR prizes named after scholars are named after men with the exception of the Joni Lovenduski prize for the best PhD in Gender and Politics and the *European Political Science* Prize, renamed in honor of Jacqui Briggs in December 2019.

REFERENCES

Abels, G., & Woods, D. R. (2015). The status of women in German political science. *European Political Science, 14*(2), 87–95.

Abu-Laban, Y. (2016). Representing a diverse Canada in political science: Power, ideas and the emergent challenge of reconciliation. *European Political Science, 15*(4), 493–507.

Abu-Laban, Y., Sawer, M., & St-Laurent, M. (2018). *IPSA gender and diversity monitoring report 2017*. Montreal. Retrieved from www.ipsa.org

Akhtar, P., Fawcett, P., Legrand, T., Marsh, D., & Taylor, C. (2005). Women in the political science profession. *European Political Science, 4*(3), 242–55.

Atchison, A. (2017). The politics of presence in academic professional associations: A research note on governance at the APSA. *PS: Political Science and Politics, 50*(4), 970–78.

Atchison, A. (2018). Towards the good profession: Improving the status of women in political science. *European Journal of Politis and Gender, 1*(1–2), 279–98.

Barnes, T. D., & Beaulieu, E. (2017). Engaging women: Addressing the gender gap in women's networking and productivity. *PS: Political Science and Politics, 52*(2), 461–66.

Bates, S., Jenkins, L., & Pflaeger, Z. (2012). Women in the profession: The composition of UK political science departments by sex. *Politics, 32*(3), 139–52.

Beal, F. M. (1970). *Double jeopardy: To be black and female*. Detroit, Michigan: Radical Education Project.

Beaulieu, E., Boydstun, A. E., Brown, N. E., Dionne, K. Y., Gillespie, A., Klar, S., Krupnikov, Y., Michelson, M. R., Searles, K., & Wolbrecht, C. (2017). Women also know stuff: Meta-level mentoring to battle gender bias in politial science. *PS: Political Science & Politics, 50*(3), 779–83.

Beckwith, K. (2015). State, academy, discipline: Regendering political science. *PS: Political Science and Politics, 48*(3), 445–49.

Begum, N., & Saini, R. (2019). Decolonising the curriculum. *Political Studies Review, 17*(2), 196–201.

Bohnet, I. (2016). *What works: Gender quality by design*. Cambridge, MA: Harvard University Press.

Bonjour, S., Mügge. L. M., & Roggeband, C. (2016). Lost in the mainstream? Gender in Dutch political science education. *European Political Science, 15*(3), 303–13.

Bowles, H. R., Babcock, L., & Lai, L. (2007). Social incentives for gender differences in the propensity to initiate negotiations: Sometimes it does hurt to ask. *Organizational Behavior and Human Decision Processes, 103*(1), 84–103.

Breuning, M., & Sanders, K. (2007). Gender and journal authorship in eight prestigious political science journals. *PS – Political Science and Politics, 40*, 347–51.

Briggs, J., & Harrison, L. (2015). The status of women in UK political science. *European Political Science, 14*, 105–15.

Brown, N. E., Horiuchi, Y., Htun, M., & Samuels, D. J. (2020). Gender gaps in perceptions of political science journals. *PS: Political Science & Politics*.

Burgess, D., & Borgida, E. (1999). Who women are, who women should be: Descriptive and prescriptive gender stereotyping in sex discrimination. *Psychology, Public Policy, and Law, 5*(3), 665–92.

Burton, D.-J., & Darcy, R. (1985). Careers of men and women in the profession: The 1970–1975 cohort. *The Western Political Quarterly, 38*(1), 132–47.

Canadian Politial Association Diversity Task Force. (2012). *Report and analysis of the Canadian Political Science Association Member Survey, May 2012.* Retrieved from https://www.cpsa-acsp.ca/documents/pdfs/diversity/2012_Diversity_Task_Force_Report.pdf, last accessed: November 27, 2019.

Colgan, J. (2017). Gender bias in international relations graduate education? New evidence from syllabi. *PS: Political Science & Politics, 50*(2), 456–60.

Collins, P. H. (1990). *Black feminist thought: Knowledge, consciousness, and the politics of empowerment.* New York, NY: Routledge.

Crenshaw, K. (1991). Mapping the margins: Intersectionality, identity politics, and violence against women of color. *Stanford Law Review, 43*(6), 1241–99.

Curtin, J. (2013). Women and political science in New Zealand. *Political Science, 65*(1), 63–83.

Davis, D. R. (2016). The journey to the top: Stories on the intersection of race and gender for African American Women in Academia and Business. *Journal of Research Initiatives, 2*(1).

Dion, M. L., Sumner, J. L., & Mitchell, S. M. (2018). Gendered citation patterns across political sciennce and social science methodology fields. *Political Analysis, 26*(3), 312–27.

Eagly, A. H., & Johnson, B. T. (1990). Gender and leadership style: A meta-analysis. *Psychological Bulletin, 108*(2), 233–56.

Eagly, A. H., Makhijani, M. G., & Klonsky, B. G. (1992). Gender and the evaluation of leaders: A meta-analysis. *Psychological Bulletin, 111*(1), 3–22.

Elizondo, A. (2015). The status of women in Spanish political science. *European Political Science, 14*, 96–104.

Emejulu, A., & Mcgregor, C. (2019). Towards a radical digital citizenship in digital education. *Critical Studies in Education, 60*(1), 131–47.

European Commission. (2009). *The gender challenge in research funding. Assessing the European national scenes.* Report. Luxembourg: Office for Official Publications of the European Communities.

European Consortium for Political Research (ECPR). *Gender study 2018.* Retrieved from https://ecpr.eu/Filestore/CustomContent/Membership/Gender_Study_2018.pdf, last accessed: February 21, 2020.

Friedan, B. (1963). *Feminine mystique.* New York: Norton.

Goede, M. De, Van Veelen, R., & Derks, B. (2016). *Financiële beloning van Mannen En Vrouwen in de Wetenschap.* Utrecht. Retrieved from https://www.lnvh.nl/uploads/moxiemanager/375.pdf, last accessed: February 21, 2020.

Gutiérrez y Muhs, G., Niemann, Y. F., Gonzalez, C. G., & Harris, A. P. (Eds.). (2012). *Presumed incompetent. The intersections of race and class for women inn academia.* Utah State University Press.

Hesli, V. L., Lee, J. M., & McLaughlin Mitchell, S. (2012). Predicting rank attainment in political science: What else besides publications affects promotion? *PS: Political Science and Politics, 45*(3), 475–92.

International Labour Organisation. (2019). *Ending violence and harassment in the world of work.* Geneva. Retrieved from www.ilo.org/publns.

Inter-Parliamentary Union, and Parliamentary Assembly of the Council of Europe. (2018). *Sexism, harassment and violence against women in parliaments in Europe.* Geneva. Retrieved from www.ipu.org.

Jaquette, J. (1971). The status of women in the profession: Tokenism. *PS: Political Science and Politics, 4*(4), 530–32.

Kantola, J. (2015). Political science as a gendered discipline in Finland. *European Political Science, 14*, 79–86. Palgrave Macmillan Ltd.

Key, E. M., & Lawrence Sumner, J. (2019). You research like a girl: Gendered research agendas and their implication. *PS: Political Science & Politics, 52*(4), 663–68.

König, T., & Ropers, G. (2018). Gender and editorial outomes at the American political science review. *PS: Political Science & Politics, 51*(4), 849–53.

LNVH. (2018). *Monitor Vrouwelijke Hoogleraren 2018.* Utrecht.

MacNell, L., Driscoll, A., & Hunt, A. (2015). What's in a name: Exposing gender bias in student ratings of teaching. *Innovative Higher Education, 40*(4), 291–303.

Maliniak, D., Powers, R., & Walter, B. F. (2013). The gender citation gap in international relations. *International Organization, 67*(4), 889–922.

Marbley, A. F., Wong, A., Santos-Hatchett, S. L., Pratt, C., & Jaddo, L. (2011). Women faculty of color: Voices, gender, and the expression. *Advancing Women in Leadership, 31*(1), 166–74.

Mattocks, K., & Briscoe-Palmer, S. (2016). Diversity, inclusion, and doctoral study: Challenges facing minority PhD students in the United Kingdom. *European Political Science, 15*(4), 476–92.

Medie, P. A., & Kang, A. J. (2018). Power, knowledge and the politics of gender in the Global South. *European Journal of Politics and Gender, 1*(1–2), 37–53.

Mitchell, S. M., Lange, S., & Brus, H. (2013). Gendered citation patterns in international relations journals. *International Studies Perspectives, 14*(4), 485–92.

Momani, B., Dreher, E., & Williams, K. (2019). More than a pipeline problem: Evaluating the gender pay gap in Canadian academia from 1996 to 2016. *Canadian Journal of Higher Education, 49*(1), 1–21.

Mügge, L., Evans, E., & Engeli, I. (2016). Gender in European political science education: Taking stock and future directions. *European Political Science, 15*(5), 281–91.

Naezer, M., & Benschop, Y. (2019). *Harassment in Dutch academia: Exploring manifestations, facilitating factors, effects and solutions commissioned by the Dutch Network of Women Professors (LNVH).* Utrecht.

Okimoto, T. G., & Brescoll, V. L. (2010). The price of power: Power seeking and backlash against female politicians. *Personality and Social Psychology Bulletin, 36*(7), 923–36.

Rai, S. M. (2015). Political performance: A framework for analysing democratic politics. *Political Studies, 63*(5), 1179–97.

Ranga, M., Gupta, N., & Etzkowitz, H. (2012). *Gender effects in research funding: A review of the scientific discussionn on the gender-specific aspects of the evaluation of funding proposals and the awarding of funding.* DFG.

Rollock, N. (2019). *Staying power: The career experiences and strategies of UK Black Female professors.* London: UCU. Retrieved from https://www.google.

co.uk/url?sa=t&rct=j&q=&esrc=s&source=web&cd=2&ved=2ahUKEwigkNays-LnAhW9RhUIHbB0DMUQFjABegQIBBAB&url=https%3A%2F%2Fwww.ucu.org.uk%2Fmedia%2F10075%2FStaying-Power%2Fpdf%2FUCU_Rollock_February_2019.pdf&usg=AOvVaw3-UgPhnDQVZhm_VpFGxJDt, last accessed: February 21, 2020.

Sampaio, A. (2006). Women of color teaching political sciennce: Examining the intersections of race, gender, and course material in the classroom. *PS: Political Sciennce & Politics*, *39*(4), 917–22.

Samuels, D. (2018). Gender and editorial outcomes at comparative political studies. *PS: Political Science & Politics, 51*(4), 854–58.

Sandberg, S. (2013). *Lean in: Women, work, and the will to lead*. New York: Alfred A. Knopf.

Sapiro, V., & Campbell, D. (2018). Report on the 2017 APSA survey on sexual harassment at annual meetings. *PS: Political Science and Politics, 51*(1), 197–206.

Savigny, H. (2019). The violence of impact: Unpacking relations between gender, media and politics. *Political Studies Review*.

Sawer, M., & Curtin, J. (2016). Organising for a more diverse political science: Australia and New Zealand. *European Political Science, 15*(4), 441–56.

Schuck, V. (1969). Women in political science: Some preliminary observations. *PS: Political Science and Politics, 2*(4), 642–53.

Slaughter, A.-M. (2015). *Unfinished business: Women, men, work, family*. New York, NY: Random House.

Smith, B. J. (2017). *American Indian tribal identity in the 21st century: Exploratory narratives of American Indian college students at predominantly white institutions* (Dissertation). Retrieved from https://hdl.handle.net/2142/97419, last accessed: November 27, 2019.

Smooth, W. G. (2016). Intersectionality and women's advancement in the discipline and across the academy. *Politics, Groups, and Identities, 4*(3), 513–28.

Stegmaier, M., Palmer, B., & Van Assendelft, L. (2011). Getting on the board: The presence of women in political science journal editorial positions. *PS: Political Science and Politics, 44*(4), 799–804.

Teele, D. L., & Thelen, K. (2017). Gender in the journals: Publication patterns in political science. *PS: Political Science & Politics, 50*(2), 433–47.

Timperley, C. (2013). Women in the academy. *Political Science, 65*(1), 84–104.

Tolleson-Rinehart, S., & Carroll, S. J. (2006). Thematic issue on the evolution of political science. *The American Political Science Review, 100*(4), 507–13.

Veelen, R. Van, & Derks, B. (2019). *Verborgen Verschillen in Werktaken, Hulpbronnen En Onderhandelingen over Arbeidsvoorwaarden Tussen Vrouwelijke En Mannelijke Wetenschappers in Nederland*. Universiteit Utrecht.

Williams, H., Bates, S., Jenkins, L., Luke, D., & Rogers, K. (2015). Gender and journal authorship: An assessment of articles published by women in three top British political science and international relations journals. *European Political Science, 14*(2), 116–30.

Williams, J. C., & Dempsey, R. (2014). *What works for women at work: Four patterns working women need to know*. New York: NYU Press.

Chapter 10

Race, Intersectionality, and Diversity in European Political Science

Shardia Briscoe-Palmer and Kate Mattocks

The "stale, male, and pale" nature of political science has been acknowledged, with a great deal of research addressing the representation of women in the profession (see Atchison, 2018; Engeli and Mügge, this volume). Savigny and Marsden (2011, p. 13) argue that political science "has tended to be dominated by white males and written as a reflection of their interests." According to the International Political Science Association's (IPSA) Gender and Diversity Monitoring Report, women make up approximately one-third of the membership of political science associations worldwide (Abu-Laban, Sawyer, & St-Laurent, 2018). While the status and inclusion of more women in the discipline has become a growing focus, a broader analysis needs to be developed that looks at other aspects of underrepresentation and marginalization in the discipline. In other words, *diversity* needs to go beyond sex and gender, to acknowledge other experiences. Additional "lenses," such as those focusing on race, ethnicity, disability, class, or sexuality, could and should be applied. To borrow an analogy from Crenshaw (1989), there is a need for multiple-axis—as opposed to single-axis—analyses of politics and "the political."

In general, the issue of race in European political science has been largely ignored. The absence of data collected on race and minimal research on this matter demonstrates the marginalized position of race in the discipline. A 2016 symposium on diversity and equality in European political science argues that the issue of "[h]ow to provide an accommodating culture is one of the most pressing questions of the 21st century" (Stockemer, Blair, Rashkova, & Moses, 2016a, p. 437). People of color are underrepresented in academia, and often have very different experiences than white counterparts, experiencing marginalization (inferior or peripheral treatment), othering (exclusion based on someone being perceived as different), discrimination, and isolation

(Bhopal, 2018; Osho, 2018; Rollock, 2018). Moreover, fruitful knowledge and expertise is lost from the discipline—other types of knowledge such as that from Indigenous communities, the Global South, formerly colonized communities—as a result of Eurocentric dominance in the (re)production of "legitimate" knowledge and knowers (Almeida, 2015, p. 81). Statistics from the United Kingdom, for example, show that more black women are employed as cleaners in universities than as academics in the same buildings (Osho, 2018).

It is against this backdrop that we set this chapter, an exploration of the lack of diversity in European political science, focusing primarily on race and ethnicity. Though this debate is usually on the fringes of academia (Law, 2017), we bring it to the fore; the chapter establishes race and ethnicity as a fundamental aspect of the debate on diversity, and diversity a fundamental aspect of political science. It does so for several reasons. First of all, for too long issues of identity and inclusion have been on the fringe of political science. For a discipline about power this is a weakness; indeed, our students are demanding more action on these issues (European Students' Union, 2017). Secondly, the world is changing rapidly, and political science must keep up in order that it remains relevant in a highly volatile political climate (Stockemer, Rashkova, Moses, & Blair, 2016b). It must also appropriately equip its students for a complex, multicultural world inclusive of different languages, religions, and beliefs. The International Association for Political Science Students' most recent annual themes—"overcoming injustice" in 2019 and "diversity and globalization" in 2018—reflect this. Therefore, on the occasion of ECPR's fifty-year anniversary, we ask: Can we celebrate our current position of diversity within European political science? At first glance there does not seem much to celebrate.

Writing a chapter on race, ethnicity, and diversity in European political science is a somewhat daunting task; as we discuss below, these terms do not have universal meanings. "Europe" and "European" are also contested terms, as is "political science." We adopt broad definitions of both, defining European as the forty-seven members of the Council of Europe. Though some of the statistics we use are from the European Union (EU), we do not conflate the EU with Europe. Political science, meanwhile, is a discipline defined by "its fixation on 'politics' *in all its myriad forms*" (Goodin & Klingemann, 1996, p. 7; emphasis added). This means that the composition of the profession is a political concern; after all, political science is about who has power and how that power is manifested. We also recognize that there is a great deal of heterogeneity in the histories, contexts, and language used around diversity across the continent (e.g., we would not expect diversity policies and procedures in British political science to be the same as diversity policy and procedures in Romanian political science).

Our objective, therefore, is to raise a series of questions and arguments on the significance of race and ethnicity—and diversity more broadly—in European political science, with the goal of provoking thought, reflection, and action. In many ways, the chapter raises more questions than it answers. What we would like readers to take from this chapter is an increased awareness of issues of race and ethnicity in the profession and a keenness to take action. We also encourage examination and exploration of our own teaching and research practices. We acknowledge that some people do not have the desire or the will to confront issues of diversity (Emejulu, 2019) and know that the chapter may make for uncomfortable reading for some. Nevertheless, the issue is important as it gets to the very core of what we study and who we are. Race in European political science must not be essentialized as an issue for a particular few but approached as a collective. The chapter first defines and contextualizes diversity. It then moves onto a discussion split into two main sections: race and ethnicity, and intersections. We finish by making recommendations and considerations for the future. We use a range of data for the chapter, including our own work on the career pipeline and professional development of early career academics in the United Kingdom, as well as information received from political science associations across the continent. Our own research has been undertaken in the United Kingdom, where the discussion of diversity is further advanced. The U.K. experience can therefore be informative for European political science in general.

1. SETTING THE SCENE: WHAT IS DIVERSITY?

Diversity is often talked about but rarely defined. Defining it is political. We take it to mean difference. In the context of an academic discipline/profession, we are mostly talking about personal characteristics. These can include race, ethnicity, disability, career stage, caring responsibilities, research focus, class, gender, religion, nationality, age, and more. Some of these are visible, some not, and some fluid, which raises further complexities in our understanding of diversity and inclusion. Difference therefore goes beyond "diversity in opinions and beliefs," which can be detached from issues of political exclusion (Phillips, 1995, p. 6). For us, diversity is closely related to the idea of *belonging*, or, to put it in another way, who or what is included in the profession and who or what is left out (Goodin & Klingemann, 1996)?

We understand diversity as *relational*, not in an essentialized, binary manner. Young (1990) describes how "groups," such as, say, lesbian women, black men, or Sikhs, share some features and do not share others. There are overlapping, shared experiences, as well as different ones. That being said, who the profession is composed of is a political matter itself: we are not disembodied from our race, gender, age, or class (Dei, 1999). It is time for increased awareness of challenges faced by underrepresented groups, as "blindness to difference disadvantages groups whose experience, culture, and socialized capacities differ from those of privileged groups" (Young, 1990, p. 164). Who we are, as individuals, matters because our own experiences and background, *in part*, shape what we consider to be "political."

Some argue that "diversity" has become an empty buzzword—a palatable alternative to race or ethnicity, or racism (Ahmed, 2012). Even with institutional or state-led initiatives to increase diversity, such as the United Kingdom's Race Equality Charter (Bhopal & Pitkin, 2018), it can remain an abstract term. Diversity alone cannot solve inequality issues or emancipate historical sufferers. European political science communities are no exception from such challenges, even if the discipline ultimately contains "varied traditions and different contemporary social and political contexts" (Berg-Schlosser, 2006, p. 163). Diversification of European political science does not require standardized action for change; rather, it requires agreed comprehension on the direction of change.

2. RACE AND ETHNICITY IN EUROPEAN POLITICAL SCIENCE

This chapter focuses specifically on race and ethnicity as a significant aspect of diversity within the discipline. While we focus on these terms, we do not shy away from their controversial nature; they have complex histories and genealogies. *Race* is defined as a vast group of people loosely bound together by historically contingent, socially significant elements of their morphology and/or ancestry (Haney-Lopez, 2000, p. 165). Race has social and political consequences: "like power, [race] is a relational concept . . . comparison, judgment, codification, hierarchy, and ultimately, inequality are the keywords that help characterize the process and relationship between the race construct, politics, and institutions" (Hanchard, 2018, p. 5, as quoted in Thompson, 2019, p. 1315). Identified commonly via ethnic groups, it can determine economic perspectives, permeate our politics and screens, and select us for the job market. *Ethnicity* is seen as an ancestral sameness, not a social pathology (Ajulu, 2010, p. 252). Creating community solidarity based on geographical ancestry and cultural commonalities among earlier colonial identities, such grouping has led to exploitations in the forms of the segregation, domination, and, at times, cleansing of particular groups. However, these terms do not have stable meanings; in Germany, for example, data on race and ethnicity is conceptualized as migrant background, whereas in Slovakia, ethnicity, religion, language, and national origin overlap, as they are highly centered on the idea of nationality (Farkas, 2017). There are challenges in trying to establish shared comprehension across cultural boundaries (Mattocks, 2018). Moreover, many European countries do not collect national statistics on race or ethnicity (see Farkas, 2017; Lentin, 2008). Scholars have named this "color-blindness" phenomenon anti-racialism. Anti-racialism "refuses a critical examination of the political conditions that enable racialization and racism" (Boulila, 2019, p. 1407).

Before turning to the discipline of political science, it is useful to put racism and discrimination into a broader context, using the 2015 Eurobarometer survey on discrimination in the EU-28.[1] Thirty percent of ethnic minority respondents indicated that they had experienced discrimination or harassment based on their ethnicity (European Commission, 2015, p. 71). Across the EU, 64 percent of respondents indicated that "they would be at ease if someone of a different ethnic origin from the majority of the population were appointed to the highest elected political position in their country" (European Commission, 2015, p. 19). Recent scholarship on race and racism in Europe has highlighted some of the nuances of these issues, particularly around migration and inclusion, broad issues that affect changing society, and, thus, the makeup of student and potential staff populations (see, for example, Boulila, 2019; Marfouk, 2019; Sadeghi, 2019).

In the context of a particular profession, racial and ethnic representation straddles many areas. We can talk about *who* the profession is composed of, as well as the structural and institutional impacts on representation. We can also discuss ideas—pedagogy, curricula, and research agendas. The first step in thinking about diversity is determining the marginalized groups in the discipline. Who are the political scientists of Europe? This is not a straightforward task: the main barrier here is a lack of data. We contacted twenty-four political science associations across the continent; of those that responded, none of them except the U.K. PSA collected statistics on or had any direct initiatives to encourage racial and ethnic diversity, although several associations mentioned that awareness was increasing on these issues. It is only with statistics that we can begin to see the true picture and then move toward a deeper understanding of people's experiences. In the absence of such figures, we make use of existing research on the profession, as well as more general research on discrimination across Europe.

Race and ethnicity affect access, belonging, and progression in academia (Harris & Gonzalez, 2012; Rollock, 2019). It is only recently that "others" have been accepted in a university setting; "[h]istorically, universities have largely catered for white privileged males, and a white, elitist, masculinist, heterosexist, able-bodied and Eurocentric culture still pervades many [of them]" (Law, 2017, p. 333). Many scholars writing on race and higher education (HE) have conceptualized universities as locales of institutionalized racism (Bhopal, 2018; Mirza, 2018; Rollock, 2019). Research has highlighted how overt and covert racism occurs in the academic space in multiple ways, including gaps in cultural awareness, exclusions of people of color from decision-making, and racist practices in hiring and promotion, as well as more direct forms such as bullying and harassment (Bhopal & Henderson, 2019).

One of the key issues in understanding the composition of the profession is the career pipeline—how do people make the transition from school to university to postgraduate studies and into an academic career?[2] Inequalities in education start from birth, not from when people complete a doctoral degree (unfortunately, space does not allow a full exploration of this literature; see Clark & Zygmunt, 2014; Haller, 1985). The narrative of "work hard enough and one will succeed" (Harris & Gonzalez, 2012) is still dominant; however, career progression is not experienced the same by everyone. As Eddo-Lodge (2018) explains, the legacy of racism does not exist without purpose. It is "not just a disempowerment from those affected by it but an empowerment for those who are not" (pp. 115–16). Evidence shows that academic gatekeepers and "insider networks" are important in progression (Bhopal, 2018; Briscoe-Palmer & Mattocks, 2020), which raises the question of who has access to these and who does not. Our own research has found that U.K. PhD researchers in political science who come from a black or minority ethnic background are less likely to want to continue in an academic career than their white counterparts. They also reported higher instances of exclusion and isolation during doctoral study (Mattocks & Briscoe-Palmer, 2016). Such experiences can make it "difficult to create sustainable scholarly communities and to find role models and mentors" (Henry et al., 2017, p. 7).

Begum and Saini (2019) argue that underrepresented groups such as people of color must work hard to fit in to an academic environment that is mostly white and middle class. The Cruel Ironies Collective (2019, p. 181), in the context of representation in Dutch academia, argue that "the critique of the absence of Black womxn[3] is valid only when articulated by a non-Black person." Pásztor's (2016) work on second-generation Turkish people navigating Austria's stratified school system demonstrates the barriers they must overcome to make it to university, let alone into postgraduate study. A recent report in the United Kingdom examines the attainment gap in black and minority ethnic students who come in with the same grades but do not achieve the same classes of degrees (Universities UK/NUS, 2019).

When we think about who occupies the spaces of learning, the student body is often much more diverse (European Students' Union, 2017; Pásztor, 2016; Universities UK/NUS, 2019). Indeed, the European Students' Union highlights inclusion as their number one current strategic priority: "big groups of potential students are left out from our higher education systems.

Not only [from] the right to study, but also to benefit from the potentials of gaining intercultural competences, networks and experiences" (European Students' Union, 2017, p. 1). Similarly, a direct quote from a respondent to a survey on the labor of doctoral research in the United Kingdom shows why this representation matters:

> I would like to stay in academia; however, the future is very bleak for black female academics within political science. I would have to break that glass ceiling which will be another hard struggle on top of all the other struggles I face. However, I would like to be able to pave a way for those undergraduates behind me who also have the same aspirations as myself but see no one like them standing in the distance. (Mattocks & Briscoe-Palmer, 2016, p. 488)

Such experiences are echoed in a recent Universities U.K./NUS (2019) report, explaining how low numbers of black, Asian, and ethnic minority staff limits an institution's capabilities to address not only the issue of racial diversity but also, consequently, the academic achievements of its students of color. Bhopal (2019) argues that the HE sector must tackle equality and diversity to create a more inclusive workforce. Formal mentorship schemes were identified as a way for black academics to advance their careers, increase confidence, and achieve job satisfaction (Bhopal, 2014).

Who the discipline is composed of is important, but so too is the politics of knowledge production, since the political also includes "who is allowed to speak, who is heard, and who is silenced" (Mattocks & Briscoe-Palmer, 2016, p. 478) in curricula. What kind of knowledge is accepted? The relationship between knowledge and power raises an important question: "In whose interest and for what purpose is knowledge constructed?" (Tickner & Sjöberg, 2006, p. 187). It has been proclaimed that knowledge production within political science is an "epistemological crisis" (Emejulu, 2019, p. 202). The curriculum is therefore also a site of inclusion or exclusion, belonging or not. The colonial past of Europe cannot be ignored in understanding and addressing race and ethnicity in the discipline. Indeed, Rodriguez de Luna (2016) frames her discussion of diversity in European political science as "the rendering of the European Political Science more inclusive to knowledge, theories and concepts produced outside of Europe or by non-western scholars" (522).

Coined initially in South Africa with the "Rhodes must fall"[4] movement, a call for a transformation of educational attitudes after colonialism and apartheid, the decolonizing movement in HE, has led to a light being shone on European academic communities. Knowledge in Europe is dominated by colonial histories about difference: "Race and racism have never been subjects for serious (read mainstream and western) social theoretical discussion because they are seen as of marginal concern. The discussion of race . . . is the discussion of *other people*, not included in the story of western social and political thought" (Lentin, 2008, p. 494). Asian, Indigenous, and African knowledge have long been considered unscientific (Dei, 1999); campaigns to decolonize the curriculum by both students and academics alike ask HE institutions across all disciplines to challenge this—to look back at our shared assumptions of the world based on colonial and imperialist hierarchies (Heleta, 2016; Le Grange, 2016). Calls to decolonize the curriculum seek broader and more inclusive sources of information that question what is worth studying and how should it be studied.

In their piece on decolonizing U.K. political science, Begum and Saini (2019) call for change and transformation by exposing the racism and sexism in political science that impacts research agendas, priorities, and therefore opportunities. They discuss marginalized and often neglected research areas that often fall into subdisciplines of *other* research, again perpetuating the saliency of "knowledge" worthy of production, impacting progression, research funding, and career networks. Their call can be expanded to European political science. Decolonizing political science does not mean *getting rid* of what has traditionally worked. Rather, it is an opportunity to include others and embrace difference, to diversify. It is a call to engage in an educational pursuit that is about not only sharing information with students but also growing intellectually (hooks, 1994):

> In a rapidly changing world, it is imperative that organizations constantly question underlying assumptions in order to keep improving the quality of their product. Exposure to diversity may show that habits and customs that were taken for granted, both by the dominant majority and by ethnic minorities, are not universal. (Essed, 1996, pp. 86–87)

Knowledge production also concerns research and publications in the discipline. Mügge, Evans, and Engeli (2016) offer an intersectional look into knowledge production and argue that academics should acknowledge not just what is taught but who is publishing in political science. Applying such an approach to pedagogy enables political scientists across Europe not only to teach a more diverse curriculum, but to engage with a diverse range of reading materials, resources, and citations (Erzeel & Mügge, 2016). Nonetheless, decolonizing the curriculum is not a "fix all" solution, when there are still structural and institutional biases and discrimination, such as the aforementioned types of racism and discrimination (Hiraldo, 2010; Pilkington, 2013).

There is also a need for further reflection on locating the self in our research, to "think about how identities and social positions are multiple, shifting, and should be interrogated throughout fieldwork and woven into our writings" (Reyes, 2018, p. 4). Factors such as our bodies, racial and ethnic identities, appearance, and accents "matter and are used to gain access and understand the field" (Reyes, 2018, p. 6). Below, we share a short extract on our own positionalities:

> I (Shardia), a masculinity scholar, research gender and race at their intersections. My research interests grew from being a mother of two black boys in the UK. It has become somewhat of a norm for me to be the only black in the academic room, especially in political science networks. Diversity in my experience cannot be integrated without the understanding of the other.

> I (Kate) research cultural policy. My thinking on belonging, cultural identity, and citizenship developed when I first moved as a masters student to the UK from my home country of Canada. I had a UK passport—and thus several rights—but didn't feel "British." These personal reflections in part led to my later intellectual inquires into the governance of cultural identity.

We often think about these factors at PhD stage, but what about post-PhD? Positionality not only affects our subjectivity but often shapes our research trajectories (Reyes, 2018). Diversity within European political science also requires increased reflectivity in our methodologies (Robertson, 2002). Moreover, who do we engage with in our research and public engagement? What methods are we utilizing in our research? How does race and ethnicity impact institutional processes such as ethical approval? Race, a fundamental element of any subjectivity, must be given a prominent role in this debate. As Eddo-Lodge (2018, p. 84) argues, "[I]n order to dismantle unjust, racist structures, we must see race."

3. INTERSECTIONS

In this section, we focus on other forms of oppression that can intersect with racism and ethnic discrimination. American legal scholar Kimberlé Crenshaw (1989) formalized the concept of "intersectionality" to interrogate the politics of antidiscrimination in the American legal system. Crenshaw's work recognizes multiple types of experiences and oppressions, focusing on race and gender. Subsequent work has developed intersectional analysis to include other oppressions including marginalized men, social class, and others (Briscoe-Palmer, 2020; Collins, 2015; Yuval-Davis, 2006). Space means that we cannot cover everything here; instead, we introduce a few key issues: class, sexuality, nationality, immigrant status, and disability.

To set this discussion in context, we again turn to the 2015 European Commission report on discrimination in the EU-28. The report detailed widespread reporting of the perception and experience of discrimination. With regards to discrimination at work—the closest we get to the subject of this chapter—overall, 83 percent of all respondents said they would be comfortable working with a black colleague, but this varied widely by country, ranging from 97 percent in Sweden to 48 percent in Slovakia. Muslims scored last in every country when it came to whether someone would be comfortable working with a colleague representing that religion (again there is a lot of difference with 89 percent indicating comfortable in Sweden and 27 percent in the Czech Republic). Finally, in terms of disability, 96 percent of respondents in Ireland and France indicated they would be comfortable working with a disabled colleague, whereas the number was 66 percent in Slovakia. 13 percent of total respondents said they would be uncomfortable working with a lesbian, gay, or bisexual colleague, and 17 percent with a transgender colleague. These numbers make for stark, uncomfortable, yet illuminating reading. We cannot generalize that these would apply to the world of academia, much less our own discipline. However, they are useful figures for context and in particular showcase some of the geographical and cultural differences across the EU-28.

The first intersection we examine is social class, which intersects with race and ethnicity to create multiple forms of oppression. Constance G. Anthony identifies social class as "the most corrosive" intersection she faced in her academic career, because it is the least socially recognized (2012, p. 307). Class creates inequalities and privileges. Race has a significant intersectional role with social class due to notions of "triple oppression" and discriminations. The "triple oppression" debate exposed by Yuval-Davis (2006, p. 195) claims, as an example, that a black woman could suffer from three different disadvantages: being black, a woman, and working class. Increased attention to these intersections would make for a more socially and politically engaged, and thus relevant, discipline.

A second area of intersecting oppression is sexuality and sexual orientation. The work of David Patternote (2018) illustrates the marginalization of sexuality in European political science. For context, 32 percent of lesbian, gay, bisexual, and transgender (LGBT) respondents to the Eurobarometer survey indicated that they had experienced discrimination or harassment on the grounds of sexual orientation (European Commission, 2015). Patternote writes that political scientists working on sexuality have often left the field because they could not find jobs, or migrated to another, more welcoming discipline. He argues that "it will be necessary to confront the implicit heteronormativity and the latent homo- and transphobia" of political science and of academic institutions themselves (Patternote, 2018, p. 64). People of color who also identify as lesbians, gays, bisexuals, transgenders, and queer (LGBTQ) may face additional challenges as a result of this identity (Brown,

2011; Collins, 2004). In 2016, the LGBT Inclusive Curriculum International Conference (United Kingdom) pioneered a discussion on diversifying the curriculum to include LGBT histories, examples, texts, and authors. The conference also formulated a best practice guide on how to as well as why diversifying the curriculum is a significant step toward inclusive change.

A third issue and potentially intersecting site of burden is belonging related to nationality. In some countries, this is closely linked to race, and in others it is not. Academia is by nature international. Grigolo, Lietaert, and Marimon (2010) argue that in countries adhering to the Continental Europe model of HE (which includes Italy, France, Spain, and Germany), the academic structures "tend to be rigid, highly centralized and regulated, while at the same time dominated by informal rules that tend to exclude outsiders—including foreigners—and favour insiders, namely internal staff and candidates" (Grigolo et al., 2010, p. 121). They also show that universities in the Scandinavian model rarely recruit outside the country. Some of our own current research demonstrates the corrosive effects, meanwhile, that the United Kingdom's referendum on EU membership has had on early career researchers in the discipline, which has made some people move or want to move away from the United Kingdom due to a divisive, unwelcoming culture (Mattocks and Briscoe-Palmer, 2019).

A final intersection is disability, including physical and mental health and well-being. Approximately 27 percent of the EU-28 population lives with a disability (European Commission, 2017);[5] moreover, "[d]iscrimination continues to be a major barrier to the full inclusion of disabled people in society" (European Commission, 2017, p. 15), with 37 percent of disabled respondents reporting discrimination or harassment on those grounds (European Commission, 2015, p. 71). Some evidence indicates that disabled people are underrepresented in academia (Brown & Leigh, 2018). A recent review of the literature of lived experiences of people with disabilities working in HE found that while there were many positive experiences, there were challenges too (Mellifont et al., 2019). These often reflect the theme of belonging. Some anecdotal conversations with colleagues across Europe have indicated that there has been gradually more awareness on issues of disability, health, and well-being. Yet, many still suffer in silence in an environment that is already highly stressful (Guthrie et al., 2017) and rewards a culture of overwork.

With only a short paragraph on a few intersections, this section sacrifices depth for breadth. Ultimately, despite advances in other disciplines, intersectionality "has not yet gained a strong foothold in political science research, particularly in Europe" (Erzeel & Mügge, 2016, p. 342). However, increased awareness of discrimination and oppression, strategies of support for diversity in HE, as well as a welcoming of a more diverse range of research ideas and knowledge production processes will have a positive impact on European political science and its intellectual inquiries.

4. CONCRETE STEPS FOR CHANGE

Fifty years on from the creation of the ECPR we can say the picture is bleak for a discipline that is approximately one-third women and overwhelmingly composed of white, able-bodied people. While there has been some progress made on women in the discipline, progress for other underrepresented groups remains a challenge, and their experiences often hidden and silenced. In this chapter, we have conceptualized the diversity debate as issues of *inclusion* and *belonging* and linked that to the wider societal relevance of political science. In this final section, we reflect on what we believe needs to be done to make the discipline more inclusive, while recognizing that academia is also a site of privilege (Stockdill & Yu Danico, 2012).

A key challenge in studying this issue, and a theme running through the chapter, is a lack of data. That only one European political science association—the U.K. Political Studies Association—collects data on race demonstrates that this is not an issue of priority. The data must be there in order to understand the full picture. As Oppenheimer argues in the case of France, "Those who wish to address the problem [of racism] are left without an important tool, while those who do not regard discrimination and inequality as an issue . . . are permitted to hide behind this lack of data" (Oppenheimer, 2008, p. 743). The scale of this challenge is shown by guidance from the European Network Against Racism (2015), whose first piece of advice is that "collecting statistics is legal" to dispel widespread belief that it is not.

In thinking about ways to increase diversity, there is ample opportunity to learn from the practices of universities and professional associations that have been more active and successful in these areas, such as the American Political Science Association (APSA) and the U.K. PSA. The U.K. PSA has recently launched a doctoral scholarship fund to encourage diverse voices in the profession (Wilson, 2019). It also has—to name a few examples—a no all-male panel policy, an anti-sexual harassment policy, and has childcare provision at its annual conference. Across the Atlantic, APSA has a number of initiatives, including funding opportunities for underrepresented racial and ethnic groups, fellowships, and a summer school program. APSA also has nine committees on the status of underrepresented and/or marginalized groups in the profession, including Asian-Pacific Americans, blacks, Latinos y Latinas, and LGBT individuals. APSA's data collection is extensive, looking at, among others, membership, conference attendance, recipients of prizes, participation and membership in (subdiscipline) sections, graduate placements, and first-generation scholars (APSA, 2018). These initiatives alone do not solve oppression or racism within the academy, but they are a start in raising awareness. There is also the need for a more comprehensive review of good practices worldwide—including those from learned associations in other disciplines—in order to build on collective knowledge.

We therefore call for political science associations across the continent to take data collection seriously, to ask your members to share more information about themselves, so that we can obtain a more accurate picture of the discipline. We recognize that there are challenges—practical, cultural, political, and otherwise. Additionally, the resources required for change may be limited. We also recognize the unrealistic expectations of increased diversity and/or inclusivity within particular geographical locations. However, without basic information on who we are as a discipline, we cannot make changes. Similar to calls from Begum and Saini (2019) and Mügge et al. (2016), we agree that European political science would benefit from an audit of the discipline, mapping the progression of marginalized groups through the academy.

Beyond professional associations, individual or national initiatives and policies can be helpful in changing experiences and raising awareness. The broader political landscape of governments, politicians, and regulators and agencies can work to create a landscape that can push for change, or that can accept the status quo.[6] The United Kingdom has been in some ways a leader on this front. National initiatives such as Stonewall, the Race Equality Charter, and Athena SWAN target LGBT, race and ethnicity, and gender inclusivity, respectively. While these are not without their critiques (see Ahmed, 2007; Tzanakou & Pearce, 2019), they do help to raise awareness. We must, though, add a note of caution here on the takeover of the concepts such as "equality" and "diversity," which, some argue, have become to be used strategically by universities and other bodies as something with "a commercial value" to be managed (Ahmed, 2012, p. 53). This raises questions regarding outward-facing initiatives, such as those for recruitment of students, and internal ones that focus on improving conditions for students and/or faculty. Instead of equality and diversity as a "thing" to be achieved, it is a living, fluid process including agency, with an emphasis on the idea of belonging.

A third and final crucial point, and one that runs through the other two, is that we encourage listening to experiences of marginalized people and then working *with* these groups, in order to avoid "assimilation" strategies which privilege those who set the rules and structures (Young, 1990). It is important to work with groups, allowing them to have a genuine voice and valuing their expertise. Borrowing from the literature on political representation, Phillips (1995, p. 13) argues that "[w]hen policies are worked out *for* rather than *with* a politically excluded constituency, they are unlikely to engage with all relevant concerns." Lentin (2008, p. 499) argues that "[t]here is no need for

Europe to integrate into its outsiders," because what is "European" has come to be seen as what is universal: outsiders must integrate into Europe. Her call for a reversal of this can be modified for our own purposes—rather than "outsiders" or people on the margins of political science having to assimilate, political science can be more inclusive and adapt to a multitude of voices, people, and experiences.

Feminist literature has strongly made the argument that experience is evidence. Thus, it often falls on the oppressed to push for change, which can create burnout (Gorski, 2019). People who raise these issues can be considered "inconvenient" (Begum & Saini, 2019), as challenging powerful structures, institutions, and individuals "opens oneself to assault, misinterpretations, abuse and denial" (Dei, 1999, p. 20). However, this is work that anyone can do—listening and paying attention to those around you and reading about others' experiences.[7] As Stockemer et al. (2016a, p. 439) argue, there is much to be done:

> We need to continue to provide support for women, black and minority ethnic (BME) and lesbian, gay, bisexual and transgender (LGBT) colleagues, as well as colleagues with disabilities. However, it is not enough to hire and support these still underrepresented groups; it is also important to create a discipline which embraces a climate of equality and diversity; a situation that does not discriminate against a particular discourse, method, approach or way of thinking. (Stockemer et al., 2016a, p. 439)

Crucially, we link this to the future of the relevance of the discipline. Stockemer et al. (2016b, p. 814) argue that the "capacity of the discipline to pay something back to society" is European political science's main strength. There is space for it to be even more relevant.

We would like to conclude with a return to the question of the purpose of education and universities in general. Most of you reading this chapter will be involved in teaching as well as research. The European Students' Union (2017, p. 3) wants to "put higher emphasis on the necessary tools to gain in-depth understanding of what we know outside formal education and how it can be used in a *changing world* for the *public good*" (emphasis added). The International Association for Political Science Students (2017), meanwhile, argues that "[f]ar more than an academic endeavour . . . the meaning of politics shapes our view of core elements of contemporary society, such as regimes, institutions, actors, conflicts, human rights or governance." We echo APSA's argument that "[e]xcellence in diversity and inclusion will strengthen and grow the profession and its capacity to address the challenging issues of the 21st Century" (APSA, 2018, p. 19). We applaud and recognize that there has been some positive change on this, but there is still more work to do to create a discipline that is reflective of the diversity of its population.

Ignoring or silencing these issues—willfully or not—does not remove their consequences (Lentin, 2008). A discipline that is more diverse and inclusive will be more representative, more equipped to tackle society's problems, more relevant, and more intellectually stimulating.

5. ACKNOWLEDGMENTS

We would like to thank the European political science associations who responded to our call for information in this chapter. We would also like to thank the editors of this volume, Gabriele Abels, Karen Celis, Beth Derks-Van Damme, Christopher Featherstone, Cherry Miller, Heather Savigny, Eniola Anuoluwapo Soyemi, and John Turnpenny.

NOTES

1. Our own exploration of this issue goes beyond the EU-28, but we still find this a useful report.

2. An important related issue is how merit and promotion are defined. For a discussion of this issue in a U.K. political science context, see Gonzalez Ginocchio, Hindmoor, and Stanley (2019).

3. Womxn refers to self-defining identity of black, queer, women, and/or gender nonbinary. It is an alternative from politicized categories of defining nonwhite women.

4. Cecil Rhodes founded the south African territory of Rhodesia (now Zimbabwe and Zambia). Serving as prime minister during the late 1800s, Rhodes was well known for his imperialist beliefs and diamond company legacies.

5. We can expect that number to be lower for the population of working age, as disability rises with age.

6. Thanks to John Turnpenny for this point.

7. See, for example, Mellifont et al. (2019) on how to be more accommodating to academics with disabilities.

REFERENCES

Abu-Laban, Y., Sawer, M., & St-Laurent, M. (2018). *IPSA gender and diversity monitoring report 2017*. Montreal: IPSA.

Ahmed, S. (2007). "You end up doing the document rather than doing the doing": Diversity, race equality and the politics of documentation. *Ethnic and Racial Studies, 30*(4), 590–609.

Ahmed, S. (2012). *On being included: Racism and diversity in institutional life*. Durham, NC: Duke University Press.

Ajulu, R. (2002). Politicised ethnicity, competitive politics and conflict in Kenya: A historical perspective. *African Studies, 61*(2), 251–68.

Almeida, S. (2015). Race-based epistemologies: The role of race and dominance in knowledge production. *Wagadu: A Journal of Transnational Women's and Gender Studies, 13*, 79–105.

American Political Science Association. (2018). *Diversity and inclusion report.* Retrieved from https://www.apsanet.org/Portals/54/diversity%20and%20inclusion%20prgms/DIV%20reports/Diversity%20Report%20Executive%20-%20Final%20Draft%20-%20Web%20version.pdf?ver=2018-03-29-134427-467 [accessed 17 May 2019].

Anthony, C. G. (2012). The port Hueneme of my mind: The geography of working-class consciousness in one academic career. In G. Gutiérrez y Muhs, Y. F. Niemann, C. G. Gonzalez, & A. P. Harris (Eds.), *Presumed incompetent: The intersections of race and class for women in academia* (pp. 300–12). Logan, UT: Utah State University Press.

Atchison, A. (2018). Towards the good profession: Improving the status of women in political science. *European Journal of Politics and Gender, 1*(1–2), 279–98.

Begum, N., & Saini, R. (2019). Decolonising the curriculum. *Political Studies Review, 17*(2), 196–201.

Berg-Schlosser, D. (2006). Political science in Europe: Diversity, excellence, relevance. *European Political Science, 5*(2), 163–70.

Bhopal, K. (2018). *White privilege: The myth of a post-racial society.* Bristol: Policy Press.

Bhopal, K. (2019). Success against the odds: The effect of mentoring on the careers of senior Black and minority ethnic academics in the UK. *British Journal of Educational Studies.* doi:10.1080/00071005.2019.1581127.

Bhopal, K., & Henderson, H. (2019). Competing inequalities: Gender versus race in higher education institutions in the UK. *Educational Review.* doi:10.1080/00131911.2019.1642305.

Bhopal, K., & Pitkin, C. (2018). *Investigating higher education institutions and their views on the Race Equality Charter.* London: University and College Union.

Boulila, S. C. (2019). Race and racial denial in Switzerland. *Ethnic and Racial Studies, 42*(9), 1401–18.

Briscoe-Palmer, S. (2020). *The politics of Black Caribbean masculinity: A (de)construction of the postcolonial other* (Unpublished doctoral thesis). Birmingham, UK: University of Birmingham.

Briscoe-Palmer, S., & Mattocks, K. (2020). Career Development and Progression of Early Career Academics in Political Science: A Gendered Perspective. Unpublished paper.

Brown, M. (2011). Gender and sexuality I: Intersectional anxieties. *Progress in Human Geography, 36*(4), 541–50.

Brown, N., & Leigh, J. (2018). Ableism in academia: Where are the disabled and ill—academics? *Disability & Society, 33*(6), 985–89.

Clark, P., & Zygmunt, E. (2014). A close encounter with personal bias: Pedagogical implications for teacher education. *The Journal of Negro Education, 83*(2), 147–61.

Collins, P. H. (2004). *Black sexual politics: African Americans, gender, and the new racism.* New York: Routledge.

Collins, P. H. (2015). Intersectionality definitional dilemmas. *Annual Review of Sociology, 41*(1), 1–20.

Crenshaw, K. (1989). Demarginalizing the intersection of race and sex: A Black feminist critique of antidiscrimination doctrine, feminist theory and anti-racist politics. *University of Chicago Legal Forum, 1989*(1), 139–67.

Cruel Ironies Collective. (2019). Cruel ironies: The afterlife of Black Women's intervention. In A. Emejulu & F. Sobande (Eds.), *To exist is to resist: Black feminism in Europe* (pp. 181–94). London: Pluto Press.

Dei, G. J. S. (1999). The denial of difference: Refraining anti-racist praxis. *Race Ethnicity and Education, 2*(1), 17–38.

Eddo-Lodge, R. (2018). *Why I am no longer talking to White people about race.* London: Bloomsbury Publishing.

Emejulu, A. (2019). Can political science decolonise? A response to Neema Begum and Rima Saini. *Political Studies Review, 17*(2), 202–6.

Erzeel, S., & Mügge, L. (2016). Introduction: Intersectionality in European political science research. *Politics, 36*(4), 341–45.

Essed, P. (1996). *Encouraging diversity: Gender, color and culture.* Amherst, MA: Massachusetts University Press.

European Commission. (2015). *Report on special Eurobarometer 437: Discrimination in the EU in 2015.* Retrieved from http://www.equineteurope.org/IMG/pdf/ebs _437_en.pdf [accessed May 17, 2019].

European Commission. (2017). *Progress report on the implementation of the European Disability Strategy (2010–2020).* Brussels: European Commission.

European Network Against Racism. (2015). *Equality data collection: Facts and principles.* Retrieved from https://www.enar-eu.org/IMG/pdf/edc-general_factsheet_final.pdf [accessed May 15, 2019].

European Students' Union. (2017). *Strategic priorities 2018–2020.* Retrieved from https://www.esu-online.org/wp-content/uploads/2018/03/BM73_7a_Strategic-Priorities-2018-20.pdf [accessed May 17, 2019].

Farkas, L. (2017). *Data collection in the field of ethnicity: Analysis and comparative review of equality data collection practices in the European Union.* Luxembourg: Publications Office of the European Union.

Gonzalez Ginocchio, B., Hindmoor, A., & Stanley, L. (2019). *Pluralism in political studies: The politics of recognition and the recognition of politics.* Paper presented at the Political Studies Association conference, Nottingham, UK, 15–17 April.

Goodin, R. E., & Klingemann, H.-D. (1996). Political science: The discipline. In R. E. Goodin & H.-D. Klingemann (Eds.), *A new handbook of political science* (pp. 3–49). Oxford: Oxford University Press.

Gorski, P. C. (2019). Racial battle fatigue and activist burnout in racial justice activists of color at predominantly White colleges and universities. *Race Ethnicity and Education, 22*(1), 1–20.

Grigolo, M., Lietaert, M., & Marimon, R. (2010). Shifting from academic "brain drain" to "brain gain" in Europe. *European Political Science, 9*(1), 118–30.

Guthrie, S., Lichten, C., van Belle, J., Ball, S., Knack, A., & Hofman, J. (2017). *Understanding mental health in the research environment: A rapid evidence assessment.* Cambridge: RAND Europe.

Haller, E. J. (1985). Pupil race and elementary school ability grouping: Are teachers biased against Black children? *American Educational Research Journal, 22*(4), 465–83.

Hanchard, M. (2018). *The spectre of race: How discrimination haunts Western democracy.* Princeton: Princeton University Press.

Hanley-Lopez, I. F. (2000). The social construction of race. In R. Delgado & J. Stefancic (Eds.), *Critical race theory: The cutting edge* (pp. 163–75). Philadelphia: Temple University Press.

Harris, A. P., & Gonzalez, C. G. (2012). Introduction. In G. Gutiérrez y Muhs, Y. F. Niemann, C. G. Gonzalez, & A. P. Harris (Eds.), *Presumed incompetent: The intersections of race and class for women in academia* (pp. 1–14). Logan, Utah: Utah State University Press.

Heleta, S. (2016). Transformation in higher education—Decolonisation of higher education: Dismantling epistemic violence and Eurocentrism in South Africa. *Transformation in Higher Education, 1*(1), 1–8.

Henry, F., Dua, E., James, C. E., Kobayashi, A., Li, P., Ramos, H., & Smith, M. S. (2017). *The equity myth: Racialization and indigeneity at Canadian Universities.* Vancouver: University of British Columbia Press.

Hiraldo, P. (2010). The role of critical race theory in higher education. *The Vermont Connection, 31*(7), 52–59.

hooks, b. (1994). *Teaching to transgress: Education as the practice of freedom.* New York and London: Routledge.

International Association for Political Science Students. (2017). *Annual theme: What is politics?* Retrieved from https://iapss.org/about/annual-theme/#1499205156560-70408769-457a [accessed August 17, 2019].

Law, I. (2017). Building the Anti-Racist University, action and new agendas. *Race Ethnicity and Education, 20*(3), 332–43.

Le Grange, L. (2016). Decolonising the university curriculum. *South African Journal of Higher Education, 30*(2), 1–12.

Lentin, A. (2008). Europe and silence about race. *European Journal of Social Theory, 11*(4), 487–503.

Marfouk, A. (2019). I'm neither racist nor xenophobic, but: Dissecting European attitudes towards a ban on Muslims' immigration. *Ethnic and Racial Studies, 42*(10), 1747–65.

Mattocks, K. (2018). "Just describing is not enough": Policy learning, transfer, and the limits of best practices. *Journal of Arts Management, Law, and Society, 48*(2), 85–97.

Mattocks, K., & Briscoe-Palmer, S. (2016). Challenges facing minority politics PhD students in the United Kingdom: Women, people of Black and ethnic minority origin, and disabled persons. *European Political Science, 15*(4), 476–92.

Mattocks, K., & Briscoe-Palmer, S. (2019). *Academic careers in uncertain times: Brexit's impacts on early career academics in the United Kingdom.* Paper presented at the Canadian Political Science Association annual conference, Vancouver, 4–6 June.

Mellifont, D., Smith-Merry, J., Dickinson, H., Llewellyn, G., Clifton, S., Ragen, J., Raffaele, M., & Williamson, P. (2019). The ableism elephant in the academy: A study examining academia as informed by Australian scholars with lived experience. *Disability & Society.* doi:10.1080/09687599.2019.1602510.

Mirza, H. S. (2018). Racism in higher education: "What then, can be done?" In J. Arday, & H. S. Mirza (Eds.), *Dismantling race in higher education: Racism, whiteness and decolonising the academy* (pp. 3–23). Cham, Switzerland: Palgrave Macmillan.

Mügge, L., Evans, E., & Engeli, I. (2016). Introduction: Gender in European political science education—taking stock and future directions. *European Political Science, 15*(3), 281–91.

Oppenheimer, D. B. (2008). Why France needs to collect data on racial identity—in a French way. *Hastings International and Comparative Law Review, 31*(2), 735–52.

Osho, Y. I. (2018). *Wearing far too many hats: BAME and female in the academy.* Discover Society. Retrieved from https://discoversociety.org/2018/11/06/wearing-far-too-many-hats-bame-and-female-in-the-academy/

Pásztor, A. (2016). Divergent pathways: The road to higher education for second-generation Turks in Austria. *Race Ethnicity and Education, 19*(4), 880–900.

Patternotte, D. (2018). Coming out of the political science closet: The study of LGBT politics in Europe. *European Journal of Politics and Gender, 1*(1–2), 55–74.

Phillips, A. (1995). *The politics of presence.* Oxford: Oxford University Press.

Pilkington, A. (2013). The interacting dynamics of institutional racism in higher education. *Race Ethnicity and Education, 16*(2), 225–45.

Reyes, V. (2018). Ethnographic toolkit: Strategic positionality and researchers' visible and invisible tolls in field research. *Ethnography.* doi:10.1177/1466138118805121.

Robertson, J. (2002). Reflexivity redux: A pithy polemic on "positionality." *Anthropological Quarterly, 75*(4), 785–92.

Rodriguez de Luna, M. (2016). Are area studies diversifying European political science? Perspectives from Germany and Portugal. *European Political Science, 15*(4), 519–35.

Rollock, N. (2019). *Staying power: The career experiences and strategies of UK Black female professors.* London: University and College Union.

Sadeghi, S. (2019). Racial boundaries, stigma, and the re-emergence of "always being foreigners": Iranians and the refugee crisis in Germany. *Ethnic and Racial Studies, 42*(10), 1613–31.

Savigny, H., & Marsden, L. (2011). *Doing political science and international relations: Theories in action.* Houndmills: Palgrave Macmillan.

Stockdill, B. C., & Danico, M. Y. (2012). The ivory tower paradox: Higher education as a site of oppression and resistance. In Brett C. Stockdill & Mary Yu Danico (Eds.), *Transforming the ivory tower: Challenging racism, sexism, and homophobia in the academy* (pp. 1–30). Honolulu: University of Hawaii Press.

Stockemer, D., Blair, A., Rashkova, E. R., & Moses, J. (2016a). Introduction: Diversity and inclusion in political science. *European Political Science, 15*(4), 437–40.

Stockemer, D., Rashkova, E., Moses, J. W., & Blair, A. (2016b). The discipline of political science in Europe: How different is it from political science in North America? *PS: Political Science & Politics, 49*(4), 813–15.

Thompson, D. (2019). Democratic hauntings: Michael Hanchard's the spectre of race and the challenge of comparison. *Ethnic and Racial Studies, 42*(8), 1313–20.

Tzanakou, C., & Pearce, R. (2019). Moderate feminism within or against the neoliberal university? The example of Athena SWAN. *Gender, Work & Organization, 26*, 1191–1211. Retrieved from https://doi.org/10.1111/gwao.12336

Universities UK/National Union of Students. (2019). *Report: Black, Asian and minority ethnic student attainment at UK universities: #closingthegap.* Retrieved from https://www.universitiesuk.ac.uk/policy-and-analysis/reports/Documents/2019/bame-student-attainment-uk-universities-closing-the-gap.pdf [accessed February 28, 2020].

Wilson, A. (2019). A note from the PSA chair: Diversity and the PSA. *Political Studies Review, 17*(2), 207–8.

Young, I. M. (1990). *Justice and the politics of difference.* Princeton and Oxford: Princeton University Press.

Yuval-Davis, N. (2006). Intersectionality and feminist politics. *European Journal of Women's Studies, 13*(3), 193–209.

Part III

EUROPEAN POLITICAL SCIENCE IN ITS ENVIRONMENT

Chapter 11

Making European Political Science Matter

Policy Advice by European Political Scientists[1]

Ivar Bleiklie, Marleen Brans, and Svein Michelsen

1. INTRODUCTION

The *advisory role* of political science—that is, what knowledge political scientists contribute to policymaking processes, how they do it, and to whom—is contested. This chapter seeks to shed light on the policy advisory roles of European political scientists, assess the scale and scope of their policy advice activities, and explore the major pathways for the provision of policy advice and the normative underpinnings of policy advice activities. Considering substantial variations in terms of arenas, advisory roles, and the extent to which political scientists play a role in them, our approach is broader than previous approaches that equated policy advice with formalized roles in public administration. Broadly speaking, political scientists may engage in and have an impact on society in a number of different ways (Stoker, Peters, & Pierre, 2015). Through academic activities—teaching and research or comments and analysis in mass media—political scientists provide knowledge and perspectives to students, politicians, public administrators, organizations, and the public at large. They may also engage more directly as consultants or members of public commissions and thereby affect public perceptions, political agendas, and public policies. We will only examine policy advice offered by political scientists who have certified academic credentials and who are researchers in universities or specialized research institutions.

We shall proceed in a stepwise fashion, first identifying different types of knowledge political scientists may provide and the advisory roles associated with these types. Next, we present a typology of different arenas in which political scientists may operate as advisers. We then examine policy advisory system(s) (PAS), which may be described as national configurations of different ways of soliciting, organizing, and delimiting policy advice activities. We also identify several dimensions—bureaucratization, professionalization, externalization, politicization, and corporatization—which may be used to characterize and analyze PAS. Finally, we explore different types of European politico-administrative system traditions (Rechtsstaat, Public Interest, Napoleonic, and Social Democratic) in order to assess to what extent characteristics of PAS vary.

Following these steps, we hope to answer the following research questions: How do different ways of organizing policy advice alongside varying politico-administrative traditions impact on perceptions and practices of political scientists in Europe? To what extent do we find clear national differences, and to what extent does political science function as a standardizing force across diverse politico-administrative systems and PAS? For the second question, we looked at: (1) data based on responses from political scientists in a pan-European survey collected in connection with COST Action CA15207 on the Professionalization and Social Impact of European Political Science; and (2) four country case studies derived from the survey on the role of political scientists employed in academic positions in higher education and research institutions—identifying norms of engagement, types of advice, relations with other actors, and arenas for the provision of policy advice.

2. POLICY ADVICE: ROLES, ARENAS, AND SYSTEMS

2.1 Forms of Advice and Arenas

We start by distinguishing between different advisory roles and the types of knowledge that may underpin them. These roles can be illuminated by a set of ideal types (Weber, 2013) that allows broad classifications of advisory roles, based on the different kinds of knowledge that underpin them. As different kinds of advice may be associated with different arenas, we seek to shed light on this by means of a typology of arenas and discuss how roles and arenas may be linked (see table 11.1).

Table 11.1   Advisory Roles and Types of Knowledge

Advisory Role	Type of Knowledge
The pure academic	Scientific (episteme)
The expert	Scientific or applied (what works) (techne)
The opinion maker	Opinionated normative science (phronesis)
The public intellectual	Episteme, techne, and phronesis

Source: Brans et al, 2019.

The *Pure Academic* operates as a researcher who primarily fulfills a duty to society by informing politicians or society at large about his or her research, broadly in the enlightenment tradition. The *Expert* is an academic more focused on application and on using scientific knowledge to help understand and/or develop practical solutions to problems defined by decision-makers. The *Opinion Maker* uses academic knowledge to draw implications from normative positions in political theory relating to current affairs or to justify normative stances in terms of political science data and empirical analyses. The *Public Intellectual* is often a noted specialist in a particular field, a well-known, recognized, learned person whose written works and other social and cultural contributions are recognized not only by academic audiences and readers but also by many members of society in general. The questions that immediately present themselves are the following: How and to what extent may policy advice provided by political scientists be fruitfully interpreted and classified according to these ideal types? Traditionally, in public administration the role of policy advice was strongly related to the role of the expert and technical expertise provided on the basis of specialized knowledge. The addition of other types of advisory roles, like the opinion maker, the public intellectual, and the pure academic, allows exploring a more diverse set of activities which may be defined as advisory in an extended sense and which take place in a variety of arenas.

In order to develop this broad conception of policy advice, we adopt a "locational" PAS model indicating the arenas from which policy advice can be provided, illustrated in figure 11.1, borrowed from Blum and Brans (2017). Applying the locational model enables us to formulate assumptions on relations between the different arenas, the different types of roles represented, and the activities associated with these role types. Starting with three partly overlapping arenas—*Internal government*, *External academic*, and *External lay*—the location of advisory actors is plotted in figure 11.1.

The *internal government arena* is dominated by bureaucrats, ministerial advisers, and parliamentary committees. We expect that political scientists' engagements in this arena will be tightly related to the role of the expert.

The *external academic arena* is made up of universities, research institutes, and individual academics where some actors may be heavily engaged in policy advice through commissioned applied research. Questions here are as follows: To what extent and where are political scientists active in this arena? To what extent are they concentrated in specific kinds of academic institutions? To what extent are they mobile through their academic careers? In this arena we would expect advisory activities to be dominated by pure academics and experts, particularly because academic institutions increasingly rely on external research funding where some level of policy advice, be it in terms of "enlightenment" or "expert advice," is explicitly expected.

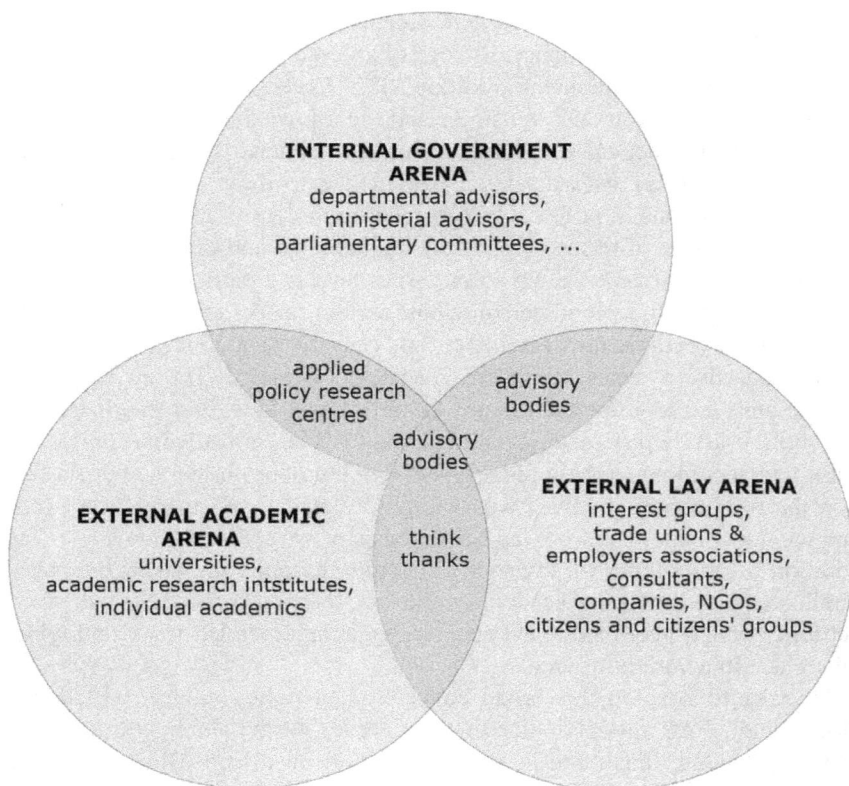

Figure 11.1   Locational Policy Advisory System Model. *Source*: Adapted from Blum and Brans (2017).

The *external lay arena* is where we find interest groups, trade unions and employers' associations, consultants, business enterprises, nongovernmental organizations (NGOs), citizen groups, and citizens. In principle, one may find political scientists providing policy advice in any capacity in the lay arena, given the wide array of organizational settings involved. We expect a wide variety of roles and variations in terms of how political scientists engage in this arena, possibly with a higher share of them operating as opinion makers or public intellectuals than in the other two arenas.

Overlapping arenas are of particular interest because organizations that are traditionally involved in policy advice are located there. Think tanks are located where the two external arenas overlap. Applied policy research centers are located where the external academic and the internal government arenas overlap. Advisory bodies such as government commissions may be formed where the internal government arena overlaps with one or both of the external arenas, depending on the nature of the bodies and composition of its members. Government commissions charged with the mission of developing, formulating, and justifying policy proposals may be corporatist in their composition, including "all affected parties" of the proposal in question. Alternatively, they may be "expert commissions," consisting of prominent researchers from universities or applied research centers, or they may be more political, composed of (former or present) politicians and senior civil servants. The locational model represents a useful heuristic for developing assumptions about relations between the different types of arenas and of advisory roles. However, relations between arenas vary in time and space. These variations can be fruitfully explored by engaging with the emerging comparative literature on PAS. In the next section, central PAS characteristics are presented and discussed, focusing on politicization, externalization, bureaucratization, professionalization, and corporatization.

2.2 Policy Advisory Systems

Traditionally, studies of the bureaucratic apparatus conceptualize policy advice rather narrowly as relations between the political and technical spheres of government (Christensen & Lægreid, 2008; Starr & Immergut, 1979) or between political structures and technical help (Jacobsen, 1965). So, policy advice would typically be considered autonomous "technical help." The concept of "policy advisory systems" (PAS) represents a new way to characterize and analyze multiple sources of policy advice utilized by governments in policymaking processes (Craft & Howlett, 2013). PAS literature maintains that advisory systems have changed as a result of the dual effects of two processes: "politicization" and "externalization." *Politicization* refers to the following: the increased use of partisan-political advice inside government itself; the strengthening of political acumen; the rising numbers and roles of political appointees in the executive; and the hiring of ministerial advisers to aid elected representatives. *Externalization* is the process whereby the locus of policy advice shifts from within public bureaucracy to sources outside the civil service. PAS literature argues that these twin dynamics have blurred the traditional sharp distinctions between inside and outside sources of advice as well as between the technical and political dimensions of policy formulation.

Much of the literature on PAS is based on Anglo-Saxon political systems, while less attention has been given to European corporatist systems. Also, in such systems, we encounter changes in relations between the political and the technical in policy formulation, but in different ways and in different directions. The dynamics of policy formulation and the role of policy advice are subjected to a "movement of political interest or control between previously accepted lines" (Starr & Immergut, 1987, p. 221). "Politicization" and "de-politicization" here refer to movements in two very different directions (ibid.), where the interactions between politicization and depoliticization have produced a complex web of advisory activities. As the state has expanded, the space for politics has become more restricted in a number of policy areas, and many issues have increasingly been discussed in technical terms. Thus, *depoliticization* can take place through *bureaucratization* as well as *professionalization* processes, to the extent that policy advice and decision-making authority is left to the discretion of bureaucrats or professional experts. More recently, the trajectory from political to technical decision-making has increasingly been reversed, as political actors progressively assert the primacy of politics in policy formation (Howlett & Craft, 2017).

The combination of politicization and depoliticization processes can change the locus of policy advice in the internal government arena, as well as in the overlapping external arenas. Policy advice may be concentrated in the ministries, dispersed to agencies working at arm's length from ministerial authority or located in areas at the intersection between the external and the internal arena. In this type of differentiated environment, policy advice might mean very different things. Several reasons for this development can be suggested, ranging from new political demands and the ability to understand political positions, identify political risks, and find points of leverage to new management skills. This conception of policy advice is completely different to the traditional idea of policy advice as technical help informed by specialized expertise and professional knowledge.

Then there is the issue of *corporatization* and the role of corporatist councils and permanent committees located at the intersection between the different arenas in the provision of policy advice. Corporatist devices are instruments for resolution and containment of political conflict, where issues are turned over to bargaining in a system where the state and organized interests share space. Politicization might imply the hollowing out and/or decline of corporatist systems, as it usually means transforming technical issues into political ones. The big question is: How and to what extent corporatist systems have been reconfigured into instruments for expert advice based on the force of expert argument rather than bargaining (Crowley & Head, 2017)? Policy advice might also be externalized to and located in new institutions like think tanks.

Summing up, the interaction of politicization and depoliticization might produce very different advisory structures and dynamics. In turn, this has implications for the shaping and reshaping of the arenas in which policy advice is provided, the extent to which they can be clearly distinguished from one another, and the degree to which they overlap. Thus, the way in which advisory arenas and roles overlap and the extent to which they do so (c.f. figure 11.1) may be better understood in light of how depoliticization—in the form of bureaucratization, professionalization, and corporatization—takes on novel forms as they interact with politicization and externalization processes. But, crucially, how these arenas and their interrelations in policy advice are formed depends on the type of politico-administrative regimes in which these activities are embedded. In the next section, we use this politico-administrative logic in order to get a better grip on the configuration of different European PAS.

2.3 Politico-Administrative Regimes and the Configuration of European PAS

European political-administrative systems in terms of PAS characteristics, their components, interactions, and dynamics, and the various nongovernmental actors that are involved have not been systematically mapped. Nor is there much literature available on the policy advisory role of political scientists. Therefore, we have to make do with other sources in order to approach the topic. Our point of departure is the literature on politico-administrative regimes and administrative traditions (Bleiklie & Michelsen, 2013; Painter & Peters, 2010; Pollitt & Bouckaert, 2004). Four different types and traditions can be identified. The Rechtsstaat tradition emphasizes rule following, correctness, and legal control, and recognizes organized interests as legitimate participants through corporatist arrangements. On the other hand, the Public Interest tradition provides a less dominant role for the state, where political rather than legal accountability mechanisms are often preferred, and where market mechanisms, quasi-markets, contracting out, and a general reduction of the distinctiveness of the public sector are favored. The Napoleonic tradition shares the Rechtsstaat focus on law as a state instrument for intervening in society, but also asserts the autonomy of the state, while limiting the role societal actors and networks can legitimately play. Therefore, interest group representatives are not usually incorporated into public administration and there is considerable selectivity surrounding participation. Finally, Social Democratic administrative traditions combine the Rechtsstaat orientation toward the law with a strong universal welfare orientation (Painter & Peters, 2010), where central bureaucracy enjoys a strong position (Olsen, 1983) and where state–society relations have been characterized by corporatism as well as extensive participatory networks (Painter & Peters, 2010). Thus, responsible bureaucracy is coupled with a complex and elaborated institutionalized landscape consisting of advisory bodies organized in various formats and shapes. This landscape also includes academics and interest group representatives.

We assume that administrative traditions and cultural characteristics matter for the articulation of policy advice in different PAS. However, the assumption that administrative traditions matter does not mean that they can explain characteristics of PAS in a straightforward way. This is even more important in the case of the role of political scientists within PAS, since the way in which political scientists are involved in policy advice may, as indicated by our research questions, vary according to national disciplinary and public-sector traditions that cannot be deduced from general administrative traditions and cultures.

3. ADVISORY ROLES AND PERCEPTIONS AMONG POLITICAL SCIENTISTS: A PAN-EUROPEAN SURVEY[2]

The pan-European survey on policy advisory activities—carried out in 2018 by the Professionalization and Social Impact of European Political Science (ProSEPS) project (COST Action CA15207)—allows us to close in on the various roles that exist for the provision of policy advice, via data on the perceptions of political scientists of a broad range of policy advice indicators and questions. The survey was administered to more than 11,000 European political scientists across thirty-seven countries in Europe plus Turkey and Israel. The response rate was just over 20 percent, yet with a highly differentiated response rate among countries, ranging from 10 percent to 64 percent. Coupled with the inevitable risk of self-selection in the responses by more publicly involved political scientists, this calls for some caution in presenting our findings as wholly representative of the policy advisory activities of the population of political scientists—"Still, to the best of our knowledge, this is the most complete survey ever realized among European Political Scientists" (ProSEPS, 2019).

3.1 Extrovert Political Scientists

Initial observations from the survey show that political scientists in Europe are rather extrovert, live outside "the ivory tower," and 80 percent engage in policy advisory activities in a broad sense. Almost half of the political scientists engage in opinion making (48%), while the second largest category is engagement in activities associated with expert advice provision (28%). Pure academics make up almost one-fifth of the sample (20%), whereas the all-round public intellectual is a rare type (4%). Measured by survey results, the majority of policy advice activities carried out by European political scientists fall into the normative, value judgment and advocacy category. The scale and scope of policy advice activities unearthed certainly merits further exploration. No doubt the inclusion of the various indicators associated with a broad range of "new" policy advisory activities (e.g., media-related activities) inflates their scores compared to traditional policy advice activities.

3.2 Professional Life Cycle Effects

Different ages seem to be associated with different types of policy advice activities. Without excluding the possibility of cohort effects, we assume that younger, early career political scientists are mainly concerned with academic work and advancing their careers. Later, when their careers are consolidated, they may publicly advocate solutions and take on expert roles or assume multiple roles. Looking at employment contracts, we find similar patterns. Nontenured scholars are arguably more focused on advancing their careers and providing expert advice within the remits of their academic positions, rather than venturing into the perils of advocacy and normative judgments.

3.3 Gender and Advisory Roles

The gender imbalance in the sample (only 33% are women) is echoed by gender imbalances in advisory roles. Female political scientists tend to refrain from giving policy advice more than their male colleagues and prefer expert roles rather than policy advocacy roles. This observation is corroborated when we look at the content of the advice. Female political scientists seem to be more engaged in technical advice, ranging from evaluations to causal analysis, and provision of facts about policies and political phenomena.

3.4 Specific Advisory Activities

What advice do political scientists actually provide in different arenas? The least frequent advisory activity is making forecasts and carrying out polls. Normative and value judgments are on the other hand provided more frequently by one-third of political scientists and by 46 percent on a less-frequent basis. In addition, political scientists are often called on to evaluate existing policies or institutions, and make recommendations on policy alternatives. But who are the recipients of political scientists' advice? And at what level are they found?

3.5 Recipients and Levels of Advice

Political scientists advise a great diversity of recipients. The top-three recipients are civil society organizations (44%), civil servants (40%), and think tanks (37%). About a third of political scientists also advise executive

(30%) or legislative politicians (30%), as well as political parties (28%). A quarter of them claim that they offer policy advice to international organizations (25%). Only 18 percent of our sample declares that their consultancy was addressed to interest groups. The national (53%) and subnational (32%) levels prevail, with less policy advice being directed at international (14%) and European Union (EU) actors (13%). This is not a small percentage, considering the physical distance of the latter actors, and not problematic either, since one out of five political scientists offer advice on international affairs and the EU.

3.6 Channels and Modes of Policy Advice Dissemination

The preferred channel of policy advice provision remains academic: publications and research reports. In second place comes traditional media articles; about one-third of respondents claimed they write a column frequently. Given the time-consuming nature of training courses for actors in different arenas, this activity, as well as writing policy briefs and memos, are less frequent. Also the use of blogs and social media for providing policy advice is limited.

3.7 Policy Areas and Subdisciplinary Expertise

Advice by political scientists is concentrated around four policy sectors, and this concentration is related to their subdisciplinary specialization. The most common substantive policy area where European political scientists provide advice is government, public administration organization, and electoral reform (33%), followed by international affairs and EU issues (27%). Next comes consultancy on civil rights, political rights and gender policies (17%), while 14 percent of respondents were involved in issues concerning immigration and ethnic minorities. The top subdisciplinary identities are political science (60%), public policy (29%), and public administration (21%).

3.8 Is Providing Policy Advice Desirable?

About 71 percent of the respondents believe that they have a professional obligation to engage in public debate and feel that they are being expected to become more involved in policymaking. Only about 20 percent agree that political scientists should refrain from direct engagement with policy actors, equaling the share of pure academics. Political scientists engage in policy advice for intrinsic rather than extrinsic motives. More than 90 percent want to make an active contribution to society, while about 45 percent think that advisory activity may expand career options outside academia, and only 35 percent claim it may help to advance their academic career.

4. COMPARING PAS ACROSS EUROPEAN COUNTRIES

Starting with the considerations above, we suggest some assumptions about PAS in European countries, based on the type of political-administrative regimes they belong to and how such regimes affect the degree of politicization, externalization, bureaucratization, professionalization, and corporatization of policy advice. Furthermore, we look at the relationship between these characteristics, the arenas in which policy advice is given and the form of policy advice that is provided in four countries: France, Germany, Norway, and the United Kingdom.

Liberal or *Anglo-Saxon* PAS are usually portrayed as formal, externalized, pluralist semiprivate systems. With centralized ministries and strong political leadership, this Public Interest model does not provide much space for bureaucratic or professional autonomy, but is fertile ground for politicization. Thus, policy advice in the United Kingdom has been characterized as follows: "highly competitive, adversarial, and politically partisan" (Bleiklie & Michelsen, 2013, p. 123). This would also imply that the external lay arena is particularly prominent and that opinion making is a major form of policy advice. Yet, the question of the specific role of political scientists in terms of their numbers, location, influence, and kind of advice they provide, is an open one. Although Germany represents the prototypical example of the *Rechtsstaat tradition*, it has also—like a number of European countries—witnessed increasing externalization of policy advice. As a decentralized and federalist system, it provides numerous access points for external policy advice. Yet, there is not much space for partisan advice, which would require a decoupling of think tank networks and dominant corporatist structures. Thus, Germany could be characterized as a formal externalized system with considerable scope for bureaucratic and professional autonomy in a context of negotiated settlements. Advice is likely to be provided where the internal government and the external lay and academic arenas overlap, and advice is likely to be of the expert kind (for a description of the German PAS, see also Blum & Jungblut, 2019; Pattyn et al., 2019).

The *Social Democratic (or Scandinavian) tradition* combines the German orientation toward the law with a strong universal welfare orientation. The Norwegian PAS is typically representative and operates within a unitary state, but shares with the Rechtsstaat tradition similar corporate mechanisms of cooperation between state and non-state actors (Rommetvedt, 2005, 2017). In addition, it is characterized by small ministries supplemented by a variety of autonomous agencies (Verhoest, Roness, Verschuere, Rubecksen, & MacCarthaigh, 2010). Although Norway finds itself in a middle European tier regarding externalization, there are reasons to assume a complex interaction between the processes of politicization and those of bureaucratization, professionalization, and corporatization, where the latter three have provided space for different forms of depoliticization, while traditional arenas have simultaneously been transformed. Thus, expert advice has become increasingly important within the corporate channel, although organized interests are still important actors (Christensen & Holst, 2017). This is exacerbated by the role played by program research, under the Research Council of Norway, that has linked public research institutions to policy advice (Bjerke, 2013). Thus, the Norwegian PAS is characterized by formal/informal advice, taking place to a considerable extent where the three major arenas overlap, and where scientific expert advice plays an important part. The *Napoleonic tradition* provides a different environment for policy advice. The centralist features of the political system offer few entry points for external actors and expertise. Policy advice takes the form of technocratic and statist expertise. In our context one might assume that PAS in this environment would be formal and internal, mainly taking place within the formal government arena, and be of a technocratic and scientific nature.

4.1 National PAS and the Policy Advisory Roles of Political Scientists: Four Case Studies

4.1.1 France (see Squevin, 2019)

Political science in France is a relatively small discipline, particularly given the country's size. In 2014, the ministry of education even called it a "rare discipline." Despite considerable growth since the 1950s, with increasing numbers of study programs hiring specialized teachers, the establishment of a national political science association, and specific research funding opportunities, it now includes only 550–600 scientists in academic positions across the country. Many of them are affiliated to universities and *grandes écoles* in and around the capital. Nationwide, there are approximately 100 professors of political science. French people know "Sciences Po" more as a prestigious educational institution—a famous "*grande école*" located in Paris—rather than as a social science discipline.

The French PAS has a distinct statist character, as opposed to more pluralist systems. The state, as the dominant actor within the PAS, exerts significant control over the many processes associated with policymaking and intervenes in numerous areas of economic and social life. The French PAS and the roles attributable to the actors therein are also conditioned by the Napoleonic tradition that still prevails in public administration (Peters & Painter, 2010). Its public administration is not particularly open to the outside, and in the civil service it is not customary to work with external actors, whether from civil society or academia.

The state's central importance in policymaking comes with the development of a specific expertise, needed to facilitate the conduct of public affairs on all fronts. This wide-ranging state expertise (*expertise d'état*) is opposed to, and usually dissociated with, other kinds of expertise such as scientific/ academic (Hauchecorne & Penissat, 2018). It is held by the "*grands corps*," which are predominantly composed of senior public servants (Biland & Gally, 2018). It can be technical or administrative and also encompasses practicing policy analysis. This state monopolization of expertise makes it difficult for academics to bring their own expertise to bear on public policy.

As to the normative views of French political scientists on policy advisory activities and public debates, the ProSEPS survey reveals that engaging in public debates is definitely not seen as imposed nor required by the profession; it is not even perceived as an essential ingredient of career advancement in France. Yet, more than 90 percent think that engaging in public debates is part of their role as social scientists and therefore given importance. Not feeling bound by professional imperatives to take part in public debates, they evaluate this participation more as a mission and a role in society. This resonates well with the tradition in French social sciences of the public intellectual, whose role it is to be engaged with and speak to society.

Normative views on policy advisory activities are overall quite positive; 57 percent of French political scientists approve of the idea of being generally involved in policymaking. French political scientists thus appear to be quite open to venturing out of the academic arena by offering advice to policy actors or being media active, even if 65 percent think that this should be done only after testing their ideas in academic publications. However, there is a discrepancy between normative views on advisory activities held by French political scientists, which are on the whole favorable, and their actual, reported participation in those activities, which is infrequent. The type of activity they carry out the most is to analyze and explain the causes and consequences of policy problems, but this activity still falls below 50 percent among respondents (46%). When it comes to less technical types of activity or more political/normative activities, they undertake these even less frequently (only 17% of respondents said they supplied value judgments/ normative arguments).

As to the recipients of advice (table 11.4), French political scientists engage most with civil society organizations and citizen groups (48%). They offer less advice to civil servants (41%), which partially corroborates the relatively closed nature of public administration. Although think tanks are generally thought to be less developed in France than in the Anglo-Saxon world, 30 percent of French political scientists turn to them to disseminate their advice. Only 7 percent of political scientists engage with interest groups in the private sector, which substantiates what is commonly accepted in France, that is, people distrust lobbies and corporate sector interest representation. Political scientists do not appear to be immune to these sentiments.

To conclude, there is a certain retrenchment of the French political science community, it is not very engaged in advisory activities, although there are signs in the data of a positive interest in such activities, normatively speaking. The French PAS, however, appears not particularly conducive to this kind of engagement.

4.1.2 Germany

Political science in Germany is an established and comparatively large discipline, which basically covers all political science subfields. Reiter and Töller (2013) identify a number of 390 political science chairs in total. What needs to be taken into account, alongside the characteristics of the German PAS outlined earlier in this chapter, are the specificities of the German academic system. It has a very low share of permanent positions compared to the rest of Europe—which could disincentivize engagement in advisory activities for all those on temporary positions (see Blum & Jungblut, 2019). Moreover, the desirability of involvement with "real-world" politics has been contested among German political scientists, with a recent intensive debate on these issues (ibid.).

Using this short depiction as a foil to look at the responses given by German political scientists, table 11.2 shows that they seem—compared to the other cases discussed in this chapter—similar when it comes to agreeing that political scientists should become involved in policymaking (60%) or engage in public debate since this is part of their role as social scientists (93%). On the other hand, there is a larger share of political scientists agreeing that they should refrain from direct engagement with policy actors (32%), which is concordant with our view that engagement in advisory activities is a contested issue among German political scientists (see Blum & Jungblut, 2019). When it comes to actual advisory activities (table 11.3), German political scientists seem to be less active, not so much regarding value judgments and normative judgments (25%), but rather evaluation activities (35%), provision of data and facts about policies and political phenomena (30.8%), as well as analysis and explanation of causes and consequences of policy problems (46%).

Regarding the actors with whom German political scientists engage in knowledge exchange, advisory, or consulting activities (table 11.4), these are most importantly civil society organizations and citizen groups (39%), followed by political parties (29%), and think tanks (27%). Looking at the position of civil servants (24%), which seems rather low when compared to the other countries, somewhat puts into perspective the expectation formulated earlier in this chapter—namely, that advice is likely to take place where

Table 11.2   Respondents Who Agreed Fully or Agreed Somewhat with the Following Statements (%)

Political Scientists Should:	FR (%)	GER (%)	NO (%)	U.K. (%)
Become involved in policymaking	57	60	51	63
Have a professional obligation to engage in public debate	39	70	82	72
Provide evidence-based knowledge and expertise outside academia, but not be directly involved in policymaking	60	65	62	51
Refrain from direct engagement with policy actors	16	32	8	8
Engage in public debate since this is part of their role as social scientists	92	93	94	88
Engage in media or political advisory activities only after testing their ideas in academic outlets	65	58	57	58
Engage in public debate because this helps them to expand their career options	20	35	25	51
	N=122	N=376	N=67	N=397

The response rates were: 21.7 percent for France, 14.7 percent for Germany, 19.7 percent for Norway, 9.9 percent for the United Kingdom. For details of the response rates, see the introduction to the general report of ProSEPS, http://proseps.unibo.it/action/deliverables/; for the exact wording of the survey questions, see http://proseps.unibo.it/wp-content/uploads/2018/10/PROSEPS-questionnaire.pdf.

Table 11.3   Respondents Who Say They Engage in Advisory Activities at Least Once a Year or More Frequently with Policy Actors (%)

	FR (%)	GER (%)	NO (%)	U.K. (%)
I make value judgments and normative arguments	17	25	13	38
I evaluate existing policies, institutional arrangements, etc.	23	35	54	51
I provide data and facts about policies and political phenomena	38	31	64	53
I analyze and explain the causes and consequences of policy problems	46	46	64	53
	N=122	N=376	N=67	N=397

the internal government and the external lay and academic arenas overlap. As table 11.5 shows, the most significant way for German political scientists to provide their advisory or consultancy services are workshops and conferences (43%), followed by face-to-face contacts with actors and organizations (39%). Of somewhat less importance are phone contacts (24%) and email contacts (22%) with actors and organizations. Finally, training courses that are provided for policy actors, administrative organizations, or other actors and stakeholders, play only a small role in the German context (17%).

Table 11.4　With Which Actors Did You Engage in Knowledge Exchange, Advisory or Consulting Activities during the Last Three Years? (%)

	FR (%)	GER (%)	NO (%)	U.K. (%)
Interest groups in the private and corporate sector	7	13	33	25
Think tanks	30	27	22	47
Advisory bodies	19	16	37	38
Civil servants	41	24	72	51
Political parties	21	29	30	21
Executive politicians	23	26	36	23
Other civil society organizations and citizen groups	48	39	45	48
N	N=122	N=376	N=67	N=397

Table 11.5　Respondents Who Say They Provide Policy and/or Consulting Services at Least Once a Year or More Frequently (%)

	FR (%)	GER (%)	NO (%)	U.K. (%)
Via workshop or conference (including events for nonacademic audiences)	41	43	51	59
By email or post to actor/organization	27	22	35	47
Over the phone to actor/organization	23	24	30	34
Face-to-face with actor/organization	44	39	7	54
Training courses for policy actors, administrative organizations, or other actors and stakeholders	29	17	18	19
	N=122	N=376	N=67	N=397

To conclude, the survey data highlight that there is—as in the other countries—significantly more support among German political scientists for "facts provision" or scientific analysis and explanation than for advising through normative arguments. However, compared to other countries, agreeing that political scientists should advise through value judgments and normative arguments is rather high.

4.1.3 Norway

Political science in Norway has gone through a period of rapid growth since World War II, and 340 political scientists, about one-third (120) female, were employed in higher education and research institutions in 2017. The considerable success of the academic discipline in educational terms is reflected by the fact that political scientists make up one of the three largest personnel groups in Norwegian ministries, alongside civil servants with degrees in law and economy.

Table 11.2 shows responses regarding the respondents' normative view on advisory activities and public debate. A large majority agree that political scientists have a professional obligation to engage in public debate. Whether such activities are useful for expanding career options seems to be of less importance. Results from the survey also indicate that research produced by political scientists is visible in public debate. More than 90 percent of the respondents agree that political science is very or quite visible in public debate, and more than two-thirds have taken part in a public debate in the media in the last three years. This underscores, yet again, a well-established characteristic of Norwegian political science: its strong focus on the general basis for democracy in Norwegian society (Underdal, 2007). The political science community is also very open to engagement in policymaking; 51 percent agree that political scientists should become involved in policymaking, not by taking part in policymaking itself but by providing evidence-based knowledge and expertise. The results could be interpreted as support of "enlightenment" and "expert" views on activities outside academia, through participation in public debate and in formal policy advice.

When it comes to actual advisory activities, table 11.3 indicates that the activity pattern of Norwegian political scientists is consistent with their normative views. The percentage that never engages in advisory activities is small. Furthermore, they engage in a wide range of advisory activities, providing facts and data, analyzing policy problems, and evaluating policies and institutional arrangements. More than 50 percent are engaged in such activities at least once a year. Making value judgments seems to be the least favored activity, with more than a third never doing so and just 13 percent doing so at least once a year. Data from the survey indicates that the national level is the most prevalent in policy advice: 80 percent engaged most frequently in policy advice or consulting activities at the national level, 9 percent engaged most frequently at the EU level, and 37 percent engaged most frequently at the subnational level.

Data from the survey (table 11.4) shows that Norwegian political scientists engage with a variety of actors. The large percentage of political scientists who have been engaged with advisory bodies corroborates the general tendency of increased representation in expert roles on advisory bodies (Holst & Christensen, 2017; Tellmann, 2016). Thirty-seven percent of the respondents have engaged with advisory bodies during the last three years. However, almost twice as many, 72 percent, have engaged with civil servants in knowledge exchange and advisory or consulting activities during the last three years. Thirty percent have engaged with political parties and 36 percent with executive politicians. Thirty-three percent have engaged in knowledge exchange or policy advice with interest groups in the private and corporate sector, 45 percent with civil society organizations, and citizen groups and 22 percent with think tanks.

Advocacy think tanks are a recent phenomenon in Norway, but they cover almost the entire political spectrum from left to right. Through their main activities, such as research, publications, seminars, and conferences as well as participation in public debate, they engage in efforts to influence political debate and policy reform proposals.

Most knowledge exchange and advisory or consulting activities take place in settings characterized by a mixture of informal and formal elements (40%) or mainly formal settings (28%). Just 3 percent have been active in purely formal settings. There is much informal exchange and discussion. Most often, policy advice is provided via workshops or conferences (see table 11.5).

Overall, the survey data corroborates the impression from other studies that the Norwegian PAS is state centered with civil servants as the most frequent actors with which the political scientists in the survey engage. Engaging in public debate is seen by most as an obligation, but at the same time the preferred type of engagement, scientific expert roles, underlines the strong position of expertise and a reluctance to engage in partisan-political debate and conflicts.

4.1.4 The United Kingdom

The U.K. PAS, as previously discussed in this chapter, is characterized by a multiplicity of sources of policy advice and—consequently—competition within the advisory spectrum. Over the last couple of decades, the U.K. PAS has evolved toward being more pluralistic, with the role of the public service as the core source of advice diminishing. It has also become more adversarial as the process of policy advice has increasingly required an involvement in the politics of decision-making (Craft & Halligan, 2017). One of the factors shaping the current PAS in the United Kingdom is its research funding system strongly incentivizing advisory and knowledge exchange activities and—consequently—shaping the supply side of policy advice. Since the introduction of the Research Assessment Exercise in 1986 (later renamed the Research Excellence Framework—REF), academic research in the United Kingdom has been subject to performance-based assessment, linked with a distribution of resources to universities, strongly shaping the process of and incentives for knowledge production for policy purposes (Bandola-Gill, 2019). In particular, since the 2014 REF exercise, the units of assessment are evaluated based not only on academic publications but also on the impact that research has on wider audiences (REF, 2019).

This science funding and incentive structure seemingly influences the advisory activities of U.K. academics as well as their attitudes toward undertaking such activities. As reflected in the survey, British academics are more willing than their counterparts to support a claim that engagement in policy advice is beneficial to their careers, with 51 percent agreeing. The majority of U.K. political scientists believe that they should become involved in policymaking (63%) and that such engagement is their professional obligation (72%). Furthermore, the U.K. academics do not support a statement that political scientists should refrain from direct engagement with policy actors, with over 90 percent disagreeing with it.

These attitudes toward advisory activities are further reflected in the types of advisory activities the British political scientists are willing to undertake. Seen from the comparative perspective, U.K. academics are more often engaged in making value judgments and normative arguments in policy, with 38 percent of academics engaging in such activities at least once a year. Akin to their counterparts in other countries, British political scientists are involved in conducting evaluations (51% do so at least once a year or more often) and policy analysis (53%), as well as providing facts and data about policies (53%). Therefore, even though, akin to other country cases, U.K. academics are more often involved in politically neutral activities, they are also more willing to engage in normative aspects of policy advice.

British political scientists target a wide variety of actors in their advisory activities, the most important one being the civil service, with 51 percent of political scientists reporting engaging with this group. The second most popular venue for knowledge exchange and advisory work, akin to other countries, is civil society (48%). More distinctive in this case was the popularity of think tanks as target groups of policy advice, with 47 percent of political scientists reporting engaging with such actors (over 20 % more than any other country). This popularity might be explained by the strong and growing position of think tanks as sources of policy ideas within the U.K. PAS (Hernando, 2019; Stone & Ladi, 2017).

Overall, the U.K. case clearly illustrates that the combination of a competitive and adversarial system of policy advice and strong incentives embedded in a research funding system shapes the advisory work of political scientists, increasing its intensity, but also their willingness to engage in normative and political aspects of policymaking.

5. CONCLUSION

Returning to the research questions, the data and our analysis demonstrate that, in the face of institutional and organizational diversity, European political scientists support and engage in various types of policy advice, primarily as opinion makers and experts. Engagement seems to increase with age. As academics become more established in their academic careers, they seem to be more willing to emerge from purely academic roles and engage in various forms of advice. There is also a tendency for male political scientists to engage more than their female colleagues. The explanation for this difference may well be similar to the explanation of age differences. Comparing the four national cases, the data indicate that, in spite of different institutional environments, political scientists share a number of common attitudes: that they should be involved in policymaking by providing evidence and analyses and engaging in public debate. However, relatively few French political scientists believe that they have a professional obligation to engage in public debate, and a slight majority of British political scientists are in favor of engaging in public debate for career-motivated reasons.

When it comes to actual engagement, it seems that fewer French and German political scientists engage than their Norwegian and British colleagues. Political scientists in all four countries engage with a wide variety of actors providing policy advice, but with a few differences. Not surprisingly, a larger share of British political scientists engages with think tanks, while Norwegian political scientists are more inclined than their colleagues in the other three countries to engage with civil servants. All in all, we may conclude that political scientists share important attitudes to policy engagement and the way in which academic and advisory roles should be balanced. Nevertheless, institutional differences across countries affect attitudes on specific dimensions and activity patterns. The data corroborate, to some extent, that the role of the *grands corps* in France, the market orientation in the United Kingdom, and the strong role of the state in Norway shape patterns of policy advice activity and contact.

NOTES

1. The authors are grateful to Pierre Squevin, Sonja Blum and Jens Jungblut, and Justyna Bandola-Gill for providing their analysis and contextualization of the French, German, and U.K. cases, respectively. They would also like to thank Athanassios Gouglas, José Real Dato, Ellen Fobé, Jens Jungblut, and Andrea Pritoni for methodological advice on the analysis of the ProSEPS survey data.

2. This section summarizes the findings of the ProSEPS survey. A complete version, including graphs and tables, is included in the report by Working Group 4 on the advisory roles of European political scientists, compiled by M. Brans, A. Timmermans and A. Gouglas as part of ProSEPS general report and is available at http://proseps.unibo.it/action/deliverables/.

REFERENCES

Bandola-Gill, J. (2019). Between relevance and excellence? Research impact agenda and the production of policy knowledge. *Science and Public Policy, 46*(6), 895–905. doi:10.1093/scipol/scz037.

Bandola-Gill, J., Flinders, M., & Brans, M. (2019). *Incentives for impact in higher education: A cross-national political science perspective.* Paper presented at WG 4 meeting of COST Action CA15207 on the Professionalization and Social Impact of European Political Science, Sheffield, March 2019.

Bjerke, C. (2012). *Konsensus eller interessekamp? Sammensetning og tildelingsmønstre i programstyrene til Norges Forskningsråd: en kvantitativ analyse av governance i norsk forskningspolitikk* (Master degree thesis). Department of Administration and Organization Theory, University of Bergen. Retrieved from https://www.uib.no/admorg/40102/masteroppgaver-2012#masterprogram-i-administrasjon-og-organisasjonsvitenskap

Biland, E., & Gally, N. (2018). Civil servants and policy analysis in central government. In C. Halpern, P. Hassenteufel, & P. Zittoun (Eds.), *Policy analysis in France* (pp. 101–18). Policy Press.

Bleiklie, I., & Michelsen, S. (2013). Comparing higher education policies in Europe. Structures and reform output in eight countries. *Higher Education, 65,* 113–33.

Blum, S., & Brans, M. (2017). Academic policy analysis and research utilization for policymaking. In M. Brans, I. Geva-May, & M. Howlett (Eds.), *Routledge handbook of comparative policy analysis* (pp. 341–59). London: Routledge.

Blum, S., & Jungblut, J. (2019). *From research to practice? The policy-advisory roles of German political scientists.* Paper presented at WG 4 meeting of COST Action CA15207 on the Professionalization and Social Impact of European Political Science, The Hague, 19–20 September 2019.

Brans, M., Timmermans, A., & Gouglas, A. (2019). *The policy advisory roles of European political scientists.* In ProSEPS "General report." Retrieved from http://proseps.unibo.it/

Christensen, T., & Lægreid, P. (2008). *Administrative reforms and competence in central government organizations* (Working Paper 7). Stein Rokkan Centre for Social Studies.

Craft, J., & Howlett, M. (2013). The dual dynamics of policy advisory systems: The impact of externalization and politicization on policy advice. *Policy and Society, 32*(3), 187–97.

Crowley, K., & Head, B. (2017). Expert advisory bodies in the policy system. In M. Brans, I. Geva-May, & M. Howlett (Eds.), *Routledge handbook of comparative policy analysis.* London: Routledge.

Hauchecorne, M., & Penissat, E. (2018). The field of state expertise. In C. Halpern, P. Hassenteufel, & P. Zittoun (Eds.), *Policy analysis in France* (pp. 191–208). Bristol: Policy Press.

Hernando, M. G. (2019). *British think tanks after the 2008 global crisis.* Basingstoke: Palgrave Macmillan.

Holst, C., & Christensen, J. (2017). Advisory commissions, academic expertise and democratic legitimacy: The case of Norway. *Science and Public Policy, 44*(6), 821–33.

Jacobsen, K. D. (1965). *Teknisk hjelp og politisk struktur*. Oslo: Universitetsforlaget.

Olsen, J. P. (1983). *Organized democracy: Political institutions in a welfare state— The case of Norway*. Oslo: Universitetsforlaget.

Painter, M., & Peters, B. G. (Eds.). (2010). *Tradition and public administration*. Basingstoke: Palgrave Macmillan.

Pattyn, V., Blum, S., Fobé, E., Pekar-Milicevic, M., & Brans, M. (forthcoming). Academic policy advice in consensus-seeking countries: The cases of Belgium and Germany. *International Review of Administrative Sciences*. Retrieved from https://doi.org/10.1177/0020852319878780.

Pollitt, C., & Bouckaert, G. (2004). *Public management reform. A comparative analysis* (2nd ed.). Oxford: Oxford University Press.

ProSEPS. (2019). *General report of COST Action CA15207 on the professionalization and social impact of European political science*. Retrieved from http://proseps. unibo.it/

Squevin, P. (2019). *The policy advisory roles of French political scientists*. Paper presented at WG 4 meeting of COST Action CA15207 on the Professionalization and Social Impact of European Political Science, The Hague, 19–20 September 2019.

REF. (2019). *Guidance on submissions*. Retrieved from https://www.ref.ac.uk/med ia/1092/ref-2019_01-guidance-on-submissions.pdf

Reiter, R., & Töller, A. E. (2013). The role of policy analysis in teaching political science at German Universities. In S. Blum & K. Schubert (Eds.), *Policy analysis in Germany* (pp. 265–77). Bristol: Policy Press.

Rommetvedt, H. (2005). Norway: Resources count, but votes decide? From neo-corporatist representation to neo-pluralist parliamentarism. *Western European Politics, 28*(4), 740–63.

Rommetvedt, H. (2017). Scandinavian corporatism in decline. In I. O. Knutsen (Red.), *The Nordic models in political science. Challenged, but still viable?* (pp. 171–90). Bergen: Fagbokforlaget.

Stoker, G., Peters, B. G., & Pierre, J. (Eds.). (2015). *The relevance of political science*. Basingstoke: Palgrave Macmillan.

Stone, D., & Ladi, S. (2017). Policy analysis and think tanks in comparative perspective. In M. Brans, I. Geva-May, & M. Howlett (Eds.), *Routledge handbook of comparative policy analysis* (pp. 324–40). London: Routledge.

Tellmann, S. M. (2016). *Experts in public policymaking: Influential, yet constrained* (Doctoral Thesis). Oslo and Akershus University College of Applied Sciences. Retrieved from https://profesjon.no/silje-maria-tellmann-experts-in-public-policymaking-influential-yet-constrained/

Underdal, A. (2007). Norsk statsvitenskap 60 år: Hvor står vi, hvor går vi. *Norsk Statsvitenskapelig Tidsskrift, 23*(3), 244–66.

Verhoest, K., Roness, P., Verschuere, B., Rubecksen, K., & MacCarthaigh, M. (2010). *Autonomy and control in state agencies*. Basingstoke: Palgrave Macmillan.

Weber, M. (2013). *Economy and society*. Berkeley, CA: University of California Press.

Chapter 12

The Engagement of European Political Scientists with Parties and Citizens

The Case of Voting Advice Applications

Diego Garzia and Alexander H. Trechsel

1. INTRODUCTION[1]

Political scientists' engagement with democratic politics and society is not limited to their direct involvement in a diverse range of advisory roles (Bleiklie et al., in this volume). The latter become ever more important as data becomes increasingly available. If the spread of survey methodology after World War II went hand in hand with the behavioral revolution in the social sciences, then computational techniques, big data, and online access to internationally coordinated data gathering efforts open up entirely new avenues for research (Dalton, in this volume). Politics and society become beneficiaries of these developments, increasingly seeking evidence-based analyses of policy impact and change (Hemerijck, in this volume). Alongside such direct forms of political scientists' engagement in (mainly institutional) politics, the growing interest of the discipline in digital transformations and the emerging potential of "civic technology" led to novel forms of engagement. In this chapter, we concentrate on a concrete example of such novel engagement with parties, candidates, and voters. The example concerns elections in the digital age, where myriad online tools for fostering voter engagement and civic competence abound. These include information-providing tools that help voters find their way around the electoral offer. These tools—originating in Europe in the late 1980s and now prominent throughout all continental democracies—are commonly labeled "Voting Advice Applications" (hereafter VAAs).

VAAs are online applications that facilitate voters' decision-making by comparing their policy preferences with the positions of political parties and/

or candidates on these policies. In doing so, VAAs engage with the supply side of politics (in order to map their policy positions) and with an unprecedented proportion of voters in the few-week span of an election campaign. As we shall detail below, the last two decades have seen VAAs become a standard feature of election campaigns in most European countries (and beyond) with millions of users resorting to them. Since 2009, VAAs have been also implemented supranationally in the context of European Parliament elections. Whenever a supranational VAA is implemented, the number of political scientists needed to facilitate such a large-scale endeavor lies in the hundreds. Admittedly, very few social science projects can count both on such large-sized research teams and on an immediate societal impact on public opinion, affecting millions of citizens. Not to mention that many VAA providers develop their tools *in collaboration* with political parties and candidates—thus expanding further the perimeter of their sociopolitical engagement. For these reasons, we believe that VAAs offer a timely and telling example of the ways in which European political science can fruitfully engage with the political process in the current information revolution.

We argue that, in addition to the traditional role played by political science in electoral processes, where preelection surveys, spin-doctoring, election night commenting, media consultancy, and postelection analyses provide for scientific—and often not-so-scientific—input; the spread of digital online technology has transformed political scientists into co-shapers of public opinion formation processes. VAAs, as we will show below, have emerged within civil society organizations, among politically interested do-gooders, and even state-sponsored initiatives. However, given the enormous and fast-growing success of these tools, political scientists began to not only be interested in the large amount of data generated by VAAs, but also in measuring, for example, their impact on public opinion and election outcomes. Increasingly, they become VAA providers themselves, working closely with tool manufacturers or even designing their own applications.

The increased involvement of political scientists in VAAs and the study of their functioning and effects are, however, not normatively void of essence. Quite to the contrary, political scientists who actively engage in such civic technology tend to adopt a particular view of democracy, elections, and political accountability. Without delving too deeply into the classic literature on types of representation, we assume that VAAs are mainly seen as tools that help maximize substantive representation, that is, a democracy, in which voters choose among parties and candidates that best represent their substantive views in politics. In times of declining party identification, sinking levels of trust, party system fragmentation, and volatility, VAAs are deemed to offer substantive information to undecided, uncertain, noninformed, and disillusioned voters. They may also serve well-informed, politicized partisans to confirm their attachments and, generally, hold the elected accountable for their electoral promises.

VAAs are also seen, by their promoters, as tools for "bringing the citizens back in," that is, for giving voters a feeling of empowerment through personalized, customized, and tailor-made information about the electoral offer. By creating transparent and politically neutral information shortcuts, voters can locate themselves more easily in the political landscape. The advantages for citizens, so the argument goes, are manifold: VAAs help citizens to escape partisan-biased propaganda; they can foster political interest and competence through a ludic form of information aggregation; and they can help immunize electoral campaigns from fake news, rumors, and other forms of information hacking in times of increasing affective polarization, social media, and the globalization of elections.

The question of whether VAAs fulfill these promises cannot be answered in this chapter. But we posit that the increased engagement of political science with VAAs and the growing academic output that has progressed from the world of obscure journals and publishing houses to the top journals in the discipline is sufficiently deep to exemplify the scholarly emancipation that has brought political science closer to citizens, public opinion, and elections. We therefore dedicate this chapter to a discussion of what VAAs are, where they come from, what effects they have, and how political science in this field is likely to develop. In doing so, we also speak to more general questions of engagement and their implications for the role of political science.

The chapters proceed as follows. In section 2, we offer a brief overview of the long-standing debate on the foundations of (political) science's public engagement. In section 3, we locate the VAA phenomenon within this debate. We highlight the distinguishing innovations brought about by the digital revolution and how this expanded the potential outreach of political science research and practice beyond academia. In section 4, we describe the origins of VAAs and map their existence and spread across Europe and beyond. We demonstrate that, over the last two decades, VAAs have become a truly global phenomenon. Section 5 then offers a brief description of the main characterizing features of VAAs, their underlying methodology, and how the "making of" VAAs corresponds to actual engagement with political parties and candidates running for election. In section 6, we review the academic literature dealing with their impact on users' political attitudes and behavior. The large amount of readily available information provided by VAAs to their users have been shown to contribute to reducing the transactional costs involved in gathering relevant political information. VAAs increase interest in, and knowledge of, political matters, leading to higher turnout figures. We then address, in section 7, the potential flaws and current limitations stemming from the implementation of VAAs. For this, we illustrate the conditions for the making of a "good VAA," building upon the *Lausanne Declaration* delivered in 2014 by a large group of academic VAA developers and researchers. Finally, we come back to the larger theme of political scientists' engagement with society and draw lessons from VAA research and implementation to address the normative implications of directly engaging with our chief objects of study.

2. POLITICAL SCIENCE AND ITS PUBLIC ENGAGEMENT: AN OVERVIEW OF THE DEBATE

The first issue that needs to be addressed is a definitional matter: What does engagement mean? Our reading of the existing literature finds that public engagement can range from the mere social media presence of academics (Wood, 2019) to their actual involvement as elected politicians (Boswell, Corbett, & Havercroft, 2019)—and everything in between (e.g., spin-doctoring, media consultancy, divulgation, and punditry). Considering the encompassing nature of this (nonexhaustive) list, we decided to rely on the epistemological understanding of engagement's nature, recently brought forward by Wood (2019). He proposes to situate engagement practices within the divergent views about the status of knowledge political science should produce. For these purposes, he distinguishes between "those who view political science as a relatively rigid *paradigmatic* set of rule-based practices aimed at generating knowledge of a privileged status . . . and those who view political science in a *pragmatic* way as a set of common rule-based practices for contributing in an eclectic manner to broader interdisciplinary or extra-disciplinary debates" (Wood, 2019, p. 4).

The paradigmatic approach is best defined by Moravcsik (2014, p. 667), who sees "scholarship as a collective enterprise—a conversation among scholars, sometimes extending to those outside academia as well." In this view, engagement equates with dissemination of research findings, whose implications will unfold autonomously on the sole basis of the normative assumptions upon which the research is initially based. The contrasting pragmatic approach is best exemplified by Sil and Katzenstein (2010, p. 418), who advocate the generation of "concrete implications for the messy substantive problems facing policymakers and ordinary social and political actors." The most recent contribution to the debate, forcefully patronizing a pragmatic understanding of public engagement, is Rainer Eisfeld's (2019) *Empowering Citizens, Engaging the Public: Political Science for the 21st Century*. He makes the case for political science to engage more deeply with the current social and political problems that the world faces, and to do so via broadly accessible public narratives, including solution-orientated normative notions.

Arguments in favor of the discipline's active engagement with the public have been increasingly voiced over the last two decades (alongside some critical voices; see Flinders and Pal, 2019). They build upon assorted grounds. For example, it is maintained that as scientific research is paid for by the public, they should receive some demonstrable benefit from it (Bandola-Gill, Brans, & Flinders, 2019). Partly related to this, it is claimed, on epistemological grounds, that by producing knowledge about the public, science bears the obligation of sharing that knowledge (Ostrom, 1998). The urgency of the call for more engagement has strengthened over the last ten years. In response to "politicians and commentators demanding 'value for money', particularly since the 2008 global financial crisis, research councils and funders now regularly integrate 'impact and engagement' criteria into their funding rules, promotion criteria reflect this, and research excellence assessments require statements of successful impact" (Wood, 2019, p. 2). Among these pleas for increasing engagement with the public, a few should be singled out as they are directly aimed at our main object of inquiry. Putnam (2003) believes that one of the key responsibilities of contemporary political science should lie with "our contribution to public understanding and to the vitality of democracy." The aforementioned Eisfeld (2019) goes as far as declaring support for active citizenship as being "mandatory" for twenty-first-century political science.

Many academic (or at least partly academic) initiatives have unfolded along these lines over the last two decades. This acceleration is due, in all probability, to a combination of factors. On the one hand, the increasing pressure to move away from the ivory tower may have provided the initial trigger. On the other hand, the digital revolution and the spread of ICTs created prime conditions for such initiatives to reach out to the wider public autonomously from all previous forms of knowledge intermediation. In all these respects, VAAs represent a specimen of political science's successful, large-scale engagement with the public in the digital age. Importantly, for our purposes VAAs also fit well with all the characteristics that are deemed constitutive of the pragmatic approach to engagement. First, because they represent a concrete example of engaged scholarship designed to bear a potential impact on millions of users in election campaigns (and beyond). Second, because they engage with their object of inquiry by (a) producing knowledge about the public, (b) sharing that knowledge with the public, and (c) doing so in real time. Indeed, this is similar to the idea of "co-production" where scholars seek to directly "co-create" research with those outside the academy (Geddes, Dommett, & Prosser, 2018). Third, because their impact is normatively loaded, since VAAs are explicitly designed to help citizens better deal with the complex issues that face the social and political world today and to increase democratic participation.

A normative assessment of VAAs as an ideal type of academic engagement is especially useful to illuminate the changes brought about by the information revolution in the relationship with our main objects of study. Today, VAAs and related technologies have (at least partly) taken on board some of the tasks undertaken, until recently, by more *paradigmatic* research projects based on, for example, mass and elite surveys. A case study of VAAs can thus shed light on the conditions under which a larger engagement perimeter, as made possible by the information revolution, can have positive spillover effects on our research populations. Obviously, we will concentrate equally attentively on those instances in which engagement could trespass the line between fostering public understanding and actually (re-)shaping people's reality.

3. PRAGMATIC OVER PARADIGMATIC: LOCATING VAAs WITHIN EXISTING ENGAGEMENT PRACTICES

Traditional methods of analysis of elites and public opinion can, by and large, be ascribed to the paradigmatic approach to public engagement. We begin by offering a brief review of established methodologies, focusing on elite surveys and mass surveys of public opinion in turn. Their core societal implications will then be compared to the more "engaging" features brought about by the availability of VAAs and related online technologies.

Over the years, political scientists have devised a multitude of techniques to assess parties' and candidates' positions on ideological and policy/issue dimensions (Marks, 2007). Established techniques include, most notably, expert surveys, such as the Chapel Hill Expert Survey program, and manifesto coding exercises, such as the Comparative Manifesto Project. More interesting for our purposes, however, are the studies conducted on the basis of internal party expertise; starting with Daalder and van der Geer's (1973) analysis of Dutch parliamentary parties, the discipline has widely resorted to surveys of political elites. Among the projects that are most representative of this approach, one must single out the Comparative Candidate Survey (Zittel, 2015). This project collects data on candidates running for national parliamentary elections through a common core questionnaire to allow for cross-country comparison. CCS Module I was conducted between 2005 and 2013, while Module II was conducted between 2013 and 2018. Both modules feature over thirty countries and thousands of candidates. Regardless of their scale, however, elite surveys' impact on the attitudes and opinions being analyzed can be considered negligible. The findings of these studies pertain mostly, if not only, to a specialized academic audience. Usually the data is analyzed and presented in an aggregated form. In other words, this makes it virtually impossible for the public to find out about a given party or candidate's attitudes and opinions.

Another major area—if not *the* major area—of political science's direct engagement with its object of study is public opinion and voting behavior analysis. Again, if the surveys are intended for academic purposes only, minimal effects can be expected. However, not all surveys are used for strictly academic purposes. In some instances, they are designed with the intention of directly manipulating voters' opinions under the guise of conducting an opinion poll, that is, the so-called *push polls*. In some other instances, polls may lack such manipulative intentions, but can still bear an indirect impact on voters when the results are made public by mainstream and new media. By providing information about the intentions of the voting population at large, opinion polls can affect voters in two different ways; these can be labeled bandwagon effects and strategic voting effects. Bandwagon effects are thought to occur whenever voters are prompted to back the party or candidate that the polls indicate as the potential winner. Empirical research in this domain shows that bandwagon effects do take place in democratic elections, though their actual impact is much lower than often purported, with the proportion of voters being influenced ranging from around 2 to 3 percent of the eligible voting population (Irwin & van Holsteyn, 2000). Strategic voting effects are relatively more common and pertain to the possibility that voters shift from their sincere preference to vote for a less preferred but generally more popular candidate. Nevertheless, existing research highlights that opinion polls only conditionally affect patterns of tactical voting through the timing of voting decisions. Undecided voters are more prone to the effects of the polls; yet, they are also potentially affected by a large array of last-minute campaign influences (McAllister & Studlar, 1991).

This picture of "minimal effects" stemming from research practices to the respective study populations was bound to be heavily affected by the spread of Information and Communication Technologies (ICTs)—for both political communication and academic engagement. Indeed, one of the defining characteristics of online political communication lies with its interactive potential. Its proliferation and peculiar effects have been hypothesized to stem from the delivery of "more detailed information [that] can be customized to a greater extent" (Prior, 2005, p. 579). In this way, users receive information—including political information—in the light of their own preferences. Parties and politicians also increasingly took advantage of the interactive possibilities of the internet to directly connect with citizens and potential voters. Existing research shows that more personalized online communication and the use of interactive features increases political involvement among online citizens (Kruikemeier, Van Noort, Vliegenthart, & De Vreese, 2013). In this picture, VAAs should be singled out as a flagship endeavor of pragmatic engagement with the public. First, because they engage directly with both the demand and the supply side of electoral politics, based on the respective emerging demands for visibility and guidance in the online world. Second, because this real-time interaction can potentially affect both sides. When parties and candidates are aware that their positions will be made visible to voters, their opinions will inevitably be subject to strategic considerations. At the same time, the users will be directly primed to consider what is their best matching party—after all, at the core of every VAA there is *voting advice*. And indeed, this will be provided to millions of voters, with potential attitudinal as well as behavioral effects of an unseen magnitude in the polling effects literature.

4. THE SPREAD OF VOTING ADVICE APPLICATIONS AMONG COUNTRIES AND CITIZENS

Over the last two decades, VAAs have mushroomed across the globe. VAAs assist and inform voters by comparing their policy preferences with the political stances of parties or candidates running for election. The users of these tools mark their positions on a range of policy statements. After comparing the user's answers to the positions of each party or candidate, the application generates a rank-ordered list or a graph indicating which party or candidate is most closely aligned to the user's policy preferences (see figure 12.1).

Whereas the advice provided by the VAA is considered a form of political communication, it must be also noted that it differs considerably from most of the campaign messages that citizens traditionally receive. Like traditional media, they relay information about parties' and/or candidates' positions to voters. Unlike other sources, however, they provide customized political information. VAAs offer an explicit ranking of viable options with the implication that this ranking is tailored according to the user's political opinions. In other words, VAAs reveal to the user the structure of the political competition *in light of her own preferences*. The ability of VAAs to reduce the costs of information at election time is one of the keys to understanding their growing success among voters (Alvarez, Levin, Trechsel, & Mair, 2014).

Nowadays, the existence of at least one VAA has been witnessed in virtually all Western democracies. An early attempt to map the distribution of national and transnational VAAs, in 2014, found almost complete coverage of the European democracies (Marschall & Garzia, 2014). On the basis of a more recent census, conducted in 2018, the global spread of this phenomenon has become even more evident. Multiple VAAs have been deployed all over the Western world, and there is now almost complete coverage of Central and South American democracies. The existence of VAAs has been also

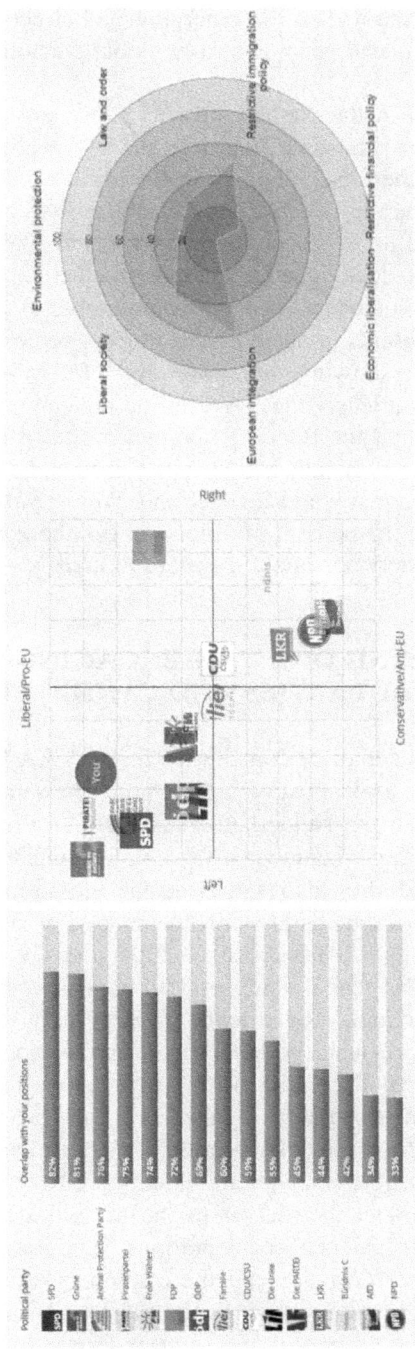

Figure 12.1   Common VAA outputs: matchlist (left) and bi-dimensional political space (centre) and spidergram (right). *Source:* http://www.euandi.eu.

witnessed in North Africa and in the emerging global economies of Asian countries. VAAs have indeed become a truly global phenomenon (see figure 12.2).

Originally developed in the Netherlands, as paper-and-pencil civic education questionnaires for first-time voters in the 1980s, by the turn of the century VAAs had reached usage figures in the millions. To mention just a few examples: the pioneering Dutch VAA *StemWijzer* was used almost seven million times in the run-up to the parliamentary election of 2017. The German VAA *Wahl-O-Mat*, developed for the federal election of the same year, peaked at over 15.7 million users. Moving from number of *usages* to number of *users*, figure 12.3 presents updated evidence from representative national election study datasets, showing the proportion of the voting population declaring to have used (at least) one VAA during the campaign.[2]

In both Scandinavia and the Benelux, the proportion of citizens resorting to VAAs at election time now falls between one-third and a half of the entire voting population. In Germany and Switzerland, *Wahl-O-Mat* and *smartvote* consistently attract over 10 percent of voters. In Southern Europe, the penetration of VAAs in society appears to be more limited.

5. THE MAKING OF A VAA: ENGAGING WITH POLITICAL PARTIES AND CANDIDATES

Among the basic features that are constitutive of the VAA family, the "nonpartisan nature" of these tools must be highlighted. The seminal *StemWijzer*-type VAAs developed in the Netherlands and Germany both originated in state-funded nonprofit organizations with a civic education background. However, the last decade has also witnessed the blossoming of academic-centered VAA endeavors such as *Stemtest,* developed by a team of political scientists at the University of Antwerp since 2004, and *smartvote*, developed in collaboration with the Universities of Lausanne and Bern in Switzerland. Supranational elections proved to be an extremely fertile ground for the development of large-scale collaborations among social and political scientists all over Europe. The series of VAAs developed for the European Parliament (EP) elections since 2009, by the European University Institute in Fiesole, have benefited from the collaboration of over 250 political scientists.

Regarding their focus, VAAs are predominantly predictive and exclusively issue oriented. They restrict themselves to the main issues at stake in the campaign, leaving aside valence considerations (e.g., retrospective evaluations of government performance and the economy). Statement selection matters because it sets the perimeter of the battleground. Different combinations of statements prime users with different understandings of the current

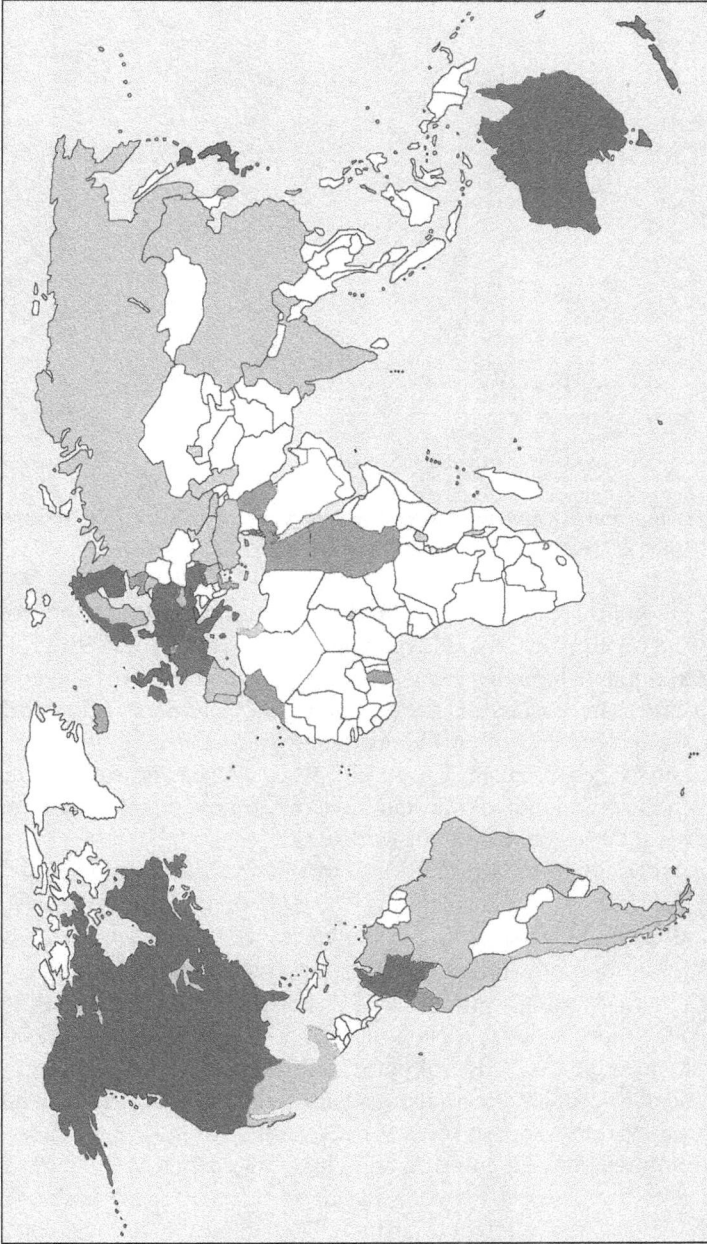

Figure 12.2   Global Distribution of VAAs. *Source:* Wahl-O-Mat-Forschung, University of Düsseldorf (last update: May 2018).

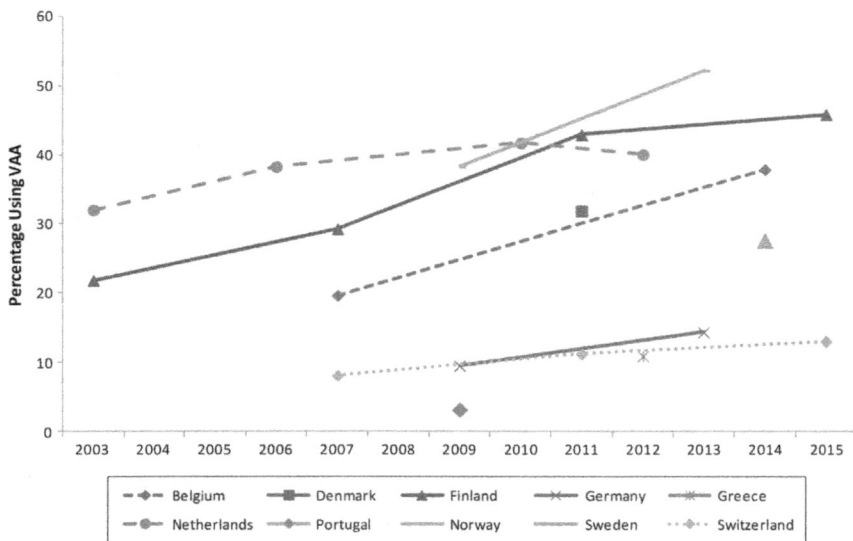

Figure 12.3 Proportion of VAA users among the voting population in selected countries.
Source: Garzia and Marschall, 2019.

dimensions of political competition, and can ultimately affect the voting advice they receive (Walgrave, Nuytemans, & Pepermans, 2009). Diverse routes lead to the development of the list of policy statements at the core of the VAA exercise. In most cases, the production of statements is undertaken by the VAA's developers, often alongside experts such as journalists and political scientists. State-linked VAAs like *Wahl-O-Mat*, however, include party actors in the production of the statements by, for example, inviting party representatives to VAA development workshops.

VAAs are generally very inclusive in terms of the parties and candidates they select. Tools like the German *Wahl-O-Mat* or the Dutch *Stemwijzer* encompass all candidates or parties in the elections, in line with their civic education background as well as their primary purpose (i.e., finding one's way through the increasingly complicated issue space of extreme multiparty systems). On the other hand, academia-based VAAs like the Belgian *Stemtest* only take into account a selection of parties. Often, this decision is grounded on both the need to exclude the numerous "irrelevant" parties on the ballot in many electoral systems, and on scientific research strategies (e.g., maximizing the attention toward parties worth studying). Interestingly, the latter type of VAAs tend to force parties to take a stance on each and every policy statement—with the tricky side effect of artificially shaping the political space to align with political science standards.

When it comes to the identification of candidates' and parties' positions, two different macro-groups of VAAs can be identified. On the one hand, candidate-based VAAs rely exclusively on the collaboration of candidates along the lines of the Comparative Candidate Survey project. Besides theoretical considerations, this operational choice is somewhat dictated by the large number of candidates targeted for inclusion. As an example, during the Swiss federal election campaign of 2019, approximately 3,900 candidates participated and answered the *smartvote* questionnaire, corresponding to a participation rate of 84 percent. Equally complex is the scenario faced by party-based systems, which host the large majority of all VAAs currently in operation. As parties are, by definition, nonunitary actors, one option for VAA developers is to determine party issue positions solely on expert assessment of the party platforms and other publicly available documentation. On the other side of the spectrum, designated party representatives are invited to identify their issue positions without these being subject to change by the tool's providers. Up until recently, however, these techniques have been used in isolation, with the unfortunate consequence that parties have been able to "manipulate" their position in the absence of an impartial check by expert observers (for the often quoted case of CDA in the Dutch election of 2006, see van Praag, 2007; see also Walgrave, van Aelst, & Nuytemans, 2008 for the case of Belgium). To avoid these drawbacks, an *iterative* method, consisting of a combination of expert judgment and party self-placement, has been pioneered by the Dutch VAA *Kieskompas* (Krouwel, Vitiello, & Wall, 2012); it has been exported to numerous countries in Europe and beyond, and it has been applied to the EP elections since 2009 (Sudulich, Garzia, Trechsel, & Vassil, 2014; Garzia, Trechsel, & De Sio, 2017).

Transnational VAAs, like the *EU Profiler* or *euandi*, represent a telling example of how their underlying methodological choices can shape the degree of pragmatic engagement with the political supply at election time. For one thing, more and more parties are agreeing to be involved in the party placement exercise. While 38 percent of all the parties contacted in 2009 by the *EU Profiler* team engaged in this cooperative endeavor, the figure rose to above 50 percent in the context of the *euandi* projects of 2014 and 2019. On the one hand, these figures are testimony to the increasing willingness of parties to be involved in—as in, be studied by—the VAA in exchange for visibility among users/voters. On the other hand, they highlight a considerable diversity in parties' strategic approach, ranging from full cooperation to explicit conflict. Examples of unconditional cooperation include the case of the Green Party of Greece in 2009, which went so far as to change some of their positions following a discussion with the academic coding team, which convincingly argued that the party's real position was—on the basis of publicly available documentation—different. A similar story applies to the Czech Pirate's Party in 2014. In other instances, the expert teams found themselves in the position of igniting a process of deliberation within the parties that led them to turn a nonattitude into an actual policy position.[3] When it comes to instances of open conflict, some parties even threaten legal action—as was the case with Fine Gael in Ireland, in 2009, and with Dimiourgia Xana in Greece, in 2014.

6. THE EFFECTS OF VAAs ON POLITICAL ATTITUDES AND BEHAVIOR: ENGAGING WITH USERS/CITIZENS

It is likely that electoral returns are the core motivation of parties' interest in VAA endeavors. Indeed, a growing body of scientific evidence points to the idea that VAAs do have an electoral effect on their users. Originally embedded in citizenship education initiatives, one central purpose of VAAs is to strengthen the capacity of citizens to engage in the political process. Having political resources, such as information and knowledge, is a key precondition for participation. With more information, citizens are better able to make sense of their own position relative to the electoral supply and thus more likely to cast their ballot in elections. In this respect, the wide amount of readily available information about politics and political parties provided by a VAA contributes to reducing the transactional costs involved in gathering relevant political information. The first studies investigating the impact of VAAs on electoral participation show that in both the 2005 and the 2009 German federal elections, more than 10 percent of users felt more motivated to vote solely due to having used *Wahl-O-Mat* (Marschall & Schmidt, 2010). In the 2007 federal elections in Switzerland, over 40 percent of respondents declared that using the *smartvote* had at least a slight and sometimes even a decisive influence on their decision to go to the polls (Ladner, Felder, & Fivaz, 2010). Later studies, relying on representative samples of the voting population and more sophisticated statistical techniques, largely confirmed these initial insights. Gemenis and Rosema's (2014) analysis of Dutch Parliamentary Election Study data estimates, by means of propensity score matching, that the presence of VAAs was responsible for over 4 percent of the reported turnout in the 2006 election. Another study by Dinas, Trechsel, and Vassil (2014), on European Election Study data, shows that even after controlling for a wide set of socio-structural, attitudinal, and behavioral variables, the probability of casting a vote in the EP election of 2009 was fourteen percentage points higher for VAA users compared to nonusers. A recent comparative study by Garzia, Trechsel, & De Angelis (2017), relying on twelve national election study datasets from Finland, Germany, the Netherlands, and Switzerland, found that—even after controlling for an exhaustive list of individual-level predictors of electoral participation—having used a VAA increased users' probability of casting a vote in elections by between two and twelve percentage points.[4] While focusing on the portion of the electorate that is mobilized due to VAA exposure, their study also finds that VAA exposure does not simply cause higher mobilization; it does so among groups in the electorate that are prone to electoral abstention: women, the young, and those less interested in politics.

Besides their ability to motivate undecided voters to participate in elections, VAAs have also been found to affect actual patterns of vote choice. In their seminal analysis of the Flemish *Stemtest*, Walgrave et al. (2008) find that the reported intention of changing behavior as a result of having used a VAA is not often matched with actual changes in voting behavior. The authors conclude that among the 8 percent of respondents who said that *Stemtest* made them doubt about their vote, only a half actually changed preferences. Interestingly, similar figures are reported in another study of VAA impact, this time focusing solely on patterns of party preference. In their cross-national analysis of the 2009 EP election, Alvarez et al. (2014) found about 8 percent of *EU Profiler* users reshuffling their party preferences to the top party proposed by the VAA. Unfortunately, their prepost design does not allow confirmation of the exact proportion of users remaining loyal in spite of a measurable VAA effect on preferences. More recently, applying a field experimental research design, Pianzola, Trechsel, Vassil, Schwerdt, and Alvarez (2019) found both a causal reinforcement effect of top-party preferences and a multiplication of electorally available parties for Swiss voters.

7. POTENTIAL FLAWS OF PRAGMATIC ENGAGEMENT: LESSONS FROM VAA IMPLEMENTATION

In this penultimate section, we build upon VAA's implementation trajectory to describe inherent risks of contaminating our object of inquiry and the ways to ethically circumvent them. To illustrate, we rely on a recent example of what could be defined as a "good engagement practice" originating in the field: the *Lausanne Declaration* delivered, in 2014, by a large group of academic VAA researchers and developers. The relevance of this declaration for the purposes of this chapter is twofold. On the one hand, it offers a paradigmatic example of the responsibility placed on the shoulders of political scientists when mingling with the political attitudes and behaviors of millions of citizens/voters. On the other hand, it also testifies to the awareness of such responsibility on behalf of political scientists as VAA developers, thus offering indications that extend far beyond the VAA realm—and, potentially, to every realm in which citizens are both analyzed and affected by means of political science methods and applications.

The signatories of the *Lausanne Declaration* agreed that, as a general rule, VAAs should be "open, transparent, impartial and methodologically sound" (§1.1). To enhance users' perception of impartiality, it is imperative that all "institutions, organisations, associations, groups, private companies and individuals financially supporting a VAA have to be made visible. Funding has to be made transparent" (§2.1).

While there is hardly any doubt that a VAA "should be freely available to all citizens" (§3.1) it is still a point of contention whether each and every party and/or candidate should be included in the VAA. *Should political scientists be put in charge of actually defining the set of parties which voters should consider?* According to the *Lausanne Declaration*, a VAA "should aim at the inclusion of as many parties/candidates that are on the ballot as possible" (§3.2). Moreover, it states that "parties and candidates should not be excluded from the tool for ideological reasons" (§3.3). These provisions highlight the contention that political scientists should refrain from altering in any way the political reality presented to citizens—regardless of the theoretical as well as methodological reasons suggested by their disciplinary knowledge—in line with the established practice of publicly funded VAA endeavors.[5]

Another critical issue raised in the *Lausanne Declaration* is that of statement selection. Early research provided clear evidence that the respective choice, composition, and wording of statements make a difference in the result indicated by a VAA. Drawing on a large-scale simulation of 500,000 different configurations of thirty-six statements, the aforementioned study by Walgrave et al. (2009) demonstrated that every possible configuration of statements produced a benefit to some parties, depending on the specific statement composition. In some instances, certain parties' shares of VAA advice multiplied several times between the least and the most favorable statement configuration. For this reason, VAA makers "ought to carefully watch that the design does not favor a party/candidate in a systematic matter" (§4.2).

Besides having an effect on the advice itself, statement selection is likely to have priming effects which have not yet been studied. A biased selection of statements may distort users' perception of the actual issues at stake in a given election—for instance, if certain relevant topics are excluded, or if certain other, less relevant, topics are included. What if VAA makers decide to exploit their visibility among the public and reshape the agenda (i.e., the list of statements) along the lines of more immediate, cognitively loaded concerns (i.e., the statements themselves) and more evocative language (i.e., question wording)? Studies from communication research can both offer insight into potential answers and raise awareness of the potentially enormous effects stemming from the widespread availability of these technologies to the general public outside the usual channels of knowledge production and intermediation, that is, a website rather than an academic journal, a few milliseconds' upload rather than a long and winding peer-review road, and so forth.

8. CONCLUSIONS

Over the last two decades, VAAs have spread throughout Europe and beyond. Social science research has begun to address the role and the effects of these tools and, especially, to consider their impact on political attitudes and voting behavior. Political scientists themselves have been increasingly involved in the making of these applications—to offer scientific standards and, also, to make use of the huge amount of VAA-generated data for empirical research purposes. Among the crucial findings of this emerging strand of research, scholars have uncovered strong effects of these technologies on their users. VAAs increase interest in, and knowledge of, political matters, and ultimately have a positive effect on individuals' propensity to take part in elections. This, combined with their massive spread among voters, enables them to impact on election turnout rates, thus counterbalancing the perils stemming from declining participation all over the Western world. What is more, VAAs do not only increase turnout. They do so among the categories most prone to electoral abstention: women, the younger generations and all those citizens with low levels of political interest.

Against the background of such encouraging outputs, one could be tempted to conclude that a pragmatic, academically driven approach to public engagement should be encouraged on the grounds of empirically measurable impact alone. However, we believe that VAAs—and related online technologies—operate within a more complex context of ethical constraints. And indeed, we concur that "there are still lingering doubts within the discipline about the ethical implications of doing impact" (Wood, 2019, p. 2). For instance, Flinders and Pal (2019) argue against the alleged obligation of the discipline to support liberal democracy. They do so on two grounds, namely the lack of unanimity in political views among political scientists and the enduring need to subject the relationship between politics and society to critical inquiry under any possible governing arrangement. We will thus conclude this chapter with our reflections about online engagement with VAAs and an attempt to situate it within this crucial disciplinary debate.

If VAAs become omnipresent features of election campaigns, if ever more citizens compare their political preferences with the electoral offer coded by VAAs, and if political scientists become indispensable partners of VAA designers, does this affect the very meaning of modern political science?

We posit that when getting actively involved in electoral campaigns, by shaping the information environment through the design of VAAs, political scientists need to reflect on their own identity. They face the epistemological problem of producing research on the politics of voters and parties while simultaneously transforming these politics. Many observers applaud higher rates of political involvement among the young, or effective instruments against fake news and disinformation. In a similar vein, exploratory studies on VAA's multiple desirable impacts would seem to offer even further hope. Garzia and Marschall (2019) argue that, by the very nature of issue-based applications, VAAs have the potential to prime issues over personality evaluations in the individual voting calculus. If VAAs follow certain criteria, they have the potential to inform voters about the "real" intentions of political parties and candidates. By prioritizing issues, VAAs could also tackle the representative deficit in some democracies in terms of fostering the responsiveness and responsibleness of political parties in office. One way is to conceptualize VAA proposals as promises that, if implemented after the election, could also be registered by modified applications, which would support the delegate model of political representation and serve the increasing number of issue voters with weaker party ties (Ladner, 2016). In all these respects, VAAs represent an undoubtedly fertile ground for disciplinary engagement with the public. Moreover, accumulated political science knowledge in VAAs serves only to provide citizens political information in the light of *their own* preferences. If bias arises, it can be fixed by the very same methods and techniques that led to its discovery in the first place. And it could be argued that it is ultimately up to citizens to decide what to do with their view of democracy when taking that information into account at election time.

This long list of promising opportunities, nonetheless, needs to be coupled with a corresponding number of potential pitfalls. Take, as an example, a VAA's promise of reengaging citizens with the political process by means of fostering turnout. Few would disagree with the general assertion that high turnout rates are a crucial measure for the vitality of a democracy. Yet, we contend that the very same assertion would be subject to much more skepticism if it came with some sort of normatively unwelcome string attached. For instance, that VAAs (or any other get-out-the-vote initiatives) increase participation among groups of citizens with illiberal inclinations—indeed a pressing issue to which we urge future scholarship to turn to. The list of potential pitfalls is large and could extend to ontological malpractice. What if political scientists—tempted by the sheer possibility to satisfy their own personal political views or to become rich and famous—manipulate the design of online engagement platforms in such ways as to help some while harming others? While we do not suggest that a return to the ivory tower may be the answer to these questions, we urge political scientists to reflect carefully about their role and the foremost societal implications of their research in the digital age.

NOTES

1. We would like to thank Mirjam Dageförde, Russell J. Dalton, Brigid Laffan, and Stefan Marschall for their insightful comments on earlier versions of this chapter, and the editors of this volume for their assistance throughout its development.

2. The data is admittedly incomplete, as it entirely relies on the existence of an item regarding VAA usage in national election studies. Nonetheless, it provides a good longitudinal overview of the developments in VAA usage in an important set of early-implementation countries.

3. Finland's Pirate Party, for instance, launched a web-survey among its EP candidates to identify a unitary party position in response to the *euandi2014* self-placement questionnaire. In Slovenia, Solidarnost even admitted that they had not taken a position on certain questions yet, and asked its self-positioning to be taken as indicative of their positions. The country team agreed to the party drawing up a list of newly taken positions and to the party sending in an official document that could be quoted.

4. This finding is supported by the replication analysis performed on Swiss data by Germann and Gemenis (2019).

5. For instance, in the case of the German *Wahl-O-Mat*, designed by the Bundeszentrale für Politische Bildung, a federal state agency, the initial noninclusion of a small party in Bavaria in 2008 resulted in a court order. In the view of the court, a state agency running a VAA was accountable to the voters and parties and therefore had to include any party contesting an election. Most recently, on 20 May 2019, the *Wahl-O-Mat*'s EP elections VAA was taken offline due to a court order. Indeed, the small German party "Volt" won the legal battle, defending its right to be included in the list of parties contesting the election.

REFERENCES

Alvarez, R. M., Levin, I., Trechsel, A. H., & Mair, P. (2014). Party preferences in the digital age: The impact of voting advice applications. *Party Politics, 20*(4), 227–36.

Bandola-Gill, J., Brans, M., & Flinders, M. (2019). *Incentives for impact in higher education: A cross-national political science perspective*. Unpublished manuscript.

Boswell, J., Corbett, J., & Havercroft, J. (2019). Politics and science as a vocation. Can academics save us from post-truth politics? *Political Studies Review*, 1–16.

Daalder, H., & van der Geer, J. P. (1977). Partijafstanden in de Tweede Kamer. *Acta Politica, 12*(3), 289–345.

Dinas, E., Trechsel, A. H., & Vassil, K. (2014). A look into the mirror: Preferences, representation and electoral participation. *Electoral Studies, 36*, 290–97.

Eisfeld, R. (2019). *Empowering citizens, engaging the public: Political science for the 21st century*. London: Palgrave Macmillan.

Flinders, M., & Pal, L. J. (2019). The moral foundations of public engagement: Does political science, as a discipline, have an ethics? *Political Studies Review*, 1–14.

Garzia, D., & Marschall, S. (2019). Voting advice applications. In S. Meisel (Ed.), *Oxford research Encyclopedia of politics*. Oxford: Oxford University Press.

Garzia, D., Trechsel, A. H., & De Angelis, A. (2017). Voting advice applications and electoral participation: A multi-method study. *Political Communication*, *55*, 1–20.

Garzia, D., Trechsel, A. H., & De Sio, L. (2017). Party placement in supranational elections: An introduction to the euandi 2014 dataset. *Party Politics*, *23*(4), 333–41.

Geddes, M., Dommett, K., & Prosser, B. (2018). A recipe for impact? Exploring knowledge requirements in the UK Parliament and beyond. *Evidence & Policy: A Journal of Research, Debate and Practice, 14*(2), 259–76.

Gemenis, K., & Rosema, M. (2014). Voting Advice Applications and electoral turnout. *Electoral Studies*, *36*, 281–89.

Germann, M., & Gemenis, K. (2019). Getting out the vote with Voting Advice Applications. *Political Communication, 36*(1), 149–70.

Irwin, G., & Van Holsteyn, J. J. (2000). Bandwagons, underdogs, the *Titanic*, and the Red Cross: The influence of public opinion polls on voters. Unpublished manuscript.

Krouwel, A., Vitiello, T., & Wall, M. (2012). The practicalities of issuing vote advice: A new methodology for profiling and matching. *International Journal of Electronic Governance, 5*(3), 223–43.

Kruikemeier, S., Van Noort, G., Vliegenthart, R., & De Vreese, C. H. (2013). Getting closer: The effects of personalized and interactive online political communication. *European Journal of Communication, 28*(1), 53–66.

Ladner, A. (2016). Do VAAs encourage issue voting and promissory representation? Evidence from the Swiss Smartvote. *Policy & Internet, 8*(4), S. 412–30.

Ladner, A., Felder, G., & Fivaz, J. (2010). More than toys? A first assessment of voting advice applications in Switzerland. In L. Cedroni & D. Garzia (Eds.), *Voting Advice Applications in Europe. The state of the art* (pp. 91–123). Napoli: Civis.

Marks, G. (Ed.). (2007). Special symposium: Comparing measures of party positioning: expert, manifesto, and survey data. *Electoral Studies, 26*(1), 1–141.

Marschall, S., & Garzia, D. (2014). Voting Advice Applications in a comparative perspective: An introduction. In D. Garzia & S. Marschall (Eds.), *Matching voters with parties and candidates. Voting Advice Applications in comparative perspective* (pp. 1–10). Colchester: ECPR Press.

Marschall, S., & Schmidt, C. K. (2010). The impact of voting indicators: The case of the German Wahl-O-Mat. In L. Cedroni & D. Garzia (Eds.), *Voting Advice Applications in Europe. The state of the art* (pp. 61–86). Napoli: Civis.

McAllister, I., & Studlar, D. T. (1991). Bandwagon, underdog, or projection? Opinion polls and electoral choice in Britain, 1979–1987. *Journal of Politics, 53*(3), 720–41.

Moravcsik, A. (2014). Transparency: The revolution in qualitative research. *PS: Political Science & Politics, 47*(1), 48–53.

Ostrom, E. (1998). A behavioral approach to the rational choice theory of collective action. *American Political Science Review, 92*(1), 1–22.

Pianzola, J., Trechsel, A. H., Vassil, K., Schwerdt, G., & Alvarez, R. M. (2019). The impact of personalized information on vote intention: Evidence from a randomized field experiment. *Journal of Politics, 81*(3), 833–47.

Prior, M. (2005). News vs. entertainment: How increasing media choice widens gaps in political knowledge and turnout. *American Journal of Political Science, 49*, 577–92.

Putnam, R. D. (2003). APSA presidential address: The public role of political science. *Perspectives on Politics, 1*(2), 249–55.

Sil, R., & Katzenstein, P. J. (2010). Analytic eclecticism in the study of world politics: Reconfiguring problems and mechanisms across research traditions. *Perspectives on Politics, 8*(2), 411–31.

Sudulich, L., Garzia, D., Trechsel, A., & Vassil, K. (2014). Party placement in supranational elections: The case of the 2009 EP elections. In D. Garzia & S. Marschall (Eds.), *Matching voters with parties and candidates. Voting Advice Applications in comparative perspective*. Colchester: ECPR Press.

Trechsel, A. H., & Mair, P. (2011). When parties (also) position themselves: An introduction to the EU profiler. *Journal of Information Technology & Politics, 8*(1), 1–20.

van Praag, P. (2007). De Stemwijzer: hulpmiddel voor de kiezers of instrument van manipulatie? Unpublished manuscript.

Walgrave, S., Nuytemans, M., & Pepermans, K. (2009). Voting aid applications and the effect of statement selection. *West European Politics, 32*(6), 1161–80.

Walgrave, S., van Aelst, P., & Nuytemans, M. (2008). "Do the vote test": The electoral effects of a popular vote advice application at the 2004 Belgian elections. *Acta Politica, 43*(1), 50–70.

Wood, M. (2019). Engaged political science. *Political Studies Review*, 1–18.

Zittel, T. (2015). Constituency candidates in comparative perspective–How personalized are constituency campaigns, why, and does it matter? *Electoral Studies, 39*, 286–94.

Chapter 13

Politics of Public Policy Revisited

Lessons from European Welfare State Research

Anton Hemerijck[1]

1. BENEFICIAL ATLANTIC CROSSINGS

Yves Mény's discretely provocative contribution to this volume, "Is There a European Touch?," concedes that, for a long time, American political science research trumped Europe's more parochial, nationally oriented research traditions in theoretical sophistication and methodological rigor. Mény highlights an important exception to the backward state of the European political science profession: comparative welfare state research. It was a British academic, Hugh Heclo, who triggered the American interest in social policy as a key component of advanced political systems, with his seminal study, *Modern Social Politics in Britain and Sweden* (1974), based on his Yale dissertation. Ever since, comparative welfare state research has become one of the most successful fields of transatlantic intellectual engagement between American and European scholars, not least due to the large numbers of highly diverse national welfare states in Europe. The landmark contribution of Danish scholar Gøsta Esping-Andersen, *The Three Worlds of Welfare Capitalism* (1990), was written at the European University Institute in Florence, the European hotbed for comparative welfare state research established by Peter Flora. Further U.S.-European collaboration flourished when Fritz W. Scharpf, director of the Max Planck Institute for the Study of Societies, teamed up with Vivien Schmidt from Boston University for the massive two-volume *Work and Welfare in the Open Economy* (2000). This was shortly followed by the extremely successful *Varieties of Capitalism* (2001) and its approach to comparative political economy, by Peter Hall from Harvard and David Soskice from the Berlin WZB. More recently, Wolfgang Streeck, also from the Cologne Max Planck Institute, and Kathleen Thelen from MIT joined forces to break new ground by explaining evolutionary modes of institutional change that are incremental and transformative at the same time. Their acclaimed edited volume *Beyond Continuity: Institutional Change in Advanced Political Economies* (2005) exposed how recent dynamics in economic, social, and political life depart in fundamental ways from traditional "punctuated equilibrium" models of stability and change, which brought political institutionalism into the academic limelight more than four decades ago.

Mény has a cunning explanation for the academic success of transatlantic scholarly engagement on the modern welfare state. European political scientists never fully heeded the grand theoretical fads from the U.S. of structural-functionalism, behaviorism and, later, rational choice and game theory, as these decontextualized theoretical approaches ran into problems in the face of heterogeneous political behavior and policy outcomes across West-European polities with highly variegated state traditions, electoral systems, and civil society relations. In other words, European political scientists never really parted with the "old" institutionalism. Then, once the "new" institutionalism made theoretical headway from the mid-1980s, European scholars, increasingly interested in doing more comparative work, were at a competitive advantage. All the milestone publications mentioned previously ensued from the leveling of the transatlantic playing field. The ferocity and dynamism of the transatlantic intellectual cross-fertilization in comparative welfare state research begs the question of whether it fed into a unified theoretical approach and methodological toolkit for the study of modern social politics? I think not, as I will exemplify below. My contention is that even in comparative welfare state research a subtle European touch remains. This is due to the contingencies of engagement and detachment that have their roots in the relative geographical proximity between American and European scholars to their objects of inquiry. American colleagues, studying the European welfare state from afar, are generally more prone to put forward and test generalizations about welfare expansion being driven by industrialization, as suggested by Harold Wilensky (1975, 2002); or to conjecture that the post-1980 "new politics of the welfare state" conjures up the "politics of the status quo," associated with the seminal work of Paul Pierson (1994, 2001); or, more recently, to claim that European Union (EU) economic integration reinforces welfare retrenchment and rising inequality across EU member states (Beckfield, 2019). In addition, this long-distance relationship inspired American scholars, more than their European colleagues, to develop detached and coherent scientific research programs in terms of theory and method (Lynch & Rhodes, 2016). European scholars, operating in close proximity to their objects of study and confronted with multifarious national- and EU-level institutional contingencies, tended to shy away from linear inferencing on the basis of *nomothetic* research programs, instead chose to particularize institutional contingencies with consequential effects for diverse welfare states in a more objectively *idiographic* fashion disciplined by the comparative method. One of these contingencies relates to the deepening and widening of the EU from six to twenty-eight member states, with nineteen sharing the single currency of the euro since the mid-1970s.

Europeanization challenges the standard methodological nationalism that U.S. research continued to adhere to. Explaining the novel two-level institutional veracity, as Maurizio Ferrera does in his magisterial study *The Boundaries of Welfare: European Integration and the New Spatial Politics of Social Protection* (2005), requires a rather open theoretical approach, with theory-building and theory-testing interacting to enrich each other with narrative detail and empirical depth. The unique exigency of intensified Europeanization, moreover, triggered a third—unforeseen—development. Since the late 1990s, national and EU-level policymakers have consulted with Gøsta Esping-Andersen, Maurizio Ferrera, myself, and many more, to advise on the future of social Europe and its de facto semi-sovereign EU welfare states. It is my contention that academic engagement with policymakers, which is constantly evolving, ultimately prepared the intellectual ground for the diffusion of social investment reform across the European continent, a policy shift that made few inroads in the United States.

Relative geographical proximity and distance to objects of scientific inquiry, I argue below, thus invoked subtly diverse traditions of welfare state research on both sides of the Atlantic, including discrete opportunities for scholarly engagement with policymakers. However, I wish to emphasize that I do not suggest that the more idiographic European emphasis is in any sense superior to more nomothetic American research. I merely wish to emphasize why they opted, in relative terms, for testing generalities vis-à-vis explaining institutional contingency. The rest of the chapter proceeds in three steps. First, section 2 surveys the rise of political institutionalism to paradigmatic hegemony in the field of comparative welfare state research since the late 1980s. I will highlight the European twist to welfare state research, to complement Mény's astute intuitions, and compare it to the American approach which maintained a stronger interest in theory and methods. Next, in an autobiographical fashion, section 3 portrays how, since the 1990s, a number of European welfare scholars were consulted by EU institutions and national governments to engage in social investment agenda-setting. In the concluding section, section 4, I argue that the kind of open institutionalism in empirical research (and policy advice) that European welfare scholars brought to comparative research, which proved indispensable to effectively exploring and explaining transformative two-level European social policy change, today faces a revitalized behavioralist counter-revolution. European political scientists are increasingly turning to bottom-up partisan competition and opinion surveys with an overriding focus on the micro-behavioral input side of the political process. As a consequence, the institutional throughput side of the political process, connecting macro regularities to micro correlates, is being shelved. The "electoral turn" confronts welfare state research with the imperative to reconstruct a form of open institutionalism, capable of interpreting and explaining the politics of welfare state recalibration. This needs to happen without throwing out the fundamental insight that extant political structures, state traditions and social policy legacies, including those at the EU-level, profile the behavior of *reflexive* reformers and facilitate policy engagement with academia, in a path-contingent but not predetermined fashion.

2. BETWIXT CLOSED AND OPEN INSTITUTIONALISM

In the 1970s, a novel field of political inquiry, comparative welfare state research, came into purview, as it became increasingly evident that the welfare state had "grown to [its] limits" (Flora & Heidenheimer, 1981). Moreover, the startling variety of national patterns of crisis management during the 1970s stagflation predicament discredited the behavioralist assumptions and functionalist convergence conjectures of postwar social science. A new generation of scholars reclaimed leverage for institutional factors—ranging from partisan control over government, electoral systems, administrative traditions, social policy legacies, to the structure of industrial relations—as independent middle-range variables better able to explain patterns of socio-economic variation across advanced Organization for Economic Cooperation and Development (OECD) democracies (Goldthorpe, 1985). For almost four decades, contributors to the vibrant field of comparative welfare state research endorsed the overarching institutional presumption that "policy shapes politics" because of the political salience of issues such as employment, care, and welfare provision, and due to the enduring character of country-specific postwar political compromise underlying domestic welfare architectures.

The founding father of the study of the politics of the welfare state, Hugh Heclo, intimated in *Modern Social Politics in Britain and Sweden* (1974) that with social spending rising to over 15 percent of GDP in the postwar era, analyzing partisan conflict and political competition over social policy no longer suffices to understand the true political weight of the modern welfare state. He urged researchers to delve into the administrative capacity of the state as an independent force in modern social politics. Heclo also brought to the fore an element of policy voluntarism on the part of nonelected policy experts. In so doing, he was the first to direct attention to the dynamics of social learning in the welfare state, driven by the complex interplay of expert consultation and political competition in the policy process (Heclo, 1974, p. 320). Fundamental to Heclo's conception of policy learning was *uncertainty*: "Politics finds its sources not only in power but also in uncertainty—men collectively wondering what to do" (Heclo, 1974, p. 305). Consequently, he defined policy learning as "relatively enduring changes in thought or behavioral intention that result from experience and/or new information with the attainment or revision of policy objectives" (ibid. 306). For Heclo, policy actors are necessarily "reflexive," suggesting that they are able to creatively diagnose problems and envision policy alternatives as solutions, under conditions of what Herbert Simon coined "bounded rationality," suggesting a world too complex for actors to comprehensively decide on the most appropriate means to privileged ends in a timely manner (Simon, 1985).

Following in the footsteps of Heclo, the research tradition of historical institutionalism took root in the United States, albeit without Heclo's strong emphasis on policy voluntarism. Theda Skocpol and Peter Katzenstein identified relatively stable features of political-administrative systems and policy legacies as important constraints to and resources for welfare state development (Evans, Rueschemeyer, & Skocpol, 1985; Katzenstein, 1985). Gøsta Esping-Andersen's pioneering breakthrough study *The Three Worlds of Welfare Capitalism*, also building on key insights from "power resources theory" (Korpi, 1983), proclaimed that the modern postwar welfare state had fundamentally recast the boundaries between politics and economics by strengthening politics against pure market forces. True to the spirit of historical institutionalism, Esping-Andersen placed additional emphasis on the critical impact of the historical legacies of religion, democratization, and political representation (see also van Kersbergen, 1995). By triangulating cross-sectional statistical analysis on stratification and redistribution and power constellations across countries in sufficient depth and detail, Esping-Andersen was able to conceptualize three "ideal-type" welfare regimes: liberal, conservative-corporatist, and social democratic. In terms of the scope of social protection and stratification, the Nordic social democratic welfare regime, based on state-guaranteed social rights, was the more generous welfare front-runner; the Anglo-Saxon liberal regime, based on the market as primary source of welfare provision, a laggard; and the conservative-corporatist regime of the European continent, based on family status differentials, fell somewhere in between. *The Three Worlds of Welfare Capitalism* represented a paradigm revolution in comparative welfare state research by bringing together institutional factors in a "configurational fashion" of distinct mixes of state, market, and family welfare provision. Esping-Andersen ultimately probed the plausibility that the "inherent logic of our three welfare state regimes seems to reproduce itself" in causally distinct path-dependent trajectories. In the Anglo-Saxon regime income inequality would become a sticking point; the Nordic model would face limits to high taxation, while the conservative welfare state was likely to confront "jobless growth."

From the late 1970s to the early 1990s, the principal research question in comparative welfare state research shifted from an emphasis on historical origins, country-specific contingencies, and political voluntarism, in explaining welfare state diversity and socioeconomic performance variation, toward explaining welfare regime "lock-in" in a more structuralist fashion, with a strong focus on self-reinforcing path-dependent feedback effects anchoring institutional stability in spite of dramatic structural change. The strongest theoretical claim of the welfare state as an *immovable object* came from Paul Pierson. In his groundbreaking study, *Dismantling the Welfare State? Reagan, Thatcher, and the Politics of Retrenchment* (1994), he was able to demonstrate how difficult it is to retrench standing social commitments, even under the ideological leadership of Margaret Thatcher and Ronald Reagan, who were zealously motivated to unburden the free market from the overloaded Anglo-Saxon welfare states in the United Kingdom and the United States in the 1980s. Pierson concluded from his two-country comparison that "the welfare state remains the most resilient aspect of the post war political economy" (Pierson, 1994, p. 179). Theoretically, he anchored his 'new politics of the welfare state' explanation of the "frozen" character of mature welfare states on the (negative) political incentives brought on by the expansion of the welfare state during the Golden Age, displacing the "old politics" of the welfare state, largely driven by "credit claiming" policy expansion. For Pierson, mature welfare states are quintessential sites of institutional self-reinforcement, making pathbreaking reform progressively more improbable, because of a generalized political fear of electoral retribution and vested interest opposition to cuts in popular social programs. In passing, he scorned Heclo's naïve mid-1970s portrayal of social policy learning by underlining that "in an atmosphere of austerity a fundamental rethinking of social policy seems a remote possibility" (1994, p. 170).

Since the publication of Pierson's famous book, the "new politics" conjecture of political inertia has been corroborated by many failed reform cases on the European continent, such as the stalemated pension reforms in Italy in 1994, which led to the downfall of the first Berlusconi government, and in France in 1995, when Prime Minister Juppé had to withdraw his social insurance reform plans after massive protests. American scholars, working on European welfare states, such as Julia Lynch (2006) on pensions, and Kimberley Morgan (2006) on working mothers, similarly sustained the change-resistant "realist" perspective of political institutionalism, leveraged on the central concept of "increasing returns" that Pierson originally borrowed from economics.

For decades, welfare states have been hard-pressed to adapt to new social and economic realities, triggered by successive economic crises, but also by demographic aging, deindustrialization, technological innovation, the rise of

the service sector, the feminization of the labor market, economic internationalization and EU market integration, and intensified migration. In spite of
mounting pressures for adaptation, *the* startling feature of the postwar welfare
state concerns its indisputable resilience, even today. In the aftermath of the
Great Recession, public spending on social protection, health and education
matched levels reached in the 1980s. However, constant aggregate spending
hides significant reallocations between the different policy programs that
make up twenty-first-century welfare states today.

The emphasis on path dependency and policy inertia is both the strength
and the weakness of institutional policy analysis. However deeply anchored,
institutions are by no means invariable (Mayntz & Scharpf, 1995; Scharpf,
1997). Mounting European anomalies in the "new politics" conjecture of
change-resistant welfare states have, since the turn of the new millennium,
led European scholars associated with the tradition of historical institutionalism, to identify more transformative trajectories of welfare adjustment.
A very influential research project in this vein found its way into the two-
volume comprehensive study *Welfare and Work in the Open Economy*,
edited by Fritz W. Scharpf and Vivien Schmidt (2000) in collaboration with
many leading European and American welfare state scholars. The Scharpf
and Schmidt research team observed how the twelve countries in the study
varied enormously in the social reforms they undertook from the late 1970s.
The challenge of intensified economic internationalization confronted each
welfare regime family, supported by specific actor-constellations, with a
distinct constellation of regime-specific adjustment syndromes and potential
reform agendas. As *Anglo-Saxon welfare states* increased the scope of the
free market and strengthened the selective nature of social programs, there
was growth in employment; the flipside of the success of the Anglo-Saxon
"jobs machine" was a significant rise in income poverty. By contrast, the
Scandinavian welfare states were best able to maintain a both generous and
universally accessible system of social security through activating labor
market policies. Problematically, *Continental welfare states* seemed caught
in a negative spiral of high gross labor costs and rising economic inactivity.
In *Southern Europe*, the Continental "inactivity trap" was exacerbated by the
stringent regime of insider-biased labor market regulation, which intensified
the exclusion of young people and, especially, women from the labor market.
In short, similar pressures led to very different policy problems across different welfare regimes, which in turn triggered diverging politicized reform
paths. In conclusion, Scharpf and Schmidt explicated that institutional characteristics shape the menu of feasible policy options, of which *Reformstau*
is one likely outcome. Blame-avoiding politics and insider-biased reform
opposition are not the only shows in town. Welfare regimes may shape
impending social problems, but they do not determine policy responses. The

Scandinavian welfare state never really experienced the astute fiscal crisis that Esping-Andersen conjectured in 1990. Apparently, active labor market policies and family-friendly services help to sustain universal social security and fiscal revenue through high levels of employment. In the United Kingdom, under New Labour, a growth-oriented macroeconomic policy allowed for an expansion of needs-based tax credits for working families, thereby temporarily improving the plight of the vulnerable, however without significantly lowering inequality. The aftermath of the oil crises of the 1970s surely inspired the political compulsion for retrenchment, but the ensuing recession also triggered more balanced adjustment responses through social pacts, supported by organized wage restraint, in the smaller political economies of Denmark, Ireland, and the Netherlands. In the 1990s, exiting the labor market early, in response to structural adjustment, invoked a severe "inactivity trap" across Continental welfare states. This, in turn, revolutionized path-shifting reforms toward more inclusive public safety nets, active labor market policies, and family service provision in the traditional male-breadwinner and female-homemaker welfare states of Germany, Austria, and Spain. In the process, Christian democracy, the political family most wedded to the male-breadwinner welfare state, slowly but surely also endorsed high levels of female employment, gender equity values, and dual-earner family roles, as it became evident that female employment warrants robust families (Hemerijck, 2013).

In other words, American "hard wired" path dependency, based on a coherent increasing returns logic, once again, ran aground on Europe's dynamic diversity, because of its inability to explain change and its insider-biased understanding of institutional actors, lacking any faculty to update cognitive, normative, and interaction orientations. While environmental changes alter the functioning of existing institutions, they also modify the interests and preferences of relevant political actors and their relative power positions to (re-)enforce their objectives. A few European researchers ventured to rehabilitate Hugh Heclo's focus on policy learning under conditions of relative austerity. For our comparative contribution to the Scharpf/Schmidt project, Martin Schludi and I explicated how very often solutions to policy problems in one area, such as wage moderation in industrial relations, may generate new problems that must subsequently be dealt with in adjacent policy areas, such as dualization in social insurance provision, triggering political pressures to reform and expand employment services. Lateral spillovers hereby create the conditions and political demands for change across interdependent areas of social and economic regulation, potentially unleashing a cascade of incremental changes across an array of policy areas, ultimately resulting in a "cumulatively transformative" refashioning of interdependent welfare policy repertoires over time (Hemerijck & Schludi, 2000; see also Visser

& Hemerijck, 1997). Preparing the ground for social policy reorientation is often attributed to expert committees and advisory councils. Cases in point are the 1993 Buurmeijer Commission in the Netherlands, which prepared the overhaul of the Dutch social insurance administration; the 1997 Swedish non-partisan expert pension reform committee, whose recommendations formed the basis of Swedish pension reform in 1998; and the 2002 Hartz Commission that precipitated Gerhard Schröder's Agenda 2010 (Clasen & Clegg, 2011).

Today, European welfare state researchers, including Maurizio Ferrera (2005) Silja Häusermann (2010), Joakim Palme (2003), Bruno Palier (2010), Jochen Clasen (2005), myself, and many more, readily acknowledge the transformative and multidimensional nature of contemporary welfare reform. In the early 2000s, Maurizio Ferrera and I developed the multidimensional concept of welfare recalibration to trace social policy change in the aftermath of the postwar golden age (Ferrera & Hemerijck, 2003). Welfare recalibration refers to policy initiatives that aim to transform the welfare state into a new configuration or *Gestalt*, beyond core social security, with the intent of effectively coping with the adaptive challenges of intensified international competition, relative austerity, gender change and demographic aging. We conceptualized an empirically grounded, multidimensional heuristic of welfare recalibration from a policy learning perspective. This suggests that reform decisions to improve policy performance nearly always pass through instances of *cognitive* assessment, *normative* judgment, *distributive* bargaining, *institutional* (re-)design, and *referential* exemplification.

Functional recalibration concerns the changing nature of social risk and the kinds of interventions that are required to effectively address it. *Distributive recalibration* involves the rebalancing of welfare provision across policy clienteles and organized interests, that is, how gains and losses associated with reform are distributed across social risk groups. *Institutional recalibration* relates to the ongoing rescaling of welfare provision, both downward from the nation-state to subnational tiers of regional and city social service provision and upward to the European level in laying down the macroeconomic parameters of domestic welfare provision. As the welfare state is based on the idea of a social contract, with citizen claims on equity, inclusion, and fairness, *normative recalibration* pertains to the changing normative orientations, values, and discourses emerging from the perceived incongruence between the broad values underpinning existing programs and adaptive pressures. Finally, *referential recalibration* refers to policymakers' ability to "borrow" effective welfare policies from other countries and muster domestic political legitimacy in an evermore competitive policy environment. At any point in time, all five dimensions of welfare recalibration can be contested politically. Actors wishing to push through reform have to be willing to confront opponents by suggesting that their (*distributive*) resistance is problematic for reasons of (*functional*) effectiveness and (*normative*) fairness in the political sphere. Ultimately, to be successful, reformers have to build political consensus (*institutional*) to gain support for proposed reforms, using foreign (*referential*) examples to portray light at the end of the tunnel (Hemerijck, 2013).

3. FROM POLITICAL "PROCESS-TRACING" TO ENGAGED SOCIAL INVESTMENT "PROCESS-MAKING"

Since the late 1990s, a fair number of European comparative welfare scholars, steeped in the tradition of political institutionalism, have been consulted to provide policy advice on welfare reform, especially in relation to widening and deepening European integration. For myself, this started in the Netherlands in 1996, when I was working with Jelle Visser on *A Dutch Miracle: Job Growth, Welfare Reform and Corporatism in the Netherlands* (1997). Civil servants from the Ministry of Social Affairs and Employment were working on a comparative study on the welfare performance of the Dutch political economy for which they sought my feedback. Next, I was invited to write a lengthy essay on *Social Policy as a Productive Factor* (1997) for a high-level policy conference under the Dutch presidency of the EU. The intention of the conference was to correct the lopsided view that comprehensive social policy provision burdens economic competitiveness, with the Dutch miracle as a good news example. For the Dutch government in 1997, led by the social democratic Wim Kok, it was essential to show the deep correlates of a strong economy and generous social policy. As this had been a primary objective of Jacques Delors, as former president of the European Commission (1985–1995), he chaired the conference. Other political figures were the Dutch ex-premier Ruud Lubbers and EU director-general of DG Employment and Social Affairs and ex-finance minister of Sweden, Allan Larsson. Esping-Andersen and Tony Atkinson, a leading expert on income inequality from Oxford Univerisity, were the keynote academics on the program. Not yet elected prime minister, Tony Blair made a dinner speech in the Rijkmuseum in front of Rembrandt's restored Night Watch painting, congratulating Wim Kok on the success of the Dutch polder model of capitalism with a human face. Ultimately, the essay *Social Policy as a Productive Factor*, weaving together arguments made at the conference, was recognized, especially by Allan Larsson, but also by Dutch Labour and Social Affairs minister Ad Melkert, as an important source of inspiration for the Employment Chapter in the Amsterdam Treaty. As an academic, I was struck how interested policymakers were in policy-relevant academic contributions to questions on welfare reform for a strong economy.

By the mid-1990s, the default background policy theory was anchored in an OECD diagnosis. In 1994, the *OECD Jobs Study* launched a critical attack on the "dark side" of double-digit unemployment figures in many European OECD member states (OECD, 1994). Hovering around 10 percent, unemployment rates in France, Germany, and Italy were twice as high as in the United States. The OECD economists argued that Europe's generous welfare states, with their overprotective job security, high minimum wages, generous unemployment insurance, heavy taxation, and overriding emphasis on coordinated wage bargaining and social dialogue, had raised the costs of labor above market-clearing levels. The OECD thus portrayed the fundamental dilemma of Europe's mature welfare states in terms of a trade-off between welfare equity and employment efficiency.

By the end of the 1990s, growing political disenchantment with the neoliberal diagnosis began to generate electoral successes for the center-left. Newly elected European social democrats such as Tony Blair, Gerhard Schröder, Wim Kok, and Poul Nyrup Rasmussen, strongly believed that European welfare states had to be transformed from passive benefits systems into activating, capacity building, social investment states. The activating welfare policy platform was inspired intellectually by Anthony Giddens' 1998 book *The Third Way: The Renewal of Social Democracy* (Giddens, 1998). By the late 1990s, Third Way ideas had found their way to the European Commission, reinforced by activating welfare reform successes in Denmark and the Netherlands.

Maurizio Ferrera and Martin Rhodes convened the European Forum on *Recasting the Welfare State* at the European University Institute (EUI) during the academic year 1998–1999. Intellectually, the Forum proved to be an important breeding ground for the U-turn in comparative welfare state research: from explaining institutional inertia per se to a more open research agenda of explaining variegated trajectories of welfare state change in times of intense socioeconomic restructuring. The "recasting" metaphor was carefully chosen so as to capture the institutionally bounded nature of the reform momentum, leading to a patchwork of old and new policies searching for greater coherence. On a number of occasions over the tenure of the European Forum, policymakers were invited to discuss our academic output. During one of the these high-level policy dialogues, Maurizio Ferrera and Martin Rhodes were approached by Portuguese officials from the Ministry of Labour to write an agenda-setting policy report for Lisbon Summit in 2000. Maurizio and Martin asked me to join the team. We wrote a small volume titled *The Future of Social Europe* (2000), which highlighted the productive importance of twenty-first-century welfare "recalibration" and the promise of the "open method of coordination" in fostering cross-country policy learning. In hindsight, the European Forum on *Recasting the Welfare State* created an "epistemic community" *avant la lettre*. Jonathan Zeitlin, who coined the term "recalibration" at the Forum, subsequently became the world expert on the "open method of coordination" (OMC). Maurizio Ferrera, Martin Rhodes, and myself presented our ideas of welfare recalibration in Lisbon in March 2000, with Tony Giddens, Fritz W. Scharpf, David Miliband, and Frank Vandenbroucke, federal minister of pensions and health care from Belgium, present. Academic engagement with policymaking enticed an important change in orientation, away from Stein Rokkan's emphasis on "retrospective diachronics" (1975)—today called processtracing—toward the exploration of what Maurizio Ferrera, inspired by Max Weber, has come to coin "prospective diachronics," referring to the analytical delineation of "possibility spaces"—that is, the identification of developmental alternatives looming in extant political structures and policy legacies for institutionally relevant change agents (2019).

The 2000 Portuguese presidency of the EU put forward an integrated political agenda of economic, employment, and social objectives, committing the Union to becoming the "most competitive and dynamic knowledge-based economy in the world, capable of sustainable economic growth with more and better jobs and greater social cohesion." The Lisbon Agenda revamped the notion of positive complementarities between equity and efficiency in the knowledge-based economy by "investing in people and developing an active and dynamic welfare state" (European Council, 2000). This broadened the notion of social policy as a productive factor beyond its traditional emphasis on inclusive and activating social protection, to include social promotion and improvement of lifelong education and training.

For the Belgian presidency of the EU that commenced in 2001, Frank Vandenbroucke, eager to build on the Lisbon Agenda's social ambitions, invited a group headed by Gøsta Esping-Andersen, including myself, to draft a bold report on a "new welfare architecture for 21st-century Europe," later published under the title *Why We Need a New Welfare State* (2002). For Vandenbroucke, a towering intellectual of the active welfare state movement in European social democracy, fundamental changes in the economy and society called for pathbreaking social policy innovation (Vandenbroucke, 1999). The assignment he gave Esping-Andersen and colleagues was to rethink the welfare state for the twenty-first century, so that "once again, labour markets and families are welfare optimizers and a good guarantee that tomorrow's adult workers will be as productive and resourceful as possible" (Esping-Andersen, Gallie, Hemerijck, & Myles, 2002, p. 25). Our report and book set a policy agenda for social investment that we believed went deeper than Tony Giddens' conception of an active welfare state as a trampoline rather than a safety net. In our work for the Belgian federal government, we emphasized—contra the Third Way—that social investment is no substitute for inclusive social protection. Adequate minimum income protection is a critical precondition for an effective social investment strategy. The overarching social investment imperative was to prepare individuals, families, and societies to preempt various risks rather than simply repair damage after misfortune engenders individual and social costs (Esping-Andersen et al., 2002, p. 5).

The core diagnosis of our work was that economic internationalization, technological innovation, demographic aging, and changing family structures in the postindustrial age increasingly foster suboptimal life chances for large parts of the population. In *Why We Need a New Welfare State*, we did not only take issue with the neoliberal axiom that generous welfare provision inevitably leads to a loss of economic efficiency. The book was equally critical about the staying power of male-breadwinner, pension-heavy, and insider-biased welfare provision in many European countries, arguing that it contributes to stagnant employment and long-term unemployment, in-work poverty, labor market exclusion, family instability, high dependency ratios, and below-replacement fertility rates. Our analysis underlined that central to the long-term financial sustainability of the welfare state is the number (*quantity*) and productivity (*quality*) of current and future employees and taxpayers. To the extent that welfare provision in a knowledge economy is geared toward maximizing employment, employability, and productivity, this sustains the so-called carrying capacity of the modern welfare state. The *work-family life course* is very much the "lynchpin" of the social investment policy paradigm. *Why We Need a New Welfare State* called for social investment policies geared toward improved resilience over the family life course, with special attention placed on avoiding career interruptions for women with small children and promoting dual-earner families, alongside gender-equal parental leave. Lengthier, more diverse, and volatile working lives harbor important implications for social policy. People are most vulnerable over critical transitions in the life course: (1) when they move from education into their first job; (2) when they aspire to have children; (3) when they—almost inevitably—experience spells of labor market inactivity; and, finally, (4) when they move to retirement. To the extent that policymakers are able to identify how economic well-being and social problems during such transitions in the life course impinge on individuals, preventive policies should be advanced to forestall cumulative social risk and poverty reproduction. The eradication of child poverty is the principal objective, alongside ensuring continuous female careers. The social investment approach hereby tilts the welfare balance from ex post compensation in times of economic or personal hardship to ex ante risk prevention through the following: early childhood education and care

(ECEC); education and training over the life course; (capacitating) active labor market policies (ALMP); work–life balance (WLB) policies, such as (paid) parental leave and flexible employment relations and work schedules; and lifelong learning (LLL).

By 2005, social democrats had been voted out of office in the larger member states of the EU, except in Britain. At this juncture, the Lisbon Agenda was criticized by a mid-term review for its lack of strategic focus and the multiplication of objectives and coordination processes; it was relaunched under the title *Working Together for Growth and Jobs* (European Commission, 2005). Social inclusion concerns and poverty reduction were not sidetracked per se in the new strategy, but they were subordinated to the reinforced priorities of growth and jobs. By the mid-2010s, more surprisingly the OECD changed orientation, away from the neoliberal retrenchment and deregulation that had characterized the *Jobs Strategy* publications of the 1990s to fully endorse the social investment priorities in studies such as *Starting Strong* (2006), *Babies and Bosses* (2007), *Growing Unequal* (2008), and *Doing Better for Families* (2011).

Academically, I felt the need to concentrate, empirically, on the extent to which EU member states had really jumped on the social investment bandwagon. By 2013, I was happy to concede that the glass was more half-full than half-empty in the monograph *Changing Welfare States*. The main takeaway from the book was that the evidence of social investment returns had become stronger in the decade leading up the global financial crisis. Competitive European welfare states, with levels of social spending hovering between 25 percent and 30 percent of gross domestic product (GDP), are best at achieving high employment, subdued poverty, and healthy public finances. This exposed the axiomatic disincentives associated with the neoliberal critique of the 1980s and 1990s as dangerous myths. At the macro-level, there were positive interaction effects between labor productivity and employment participation. The shift toward social investment, in terms of spending, proved to be unaffected by the redistributive strength of the welfare state, indicating that social investment services, childcare, and educational benefits may in effect smooth gaps in income distribution.

In 2012, I was approached by László Andor, commissionar for Employment, Social Affairs and Inclusion of the European Commission from 2010 to 2014, to join the Social Investment Expert Group for DG Employment and Social Affairs, together with Maurizio Ferrera, Bruno Palier, Frank Vandenbroucke, and others. I was able to supply evidence to the EU's most recent assertive embrace of social investment, the *Social Investment Package for Growth and Social Cohesion* in 2013. Next, DG Employment invited Brian Burgoon and myself to confront social investment returns with micro-level statistical testing (Hemerijck, Burgoon, Di Pietro, &

Simon, 2016). We were able to demonstrate how ALMP and ECEC, as exemplar social investments, positively relate to an individual's employment while mitigating household poverty, using individual-level data from Eurostat and EU-SILC.

When the ASIS report was published, Marianne Thyssen, a Belgian Christian democrat, had taken over from Andor as social affairs commissioner. She did not wholeheartedly embrace social investment, in part because she wished to dissociate herself from her social democratic predecessor. By 2015, many more countries had jumped on the social investment reform bandwagon in child care, active labor market policy, parental leave, dual-earner family services, and long-term care. In 2016, the Commission's social agenda again refocused on social investment, on the initiative of the cabinet of Commission President Juncker, with the Pillar of Social Rights. Allan Larsson, ex-commissionar of Social Affairs, a staunch defender of "social policy as productive factor," made sure that out of the twenty principles articulated in the 2017 Pillar of Social Rights, about a quarter were anchored on social investment. By 2019, the Employment and Social Developments in Europe Report of the Commission devoted a special feature to social investment policy progress in an empirically even-handed manner (European Commission, 2019).

Practical involvement in social investment agenda-setting across the EU taught me four lessons. First and foremost, responsible policymakers are aficionados of reform ideas and policy analysis. The emphasis on social investment started with the political imperative of Third Way leaders to explore an alternative policy theory to the one offered by OECD economists. They found cues in the writings of the late Tony Atkinson, Gøsta Esping-Andersen, Maurizio Ferrera, myself, and others. An additional advantage of our political contribution was that our comparative diagnoses and policy options were recognizant of the variegated social and institutional conditions across the EU, factors that are given little weight by economists. The linear studies of the OECD, ranking countries on numeric indicators from good to bad performers, as such, also lacked serious reflection on how different dimensions of reform success and failure come together institutionally. Also our multi-dimensional conception of welfare recalibration enabled us to engage with a normative agenda of policy improvement in terms of mitigating poverty and inequality through social investment welfare provision.

A second lesson is that the European Commission, especially DG Employment, should be given credit as a central "ideas broker" in the saga, courageously raising the stakes for social investment at a time when the available evidence was not as strong as it is today. Ever since 1997, the Commission has helped to anchor the social investment edifice, from the stepping stones in the Lisbon Agenda of 2000 to a full-fledged welfare paradigm with the

publication of the Social Investment Package in 2013, whose recommendations were codified into the 2017 Pillar of Social Rights.

On a less sanguine note, a third lesson is that Eurozone members in dire
fiscal straits since the Great Recession continue to be perversely obliged to
cut active labor market policies, vocational training, and family and childcare
services. From a social investment perspective, we know this critically erodes
job opportunities for men, women, and youth, resulting in higher levels of
child poverty and declining levels of fertility, hence undermining the carrying
capacity of the welfare state to shoulder the future aging burden.

Academically, fourth and finally, at least for myself, intellectual engagement with policymakers has had a lasting effect on strategies and methods
of knowledge production, with a strong appreciation for latent possibilities
in diverse policy environments, to be exploited by reformers, despite equally
relevant institutional constraints.

4. STILL A EUROPEAN TOUCH?

Evidently, there is a European touch to comparative welfare state research!
Perhaps, its spirit has been best captured by Albert O. Hirschman—a transatlantic intellectual par excellence—when he urged comparative political economy researchers in the early 1980s to bring to the fore "a little more reverence
for life, a little less straight-jacketing of the future, and a little more allowance
for the unexpected" (Hirschman, 1981, p. 85). There is a price tag, however,
attached to the open institutionalist research agenda, and that is the lack of
"hard core" theory and methods, which are a strength in the more realist
American institutionalist tradition. In their review on welfare state research
in Europe for the 2016 *Oxford Handbook of Historical Institutionalism*, Julia
Lynch and Martin Rhodes underscore the importance of a coherent research
program to demarcate political institutionalism from other kinds of research
on the welfare state. Rhodes and Lynch, respectively co-convener and fellow
of the EUI European Forum on Recasting the Welfare State, curiously fail
to cite Maurizio Ferrera's work on Southern Europe and his 2005 landmark
study on two-level EU social policy change. Also, there is no mention of the
seminal 2000 Scharpf/Schmidt volume, to which Rhodes himself contributed.
In their defense, it can be argued that Ferrera's *The Boundaries of Welfare*
and the Scharpf/Schmidt volume *Work and Welfare in the Open Economy*
both lack a well-defined theoretical "hard core" with a distinct methodology
which Lynch and Rhodes hold as definitive for an effective research program.
But should the strengths of theory and methodology not ultimately be judged
by empirical validation? What Ferrera, Scharpf, and Schmidt brought to the
table was that the "new politics" of "frozen" welfare states, when taken too

far, offer little empirical purchase on the complex processes of profound post-formative welfare state change across Europe since the 1990s.

Social reform is difficult, but it happens. In the new millennium, the academic focus in European comparative welfare state research has shifted assertively from change-resistant welfare states to probe a more open insti-tutionalist explanation of how welfare states in effect do change over time and in what direction, against the background of progressive EU economic integration. We obviously live in a world of path-contingent solutions, but institutional density does not preclude transformative welfare change.

In recent years, somewhat paradoxically, I have come to concede that perhaps a fundamental reason why social investment reform took off so swiftly in Austria, Germany, and the Netherlands, countries with strong male-breadwinner policy legacies, does lie in the political predicament that welfare retrenchment is difficult in countries where compensatory precom-mitments, especially in the area of pensions, are vast. When benefit retrench-ment is difficult, it is my contention, in tune with Heclo and in contrast to Pierson, that fiscally responsible governments are inadvertently forced to explore new reform alternatives in a policy-learning fashion. To the extent that social investment reforms raise employment participation and labor productivity, and, by implication, do not reign in standing commitments per se, they position the carrying capacity of expensive yet popular welfare states on a more sustainable fiscal footing. It could thus be argued that high-spending Continental welfare states entertain a "productive constraint" that institutionally privileges upward social investment recalibration, precisely because intrusive retrenchment reform is politically impeded by comprehen-sive benefit commitments. Later, as social investment policy profiles become institutionalized, they in create their own clienteles, which in turn drive up quality standards in capacitating social services, as was the case with social insurance provision in the postwar decades. As such, social investment reca-libration may place manageable demands on political leadership to build coalitions on a platform of what Giuliano Bonoli aptly coins "affordable credit-claiming" (2013).

In the final analysis, coming back to the academic study of comparative welfare state politics, I see a cloud on the horizon. Over the past decade, both the institutional factor and the diachronic (inter-)temporal character of comparative welfare state research have lost intellectual allure in the face of a strong comeback of political behavioralism both in Europe and the United States. Scholars advocating an "electoral turn" have shifted atten-tion to bottom-up electoral behavior and partisanship mobilization, steeped in public opinion survey research (and experiments) on welfare- and work-related issues, to the input side of the political process (Beramendi et al., 2015). There is a distinct departure from the core institutional insight that "policy shapes social politics," as scholars under the umbrella of the "electoral turn" assume parties to respond in a synchronic short-term fashion, congruent to electoral preferences, harking back to the pre-institutional presumption that "politics creates policy." An illuminating example of the electoral turn is found in the commanding book *Democracy and Prosperity: Reinventing Capitalism through a Turbulent Century*, by Torben Iversen and David Soskice (2019), erstwhile core Varieties and Capitalism scholars. However much I share their understanding of capitalism and democracy in symbiotic terms, I take issue with anchoring the stability of this symbiosis straightforwardly in middle-class electorates. Following Iversen and Soskice, there is no longer a need to seriously study the administrative capabilities of the modern state, curiously at a time when about 40 percent of GDP is channeled through the public purse. They simply infer that "those with high education and income may simply understand the constraints on government better than others" by citing as an obvious example "the need for countercyclical fiscal policies" (p. 25). The fresh experience of the Eurozone crisis, however, suggests a different, more institutional, explanation. With Mario Draghi at the helm of the independent ECB, an institutional actor par excellence, the euro was saved through heterodox negative interest rates and large-scale sovereign debt purchases, which effectively brought the Eurozone unemployment spike to a halt. A more malignant institutional predicament remains. The need for a euro-area fiscal capacity of adequate size and design to further stabilize the monetary union continues to fall on deaf ears in Germany, Finland, and the Netherlands. Draghi's vow to do "whatever it takes" surely raised the appreciation for countercyclical ideas, but I doubt whether middle-class electorates across Europe understand EMU monetary and EU fiscal policy in times of lowflation and negative interest rates.

On social investment, Garritzmann et al. (2018) have likewise ventured into "electoral turn" opinion research whereby citizens are being asked whether they would support social investment reform if it meant pension retrenchment. While the overall macro evidence suggests that pensions are more sustainable in social investment welfare states, such a survey question inescapably creates a "false necessities" in survey results. In an age of negative interest rates, there is not even a time inconsistency between social investment and pension spending. Although I support the electoral turn in political science in our times of intensified electoral volatility, I remain skeptical of its reductionism in explaining policy reform in troubled times. To the extent that policies are important levers and signifiers of change, shying away from policy substance and institutional characteristics, impoverishes our understanding of the dynamics of welfare reform that have intensified since the Great Recession.

These recent developments compel me, after the late Hirschman, to incessantly, bring forth the consequential importance of the "unexpected" in welfare state futures, in line with an open institutionalist research agenda. My quest remains to explain institutional variation of the "middle range" across different levels of governance, with consequential outcomes in terms of macroeconomic performance and their micro-level distributive correlates. Welfare reform needs to be studied over lengthy chains of causation, in a path-contingent possibilist—not predetermined—fashion.

NOTE

1. Besides the editors, I would especially like to thank Brigid Laffan for her trenchant comment to streamline and focus the argument and Maurizio Ferrera for pointing out the roots of open institutionalism to Max Weber and Stein Rokkan.

REFERENCES

Beckfield, J. (2019). *Unequal Europe. Regional integration and the rise of European inequality.* Oxford: Oxford University Press.

Beramend, P., Häusermann, S., Kitschelt, H., & Kriesi, H. (2015). *The politics of advanced capitalism.* Cambridge: Cambridge University Press.

Bonoli, G. (2012). Blame avoidance and credit claiming revisited. In G. Bonoli & D. Natali (Eds.), *The politics of the new welfare state* (pp. 94–110). Oxford: Oxford University Press.

Clasen, J. (2005). *Reforming European welfare states: Germany and the United Kingdom compared.* Oxford: Oxford University Press.

Clasen, J., & Clegg, D. (Eds.). (2011). *Regulating the risk of unemployment. National adaptations to post-industrial labour markets in Europe.* Oxford: Oxford University Press.

Esping-Andersen, G. (1990). *The three worlds of welfare capitalism.* Cambridge: Polity Press.

Esping-Andersen, G., Gallie, D., Hemerijck, A., & Myles, J. (Eds.). (2002). *Why we need a new welfare state.* Oxford: Oxford University Press.

European Commission. (2005). *Working together for growth and jobs.* Brussels: European Commission.

European Commission. (2013). *Social investment package for growth and social cohesion.* Brussels: European Commission.

European Commission. (2017). *European pillar of social rights.* Brussels: European Commission.

European Commission. (2019). *Employment and social development in Europe. Sustainable growth for all. Choices for the future of social Europe.* Brussels: European Commission.

European Council. (2000). *Presidency conclusions Lisbon European Council*. 23–24 March. SN 100/00. Council of the European Union.

Evans, P. B., Rueschemeyer, D., & Skocpol, T. (Eds.). (1985). *Bringing the state back in*. Cambridge: Cambridge University Press.

Ferrera, M. (2005). *The boundaries of welfare: European integration and the new spatial politics of social protection*. Oxford: Oxford University Press.

Ferrera, M. (2019). Objectivity, political order, and responsibility in Max Weber's thought. *Critical Review* (I), 1–19.

Ferrera, M., & Hemerijck, A. (2003). Recalibrating European welfare regimes. In J. Zeitlin & D. Trubeck (Eds.), *Governing work and welfare in a new economy: European and American experiments* (pp. 88–128). Oxford: Oxford University Press.

Ferrera, M., Hemerijck, A., & Rhodes, M. (2000). *The future of social Europe: Recasting work and welfare in the new economy*. Report prepared for the Portuguese Presidency of the EU. Oeiras: Celta Editora.

Flora, P., & Heidenheimer, A. J. (Eds.). (1981). *The development of welfare states in Europe and America*. New Brunswick, NJ: Transaction Books.

Garritzmann, J. L., Busemeyer, M. R., & Neimanns, E. (2018). Public demand for social investment: New supporting coalitions for welfare state reform in Western Europe? *Journal of European Public Policy, 25*(6), 844–61.

Giddens, A. (1998). *The third way: The renewal of social democracy*. Cambridge: Polity.

Goldthorpe, J. H. (Ed.). (1985). *Order and conflict in contemporary capitalism*. London: Oxford University Press.

Hall, P., & Soskice, D. (2001). *Varieties of capitalism: The institutional foundation of comparative advantage*. Oxford: Oxford University Press.

Häusermann, S. (2010). *The politics of welfare state reform in continental Europe: Modernization in hard times*. Cambridge: Cambridge University Press.

Heclo, H. (1974). *Modern social politics in Britain and Sweden*. New Haven: Yale University Press.

Hemerijck, A. (1997). *Social policy as a productive factor*. The Hague: Ministry of Social Affairs and Employment; Brussels: European Commission.

Hemerijck, A. (2013). *Changing welfare states*. Oxford: Oxford University Press.

Hemerijck, A., & Schludi, M. (2000). Sequences of policy failures and effective policy responses. In F. W. Scharpf & V. A. Schmidt (Eds.), *Welfare and work in the open economy, I. From vulnerability to competitiveness* (pp. 125–28). Oxford: Oxford University Press.

Hemerijck, A., Burgoon, B., Di Pietro, A., & Simon, V. (2016). *Assessing Social Investment Synergies (ASIS)*. Report written for the European Commission —DG-EMPL.

Hirschman, A. O. (Ed.). (1981). *Essays in trespassing: Economics to politics and beyond*. Cambridge: Cambridge University Press.

Iversen, T., & Soskice, D. (2019). *Democracy and prosperity: Reinventing capitalism through a turbulent century*. Princeton: Princeton University Press.

Katzenstein, P. J. (1985). *Small states in world markets: Industrial policy in Europe*. Ithaca, NY: Cornell University Press.

Kersbergen, K. Van. (1995). *Social capitalism: A study of Christian democracy and the welfare state*. London: Routledge.

Korpi, W. (1983). *The democratic class struggle*. London: Routledge.

Lynch, J., & Rhodes, M. (2016). Historical institutionalism and the welfare state. In O. Fioretos, T. G. Falleti, & A. Sheingate (Eds.), *The Oxford handbook of historical institutionalism*. Oxford: Oxford Univerisity Press.

Mayntz, R., & Scharpf, F. W. (1995). Der ansatz des akteurzentrierten institutionalismus. In R. Mayntz & F. W. Scharpf (Eds.), *Steuerung und selbstorganisation in staatsnahen sektoren* (pp. 39–72). Frankfurt am Main: Campus.

OECD. (1994). *The OECD jobs study: Facts, analysis, strategies*. Paris: OECD Publishing.

OECD. (2006). *Starting strong: Early childhood education and care*. Paris: OECD.

OECD. (2007). *Babies and bosses: Reconciling work and family life*. Paris: OECD.

OECD. (2008). *Growing unequal*. Paris: OECD.

OECD. (2011). *Doing better for families*. Paris: OECD.

Palier, P. (Ed.). (2010). *A long goodbye to Bismarck?* Amsterdam: Amsterdam University Press.

Palme, J., Bergmark, A., Bäckman, O., Estrada, F., Fritzell, J., Lundberg, O., Sjöberg, O., Sommestad, L., & Szebehely, M. (2003). A welfare balance sheet for the 1990s. *Scandinavian Journal of Public Health, 60*, 7–143.

Pierson, P. (1994). *Dismantling the welfare state? Reagan, Thatcher, and the politics of retrenchment*. Cambridge: Cambridge University Press.

Pierson, P. (2001). *The new politics of the welfare state*. Oxford: Oxford University Press.

Rokkan, S. (1975). Entries, voices, exits: Towards a possible generalization of the Hirschman model. *Social Sciences Information, 13*(1), 39–53.

Scharpf, F. W. (1997). *Games real actors play: Actor-centered institutionalism in policy research*. Oxford: Westview.

Scharpf, F. W., & Schmidt, V. A. (Eds.). (2000). *Welfare and work in the open economy* (Two volumes). Oxford: Oxford University Press.

Simon, H. (1985). Human nature in politics: The dialogue of psychology with political science. *American Political Science Review, 79*, 293–304.

Steinmo, S., Thelen, K., & Longstreth, F. (Eds.). (1992). *The new institutionalism: State, society and economy*. Cambridge: Cambridge University Press.

Streeck, W., & Thelen, K. (2005). *Beyond continuity: Institutional change in advanced political economies*. Oxford: Oxford University Press.

Vandenbroucke, F. (1999). *The active welfare state: A European ambition*. Den Uyl lecture, Amsterdam.

Visser, J., & Hemerijck, A. (1997). *A Dutch miracle: Job growth, welfare reform and corporatism in the Netherlands*. Amsterdam: Amsterdam University Press.

Wilensky, H. L. (1975). *The welfare state and equality: Structural and ideological roots of public expenditures*. Berkeley, CA: University of California Press.

Wilensky, H. L. (2002). *Rich democracies: Political economy, public policy and performance*. Berkeley, CA: University of California.

Chapter 14

Political Science at Risk in Europe

Frailness and the Study of Power

David Paternotte and Mieke Verloo

During the summer of 2018, Victor Orban's government announced its intention to revoke the accreditation of gender studies programs, unjustly claiming gender studies to be "ideological" and graduates "not to be able to find jobs." This decision, imposed upon Hungarian academic authorities (including Central European University (CEU)), sparked massive international outcry but was finally adopted in October 2018, forcing both the CEU and Eötvös Loránd University to stop enrolling students for the next academic year.[1] This was not the first attack on academic freedom in the country (Helms & Kriszan, 2017; Pető, 2018). In recent years, CEU has been under assault regularly, a process that culminated with the adoption of the "Lex CEU" in 2017 (Trencsényi et al., 2017) and the forced relocation of CEU's teaching activities to Vienna in 2019. This institution was also forced to close down programs for registered refugees and asylum seekers and to stop research projects related to migration. Finally, Hungarian scholars have been regularly exposed in public debates, with lists of names published in media close to the government. It would be a mistake to attribute these attacks to the specificities of the institution under attack and to the kind of knowledge under scrutiny. Time has shown that these attacks were not restricted to CEU or to minority studies but belonged to wider efforts to increase centralization and state power in higher education (Craciun & Mihut, 2017; Enyedi, 2018). The attacks on CEU were rapidly followed by an assault on the institutional and financial autonomy of the Hungarian Academy of Sciences, the country's main research institution, and applied this time to all fields of study including STEM and economics.[2] Important academic institutions like the post-1945 collections of the National Archives and the National Library were also forced to leave their premises without a clear relocation.

Hungary undoubtedly provides some of the most spectacular examples of recent attacks on academic freedom in Europe today. Yet, such assaults do not happen only in the so-called "illiberal" regimes but are part of a wider phenomenon of democratic backsliding (Cole, 2017; Pető, 2019; Stockemer & Kim, 2018). We contend that such attacks do not merely target political science, but social sciences and humanities as a wider field of knowledge and universities as specific social institutions. Ongoing political, social, and economic changes are closely intertwined with changes in the politics of knowledge. Researchers' freedoms of inquiry and expression are increasingly contested and power rulers show a growing interest in controlling research processes and outputs. Hostile public debates undermine the legitimacy of several fields of research and institutional autonomy is under threat in different parts of Europe. These transformations are further helped by structural—especially neoliberal—reforms of academia. Because of its object, political science appears as particularly frail when opposing power, and these changes are threatening its quality and future existence in Europe. It is therefore urgent for political science as a discipline to develop a strategic response to these challenges.

To apprehend the risks for political science in the current political landscape, we rely on the notion of academic freedom, defined by UNESCO as "the right, without constriction by prescribed doctrine, to freedom of teaching and discussion, freedom in carrying out research and dissemination and publishing the results thereof, freedom to express freely opinions about the academic institution or system in which one works, freedom from institutional censorship and freedom to participate in professional or representative academic bodies."[3] Academic freedom depends on the observance of a set of rules in the process of knowledge production and on the relation between a scholar and a community of peers, which assesses collectively the validity of the knowledge produced in the field. This form of disciplinary validation avoids being controlled by an external institution such as the market or the state (Calhoun, 2009; Ménand, 1996; Scott, 2019). Academic freedom is strengthened by the upholding of institutional autonomy, that is the capacity of an academic institution to decide on its modes of organization and its priorities independently from the market or the state. Institutional autonomy can be either substantive (about the goals of an institution and the content of its programs) or procedural (about the process of decision-making over the goals and programs) (Aberbach & Christensen, 2017; Berdahl, 1990). Therefore, attacks on institutional autonomy as those on CEU and the Hungarian Academy of Sciences directly undermine the academic freedom of researchers active in both institutions. Academic freedom is also closely linked to the right to free expression for researchers (Calhoun, 2009). Indeed, if academic freedom and free speech imply different types of rights enjoyed by distinctive constituencies (academics in the first case, every citizen in the second one)

(Butler, 2018; Scott, 2019), researchers are expected to intervene in public debate more than average citizens because of their expertise (Göle, 2017).

In this chapter, we define political science as the study of power dynamics, both in the public sphere and more broadly. Politics can therefore not be examined without understanding the wider society in which they take place, and this chapter delves into the complex relationship between political science and its academic, political, and social context to highlight some of the risks that political sciences run into in these turbulent times. It also addresses the internal complexity of political science, which is made of numerous sub-disciplines, as power dynamics in current European societies affect political philosophy, international relations, gender and sexuality studies, minority studies or comparative politics differently. Finally, political science cannot be isolated from other social sciences, although these are not necessarily equally exposed to current political transformations. This piece offers a first exploration of the current situation in Europe, and tries to go beyond specific national case studies (Karran, 2010; Karran, Beiter, & Appiagyei-Atua, 2017). It relies on analyzing existing academic literature, the specialized press and reports by organizations such as Scholars at Risk and the European University Association, as well as informal exchanges with numerous colleagues across the continent. As will become clearer throughout this exploratory chapter, threats to political science in Europe cannot be dissociated from broader debates on academic freedom. In exploring the risks involved, the responses that can be detected, and those that we deem to be necessary for the future, we urge colleagues to become more and more visibly active in serious debates and actions in our profession.

This chapter starts with a reflection on political science as a discipline, and the implications of its oscillating relation to formal state power for its current and future quality. It then continues with exploring how political science is shaped by material resources and the relation of academia to the market and to market logics. The next section investigates the frames used to attack academic freedom, as well as the main tools and tactics used in this battle. After exposing how political science is at risk in Europe, we turn to actual and needed responses, before ending with a call for action resulting from our exploration and analysis.

1. THE PENDULUM OF POLITICAL SCIENCE: ACCOMMODATION AND RESISTANCE TO POWER

Science is shaped by power and politics, an observation which holds true for political science as well (Ravecca, 2019). Indeed, the relations between political science and political power have constantly oscillated between two poles with a differentiated impact on research access to politics and the political as well as on academic freedom. Like a pendulum, political science has swung between a pole aiming at knowledge production that supports existing power actors or institutions, and another pole aiming at providing a distanced critical analysis of the origins, dynamics, and impacts of existing power actors and institutions. While other disciplines such as law or economics have also been closely associated with the exercise of political power, political science appears as particularly exposed because of its unique ambition in dissecting and analyzing the actual workings of power.

Historically, drawing on the tradition of Machiavelli and Hobbes, the discipline has developed as a science of power and government, and it remains so in many contexts, as reminded by the numerous "schools of government" and the proximity to law in many countries. This feature makes political science attractive to the powerful who can regard it as a vehicle to consolidate power. Political science produces "political engineering" knowledge that can be used to justify and secure power. For example, Spanish political science significantly developed under Franco, with the key involvement of crucial figures of the regime (Jerez Mir, 2002). In this volume, Luciana Alexandra Ghica similarly reminds us the limits of scientific socialism in Central and Eastern Europe. If political science is very close to, intertwined with, or has not enough distance to political power, then constraints on academic freedom are likely to be expected. At the other end of the ideal-typical spectrum, political science has emancipated itself from the state. This emancipation has been encouraged by the production of more independent knowledge about political dynamics in academia, but also in social movements. From these movements came a strong impulse to expand the understanding of what constitute "politics" beyond the state and state-related actors. Socialist, feminist, and civil rights movements have broadened the study of politics to the politics in society at large, aiming at a critical reflection on the effects of formal and informal politics on society (such as the relation of politics to inequalities). This understanding of politics necessarily distances itself from actual political power, and when and where such a critical distance is not appreciated by actual political power, academic freedom may be at risk. Indeed, a more critical political science may appear as threatening to authoritarian powers and various attempts of *kulturkampf*, for it interrogates what is generally taken for granted in a society and unveils the actual working of power.

In Europe today, the study of formal politics remains dominant within the discipline, although political science research has for some time now reached out to the study of political dynamics outside formal political arenas such as parliaments, elections, governments, states, and supranational political institutions. At the same time, the discipline has clearly responded to the growing need to include the political dynamics of policymaking and policy implementation, and the political dynamics in other domains such as the economy and the private sphere. All this implies that in the practice of political science as a discipline, one can find examples with elements situated all over the range of the pendulum between the critique of political power and the engineering of political power. Scholars who are situated close to political power can expect to enjoy good access to political actors and processes, at least as long as they remain visibly useful and deliver well-trained candidates for political and administrative positions. For them, the degree of academic freedom they can expect depends on the openness and the democratic nature of political power. To function properly, they need to be able to make their analyses public, even when critical of existing power. This mostly happens in democratic systems, as they provide the freedom and the absence of strong repercussions necessary to make this work. Defending broader and more critical forms of analysis, colleagues located at the other end of the spectrum are even more in need of a free and open society to function properly. They need a regime that allows societal and political dynamics to be observed, measured, analyzed, reflected upon, assessed, and debated publicly without personal risks or dangers. Finally, in between both ends of the spectrum stand researchers who articulate new types of critique or critical analyses of social and political phenomena that are highly salient in formal politics or highly polarized across the political spectrum. Those are highly vulnerable to direct attacks from political actors, and strongly in need of an open and democratic space to function properly.

All in all, whatever the exact position in the course of the pendulum, under the current conditions of strong political and social polarization, the innovative power of the discipline and its capacity to deliver knowledge that is most relevant to political life is significantly at risk. Regardless of the focus on formal politics or politics in a broader understanding, all political science needs is a democratic setting to function properly. Indeed, all innovative and critical political science relies on free speech and academic freedom. Furthermore, as argued by many authors, academic freedom is best defended in a democratic polity (Cole, 2017; Pető, 2019; Stockemer & Kim, 2018). Therefore, democracy appears as a vital condition for political science and a crucial prerequisite for its ongoing capacity of renewal. In other terms, the current backsliding of democracy in Europe may threaten the future of political science.

2. ACADEMIC CAPITALISM AND
ACADEMIC FREEDOM

The future of political science is not only shaped by the kind of political regime, but also by economics and by the material resources available for research and teaching. The neoliberal turn and its impact on the emergence of academic capitalism have crucially transformed universities and altered the space in which academics pursue their work (Mirowski, 2011). As argued by Craig Calhoun (2009), the restructuration of universities has profoundly impacted the conditions of academic freedom in Western countries, through interventions in university autonomy that weakened the capacity of universities to guarantee and promote their members' academic freedom and freedom of speech.

In a piece on academic freedom and performance-based research funding, Butler and Mulgan (2013) argue that academic freedom rests on four broad paradigms of independence: economic, institutional, social, and professional. All four are to some extent impacted by economy-related factors. Economic independence is the degree to which universities can make decisions about their functioning without being restricted strongly by budgetary concerns. The idea is that research choices should not result from economic power, just as they should not result from political power. However, for decades, the economic autonomy of universities has been under threat by defunding and austerity, either motivated politically or based on market considerations. Professional independence is the degree to which academic professionals can base their research and teaching decisions on their expertise, and their motivation to drive the discipline forward. It has been negatively impacted by the introduction of new public management style of leadership in universities, that is, giving the top management control through elaborate instruments of numerical quality measurement, monitoring, and rewards. Social independence refers to the degree to which universities and academics can depart from social and political expectations about what they should teach or research. For instance, war research is often driven by state and military concerns.[4] Strong populist accusations against universities and academics can inspire fear or evasion from certain topics and more, adaptation to the new public management. Finally, institutional independence is the degree to which an academic institution can make fundamental decisions about research and teaching. Here, apart from direct political interference, academic freedom can be encroached upon by increase of conditional money for which universities have to compete among each other under market conditions.

All this highlights how the neoliberal politics of academia have decreased institutional autonomy directly and indirectly, making universities less independent from the market and the state. These transformations have impacted negatively the capacity of universities and academics working within them to decide autonomously about their goals, content of programs and modus operandi of teaching and research. While this applies to academia in general, political science is seriously affected by these processes, and neoliberal mechanisms of decreasing institutional autonomy and academic freedom are also some of the tools used by authoritarian governments to further restrict academic freedom.

The notion of academic capitalism (Slaughter & Leslie, 1997) insists on the ways public universities respond to neoliberal pressures rather than on what they end up as (that is neoliberal institutions). It highlights the shift toward managerial authority, accountability to economic productivity standards, quantitative performance auditing, and the instrumental use of research to serve national economic interests (Ferree & Zippel, 2015). In academia, such neoliberal changes have resulted in managerial governance, a stronger managerial class, commercialization of knowledge, and adapting corporate practices and ideologies to higher education (Deem, 2007; Tuchman, 2009). Academic capitalism has introduced norms and values that disrupt those of the classic liberal-humanistic university, including its elitist professorial authority relations, old boys' networks, and internalized disciplinary standards (Slaughter & Leslie, 1999). While the classic academic model was also flawed (for it was largely reflecting the interests of privileged populations), Ferree and Zippel (2015) rightly point out that neoliberalized academia has its own weaknesses and threats, and that it accepts and strengthens, rather than challenges, the bias toward economic and political elites that was present in the classic politics of knowledge.

Although academic capitalism has strong negative impacts, its effects are by no means homogeneous in Europe. Across countries, neoliberalism is a collection of nationally specific, importantly different projects with some common elements (Brenner, Beck, & Theodore, 2010). While problems result from a general underfunding of science in some countries, in others the main issue lies in the modes of allocation of resources. Another research project shows that there is both a general shift toward market models of governance and a differentiation across countries, and that the shift to a market model is more likely to lead to a loss of economic and professional autonomy (Dobbins & Knill, 2017).

Overall, the shift to market governance has had negative implications for academic freedom. The development of neoliberalism has led to an overall reduction of public funding for research and teaching, induced an increase of funding through projects, and made research and teaching more dependent on the market. This has reset criteria for quality and excellence through mimicking market competition dynamics in judging quality and excellence in research and teaching, at the expense of other criteria. The changing academic governance from relatively slower processes of internal co-optation, peer review, or academic democracy to fast-paced processes of new public management has further helped facilitate the exclusive use of economic productivity criteria in judging academic excellence and in promotion or granting possibilities. The new public management inspired procedures of hyper detailed monitoring have resulted in an academic panopticon, reducing the space for free thinking. These academic capitalism changes have also led to a very substantial decrease of job security in academia, leading to an increase in academic precariousness, which further harms academic freedom.

3. ACADEMIA IN CHANGING DEMOCRACIES

Many have noticed an increased polarization of social and political debates in Europe (Ignatieff, 2018, p. 5). Debates are often trapped into binary oppositions, political opponents are described as enemies, violence against politicians is rising (Krook, 2017), all of which diminishes the likelihood of democratic debate between citizens or politicians at the opposite ends of political positions. Public debate is moving away from the Enlightenment ideal of a rational and democratic conversation in which people listen to each other and try to justify their arguments in reason. Moreover, as shown by the development of fake news and the role of emotions in social media hypes, truth and accuracy are no longer necessary requirements for public debate. Even if scholars have also unveiled the problematic assumptions historically underpinning this ideal of public rationality, and highlighted the positionality and the location of any producer of knowledge, these new developments harm the potential of truth claims based on rational inquiry. If scientific debates have never been democratic, insofar as they were necessarily based on the recognition of disciplinary vertical authority (Scott, 2019), they were ruled by a similar understanding of reason, and scientists have often contributed to social and political discussions on the basis of their expertise. The current developments that are detrimental to public debate are also harmful for knowledge production through science.

The newly developing new debate culture is linked to current attacks on academic freedom, inasmuch as both contribute to delegitimize science as a highly valued source of knowledge and expertise and threaten both the autonomy of science and its role in public debate. Scientists are no longer seen as the owners and producers of a type of knowledge judged as particularly valuable because of its distinctive modes of production and collective validation. Opinion and scholarship are often equated in the name of free speech, leading to a "worrisome relativizing of scholarship as 'opinions' in society at large" (Bracke, 2018). This type of attacks does not only happen in increasingly authoritarian regimes, but also in consolidated democratic societies. They are perpetrated by a wide range of actors, including states, university administrations, political party followers, citizens' groups, or media outlets. In this section, we highlight some of the frames used to attack academic freedom, as well as the tools and tactics used in this battle.

3.1. Framing Attacks on Science

An analysis of attacks on science across Europe has allowed us to identify five major frames currently circulating in Europe: they serve as the discursive foundation of this offensive on academia, and more specifically on social sciences and humanities. They are not mutually exclusive and can be combined in various ways: the "academics as elite" frame, the "absence of free speech for the Right" frame, the "identity politics" frame, the "cultural Marxism" frame, and the "academics are lazy" frame. Most attempt to destroy the truth claim of science by framing science as ideological. They are generally voiced from outside of academia by public intellectuals, media pundits, and politicians. When they are raised by scientists, the latter often speak outside of their discipline or area of expertise, as exemplified by the examples of Alan Sokal and Jean Bricmont (1999) or by Canadian psychologist Jordan Peterson in recent years. These frames do not only come from religious or far-right circles as one could expect, but can be warped into or disguised as a defense of Enlightenment (and positivism) against the fantasies and the illusions of "postmodernism."

The first frame—*academics as elite*—articulates a criticism with roots in the current populist wave. It opposes academics to average citizens, and portrays them as another privileged group or as belonging to the elites. It reclaims common sense against what is portrayed as pseudoscientific imaginations and accuses scientists of wasting taxpayer's money. Promoting anti-intellectualism, it depicts academics as people who have lost connection with "normal citizens" and do not understand everyday concerns. In brief, as claimed by Recep Tayyip Erdogan in response to the Academics for Peace's petition, academics are not necessarily enlightened and do not always pursue the common good (Erdogan, 15 January 2016, quoted in Özkirimli, 2017, p. 851). Former Belgian secretary of state for Asylum and Migration Theo Francken (NV-A) similarly responded to a joint letter sent by all Belgian university chancellors and to an open letter signed by more than 1,000 Belgian scholars, both asking for clarity in the murder of an underage asylum seeker by the police, by threatening them and emphasizing the gap between academic elites and average citizens around issues of migration[5] (see table 14.1).

Table 14.1 Main Frames against Science

Academics as elite
Absence of free speech for the Right
Identity politics
Cultural Marxism
Academics are unproductive

A second frame—*absence of free speech for the Right*—invokes the concept of academic freedom to denounce how "political correctness" would impose restrictions on free speech in universities (for recent examples, see Bock-Côté, 2018; Griffiths, 2018; Legutko, 2016; Onfray, 2019). According to these critics, certain truths could no longer be said because they embarrass some groups with power, and universities are submitted to a new police of thought and language, a new kind of dictatorship. In the name of equality and nondiscrimination, it would actually lead to a normalization of knowledge and restrict the rights of certain groups, especially on the right. Often, critics denounce the imbalance between various types of discourse in academia and, by insisting on limitations to freedom of expression, they confuse academic freedom with free speech (Scott, 2017). Furthermore, they usually claim that "political correctness" is a U.S. import that threatens national culture and could dislocate the nation (Fassin, 2008). Often, academics are hence portrayed as "external agents, as enemies of the nation" (Göle, 2017, p. 876).

This frame is often combined with, and explained by, another one—the *identity politics* frame—that is, the claim that universities are confiscated by various sorts of minorities. Often used as a vague term coined to insist on the new political relevance of identities, "identity politics" serves here to target so-called minority studies, sometimes presented as "grievance studies."[6] According to detractors, these fields of research would endanger the universal and reuniting project of science the same way it undermines the unity of the people and the nation (Fukuyama, 2018; Lilla, 2017). They would also misuse the name of science to pursue political goals under cover, and are accused of promoting cultural relativism or political correctness and of misreading social complexity though binary—and hence ideological—frames such as of men/women, of blacks/whites, straight/gay, as well (paradoxically) as of those relying on postmodern foundations, which are often denigrated as "fake science" (Kuby, 2015; Ruse, 2017). As a result, universities would have become a dangerous space for white heterosexual men, who would be exposed to forms of discrimination.

Through a fourth frame—the *cultural Marxism* frame—several actors criticize the presumed intellectual power of the Left and its alleged domination over campuses. In this frame, since the cultural revolution of the 1960s, the Left would have massively invested academia, turning it into a hostile space for conservatives. This would have strengthened after the fall of the Berlin Wall, when former socialists understood that they need to fight in the field of ideas to conquer society. Again, knowledge is presented as a tool of power and this reading, which relies on a simplified version of Gramsci's theory of cultural hegemony, labels this strategy as "cultural Marxism." Recent debates in the Netherlands illustrate the relevance of such arguments. As argued by Verloo (2018), leading politicians of Thierry Baudet's Forum voor Democratie, but also from Wilders' party, have repeatedly declared that universities and academics have been taken over by a leftist cabal propagating "cultural Marxism" as the entry point for Islamization. A recent controversy in Dutch politics in 2017, with parliamentary inquiries on this supposedly Left dominance, even resulted in a policy brief to the Dutch government on "Freedom of Academic science in the Netherlands" by the Dutch Royal Academy (KNAW) that concludes that there is no indication of serious restrictions to academic freedom in the Netherlands.[7] Similar debates also reached the Flemish press.[8]

These four frames are often combined with a fifth one, which is much more diffuse: *"academics are unproductive."* In many places, academics are presented as idle, unproductive, and therefore an expensive and unnecessary luxury. This depiction fits well into the elitist picture of academics of the first frame, turning academics into people wasting taxpayers' money. Moreover, there would be no reason to protect them if they pursue ideological enterprises instead of further developing science, as entailed in several of the other frames. Crucially, this frame also fits very well with neoliberal forms of bureaucratic control and competition for funding, as well as the abolishment of permanent positions, that can then be portrayed as a response or cure.

3.2. Repertoire of Action: The Main Weapons against Academic Freedom

These five frames are supported and embodied in a series of tools and tactics that have been spreading across Europe. This repertoire of action can be divided into two categories. Attacks can take the appearance of "business as usual" and engage with science management and university administration. Alternatively, they can wage the fight from outside academia. The weapons described in this sections have been used against a wide range of targets, including mainstream political science topics such as Brexit, terrorism, Islam, far-right parties, Israel-Palestine relations, environmental politics, or social movements.

Internal weapons against academic freedom fall into five categories (see table 14.2). First, as shown by the Hungarian attack on gender studies, *accreditation politics* are crucial. They allow politicians to decide on what is taught and to obstruct the development of entire fields of studies. In 2018,

Table 14.2 Internal Weapons against Academic Freedom

Accreditation politics
Funding
(Self)censorship
Department/university closure
Alternative academic venues

Polish authorities also decided to erase ethnology and social anthropology as specific disciplines and to merge them into a new field called "the study of culture and religion."[9]

Funding is a second decisive means, with impact on both teaching and research. Recent examples show the various forms this weapon may adopt. Whole areas of research may be defunded, as happened to gender studies after Valérie Pécresse (LR)'s election as the president of the region Ile-de-France in 2015. Projects may also be rejected on political grounds, despite positive reviews or even after they had passed all the steps of the review process, as happened recently in Bulgaria (Darakchi, 2018).

Third, cases of *censorship and self-censorship* have been reported in many places. They can take the form of direct political interventions in the research process. For instance, in Italy, in December 2018, the Italian education minister blocked a research of the Università di Perugia on homophobic and racist school bullying funded by the Region of Umbria, because of disagreements with the questionnaire.[10] In April 2019, representatives of Lega Nord contacted the Università di Bologna because of a political science course using a book in which their party was labeled as far right and required the application of antidiscrimination regulations for right-wing students who could feel offended by such a reading.[11] In Poland, the government has—unsuccessfully—required university authorities to establish lists of scholars working in gender studies and, in 2017 in Britain, a Tory MP famously asked several British universities to provide lists of scholars teaching European affairs, particularly in relation to Brexit.[12]

In many cases, however, scholars or institutions themselves prefer not to engage in controversial research or teaching initiatives out of a fear for potential attacks (Aktas, Nilsson, & Borell, 2018; Kondakov, 2016). For this reason, scholars may revise the content of a program, a course, a syllabus, a seminar series, or a publication to make sure they do not contain anything that could be labeled as "problematic." This happened recently at the University of Zagreb with courses around gender and sexuality in human rights and in sociology, which were removed from the programs under the false argument of a lack of students. Similarly, in Britain, the content of some courses and the list of guest speakers have been amended to comply with the 2015 Counter Terrorism and Security Act,[13] at the same requirements for ethical clearances were increased (Spiller, Awan, & Whiting, 2019).[14] Finally, various observers, from both left and right, have started to worry about the threats on academic freedom in result of the debates on safe spaces, trigger warnings, and micro aggressions, which are currently traveling from the United States and Australia to Europe.[15] By asking universities to protect students from the knowledge that could hurt them, these developments would infantilize students and obstruct critical thinking because of paternalism. Symptomatic of the neoliberal university, these debates would imply the individualization of critical thinking on collective processes of oppression and pay too much attention to psychological harm and injury, diverting students from politics in favor of personal comfort (Scott, 2019; for a conservative critique, Furedi, 2017).

Fourth, *closing a department or an institution or threatening to do so*—by suspending or revoking its license—appears as a more extreme means to achieve similar objectives. CEU is not the only institution threatened with close down: the European University at Saint-Petersburg was temporarily closed down in 2008[16] and had no license for a bit more than a year between 2017 and 2018[17] (Dubrovskiy, 2017). Several departments have also been threatened or even been shut down under suspicions of political and ideological reasons, including some in Russia (Butterfield & Levintova, 2011) and Israel.[18] Institutions are not the only victims and, as shown by the dramatic example of Turkey, where at least 8,535 university staff members lost their job (SAR, 2018), critical colleagues may also be disciplined or even dismissed by higher education authorities, especially when they are not tenured. Not promoting them is another strategy, as recently reported in the Czech Republic.[19]

Finally, *creating alternative academic venues* is another strategy to engage in the production of academic knowledge. These include the creation of new departments or institutions, such as Marion Maréchal-Le Pen's "Institut des sciences sociales, économiques et politiques de Lyon," publishing houses and even journals such as *The Natural Family: An International Journal of Research and Policy*, which is run by the anti-choice World Congress of Families and has recently published a speech by Victor Orban, and research results by controversial U.S. sociologist Mark Regnerus.

Six external means of action, as they take place mostly outside of academic and administrative circuits, must be discussed (see table 14.3). First, *"public online target harassment"* (Ferber, 2018), *stalking, ad hominem attacks, and physical and death threats* have become a common experience for many colleagues, especially on Twitter and other social media. A bomb alert against the Swedish Secretariat for Gender Research was even reported in Gothenburg in 2018.[20] Such threats happen in many countries (Belgium, Britain, Bulgaria, Finland, France, Germany, Greece, Hungary, the Netherlands,

Table 14.3 External Weapons against Academic Freedom

Harassment, stalking, personal threats, and attacks
Naming, blaming, blacklisting scholars/disciplines
Protest
Recording
Constraints on freedom of circulation
Policing and prosecution

Turkey, etc.) and colleagues working on the far right, Islam, or migration are particularly at risk, along with women and minorities (Savigny, 2019).

Second, *naming, blaming, and blacklisting* scholars and disciplines, online or in the press, have become common practices in Europe. If Hungarian or Turkish lists have been widely publicized, France has experienced a similar phenomenon in relation to the (timid) development of post- and decolonial studies. Leading public intellectuals (including Elisabeth Badinter, Alain Finkielkraut, and Pierre Nora) have publicly warned against the alleged dangers of this field of study,[21] and major media outlets like *Le Point*, *Le Nouvel Observateur* or *Le Figaro* have published detailed accounts of the activities of these supposedly dangerous colleagues.[22] Specific websites, sometimes run by (former) scholars, watch research activities, like the German website Sciencefiles. In Britain and the Netherlands, critical academics have been regularly exposed in the press (Miller, Mills & Harkins, 2011; Moors, 2018).

This trend may be accompanied by the delegitimizing of entire fields of study. For instance, in 2015 and 2016, former French prime minister Manuel Valls has—along with other French public figures—repeatedly accused sociology of promoting a "culture de l'excuse," that is, of justifying mischief (including terrorism) and exonerating perpetrators of part of their responsibility through attempts of understanding their motivations and the context in which these acts are perpetrated (Bronner & Géhin, 2017; Lahire, 2016). Similarly, in many countries, researchers on Islam, who are often denigrated though the use of the derogatory term "islamo-leftists," are accused of being too benevolent toward their object of study and the alleged radicalization of part of the Muslim community.[23]

Third, *protest* against academic events or specific courses[24] has increased. In February 2019, Polish nationalists severely disturbed a conference on the Shoah organized at the Ecole des hautes études en sciences sociales in Paris, forcing the president of the school to write an open letter to the Polish ambassador and to contact judicial authorities and the French government to contact its Polish counterpart.[25] Although this incident was particularly dramatic, it is not the first-time activists try to disturb an academic event. In October 2017, the authorities of the University Lyon 2 canceled a conference on islamophobia under pressures from both far-right and secularist groups.[26] Similar forms of protest led the head of the University of Verona to cancel a conference on LGBT asylum seekers in May 2018.[27] States may sometimes pressure the organizers of academic events, as happened in July 2018 at the Jewish Museum of Berlin with the cancellation of a lecture about being Queer and Palestinian in East-Jerusalem because of support to Boycott, Divestment and Sanctions (BDS).[28] Finally, such attacks are not exclusively fomented by right-wing groups, as happened with several academic events on surrogacy or sex work in Spain in 2019 or on trans rights in the United Kingdom since 2018.[29]

Fourth, various groups encourage students to *record* controversial lecturers[30] and to *report* their ideas and activities, for instance, to specific websites or hotlines. Dutch politician Thierry Baudet offered one of the most recent examples of this strategy. Following the statement made in the speech following his electoral victory in the 2019 provincial elections that universities are one of the forces undermining the Netherlands,[31] the Forum voor Democratie announced the establishment of a hotline against indoctrination where pupils and students can denounce their teachers before freezing the initiative for concerns related to breach of privacy.[32]

Fifth, constraints on the *freedom of circulation* for researchers exist in different countries, preventing them from leaving the country, even to attend conferences. This strategy is common in Turkey against academics who signed the Academics for Peace petition. Israel has also restricted access to visiting scholars supporting BDS. The reverse strategy, forcing academics to leave their country to pursue their activities, has also been reported in Turkey, in Russia, and increasingly in Hungary. In some countries like Russia or Hungary, state officials also claim to combat the influence of foreign education in higher education (Dubrovskiy, 2017).

Finally, *legal and police means*, including blackmail, surveillance, prosecution, and incarceration, have been used against scholars, Turkey being the most dramatic example, with several hundreds of university employees and students arrested since January, and thousands of staff members dismissed, leading to cases of "civil deaths" (Aktas, Nilsson, & Borell, 2018; see also Baser, Akgönül, & Öztürk, 2017).[33] It takes less spectacular forms in most European countries. Several researchers have been attacked and sometimes prosecuted for the use of private data acquired without the consent of its owner, threatened with legal action for defamation because they had raised concerns of plagiarism or suggested a line of analysis which was not shared by the interviewees or because they have used their knowledge to support a cause they believe in, as happened with several law and political science professors advising the Catalan government on the 2017 independence referendum.[34]

4. HOW TO RESPOND?

European political scientists deserve better responses, in terms of both prevention and protection. It is urgent to prevent that more colleagues become "scholars at risk," and there is a need for protection at institutional, collective, and individual levels. As recent events have shown in different parts of the region, it is a serious mistake to treat statements of intention about the politics of knowledge, academia, research, and teaching, social sciences and humanities by politicians and other powerful actors as "just talk." Moreover, against the belief that academic institutions are strong and resilient, recent events have exposed their fragility and the speed with which they can be attacked and dismantled. It is of the highest urgency to study the actors and dynamics behind the attacks, and to revise our assumptions about the state of academic freedom in Europe (Gessen, 2017).[35]

On the one hand, this requires better knowledge. Instead of assuming that we know already what is happening, we need to collect more empirics, to adjust and to refine our theories, and to confront more systematically our analytical frames to new political and social developments. We need knowledge on oppositional frames, tactics and tools, and the way they travel across borders, for the case of Hungary indicates, for instance, a diffusion of bad practices from Israel, Poland, and Russia. We should also trace more carefully how neoliberal reforms have provided a fertile ground for recent attacks. Finally, we need to articulate research on academic freedom to the flourishing literature on the growth of populism, nationalism, and the far right in Europe, as well as study more thoroughly the interactions between de-democratization or democratic backsliding and attacks or restrictions to academic freedom to detect possible feedback loops (Verloo, 2018).

Better knowledge also implies a better understanding of the articulation between academic freedom and freedom of speech: for instance, academic freedom and rights of political expression converge when academics who speak "extramurally" suffer retaliation or punishment within the university or are threatened with the loss of their positions (Butler, 2017). Finally, we have to produce more knowledge on effective political pressure (lobbying, networking, interventions in public debates) to keep the space for academic reflection on political turbulence open.

On the other hand, it is crucial to improve the protection of political scientists against such attacks, not only when these happen but also preemptively. Such protection requires the intervention of various types of actors, improved interactions between political, institutional, and professional levels, and coalitions across countries and disciplines to break the isolation of some scholars and to overcome national logics (Bouvart, De Proost, & Norocel, 2018).

At political level, European states and supranational institutions must play a more proactive role, both within Europe and beyond. Building on the work of UNESCO mentioned earlier, we need stronger international standards for academic freedom, and indicators, milestones, and monitoring systems to follow closely what is happening in Europe. These institutions also need to ensure political scientists can still work in increasing authoritarian or illiberal contexts such as Hungary or Turkey, which implies the development of measures to be deployed to enforce these standards and sanctions for those who infringe them.

Given its competences and legacy in research policy, the European Union (EU) should play a leading role. However, this has not been the case until now. The strong dependence on high competition for the allocation of its research money has strengthened neoliberal understandings of individual excellence instead of solidarity. Moreover, while the Parliament has repeatedly raised the issue, the European Commission has been particularly mild when condemning attacks on academic freedom in Hungary. Among what could be done, we would like to emphasize three ideas that would fit well within the EU's research policy. First, calls for applications could include requirements on academic freedom and institutional autonomy, echoing what has been done with gender equality. Second, direct funding could be devoted to research on understanding breaches of academic freedom in Europe. Third, the European Research Area must be consolidated across the East-West and North-South divide. Indeed, European states have a large responsibility to enforce broader conditions for academic freedom and institutional autonomy, but their track record so far is weak, and some states are among the biggest offenders. Therefore, more equality across European states is needed to avoid having (social) science deserts.

At the academic level, universities and group of universities, such as the newly created "European universities" and leagues and organizations as different as the European University Association (EUA), the Russell Group, or the Network of Universities from the Capitals of Europe (UNICA), must ensure their employees are adequately protected against potential attacks and provide them with adequate institutional responses whenever it is the case. This implies the development of protocols and worst-case scenarios, as well as sufficient provisions of financial, legal, security, psychological, and social support. A thorough reflection on how to decrease risks is also urgent (for instance, when scholars are urged by their institution to become active on platforms such as Twitter without proper training about the dangers it entails).

Academic institutions can also be instrumental in building concrete forms of solidarities with colleagues in more hostile contexts, for instance by issuing clear statements condemning attacks on academic freedom. Statements can also be part of lobbying strategies, both to increase pressure on problematic governments or institutions and to ask political institutions to intervene. For instance, in addition to statements on individual worrying cases like Hungary, All European Academies (ALLEA), the European University Association (EUA) and Science Europe issued a joint statement on 10 April 2019 on the urgent need to back commitments to academic freedom and university autonomy with solid actions,[36] and also support together the need for "stronger human and societal approaches across the new Horizon Europe program."[37] Statements are also regularly made by single institutions, and some have even developed policies to ensure a representation at trials against scholars in countries such as Turkey.

Fellowship programs for scholars at risk offer another way of achieving concrete solidarity.[38] These may be restricted to scholars from specific countries or disciplines or be open more broadly and are offered by various institutions in Europe today, such as the Réseau français des instituts d'études avancées (RFEIA, French network of Institutes for Advanced Studies) and the Université libre de Bruxelles. These grants are however often of limited duration and remain scarce in Europe, raising concerns about the future of scholars at risk once they terminate their fellowship. Broader and more ambitious international solidarity schemes are needed, be it as grants or in other forms, and several initiatives must be mentioned. In France, the Pause Program (Programme national d'aide à l'accueil en urgence des scientifiques en exil) was created in 2017 to welcome scholars at risk in French academic institutions.[39] Hosted at the Collège de France and supported by the French State, it aims at welcoming 100 scholars at risk per year. Under a different model, the Philipp Schwartz Program at Humboldt Foundation pursue a similar goal in Germany with the support of Federal authorities and various foundations.[40] The NGO Council for At-Risk Academics (CARA) gathers a network of 119 U.K. universities to protect academic freedom and welcome scholars at risk in Britain. It is helped by numerous foundations and social actors.[41]

At professional level, national, European, and international scientific organizations such as the ECPR have a tremendous responsibility in protecting the field and those who practice it. First, access to ECPR conferences and activities must be ensured or enabled, also for colleagues from endangered contexts. This implies paying more attention to cross-national inequalities in higher education, economic disparities, and sometimes visa issues, as well as looking for more concrete solutions than the rhetorical mantra of academic excellence. A policy of avoiding countries and institutions known for not upholding academic freedom could also be more systematically implemented.

Professional organizations could also be spaces to gather and exchange knowledge and solutions, for instance through the setting up of an observatory of academic freedom or a helpdesk for scholars at risk in Europe. This aim could be pursued with organizations from different countries and disciplines. Professional organizations could also offer fora to raise awareness of these attacks among scholars, the media, and social and political actors more generally. They could finally promote the public role of political science as a strategy to avoid a break with citizens and social and political actors in specific countries. Lastly, professional organizations should act to protect their members against their own institutions when these are not complying with their obligations or cannot act in systems of direct dependency on hostile state authorities.

Having said all this, critical self-reflection is also required, for political science can only endure if it considers its own limits. These include a lack of diversity and inclusiveness, blindness to social inequalities within the profession, a burdensome legacy of colonialism and Eurocentrism, wide inequalities in access to the discipline and in the organization of the discipline, and—often—a lack of transparent forms of internal governance. A thorough interrogation of disciplinary divides and further promotion of interdisciplinarity are also needed, especially as many opponents do not make complex distinctions about who belongs to what. Further work on ethics, integrity, and transparency is required, especially in light of the pressures faced by scholars under neoliberalism.

Backing up our recommendations for responses, we conclude that it is urgent to lose our naivety when facing our increasingly less bright future and to further investigate the threats that seriously endanger the discipline. These are also attacks against scholars, and we need to face and understand them instead of behaving like ostriches and keeping quiet until the storm will be gone. To achieve this goal, it is urgent for political scientists to reflect on the purpose of their discipline: What should political sciences be for and for whom? This would offer a stronger base and vision from which to act against current attacks.

NOTES

1. At least for their Hungarian programs: https://www.newsweek.com/hungarys-l eader-orban-bans-gender-studies-all-universities-because-its-not-1174069?fbclid= IwAR05Hs1djM7HB6FxyBt-PJHAiuX1zzyW2y3oy48BoyJPaftY2w16T7B42jw.

2. https://www.nature.com/articles/d41586-019-02107-4?fbclid=IwAR022 Yx5eZAzzbLR5fspA3ijZEKbNXcbvICYUdu1yGBsuM5XpWS_Go7Dt6g&_ga=2 .144915956.1379537620.1562610032-1005911596.1559666081.

3. https://unesdoc.unesco.org/ark:/48223/pf0000109075.

4. https://zilsel.hypotheses.org/3052.

5. http://www.standaard.be/cnt/dmf20180608_03551810.

6. https://areomagazine.com/2018/10/02/academic-grievance-studies-and-the -corruption-of-scholarship/.

7. https://www.knaw.nl/nl/actueel/publicaties/vrijheid-van-wetenschapsbeoefeni ng-in-nederland. The report states that academic freedom could be threatened by the preference for societal impact of research and funding by third parties can lead to some restrictions or unwanted interference of research.

8. https://www.standaard.be/cnt/dmf20190920_04619294?articlehash=339 0F384E257555F7954758283930F2AC9722781DE03B9EA2F83F4E24C2B85A BA74DD9A59B6957B1E3E9A6C3D33E514CC283C8F7CA0A3FAA394395 CAD24F30B2.

9. http://www.anthropology-news.org/index.php/2018/12/07/erasing-polish-anthropology/.

10. https://www.corriere.it/cronache/18_dicembre_09/umbria-questionario-gender-pillon-lega-fa-bloccare-ricerca-sull-omofobia-058c7ba2-fbab-11e8-b5c8-9e33310709fc.shtml.

11. https://www.independent.co.uk/voices/italy-far-right-salvini-lega-league-un iversity-bologna-fascism-a8870736.html.

12. https://www.theguardian.com/education/2017/oct/24/universities-mccarth yism-mp-demands-list-brexit-chris-heaton-harris.

13. https://www.theguardian.com/education/2018/nov/11/reading-university-warns-danger-left-wing-essay.

14. Regulations limiting the action of social movements have also been used against those studying them: for instance, http://www.notav.info/post/studiare-il-movimento-notav-e-considerato-criminale/.

15. https://www.newstatesman.com/education/2014/10/why-uk-universities-must-steer-clear-trigger-warnings; https://www.theguardian.com/education/2019/feb/02/government-tells-universities-to-protect-free-speech-on-campus.

16. https://www.opendemocracy.net/en/odr/closure-of-european-university-at -st-petersburg-dead-cert/.

17. https://eu.spb.ru/en/news/19178-375-days-without-a-license?fbclid=IwAR 3ffMBX8xNfYKseN9st2hRk9nzIeoP62y3UVU4HMP3rH65lwijKK2_X_kA.

18. http://www.deliberatelyconsidered.com/2012/09/academic-freedom-attacked-in-israel/.

19. https://www.timeshighereducation.com/news/czech-president-blocks-professor-ships-academic-critics.

20. https://www.opendemocracy.net/en/can-europe-make-it/swedish-model-dismantled-premature-closure-of-gender-equality/.

21. https://www.lepoint.fr/politique/le-decolonialisme-une-strategie-hegemonique-l-appel-de-80-intellectuels-28-11-2018-2275104_20.php.

22. https://www.nouveau-magazine-litteraire.com/université/la-guerre-du-canon-n'aura-pas-lieu.

23. https://plus.lesoir.be/79159/article/2017-01-25/gilles-kepel-luniversite-est-sou mise-des-pressions-islamo-gauchistes.

24. Like the course on the history of homosexuality created at the Università di Torino in 2019 (https://www.vice.com/it/article/bj7mgz/storia-omosessualita-forza -nuova-torino) or the one on identity politics from a literature and queer perspective at the University of Sofia (https://www.uni-sofia.bg/index.php/bul/novini/novini_i_ s_bitiya/svobodata_e_v_rhovna_cennost_zaschitata_na_svobodata_v_rhoven_d_lg).

25. https://www.lemonde.fr/societe/article/2019/03/01/un-colloque-sur-l-histoire-de-la-shoah-perturbe-par-des-nationalistes-polonais_5429753_3224.html.

26. https://www.lemonde.fr/religions/article/2017/10/11/l-annulation-d-un-collo que-universitaire-sur-l-islamophobie-fait-debat-a-lyon_5199309_1653130.html.

27. https://www.opendemocracy.net/en/can-europe-make-it/academic-freedom-under-threat-workshop-on-lgbt-asylum-is-cen/.

28. https://www.jpost.com/Diaspora/Israels-ambassador-convinces-Berlins-Jewish-Museum-to-cancel-BDS-speaker-563220.

29. https://www.pikaramagazine.com/2019/05/manifiesto-contra-la-quema-de-brujas-y-las-practicas-inquisitoriales-de-ciertas-plataformas-feministas/; https://www.eldiario.es/sociedad/Universidad-Coruna-suspende-jornadas-criticas_0_941056797.html.

30. https://www.timeshighereducation.com/news/online-intimidation-left-biased-academics-spreads-worldwide.

31. http://www.advalvas.vu.nl/nieuws/forum-voor-democratie-wil-extreem-linkse-hoogleraren-vervangen?fbclid=IwAR3u2Upgu4cq6SF7UyIydVvGPFYBiP ytFlHzw0mMM8C7VA3gGbvntZuZYeY.

32. https://nos.nl/artikel/2277889-onderwijs-en-politiek-vallen-hard-over-meldpunt-indoctrinatie.html?fbclid=IwAR1u_4eRKBAHsiYol7JAO4Bs8OVTtDyPsUO9s5tt FKV6fb_D3ObJfOEn4PY.

33. For numbers: https://www.scholarsatrisk.org/wp-content/uploads/2018/01/Scholars-at-Risk-Letter-Brief-on-Turkey-2018.01.15.pdf.

34. https://eldebatedehoy.es/politica/proces-comunidad-cientifica/.

35. Masha Gessen's (2017) rules are: Believe the autocrat; Do not be taken in by small signs of normality; institutions will not save you; Be outraged; Pay attention to the ways in which the Trump presidency breaks the moral compass; Remember the future.

36. https://allea.org/allea-eua-and-science-europe-publish-joint-statement-on-academic-freedom-and-institutional-autonomy/.

37. https://eua.eu/downloads/publications/universities-united-for-the-best-horizon-europe.pdf.

38. See the project Academic Dugnad, a term first used by the University of Oslo, targeting refugee scholars and students. It is promoted by UNICA: http://www.unica-network.eu/category/content/academic-dugnad-refugees-academia.

39. https://www.college-de-france.fr/site/programme-pause/index.htm.

40. https://www.humboldt-foundation.de/web/philipp-schwartz-initiative-en.html.

41. https://www.cara.ngo.

REFERENCES

Aberbach, J. D., & Christensen, T. (2017). Academic autonomy and freedom under pressure: Severely limited, or alive and kicking? *Public Organization Review, 18*(4), 487–506.

Aktas, V., Nilsson, M., & Borell, K. (2019). Social scientists under threat: Resistance and self-censorship in Turkish academia. *British Journal of Educational Studies, 67*(2), 169–86.

Awan, I., Spiller, K., & Whiting, A. (2019). *Terrorism in the classroom. Security, surveillance and a public duty to act.* Basingstoke: Palgrave.

Baser, B., Akgönül, S., & Öztürk, A. E. (2017). "Academics for peace" in Turkey: A case of criminalizing dissent and critical thought via counterterrorism policy. *Critical Studies on Terrorism, 10*(2), 274–96.

Berdahl, R. (1990). Academic freedom, autonomy and accountability in British universities. *Studies in Higher Education, 15*(2), 169–80.

Bock-Côté, M. (2019). *L'empire du politiquement correct*. Paris: Editions du Cerf.

Bouvart, A., De Proost, M., & Norocel, O. V. (2018). I've got a gender and I do not hesitate to use it. *Journal of the International Network for Sexual Ethics and Politics*. Forthcoming. Retrieved from https://www.insep.ugent.be

Bracke, S. (2018). *Peterson on campus: Thinking through the failures*. Paper presented at the AISSR lunch: public speaking and debate in academia.

Brenner, N., Peck, J., & Theodore, N. (2010). Variegated neoliberalization: Geographies, modalities, pathways. *Global Networks, 10*(2), 182–222.

Bronner, G., & Géhin, E. (2017). *Le danger sociologique*. Paris: Presses universitaires de France.

Butler, J. (2017). Academic freedom and the critical task of the University. *Globalizations, 14*(6), 857–61.

Butler, J. (2018). What is free and open inquiry? Academic freedom and political expression. Keynote lecture delivered at the Scholars at Risk Global Congress in Berlin. Retrieved from https://www.scholarsatrisk.org/resources/prof-dr-judith -butler-university-of-california-berkeley-what-is-free-and-open-inquiry-academic -freedom-and-political-expression-keynote/

Butler, P., & Mulgan, R. (2013). Can academic freedom survive performance-based research funding. *Victoria University of Wellington Law Review, 44*, 487–520.

Butterfield, J., & Levintova, E. (2011). Academic freedom and international standards in higher education: Contestation in journalism and political science at Moscow State University. *Communist and Post-Communist Studies, 44*(4), 329–41.

Cole, J. R. (2017). Academic freedom as an indicator of a liberal democracy. *Globalizations, 14*(6), 862–68.

Craciun, D., & Mihut, G. (2017). Requiem for a dream: Academic freedom under threat in democracies. *International Higher Education, 90*, 15–16.

Darakchi, S. (2018). Emergence and development of LGBTQ studies in post-socialist Bulgaria. *Journal of Homosexuality*. doi:10.1080/00918369.2018.1534413.

Deem, R. (2007). Managing a meritocracy or an equitable organisation? Senior managers' and employees' views about equal opportunities policies in UK universities. *Journal of Education Policy, 22*(6), 615–36.

Dobbins, M., & Knill, C. (2017). Higher education governance in France, Germany, and Italy: Change and variation in the impact of transnational soft governance. *Policy and Society, 36*(1), 67–88.

Dubrovskiy, D. (2017). Escape from freedom: The Russian academic community and the problem of academic rights and freedoms. *Interdisciplinary Political Studies, 3*(1), 171–89.

Enyedi, Z. (2018). Democratic backsliding and academic freedom in Hungary. *Perspectives on Politics, 16*(4), 1067–74.

Fassin, E. (2008). L'empire du genre. L'histoire politique ambiguë d'un outil conceptuel. *L'Homme, 187–188*, 375–92.

Ferber, A. L. (2018). "Are you willing to die for this work?" Public targeted online harassment in higher education. *Gender & Society, 32*(3), 301–20.

Fukuyama, F. (2018). *Identity: The demand for dignity and the politics of resentment*. New York: Farrar, Straus and Giroux.

Furedi, F. (2016). *What's happened to the university? A sociological exploration of its infantilization.* London: Routledge.

Gessen, M. (2017, 8 November). One year after Trump's election, revisiting "Autocracy: Rules for survival." *New Yorker.*

Göle, N. (2017). Undesirable public intellectuals. *Globalizations, 14*(6), 877–83.

Griffiths, R. (Ed.). (2018). *Political correctness. Dyson and Goldberg vs. Fry and Peterson. The Munk Debates.* Toronto: House of Anansi.

Helm, E., & Krizsan, A. (2017). Hungarian government's attack on Central European University and its implications for gender studies in Central and Eastern Europe. *Femina Politica, 2,* 169–73.

Ignatieff, M. (2018). Academic freedom from without and within. In M. Ignatieff & S. Roch (Eds.), *Academic freedom: The global challenge* (pp. 1–10). Budapest: CEU Press.

Jerez Mir, M. (2002). La constitution de la science politique espagnole. *Pôle Sud, 16,* 157–71.

Karran, T. (2009). Academic freedom in Europe: Reviewing UNESCO's Recommendation. *British Journal of Educational Studies, 57*(2), 191–215.

Karran, T., Beiter, K., & Atua, K. A. (2017). Measuring academic freedom in Europe: A criterion referenced approach. *Policy Reviews in Higher Education, 1*(2), 209–39.

Kondakov, A. (2016). Teaching queer theory in Russia. *QED: A Journal in GLBTQ Worldmaking, 3*(2), 107–18.

Krook, M. L. (2017). Violence against women in politics. *Journal of Democracy, 28*(1), 74–88.

Kuby, G. (2015). *The global sexual revolution: Destruction of freedom in the name of freedom.* Brooklyn: Angelico Press.

Lahire, B. (2016). *Pour la sociologie. Et pour en finir avec une prétendue "culture de l'excuse."* Paris: La Découverte.

Legutko, R. (2016). *The demon in democracy: Totalitarian temptations in free societies.* New York: Encounter Books.

Lilla, M. (2017). *The once and future liberal: After identity politics.* New York: HarperCollins.

Ménand, L. (1996). The limits of academic freedom. In L. Ménand (Ed.), *The future of academic freedom* (pp. 3–19). Chicago: University of Chicago Press.

Mills, D., Mills, T., & Harkins, S. (2011). Teaching about terrorism in the United Kingdom: How it is done and what problems it causes. *Critical Studies on Terrorism, 4*(3), 405–20.

Mirowski, P. (2011). *Science-mart: Privatizing American science.* Cambridge, MA: Harvard University Press.

Moors, A. (2019). No escape: The force of the security frame in academia and beyond. In N. Fadil, F. Ragazzi, & M. de Koning (Eds.), *Radicalization in Belgium and The Netherlands: Critical perspectives on violence and security* (pp. 245–61). London: I.B. Tauris.

Onfray, M. (2019). *Théorie de la dictature.* Paris: Robert Laffont.

Özkirimli, U. (2017). How to liquidate a people? Academic freedom in Turkey and beyond. *Globalizations, 14*(6), 851–56.

Pető, A. (2018). Attack on freedom of education in Hungary. The case of gender studies. *Engenderings*. Retrieved from https://blogs.lse.ac.uk/gender/2018/09/24/attack-on-freedom-of-education-in-hungary-the-case-of-gender-studies/

Pető, A. (2019). Intellectual Freedom and its new enemies. *Project Syndicate*. Retrieved from https://www.project-syndicate.org/commentary/eastern-europea n-governments-attack-scientific-knowledge-by-andrea-peto-2019-02

Ravecca, P. (2019). *The politics of political science. Re-writing Latin American experiences*. New York: Routledge.

Ruse, A. (2017). *Fake science: Exposing the Left's skewed statistics, fuzzy facts, and dodgy data*. Washington: Regnery.

Savigny, H. (2019). The violence of impact: Unpacking relations between gender, media and politics. *Political Studies Review*. doi:10.1177/1478929918819212.

Scott, J. W. (2017). On free speech and academic freedom. *Journal of Academic Freedom, 8*. Retrieved from https://www.aaup.org/JAF8/free-speech-and-aca demic-freedom#.XObEwi_pOL9

Scott, J. W. (2019). *Knowledge, power and academic freedom*. New York: Columbia University Press.

Slaughter, S., & Leslie, L. (1999). *Academic capitalism: Politics, policies and the entrepreneurial university*. Baltimore: Johns Hopkins University Press.

Sokal, A., & Bricmont, J. (1999). *Fashionable nonsense: Postmodern intellectuals' abuse of science*. New York: Picador.

Stockemer, D., & Kim, M. (2018). Introduction: Academic freedom in danger: Case studies of Turkey, Hungary and Japan. *European Political Science*. doi:10.1057/s41304-018-0172-9.

Trencsényi, B., Rieber, A. J., Iordachi, C., & Hîncu, A. (2017). Academic freedom in danger. Fact files on the "CEU Affair." *Südosteuropa, 65*, 412–67.

Tuchman, G. (2009). *Wannabe U: Inside the corporate university*. University of Chicago Press.

Verloo, M. (2018). Gender knowledge, and opposition to the feminist project: Extreme-right populist parties in the Netherlands. *Politics and Governance, 6*(3). doi:10.17645/pag.v6i3.1456.

POSTFACE

Chapter 15

The Boundaries of Political Science in Europe

Kris Deschouwer

1. THE FOUNDING BOUNDARIES

When, in 1970, a few political scientists decided that political science in Europe needed a boost and therefore decided to set up the European Consortium for Political Research (ECPR), they were thinking in terms of boundaries. In the first place, there was the boundary between Europe and the United States. All those who stood at the cradle of the ECPR were familiar with the state of the discipline in the United States and felt that political science in Europe would continue lagging behind if nothing was done. They saw a boundary between the two continents that needed to be bridged. They wanted to bring political science in Europe to the superior level of the discipline in the United States. The Europeans needed professionalization, rigorous and systematic training of their graduate students, decent data gathering and archiving, and opportunities for increased dialogue and communication of research results. On the American side of that boundary, they found the generous funds that would help them to make that happen.

The second boundary was one that should not be crossed. For them, political science could only truly develop in democratic regimes. Authoritarian regimes had therefore to be excluded from their endeavor. At that time, this reduction of what "Europe" meant in "political science in Europe" was important. Not only was there the division between Western and Eastern Europe, but in the early 1970s countries like Spain, Portugal, and Greece did not belong to the family of democratic states. Political science in Europe was thus in fact political science in North-West Europe.

While these two boundaries were explicitly present in the thinking and actions of the founding fathers of the ECPR, they also drew other important lines, albeit in less conscious ways. They defined the boundaries of a "good" discipline by stating how political phenomena should be analyzed. They focused on comparative analysis and on describing, classifying, and comparing political institutions, movements, and processes. They also focused on the gathering of data, on measuring political actors and institutions and on overcoming the fear for quantitative methods.

> The collection of facts has to come . . . before the development of theory. It is just not true that we need theory to amass the facts; on the contrary, we need the facts to be able to even contemplate what the theory might be about. (Blondel, 1997, p. 117)

And, finally, the founding fathers were—as children of their time—unconsciously but firmly drawing a clear picture of the community of political scientists. It was—to quote Briscoe-Palmer and Mattocks in this volume—very much "stale, male and pale." The founding fathers were all "fathers," that is, they were all men. Equally, if one looks at other actors who were involved on both the American and the European side, one only comes across men. The first executive committee of the ECPR was composed of men only, and this only changed in 1979 when Jeanne Becquart-Leclercq from the University of Lille II joined the team. There was another all-male executive committee from 1982 to 1985, after which there has been always at least one woman among the twelve-member committee. It is only recently that the proportion of female members in the leading organ of the ECPR has reached one-third, and only thanks to a hard quota will it reach 50 percent in 2021.

2. THE STATES OF EUROPE

This collection of chapters reflecting on the achievements, challenges, and prospects of political science shows a continuing preoccupation with boundaries—with the external boundaries of the discipline and of the community, and with its internal divisions, with old and new walls that are still drawing hard lines and creating divisions. It should not come as a surprise, but it deserves to be stressed explicitly that the boundaries of the national states are prominently present in the discussions. There are many views and opinions on the question of whether or not there is today a specific European touch or taste in political science, but the one thing that cannot be ignored when looking for differences between the United States and Europe is the importance and centrality of the national state in European politics and therefore also in European political science. We owe to Stein Rokkan the understanding of how the processes of state formation, the closure of boundaries, the creation of distinct political communities inside state boundaries, the background and identity of state-building actors, the timing and trajectory of state formation, and the geographical location in the European space account for a number of similarities and many important differences between the political systems of the different states (Flora, Kuhnle, & Urwin, 1999). Europe is a fantastic laboratory for comparative analysis of party systems and voting behavior, social movements, parliaments and governments, judicial systems, and policy outputs, to name only the most obvious institutions and processes that developed in different ways in different countries and have inspired research trying to make sense of similarities and varieties. Probably the most striking indicator of the importance of the state in political science research is the large number of edited volumes or special issues of journals that focus on one aspect of a political system and analyze it in chapters that look at the specificities of a specific country, while the editors provide an introduction or a conclusion in which they try to summarize and possibly explain why new parties, or voting behavior in parliament, or central banks, or heads of states, or political careers, or gender regimes in different countries are not all the same.

Political scientists have become more mobile, as Norris is this volume has shown. In several—but certainly not in all—countries, the academic labor market for political scientist has opened to nonnationals. Yet that does not mean that political scientists have become country neutral. Not only is the proportion of those who migrate relatively low (not counting short research stays or exchanges), but those who move to go and work abroad always remain from somewhere. They are more familiar than others with the politics of their original country, which they keep on following closely. They remain an expert of their own country, because they have been trained and socialized there, because they have discovered theories and models of political science by learning at the same time to what extent their own country is a typical example of more general patterns or to the contrary an interesting exception. They might have easier access to political actors and are able to read documents in the country's language. That makes them distinct from colleagues who come from another place.

One should not underestimate the role and importance of language in the European sphere. Certainly, the evolution of English into the lingua franca of scientific communication has facilitated the crossing of borders, international exchanges, the organization of workshops and conferences, the proliferation of multicountry projects, job mobility, and the publication of research results. The presence of a common language is not an issue in American academia, but it is in Europe. It is only because one of the languages spoken in Europe has become a common language that boundaries between states and thus between languages have been eroded to create a scientific community. Yet while the use of English has eroded and opened boundaries, it has also created new ones. The use of English might today seem obvious, but one should not forget that for most political scientists in Europe English is a second or a third language. It requires additional training and lots of practice to become able to communicate well and accurately in a language that is not one's mother tongue. Speaking, writing, and thinking in English is easier for some than for others. The familiarity with English is also not randomly spread but depends on the country of socialization. Smaller language communities are generally more open to English, while the larger ones can more easily survive on their own. The list of countries where English-language movies are shown with subtitles and the countries where the actors are dubbed in the local language presents a good (but not perfect) classification of the degree to which people are exposed to English and to which the need to learn English leads to a better mastering of it. The simple point is that the use of English has also created a division—that is only gradually eroding—between countries where it is either easier or more difficult to function in English. This division is not neutral. It builds in inequalities, an uneven distribution of opportunities to become fully part of the "European" political science community. When half a century ago the definition of "Europe" in "political science in Europe" was to a large extent North-West Europe, that difference can still be seen today. Whether one looks at the membership of the larger scholarly organizations (see Boncourt, in this volume) or at the authors in the major (English-language) journals, one can still see the underrepresentation of southern Europe and of East-Central Europe.

Another reason why state boundaries remain relevant for political science in Europe is the dependence on public funding. That is something political science shares with other social and behavioral sciences. Its research results are not meant to produce any advantage for profit-seeking companies, and therefore funding comes from the public authorities or possibly from (domestic) social and political actors like pressure groups and political parties. Funding programmes of the European Union (EU) have offered great opportunities for seeking funding outside home nations and opportunities for setting up research teams across national boundaries. These EU funding schemes have, however, by no means replaced domestic ones. Most political science researchers are for their work (and their job) dependent on their university and on the university system embedded in their national context. Applications to the national (or subnational) funding agencies are now mostly all in English, and are peer-reviewed by international colleagues, but funding is often made dependent on the ability to show the societal relevance of the project and some obligation to "valorize" the results, that is, to communicate them beyond the community of political scientists and in ways that are accessible for a wider public. That means—again—the use of the national language for communicating the research results.

As Bleiklie, Brans, and Michelsen in this volume have shown, researchers in political science have developed close links with public authorities, for whom they act as experts. It is an important way of making political science and its research findings relevant and useful, and at the same time remaining close to those who can decide on the further funding of projects, both for fundamental and for more applied research. These "policy advice systems," which do—again—vary between countries, are one side of the pendulum that is described in the chapter by Paternotte and Verloo:

> Like a pendulum, political science has swung between a pole aiming at knowledge production that supports existing power actors or institutions, and another pole aiming at providing a distanced critical analysis of the origins, dynamics and impacts of existing power actors and institutions.

This puts political science in an awkward position, constantly in search of the right distance from power and government. The close relationship—especially because of the funding power of those in control of government—also makes political science vulnerable. Paternotte and Verloo in this volume do not paint a bright picture in this respect. They describe the increasing hostility to and distrust of science in general and of social science in particular. There are now too many examples of political parties and governments in Europe that seize every opportunity to delegitimize political science and to cut its wings, its funding, and even its right to exist as an academic discipline.

The attacks on academic freedom in the social sciences are stronger in some countries than in others. The democratic backsliding of which this is an integral part is present in many places but has become acute in some countries of East-Central Europe. It is one of the ways in which the division between West and East is kept alive inside the discipline of political science. When in postwar Europe the countries from East-Central (and southern) Europe were not included in the community of "normal" political science, that was because of the authoritarian nature of the regimes. The authoritarian regimes of East-Central Europe disappeared three decades ago but the dividing line is still visible. Luciana Ghica in this volume explains how postcommunist Europe has remained on the periphery of the Western "normal" to which it is supposed to catch up and converge. Different national patterns and processes are too easily underestimated or even ignored in this Western definition of East-Central Europe and the communalities are not conducive to bring about this desired convergence. Ghica points at the fact that major debates and major projects are dominated by the (North-)West and that playing a leading role in them is extremely difficult for scholars from East-Central Europe. Their national university systems and national contexts result in lower institutional capacity, less funding, and lower wages, which make it more difficult to afford international conference attendance. On top of that comes the difference in the English-language competence that is needed to play a prominent role and, in recent years, democratic backsliding. This is a boundary inside the community of political science in Europe that appears to be extremely resilient.

3. THE BOUNDARIES OF THE DISCIPLINE

National and regional boundaries are important and typical for the society or societies of Europe. These geographical boundaries are not unrelated to others. As Giraudon in this volume rightly notes, the pluralism in European political science is not an accident but is constitutive of the discipline. This refers to the fact that political science in Europe was historically rooted in and related to history, law, or geography. It also means that the way in which political science became a more independent discipline depended on how these links and connections with other disciplines were made and unmade in different countries.

When political science became a more stand-alone discipline and developed links across national boundaries, comparative political analysis was at its core. That is also the way in which the founding fathers of ECPR in 1970 defined the discipline and tried to further develop and strengthen it. Things have changed though. This narrow definition of political science is no longer valid. The discipline has extended its boundaries and is a broader and more varied house in which there is a place for many topics, approaches, and material objects that qualify as political and that deserve the attention of political science scholars. In a way political science has expanded again in the direction of neighboring disciplines like sociology, anthropology, history, and geography and has enlarged its methodological toolbox such that it now includes a wider variety of approaches and techniques. The list of Standing Groups and Research Networks of the ECPR is a nice illustration of that: there are more than fifty and they are defined in terms of geographical areas, methodological approaches, and different aspects of the political. This wide and open approach to what political science can be—Giraudon calls it ecumenical—is not without risks. It does reduce the possibility to talk to each other. The broad and ecumenical house with its many rooms keeps many internal doors closed. Each group, and each approach, forms a community of its own: its own journals, projects, workshops, panels at large conferences, and, for some, entire conferences to cater for people with the same research interests and speaking the same theoretical and methodological language. Variety can lead to disintegration. The expanded and vaguer external boundaries of the discipline have also led to the voicing of discontent by those who believe in a neater and more homogenous political science. The creation of the European Political Science Association (EPSA) in 2010 is a clear sign of that. The question of what the discipline of political science exactly is, what it should do, how it should conduct research, and how it relates to other disciplines remains unanswered. The boundaries of the discipline are contested.

There is one final boundary that deserves our attention. It is the one defining the community of political scientists. For a long time, political science in Europe has been to a large extent a white male affair. Both the chapters by Engeli and Mügge and by Briscoe-Palmer and Mattocks in this volume detail the ways and mechanisms by which this original definition of the political scientist is constantly being reproduced. Inequalities are deeply entrenched in the ways in which political science—like all other disciplines—selects, evaluates, promotes, and rewards its scholars. Political science is—like all other disciplines—part of its society, and it reflects the inequalities, thresholds, and role models that are omnipresent. Yet as a science that is focused on power and on the way in which it functions, political science should have the vocation to analyze, decipher, and counter these inequalities more than others.

For the lack of gender balance there has been at least an increasing awareness and a willingness to search for corrective mechanisms. If we think of diversity beyond gender however, as Briscoe-Palmer and Mattocks do in their chapter, the conclusion must be that there is still a long way to go. People of color and people with a migration background are dramatically underrepresented in academia. This is not without consequences for the way in which research questions are selected and formulated, for the choice of theories, concepts, and methods, for the awareness (or the lack thereof) of one's own position in the research process, and, not in the least, for funding opportunities and possibilities to publish. One must keep in mind that for scholars with a migration background who do not live in a country where English is the national language—that is, most of them—the English that is required to be fully part of the scientific dialogue is often one extra language away from their mother tongue. Here are scholars and potential scholars trying to move from the margin of the scientific community to its core, who are knocking on the doors, who are asking for attention, and who are hoping that hard boundaries can be softened and eventually removed.

4. ACHIEVEMENTS, CHALLENGES, AND PROSPECTS

This volume has looked back at fifty years of political science in Europe. That is a fascinating story of five decades of substantial change. Political science has grown. The scientific community has become much larger and is still expanding. Political science has widened its scope. The material object—the political—does not only include the formal institutions of government, but a wider variety of processes and of actors who participate in the way in which societies are being organized and governed. Political science has become more professional, with good training both in universities and in both smaller and larger international networks and organizations. Political science in Europe has indeed also become more international, with these networks and organizations offering numerous possibilities for collaboration, collective projects, and multiauthored publications. Political science in Europe has moved beyond several boundaries that limited its size and scope half a century ago.

Yet not all the boundaries have gone. The differences between states—and in some countries, also between substates—remain highly relevant. They belong to the very nature of Europe's political organization, and national traditions, variations, and languages will always draw boundaries within the discipline while offering a beautiful laboratory for comparative analysis, for research trying to understand the communalities and the differences in the ways the political objects of research take shape. Some of these internal European boundaries are problematic, because they reflect inequalities and the lack of true integration. The dominance of the North-West of Europe in what is considered to be the mainstream defines and treats especially East-Central Europe as peripheral. Further, while the community of political science has greatly expanded, it does remain rather homogenous, with only a gradual and slow improvement in the gender balance and with a striking underrepresentation of people of color.

Political science in Europe has traveled a long way. It is now stronger than before. But in times when facts, figures, and scientific underpinning are losing their legitimacy, when populism is rising, when those in power increasingly prefer a gut feeling over sound and scientific policy advice, and when some of those in power are directly and effectively attacking the very existence of a science critical of power, it will need strength and persistence. It will need a strong and diverse community of scholars who are committed to political science and who believe in its necessity and in its relevance. There are many achievements to look back on, as well as many challenges to be aware of, but also great prospects for a bright future.

REFERENCES

Blondel, J. (1997). Amateurs into professionals. In H. Daalder (ed.), *Comparative European politics. The story of a profession* (pp. 115–26). Pinter: London & Washington.

Flora, P., Kuhnle, S., & Urwin, D. (1999). *State formation, nation-building, and mass politics in Europe. The theory of Stein Rokkan.* Oxford: Oxford University Press.

Index

Page references for figures and tables are italicized

Author Biographies

Ivar Bleiklie is Professor Emeritus of Political Science at the University of Bergen, Norway. He has been the director of the Norwegian Research Center in Organization and Management and a visiting scholar/professor at Stanford University, Harvard University, Boston College, and Science Po. Bleiklie has directed and participated in a number of comparative projects on higher education policies and organizational change in Western Europe, and he has published a number of books, book chapters, and articles about social services, health policy, and policy and organizational change in higher education.

Thibaud Boncourt is Associate Professor at University Paris 1 Panthéon-Sorbonne and a researcher at Centre Européen de Sociologie et de Science Politique (CESSP). He earned his PhD in 2011 at the Institute of Political Studies of Bordeaux and later held a Max Weber fellowship at the European University Institute (2013–2014). His research interests include the history and sociology of science, the relationships between knowledge and power, and internationalization dynamics. He recently coedited, with Johan Heilbron and Gustavo Sora, *The Social and Human Sciences in Global Power Relations* (2018).

Marleen Brans is Professor at the KU Leuven Public Governance Institute and Treasurer of the International Public Policy Association. Her research focuses on the production and use of policy advice, with special attention on the uptake of scientific research and the role of ministerial advisers.

Shardia Briscoe-Palmer is an early career academic fellow at De Montford University in Leicester, United Kingdom. Her research specialisms intersect across the politics of gender, race, and social injustices. Her research focus explores the politics of black masculinity while (de)constructing postcolonial identities. Her research interests also include academic diversity and inclusivity challenges faced by minority groups within higher education. She completed her doctorate at the University of Birmingham in political science and international studies. She is a strong advocate on why and how race and its intersections must be addressed adequately in the discipline.

Terrell Carver is Professor of Political Theory at the University of Bristol, United Kingdom. He first attended an ECPR Joint Sessions in 1978 and in subsequent years has been a workshop director and official representative. He has published extensively on Critical Theory, Gender Theory, and Philosophy of the Social Sciences, and regularly teaches Discourse and Visual Analysis for the IPSA Methods School in Singapore.

Russell J. Dalton is Research Professor at the Center for the Study of Democracy at UC Irvine. His research focuses on the role of citizens in the democratic process, involving the topics of political culture, electoral politics, and political representation. Dalton's most recent books include *The Good Citizen* (2020), *Political Realignment—Economics, Culture and Electoral Change* (2018), *The Participation Gap* (2017), and *The Civic Culture Transformed* (2015). He has received a Fulbright Professorship at the University of Mannheim, a Barbra Streisand Center Fellowship, German Marshall Research Fellowship, and a POSCO Fellowship at the East/West Center.

Kris Deschouwer is Emeritus Professor of Political Science at the Vrije Universiteit Brussel. He is Chair of the ECPR (2018–2021).

Isabelle Engeli is Professor of Public Policy at the University of Exeter. Her research specializes in comparative public policy with a focus on the politics of gendering policy action and implementation, regulating biotechnology and the comparative turn in policy research. Her work appears in the *European Journal of Public Policy, Regulation & Governance, West European Politics, Comparative European Politics, Journal of Comparative Policy Analysis*. She is the recipient of the APSA 2012 Best Comparative Policy Paper Award, and the 2011 Carrie Chapman Catt Prize. She serves as coeditor-in-chief of the *European Journal of Political Research* and founding editor of the *European Journal of Politics & Gender.*

Diego Garzia is an SNSF Eccellenza Professor of Political Science at the University of Lausanne, and also a recurring Visiting Fellow at the Robert Schuman Centre for Advanced Studies in Fiesole. He held a Jean Monnet

Fellowship at the European University Institute (2012–2014) and an SNSF Ambizione Fellowship at the University of Lucerne (2017–2019). He currently serves as founding convenor of the ECPR Research Network on Voting Advice Applications and as a member of the Scientific Committee of the Italian National Election Study (ITANES). With ECPR Press, he has already published *Matching Voters with Parties and Candidates* (2014).

Luciana Alexandra Ghica is Associate Professor of International Relations and European Studies at the Faculty of Political Science, University of Bucharest (Romania), where she also acts as founding director of the Centre for International Cooperation and Development Studies (IDC). She studied political science and international relations at the University of Bucharest, Central European University (Budapest, Hungary), and Oxford University, where she specialized in the analysis of international cooperation processes, with a focus on the institutional and discursive impact of democratization on policymaking. Author of several studies on democratization, foreign policy, and international cooperation, she is also the editor of the first Romanian encyclopedia of the European Union (c. 2005, 2nd ed. 2006, 3rd ed. 2007).

Virginie Guiraudon is CNRS research director at the Sciences Po Center for European and Comparative studies in Paris. She holds a PhD in Government from Harvard University (1997). She has been Marie Curie Professor at the EUI and a visiting professor and scholar in various universities (Princeton, UCLA, Doshisha University in Kyoto, the CEPC in Madrid). Her current work focuses in part on European integration. She is coeditor (with Adrian Favell) of *Sociology of the European Union* (2011). She has been very active in developing European studies, notably as executive board member successively of EUSA, the Council for European Studies, and the ECPR Standing Group on the European Union. She is the 2013 recipient of the ECPR Mattei Dogan Prize in European Political Sociology.

Anton Hemerijck is Professor of Political Science and Sociology at the European University Institute (EUI) in Florence. Between 2001 and 2009, he directed the Scientific Council for Government Policy (WRR), while holding a professorship in Comparative European Social Policy at the Erasmus University Rotterdam. Over the past two decades, he advised the European Commission and several EU presidencies on European social policy developments. Important book publications include *Why We Need a New Welfare State* with Gøsta Esping-Andersen, Duncan Gallie, and John Myles (2002) and the monograph *Changing Welfare States* (2013). His most recent book publication is the edited volume *The Uses of Social Investment* (2017).

Kate Mattocks is a Lecturer in Politics at the University of East Anglia in Norwich, United Kingdom. Her research interests lie in two main areas, the politics of cultural policy and academic labor. Her cultural policy research focuses on the governance of policies to do with the arts and culture, with a particular focus on cultural identity and diversity. Her research on academic labor has examined the experiences of doctoral researchers and early career academics in the United Kingdom. She holds a doctorate from City, University of London (2017) and has held teaching positions at Liverpool Hope University and Richmond University.

Yves Mény is Emeritus President of the European University Institute (2002–2009) and former president of the Sant'Anna School for Advanced Studies in Pisa and IUSS, Pavia. He is also former chair of the ECPR Executive Committee (2000). His academic career includes positions in Rennes, Paris II, Sciences Po, and the European University Institute. He has taught in many American and European Universities and is an honorary member of the Irish Academy. He has published extensively in the field of French and comparative politics, public policies, and administration. Later, his publications have focused on corruption and populism. In 2019, his book on *Imperfect democracies* was simultaneously published in Italy and France (Il Mulino and Presses de SciencesPo).

Svein Michelsen is Professor of Political Science at the Department of Administration and Organization Theory at the University of Bergen. His main interests are focused on higher education and vocational education and training systems and policies in Western European countries.

Liza Mügge is Associate Professor of Political Science at the University of Amsterdam (UvA). At the UvA, she also chairs the Taskforce on Social Safety and coleads the "Diverse Europe" research group of the Amsterdam Centre for European Studies (ACES). She is cofounding editor of the *European Journal of Politics & Gender* and PI of a five-year project on political representation and diversity funded by the Netherlands Organisation for Scientific Research (NWO).

Pippa Norris is a comparative political scientist who has taught at Harvard University for a quarter century. Her research compares public opinion and elections, democratic institutions and cultures, gender politics, and political communications in many countries worldwide. Major honors include APSA's Charles Merriam Award, fellowship of the American Academy of Arts and Sciences, the PSA's Isaiah Berlin Lifetime Achievement Award, IPSA's Karl Deutsch Award, the 2011 Johan Skytte prize in political science, and the ARC's 2011 Kathleen Fitzpatrick Australian Laureate Fellowship, she has published around fifty books. The most recent include *Cultural Backlash: Trump, Brexit and Authoritarian Populism* (authored with Inglehart, 2019) and *Electoral Integrity in America* (coedited, 2019).

David Paternotte is Associate Professor in Sociology at the Université libre de Bruxelles, Belgium. He is also vice dean for International Affairs and chair of the interdisciplinary master in gender studies that unites the French-speaking universities. After research on same-sex marriage advocacy and LGBT activism, he studied anti-gender campaigns and attacks on academic freedom in Europe. In addition to numerous articles and book chapters, he has authored the book *Revendiquer le "mariage gay": Belgique, France, Espagne* (2011). He is the codirector of the book series *Global Queer Politics* (Palgrave) and *Genre(s) & Sexualité(s)* (Editions de l'Université de Bruxelles).

Alexander H. Trechsel is Professor of Political Science at the University of Lucerne. He obtained his PhD in Political Science at the University of Geneva in 1999. From 2005 to 2016 he held the Swiss Chair in Federalism and Democracy at the European University Institute in Fiesole. In addition, he was from 2013 to 2016 Head of the Department for Political and Social Sciences at the same institute. Also, from 2012 to 2015, he was Faculty Fellow at the Berkman Center for Internet and Society at Harvard University.

Mieke Verloo is Professor of Comparative Politics and Inequality Issues at Radboud University in the Netherlands, and Non-Residential Permanent Fellow at the IWM, Institute for Human Sciences in Vienna. She is the winner of the 2015 ECPG Gender and Politics Career Achievement Award. She was scientific director of large research projects on gender equality policymaking in Europe and has extensive consultancy and training experience on gender mainstreaming and intersectionality for several European governments and institutions. Publications from her work on opposition to feminist politics include the edited volume on *Varieties of opposition to gender equality in Europe* (2018).